MW01690435

GOD'S AMAZING GRACE

Daily devotional books
from the writings of
Ellen G. White

Christ Triumphant
Conflict and Courage
The Faith I Live By
God's Amazing Grace
In Heavenly Places
Lift Him Up
Maranatha—The Lord Is Coming
My Life Today
Our High Calling
Reflecting Christ
Sons and Daughters of God
That I May Know Him
This Day With God
The Upward Look
Ye Shall Receive Power

God's Amazing Grace

ELLEN G. WHITE

"Never was there a time when the Lord would manifest His great grace unto His chosen ones more fully than in these last days when His law is made void."—Ellen G. White.

REVIEW AND HERALD® PUBLISHING ASSOCIATION
Since 1861 | www.reviewandherald.com

Texts credited to ARV are from *The Holy Bible,* edited by the American Revision Committee, Thomas Nelson and Sons, 1901.

Texts credited to NEB are from *The New English Bible.* © The Delegates of the Oxford University Press and the Syndics of the Cambridge University Press 1961, 1970. Reprinted by permission.

Bible texts credited to RSV are from the Revised Standard Version of the Bible, copyright © 1946, 1952, 1971, by the Division of Christian Education of the National Council of the Churches of Christ in the U.S.A. Used by permission.

Texts credited to RV are from *The Holy Bible,* Revised version, Oxford University Press, 1911.

Cover designed by Gerald Lee Monks
Cover design resources from iStockphoto.com/wingmar
Interior design by Toya Koch
Typeset: 11/14 Berkley Book

Printed by Pacific Press® Publishing Association
PRINTED IN U.S.A.

LIBRARY OF CONGRESS CATALOG CARD NO. 73-83097

ISBN 978-0-8280-2844-8

Foreword

The hymn "Marvelous Grace" has been a favorite with Christians for many years. Joyfully and enthusiastically they have sung:

"Marvelous grace of our loving Lord,
Grace that exceeds our sin and our guilt!
Yonder on Calvary's mount outpoured—
There where the blood of the Lamb was spilt.
Grace, grace, God's grace,
Grace that will pardon and cleanse within;
Grace, grace, God's grace,
Grace that is greater than all our sin!"
—*The SDA Hymnal,* No. 109

Ellen White described grace as "an attribute of God exercised toward undeserving human beings. We did not seek after it," she marveled, "but it was sent in search of us" (*The Ministry of Healing,* p. 161). She was overwhelmed by the thought that God in His infinite love has extended grace to beings who are in rebellion against Him. Over and over she returned to this theme in her writings, always pointing to the cross of Christ as proof that divine grace knows no limits. In various contexts the word "grace" appears more than13,000 times in her published writings.

The present volume has been produced under the direction of the trustees of the Ellen G. White Estate. In many cases the reading for the day consists of a number of choice quotations grouped together as a composite statement. These quotations have been drawn from Ellen White books presently in circulation, as well as from such periodicals as the *Review and Herald,* the *Youth's Instructor,* and *Signs of the Times.* Individual source credits and a Scripture index may be found at the close of the volume.

It is our hope that every person who reads the inspired messages in this book will be led into a more intimate experience with Jesus, and thus receive the ultimate benefit of God's grace—eternal life (1 John 5:11, 12).

The Trustees of the
Ellen G. White Estate

Silver Spring, Maryland
January 2001

Monthly Topics

Amazing Grace

Amazing grace! how sweet the sound
That saved a wretch like me!
I once was lost, but now am found;
Was blind, but now I see.

'Twas grace that taught my heart to fear,
And grace my fears relieved;
How precious did that grace appear,
The hour I first believed!

Through many dangers, toils, and snares,
I have already come;
'Tis grace hath brought me safe thus far,
And grace will lead me home.

The Lord has promised good to me,
His word my hope secures;
He will my shield and portion be,
As long as life endures.

The earth shall soon dissolve like snow,
The sun forbear to shine;
But God, who called me here below,
Will be for ever mine.

When we've been there ten thousand years,
Bright shining as the sun,
We've no less days to sing God's praise
Than when we first begun.

—John Newton*

*Stanzas 1, 2, 3, 5—*Hymns and Tunes,* No. 441
Stanza 4—E. E. White, *Singing With Understanding,* No. 295
Stanza 6—from *He's Everything to Me, Plus 53,* published by "Sacred Songs," Waco, Texas.

Good News of the Kingdom

And Jesus went about all Galilee, teaching in their synagogues, and preaching the gospel of the kingdom. Matt. 4:23.

He opened his mouth, and taught them, saying, Blessed are the poor in spirit: for theirs is the kingdom of heaven" (Matt. 5:2, 3). As something strange and new, these words fall upon the ears of the wondering multitude. Such teaching is contrary to all they have ever heard from priest or rabbi. They see in it nothing to flatter their pride or to feed their ambitious hopes. But there is about this new Teacher a power that holds them spellbound. The sweetness of divine love flows from His very presence as the fragrance from a flower. . . .

In the throng that surrounded Jesus there were some who had a sense of their spiritual poverty. . . . There were souls who, in the presence of His purity, felt that they were "wretched, and miserable, and poor, and blind, and naked" (Rev. 3:17); and they longed for "the grace of God that bringeth salvation" (Titus 2:11). . . .

Of the poor in spirit Jesus says, "Theirs is the kingdom of heaven." This kingdom is not, as Christ's hearers had hoped, a temporal and earthly dominion. Christ was opening to them the spiritual kingdom of His love, His grace, His righteousness. . . . His subjects are the poor in spirit, the meek, the persecuted for righteousness' sake. The kingdom of heaven is theirs. Though not yet fully accomplished, the work is begun in them which will make them "meet to be partakers of the inheritance of the saints in light" (Col. 1:12).

All who have a sense of their deep soul poverty, who feel that they have nothing good in themselves, may find righteousness and strength by looking unto Jesus. . . . He bids you exchange your poverty for the riches of His grace. We are not worthy of God's love, but Christ, our surety, is worthy, and is abundantly able to save all who shall come unto Him. Whatever may have been your past experience, however discouraging your present circumstances, if you will come to Jesus just as you are, weak, helpless, and despairing, our compassionate Saviour will meet you a great way off, and will throw about you His arms of love and His robe of righteousness.[1]

For Sinners Only

For the grace of God that bringeth salvation hath appeared to all men.
Titus 2:11.

By disobeying the commands of God, man fell under the condemnation of His law. This fall called for the grace of God to appear in behalf of sinners. We should never have learned the meaning of this word "grace" had we not fallen. God loves the sinless angels, who do His service, and are obedient to all His commands; but He does not give them grace. These heavenly beings know naught of grace; they have never needed it; for they have never sinned. Grace is an attribute of God shown to undeserving human beings. We did not seek after it, but it was sent in search of us. God rejoices to bestow this grace upon every one who hungers for it. To every one He presents terms of mercy, not because we are worthy, but because we are so utterly unworthy. Our need is the qualification which gives us the assurance that we shall receive this gift.

But God does not use His grace to make His law of none effect, or to take the place of His law. . . . God's grace and the law of His kingdom are in perfect harmony; they walk hand in hand. His grace makes it possible for us to draw nigh to Him by faith. By receiving it, and letting it work in our lives, we testify to the validity of the law; we exalt the law and make it honorable by carrying out its living principles through the power of the grace of Christ; and by rendering pure, whole-hearted obedience to God's law, we witness before the universe of heaven, and before an apostate world that is making void the law of God, to the power of redemption.[2]

Not because we first loved Him, does God love us; but "while we were yet sinners" (Rom. 5:8) Christ died for us, making full and abundant provision for our redemption. Although by our disobedience we have merited God's displeasure and condemnation, He has not forsaken us; He has not left us to grapple with the power of the enemy in our own finite strength. Heavenly angels fight our battles for us; and co-operating with them, we may be victorious over the powers of evil. Trusting in Christ as our personal Saviour, we may be "more than conquerors through him that loved us" (Rom. 8:37).[3]

At God's Appointed Time

When the fulness of the time was come, God sent forth his Son, . . . to redeem them that were under the law, that we might receive the adoption of sons. Gal. 4:4, 5.

In heaven's council the hour for the coming of Christ had been determined. When the great clock of time pointed to that hour, Jesus was born in Bethlehem. . . . Providence had directed the movements of nations, and the tide of human impulse and influence, until the world was ripe for the coming of the Deliverer. . . .

The deception of sin had reached its height. All the agencies for depraving the souls of men had been put in operation. The Son of God, looking upon the world, beheld suffering and misery. With pity He saw how men had become victims of satanic cruelty. He looked with compassion upon those who were being corrupted, murdered, and lost. . . . It was demonstrated before the universe that, apart from God, humanity could not be uplifted. A new element of life and power must be imparted by Him who made the world.

With intense interest the unfallen worlds had watched to see Jehovah arise, and sweep away the inhabitants of the earth. . . . But instead of destroying the world, God sent His Son to save it. . . . At the very crisis, when Satan seemed about to triumph, the Son of God came with the embassage of divine grace. Through every age, through every hour, the love of God had been exercised toward the fallen race. Notwithstanding the perversity of men, the signals of mercy had been continually exhibited. And when the fullness of the time had come, the Deity was glorified by pouring upon the world a flood of healing grace that was never to be obstructed or withdrawn till the plan of salvation should be fulfilled.

Satan was exulting that he had succeeded in debasing the image of God in humanity. Then Jesus came to restore in man the image of his Maker. None but Christ can fashion anew the character that has been ruined by sin. He came to expel the demons that had controlled the will. He came to lift us up from the dust, to reshape the marred character after the pattern of His divine character, and to make it beautiful with His own glory.[4]

The Message of the First Advent

Jesus came into Galilee, preaching the gospel of the kingdom of God, and saying, The time is fulfilled, and the kingdom of God is at hand: repent ye, and believe the gospel. Mark 1:14, 15.

As Jesus traveled through Galilee, teaching and healing, multitudes flocked to Him from the cities and villages. Many came even from Judea and the adjoining provinces. Often He was obliged to hide Himself from the people. The enthusiasm ran so high that it was necessary to take precautions lest the Roman authorities should be aroused to fear an insurrection. Never before had there been such a period as this for the world. Heaven was brought down to men. Hungering and thirsting souls that had waited long for the redemption of Israel now feasted upon the grace of a merciful Saviour. . . .

The gospel message, as given by the Saviour Himself, was based on the prophecies. The "time" which He declared to be fulfilled was the period made known by the angel Gabriel to Daniel. . . . "Know therefore and understand, that from the going forth of the commandment to restore and to build Jerusalem unto the Messiah the Prince shall be seven weeks, and threescore and two weeks" (Dan. 9:25), sixty-nine weeks, or four hundred and eighty-three years. The commandment to restore and build Jerusalem, as completed by the decree of Artaxerxes Longimanus (see Ezra 6:14; 7:1, 9, margin), went into effect in the autumn of 457 B.C. From this time four hundred and eighty-three years extend to the autumn of A.D. 27. According to the prophecy, this period was to reach to the Messiah, the Anointed One. In A.D. 27, Jesus at His baptism received the anointing of the Holy Spirit, and soon afterward began His ministry. Then the message was proclaimed, "The time is fulfilled." . . .

The time of Christ's coming, His anointing by the Holy Spirit, His death, and the giving of the gospel to the Gentiles, were definitely pointed out. . . . "The Spirit of Christ which was in them" "testified beforehand the sufferings of Christ, and the glory that should follow" (1 Peter 1:11). . . . As the message of Christ's first advent announced the kingdom of His grace, so the message of His second advent announces the kingdom of His glory.[5]

A Spiritual Kingdom

Jesus answered, My kingdom is not of this world. John 18:36.

The kingdom of God comes not with outward show. The gospel of the grace of God, with its spirit of self-abnegation, can never be in harmony with the spirit of the world. The two principles are antagonistic. . . .

But today in the religious world there are multitudes who, as they believe, are working for the establishment of the kingdom of Christ as an earthly and temporal dominion. They desire to make our Lord the ruler of the kingdoms of this world, the ruler in its courts and camps, its legislative halls, its palaces and market places. They expect Him to rule through legal enactments, enforced by human authority. Since Christ is not now here in person, they themselves will undertake to act in His stead, to execute the laws of His kingdom. The establishment of such a kingdom is what the Jews desired in the days of Christ. They would have received Jesus, had He been willing to establish a temporal dominion, to enforce what they regarded as the laws of God, and to make them the expositors of His will and the agents of His authority. But He said, "My kingdom is not of this world." He would not accept the earthly throne. . . .

Not by the decisions of courts or councils or legislative assemblies, not by the patronage of worldly great men, is the kingdom of Christ established, but by the implanting of Christ's nature in humanity through the work of the Holy Spirit. . . . Here is the only power that can work the uplifting of mankind. And the human agency for the accomplishment of this work is the teaching and practicing of the Word of God. . . .

Now, as in Christ's day, the work of God's kingdom lies not with those who are clamoring for recognition and support by earthly rulers and human laws, but with those who are declaring to the people in His name those spiritual truths that will work in the receivers the experience of Paul: "I am crucified with Christ: nevertheless I live; yet not I, but Christ liveth in me" (Gal. 2:20).[6]

Unlike Earthly Kingdoms

And he said, Whereunto shall we liken the kingdom of God? or with what comparison shall we compare it? Mark 4:30.

Christ found the kingdoms of the world corrupt. After Satan was expelled from heaven, he erected his standard of rebellion on this earth, and sought by every means to win men to his standard. . . . His purpose was to establish a kingdom which would be governed by his own laws, and carried on with his own resources, independent of God; and so well did he succeed, that when Christ came to the world to establish a kingdom, He looked upon the governments of men, and said, "Whereunto shall we liken the kingdom of God?" Nothing in civil society afforded Him a comparison. . . .

In striking contrast to the wrong and oppression so universally practised were the mission and work of Christ. . . . He planned a government which would use no force; His subjects would know no oppression. . . . Not as a fierce tyrant did He come, but as the Son of man; not to conquer the nations by His iron power, but "to preach good tidings unto the meek;" "to bind up the brokenhearted, to proclaim liberty to the captives, and the opening of the prison to them that are bound;" "to comfort all that mourn" (Isa. 61:1, 2). He came as the divine Restorer, bringing to oppressed and downtrodden humanity the rich and abundant grace of Heaven, that by the power of His righteousness, man, fallen and degraded though he was, might be a partaker of divinity. . . .

Christ taught that His church is a spiritual kingdom. He Himself, "the Prince of peace," is the head of His church. In His person humanity, inhabited by divinity, was represented to the world. The great end of His mission was to be a sin-offering for the world, that by the shedding of blood an atonement might be made for the whole race of men. With a heart ever touched with the feelings of our infirmities, an ear ever open to the cry of suffering humanity, a hand ever ready to save the discouraged and despairing, Jesus, our Saviour, "went about doing good" (Acts 10:38). . . .

And all who are members of the kingdom of Christ will represent Him in character and disposition.[7]

The Ensign of Christ's Kingdom

Behold the Lamb of God, which taketh away the sin of the world. John 1:29.

To Daniel was given a vision of fierce beasts, representing the powers of the earth. But the ensign of the Messiah's kingdom is a lamb. While earthly kingdoms rule by the ascendancy of physical power, Christ is to banish every carnal weapon, every instrument of coercion. His kingdom was to be established to uplift and ennoble fallen humanity.[8]

To Adam, the offering of the first sacrifice was a most painful ceremony. His hand must be raised to take life, which only God could give. . . . As he slew the innocent victim, he trembled at the thought that his sin must shed the blood of the spotless Lamb of God. This scene gave him a deeper and more vivid sense of the greatness of his transgression, which nothing but the death of God's dear Son could expiate. And he marveled at the infinite goodness that would give such a ransom to save the guilty.[9]

The types and shadows of the sacrificial service, with the prophecies, gave the Israelites a veiled, indistinct view of the mercy and grace to be brought to the world by the revelation of Christ. . . . Only through Christ can man keep the moral law. By transgression of this law man brought sin into the world, and with sin came death. Christ became the propitiation for man's sin. He proffered His perfection of character in the place of man's sinfulness. He took upon Himself the curse of disobedience. The sacrifices and offerings pointed forward to the sacrifice He was to make. The slain lamb typified the Lamb that was to take away the sin of the world. . . .

The law and the gospel are in perfect harmony. Each upholds the other. In all its majesty the law confronts the conscience, causing the sinner to feel his need of Christ as the propitiation for sin. The gospel recognizes the power and immutability of the law. "I had not known sin, but by the law" (Rom. 7:7), Paul declares. The sense of sin, urged home by the law, drives the sinner to the Saviour. In his need man may present the mighty arguments furnished by the cross of Calvary. He may claim the righteousness of Christ; for it is imparted to every repentant sinner.[10]

God's Kingdom in the Heart

Behold, the kingdom of God is within you. Luke 17:21.

The government under which Jesus lived was corrupt and oppressive; on every hand were crying abuses—extortion, intolerance, and grinding cruelty. Yet the Saviour attempted no civil reforms. He attacked no national abuses, nor condemned the national enemies. He did not interfere with the authority or administration of those in power. He who was our example kept aloof from earthly governments. Not because He was indifferent to the woes of men, but because the remedy did not lie in merely human and external measures. To be efficient, the cure must reach men individually, and must regenerate the heart.[11]

Some of the Pharisees had come to Jesus demanding "when the kingdom of God should come" (Luke 17:20). More than three years had passed since John the Baptist gave the message that like a trumpet call had sounded through the land, "The kingdom of heaven is at hand" (Matt. 3:2). And as yet these Pharisees saw no indication of the establishment of the kingdom. . . .

Jesus answered, "The kingdom of God cometh not with outward show [margin]: neither shall they say, Lo here! or lo there! for, behold, the kingdom of God is within you." The kingdom of God begins in the heart. Look not here or there for manifestations of earthly power to mark its coming.[12]

The works of Christ not only declared Him to be the Messiah, but showed in what manner His kingdom was to be established. . . . It comes through the gentleness of the inspiration of His word, through the inward working of His Spirit, the fellowship of the soul with Him who is its life. The greatest manifestation of its power is seen in human nature brought to the perfection of the character of Christ. . . .

When God gave His Son to our world, He endowed human beings with imperishable riches—riches compared with which the treasured wealth of men since the world began is nothingness. Christ came to the earth and stood before the children of men with the hoarded love of eternity, and this is the treasure that, through our connection with Him, we are to receive, to reveal, and to impart.[13]

Like Mustard Seed

The kingdom of heaven is like to a grain of mustard seed, . . . which indeed is the least of all seeds: but when it is grown, it is the greatest among herbs, and becometh a tree, so that the birds of the air come and lodge in the branches thereof. Matt. 13:31, 32.

The germ in the seed grows by the unfolding of the life-principle which God has implanted. Its development depends upon no human power. So it is with the kingdom of Christ. It is a new creation. Its principles of development are the opposite to those that rule the kingdoms of this world. Earthly governments prevail by physical force; they maintain their dominion by war; but the founder of the new kingdom is the Prince of Peace. . . . Christ implants a principle. By implanting truth and righteousness, He counterworks error and sin. . . .

The kingdom of Christ in its beginning seemed humble and insignificant. Compared with earthly kingdoms it appeared to be the least of all. By the rulers of this world Christ's claim to be a king was ridiculed. Yet in the mighty truths committed to His followers the kingdom of the gospel possessed a divine life. And how rapid was its growth, how widespread its influence! When Christ spoke this parable, there were only a few Galilean peasants to represent the new kingdom. . . . But the mustard seed was to grow and spread forth its branches throughout the world. When the earthly kingdoms whose glory then filled the hearts of men should perish, the kingdom of Christ would remain, a mighty and far-reaching power.

So the work of grace in the heart is small in its beginning. A word is spoken, a ray of light is shed into the soul, an influence is exerted that is the beginning of the new life; and who can measure its results? . . .

In this last generation the parable of the mustard seed is to reach a signal and triumphant fulfillment. The little seed will become a tree. The last message of warning and mercy is to go to "every nation and kindred and tongue" (Rev. 14:6-14), "to take out of them a people for his name" (Acts 15:14; Rev. 18:1). And the earth shall be lightened with His glory.[14]

Like Yeast

The kingdom of heaven is like unto leaven, which a woman took, and hid in three measures of meal, till the whole was leavened. Matt. 13:33.

In the Saviour's parable, leaven is used to represent the kingdom of heaven. It illustrates the quickening, assimilating power of the grace of God. . . .

The grace of God must be received by the sinner before he can be fitted for the kingdom of glory. All the culture and education which the world can give will fail of making a degraded child of sin a child of heaven. The renewing energy must come from God. . . . As the leaven, when mingled with the meal, works from within outward, so it is by the renewing of the heart that the grace of God works to transform the life. . . .

The leaven hidden in the flour works invisibly to bring the whole mass under its leavening process; so the leaven of truth works secretly, silently, steadily, to transform the soul. The natural inclinations are softened and subdued. New thoughts, new feelings, new motives, are implanted. A new standard of character is set up—the life of Christ. The mind is changed; the faculties are roused to action in new lines. . . . The conscience is awakened. . . .

The heart of him who receives the grace of God overflows with love for God and for those for whom Christ died. Self is not struggling for recognition. . . . He is kind and thoughtful, humble in his opinion of himself, yet full of hope, always trusting in the mercy and love of God. . . .

The grace of Christ is to control the temper and the voice. Its working will be seen in politeness and tender regard shown by brother for brother, in kind, encouraging words. An angel presence is in the home. The life breathes a sweet perfume, which ascends to God as holy incense. Love is manifested in kindness, gentleness, forbearance, and long-suffering. The countenance is changed. Christ abiding in the heart shines out in the faces of those who love Him and keep His commandments. . . . As these changes are effected, angels break forth in rapturous song, and God and Christ rejoice over souls fashioned after the divine similitude.[15]

Established by Christ's Death

Who his own self bare our sins in his own body on the tree, that we, being dead to sins, should live unto righteousness: by whose stripes ye were healed. 1 Peter 2:24.

At the very time when they [Christ's disciples] expected to see their Lord ascend the throne of David, they beheld Him seized as a malefactor, scourged, derided, and condemned, and lifted up on the cross of Calvary. . . .

The announcement which had been made by the disciples in the name of the Lord was in every particular correct, and the events to which it pointed were even then taking place. "The time is fulfilled, and the kingdom of God is at hand" (Mark 1:15), had been their message. . . . And the "kingdom of God" which they had declared to be at hand was established by the death of Christ. This kingdom was not, as they had been taught to believe, an earthly empire. Nor was it that future, . . . everlasting kingdom, in which "all dominions shall serve and obey him" (Dan. 7:27). As used in the Bible, the expression "kingdom of God" is employed to designate both the kingdom of grace and the kingdom of glory. . . .

The kingdom of grace was instituted immediately after the fall of man. . . . Yet it was not actually established until the death of Christ. Even after entering upon His earthly mission, the Saviour . . . might have drawn back from the sacrifice of Calvary. In Gethsemane the cup of woe trembled in His hand. He might even then have wiped the blood-sweat from His brow, and have left the guilty race to perish in their iniquity. . . . But when the Saviour yielded up His life, and with His expiring breath cried out, "It is finished," then the fulfillment of the plan of redemption was assured. The promise of salvation made to the sinful pair in Eden was ratified. The kingdom of grace, which had before existed by the promise of God, was then established.

Thus the death of Christ—the very event which the disciples had looked upon as the final destruction of their hope—was that which made it forever sure. . . . The event that had filled them with mourning and despair was that . . . in which centered the future life and eternal happiness of all God's faithful ones in all the ages.[16]

Its Principles of Government

Wherefore the law is holy, and the commandment holy, and just, and good. Rom. 7:12.

The law of God, from its very nature, is unchangeable. It is a revelation of the will and the character of its Author. God is love, and His law is love. Its two great principles are love to God and love to man. . . . The character of God is righteousness and truth; such is the nature of His law. . . .

In the beginning, man was created in the image of God. He was in perfect harmony with the nature and the law of God; the principles of righteousness were written upon his heart. But sin alienated him from his Maker. He no longer reflected the divine image. His heart was at war with the principles of God's law. . . . But "God so loved the world, that he gave his only-begotten Son," that man might be reconciled to God. Through the merits of Christ he can be restored to harmony with his Maker. His heart must be renewed by divine grace; he must have a new life from above. This change is the new birth. . . .

The first step in reconciliation to God is the conviction of sin. . . . "By the law is the knowledge of sin" (Rom. 3:20). In order to see his guilt, the sinner must test his character by God's great standard of righteousness. It is a mirror which shows the perfection of a righteous character and enables him to discern the defects of his own. The law reveals to man his sin. . . . It declares that death is the portion of the transgressor. The gospel of Christ alone can free him from the condemnation or the defilement of sin. He must exercise repentance toward God, whose law has been transgressed; and faith in Christ, his atoning sacrifice. . . .

In the new birth the heart is brought into harmony with God, as it is brought into accord with His law. When this mighty change has taken place in the sinner, he has passed from death unto life, from sin unto holiness, from transgression and rebellion to obedience and loyalty. . . .

The followers of Christ are to become like Him—by the grace of God to form characters in harmony with the principles of His holy law. This is Bible sanctification.[17]

Our Top Priority

Seek ye first the kingdom of God, and his righteousness; and all these things shall be added unto you. Matt. 6:33.

The people who listened to the words of Christ were still anxiously watching for some announcement of the earthly kingdom. While Jesus was opening to them the treasures of heaven, the question uppermost in many minds was, How will a connection with Him advance our prospects in the world? Jesus shows that in making the things of the world their supreme anxiety they were like the heathen nations about them. . . .

"All these things," said Jesus, "do the nations of the world seek after" (Luke 12:30). . . . I have come to open to you the kingdom of love and righteousness and peace. Open your hearts to receive this kingdom, and make its service your highest interest. Though it is a spiritual kingdom, fear not that your needs for this life will be uncared for. . . .

Jesus does not release us from the necessity of effort, but He teaches that we are to make Him first and last and best in everything. We are to engage in no business, follow no pursuit, seek no pleasure, that would hinder the outworking of His righteousness in our character and life. Whatever we do is to be done heartily, as unto the Lord.

Jesus, while He dwelt on earth, dignified life in all its details by keeping before men the glory of God, and by subordinating everything to the will of His Father. If we follow His example, His assurance to us is that all things needful in this life "shall be added." Poverty or wealth, sickness or health, simplicity or wisdom—all are provided for in the promise of His grace.[18]

Difficulties will be powerless to hinder him who is determined to seek first the kingdom of God and His righteousness. . . . Looking to Jesus, . . . the believer will willingly brave contempt and derision. And help and grace sufficient for every circumstance are promised by Him whose word is truth. His everlasting arms encircle the soul that turns to Him for aid. In His care we may rest safely, saying, "What time I am afraid, I will trust in thee" (Ps. 56:3).[19]

Entrance Requirement

Jesus answered and said unto him, Verily, verily, I say unto thee, Except a man be born again, he cannot see the kingdom of God. John 3:3.

In the interview with Nicodemus, Jesus unfolded the plan of salvation and His mission to the world.[20]

He came directly to the point, saying solemnly, yet kindly, "Verily, verily, I say unto thee, Except a man be born from above, he cannot see the kingdom of God" (John 3:3, margin). . . . Raising His hand with solemn, quiet dignity, He pressed the truth home with greater assurance, "Verily, verily, I say unto thee, Except a man be born of water and of the Spirit, he cannot enter into the kingdom of God.". . .

By nature the heart is evil. . . . The fountain of the heart must be purified before the streams can become pure. He who is trying to reach heaven by his own works in keeping the law is attempting an impossibility. There is no safety for one who has merely a legal religion, a form of godliness. The Christian's life is not a modification or improvement of the old, but a transformation of nature. There is a death to self and sin, and a new life altogether. This change can be brought about only by the effectual working of the Holy Spirit. . . . It can no more be explained than can the movements of the wind. . . .

While the wind is itself invisible, it produces effects that are seen and felt. So the work of the Spirit upon the soul will reveal itself in every act of him who has felt its saving power. When the Spirit of God takes possession of the heart, it transforms the life. Sinful thoughts are put away, evil deeds are renounced; love, humility, and peace take the place of anger, envy, and strife. Joy takes the place of sadness, and the countenance reflects the light of heaven. . . . The blessing comes when by faith the soul surrenders itself to God. Then that power which no human eye can see creates a new being in the image of God. . . .

Like Nicodemus, we must be willing to enter into life in the same way as the chief of sinners. Than Christ, "there is none other name under heaven given among men, whereby we must be saved" (Acts 4:12).[21]

By God's Grace

Being justified freely by his grace through the redemption that is in Christ Jesus. Rom. 3:24.

In many of His parables, Christ uses the expression, "the kingdom of heaven," to designate the work of divine grace upon the hearts of men. . . . The kingdom of grace was instituted immediately after the fall of man, when a plan was devised for the redemption of the guilty race. It then existed in the purpose and by the promise of God; and through faith, men could become its subjects.[22]

The exercise of force is contrary to the principles of God's government; He desires only the service of love. . . . To know God is to love Him; His character must be manifested in contrast to the character of Satan. This work only one Being in all the universe could do. Only He who knew the height and depth of the love of God could make it known. . . .

The plan for our redemption was not an afterthought, a plan formulated after the fall of Adam. It was a revelation of "the mystery which hath been kept in silence through times eternal" (Rom. 16:25, RV). It was an unfolding of the principles that from eternal ages have been the foundation of God's throne. . . . God did not ordain that sin should exist, but He foresaw its existence, and made provision to meet the terrible emergency. So great was His love for the world, that He covenanted to give His only-begotten Son, "that whosoever believeth in him should not perish, but have everlasting life."[23]

As soon as there was sin, there was a Saviour. Christ knew that He would have to suffer, yet He became man's substitute. As soon as Adam sinned, the Son of God presented Himself as surety for the human race, with just as much power to avert the doom pronounced upon the guilty as when He died upon the cross of Calvary.[24]

What love! What amazing condescension! The King of glory proposes to humble Himself to fallen humanity! He would place His feet in Adam's steps. He would take man's fallen nature, and engage to cope with the strong foe who triumphed over Adam. He would overcome Satan, and in thus doing He would open the way for the redemption from the disgrace of Adam's failure and fall, of all those who would believe on Him.[25]

The Royal Robe

And to her was granted that she should be arrayed in fine linen, clean and white: for the fine linen is the righteousness of saints. Rev. 19:8.

The parable of the wedding garment [Matt. 22:1-14] opens before us a lesson of the highest consequence. . . . By the wedding garment in the parable is represented the pure, spotless character which Christ's true followers will possess. . . . The fine linen, says the Scripture, "is the righteousness of saints." It is the righteousness of Christ, His own unblemished character, that through faith is imparted to all who receive Him as their personal Saviour.

The white robe of innocence was worn by our first parents when they were placed by God in holy Eden. They lived in perfect conformity to the will of God. . . . A beautiful soft light, the light of God, enshrouded the holy pair. . . . But when sin entered, they severed their connection with God, and the light that had encircled them departed. Naked and ashamed, they tried to supply the place of the heavenly garments by sewing together fig leaves for a covering.[26]

We cannot provide a robe of righteousness for ourselves, for the prophet says, "All our righteousnesses are as filthy rags" (Isa. 64:6). There is nothing in us from which we can clothe the soul so that its nakedness shall not appear. We are to receive the robe of righteousness woven in the loom of heaven, even the spotless robe of Christ's righteousness.[27]

God has made ample provision that we may stand perfect in His grace, wanting in nothing, waiting for the appearing of our Lord. Are you ready? Have you the wedding garment on? That garment will never cover deceit, impurity, corruption, or hypocrisy. The eye of God is upon you. It is a discerner of the thoughts and intents of the heart. We may conceal our sins from the eyes of men, but we can hide nothing from our Maker.[28]

Let the youth and the little children be taught to choose for themselves that royal robe woven in heaven's loom—the "fine linen, clean and white," which all the holy ones of earth will wear. This robe, Christ's own spotless character, is freely offered to every human being. But all who receive it will receive and wear it here.[29]

An Inheritance in Heaven

To an inheritance incorruptible, and undefiled, and that fadeth not away, reserved in heaven for you. 1 Peter 1:4.

Christ was teaching, and, as usual, others besides His disciples had gathered about Him. . . . But there were many who desired the grace of heaven only to serve their selfish purposes. They recognized the marvelous power of Christ in setting forth the truth in a clear light. . . . Would He not lend His power for their worldly benefit?

"And one of the company said unto him, Master, speak to my brother, that he divide the inheritance with me" (Luke 12:13). . . . In the midst of the solemn instruction that Christ had given, this man had revealed his selfish disposition. He could appreciate that ability of the Lord which might work for the advancement of his own temporal affairs; but spiritual truths had taken no hold on his mind and heart. . . . [Jesus] was opening to him the treasures of divine love. The Holy Spirit was pleading with him to become an heir of the inheritance that is "incorruptible, and undefiled, and that fadeth not away.". . . [But] his eyes were fixed on the earth. . . .

The Saviour's mission on earth was fast drawing to a close. Only a few months remained for Him to complete what He had come to do, in establishing the kingdom of His grace. Yet human greed would have turned Him from His work to take up the dispute over a piece of land. But Jesus was not to be diverted from His mission. His answer was, "Man, who made me a judge or a divider over you?" . . . Christ virtually said, It is not My work to settle controversies of this kind. He came for another purpose, to preach the gospel, and thus to arouse men to a sense of eternal realities. . . .

When He sent forth the twelve, He said, "As ye go, preach, saying, the kingdom of heaven is at hand . . ." (Matt. 10:7, 8). They were not to settle the temporal affairs of the people. Their work was to persuade men to be reconciled to God. In this work lay their power to bless humanity. The only remedy for the sins and sorrows of humanity is Christ. The gospel of His grace alone can cure the evils that curse society. . . . He alone, for the selfish heart of sin, gives the new heart of love.[30]

The Gracious Invitation

Come unto me, all ye that labour and are heavy laden, and I will give you rest. Matt. 11:28.

Christ sought to teach the disciples the truth that in God's kingdom there are no territorial lines, no caste, no aristocracy; that they must go to all nations, bearing to them the message of a Saviour's love.[31]

Christ tears away the wall of partition, the self-love, the dividing prejudice of nationality, and teaches a love for all the human family. . . . He teaches us to look upon every needy soul as our neighbor and the world as our field. As the rays of the sun penetrate to the remotest corners of the globe, so God designs that the light of the gospel shall extend to every soul upon the earth.[32]

All over the world men and women are looking wistfully to heaven. Prayers and tears and inquiries go up from souls longing for light, for grace, for the Holy Spirit. Many are on the verge of the kingdom, waiting only to be gathered in. . . .

In the trust given to the first disciples, believers of every age have shared. Every one who has received the gospel has been given sacred truth to impart to the world. God's faithful people have always been aggressive missionaries, consecrating their resources to the honor of His name, and wisely using their talents in His service. . . .

Everyone who has received Christ is called to work for the salvation of his fellow men. "The Spirit and the bride say, Come. And let him that heareth say, Come" (Rev. 22:17). The charge to give this invitation includes the entire church. Every one who has heard the invitation is to echo the message from hill and valley, saying, "Come.". . .

Long has God waited for the spirit of service to take possession of the whole church, so that every one shall be working for Him according to his ability. When the members of the church of God do their appointed work in the needy fields at home and abroad, in fulfillment of the gospel commission, the whole world will soon be warned and the Lord Jesus will return to this earth with power and great glory.[33]

Embraces the Whole World

Ask of me, and I shall give thee the heathen for thine inheritance, and the uttermost parts of the earth for thy possession. Ps. 2:8.

The field is the world" (Matt. 13:38). We understand better what this saying comprehends than did the apostles who received the commission to preach the gospel. The whole world is a vast missionary field.[34]

The terrible condition of the world would seem to indicate that the death of Christ has been almost in vain, and that Satan has triumphed. . . . But we have not been deceived. Notwithstanding the apparent triumph of Satan, Christ is carrying forward His work in the heavenly sanctuary and on the earth. . . .

The solemn, sacred message of warning must be proclaimed in the most difficult fields and in the most sinful cities, in every place where the light of the great threefold gospel message has not yet dawned. Every one is to hear the last call to the marriage supper of the lamb. From town to town, from city to city, from country to country, the message of present truth is to be proclaimed, not with outward display, but in the power of the Spirit.[35]

Before man can belong to the kingdom of Christ, his character must be purified from sin and sanctified by the grace of Christ. . . . Christ longs to manifest His grace, and stamp His character and image upon the whole world. He was offered the kingdoms of this world by the one who revolted in heaven, to buy His homage to the principles of evil; but He came to establish a kingdom of righteousness, and He would not be bought; He would not abandon His purpose. This earth is His purchased inheritance, and He would have men free and pure and holy. . . . Though Satan works through human instrumentalities to hinder the purpose of Christ, there are triumphs yet to be accomplished through the blood shed for the world, that will bring glory to God and to the Lamb. His kingdom will extend, and embrace the whole world. . . . Christ will not be satisfied till victory is complete. But "he shall see of the travail of his soul, and shall be satisfied." "So shall they fear the name of the Lord from the west, and his glory from the rising of the sun" (Isa. 53:11; 59:19).[36]

Ambassadors of the Kingdom

Now then we are ambassadors for Christ, as though God did beseech you by us: we pray you in Christ's stead, be ye reconciled to God. 2 Cor. 5:20.

Since His ascension, Christ the great Head of the church, has carried forward His work in the world by chosen ambassadors, through whom He speaks to the children of men, and ministers to their needs. The position of those who have been called of God to labor in word and doctrine for the upbuilding of His church, is one of grave responsibility. In Christ's stead they are to beseech men and women to be reconciled to God. . . .

Christ's ministers are the spiritual guardians of the people entrusted to their care. Their work has been likened to that of watchmen. In ancient times, sentinels were often stationed on the walls of cities, where, from points of vantage, they could overlook important points to be guarded, and give warning of the approach of an enemy. Upon their faithfulness depended the safety of all within. . . .

To every minister the Lord declares: "O son of man, I have set thee a watchman unto the house of Israel; therefore thou shalt hear the word at my mouth, and warn them from me . . ." (Eze. 33:7-9). These words of the prophet declare the solemn responsibility resting upon those who are appointed as guardians of the church, stewards of the mysteries of God. . . .

It is the privilege of the watchmen on the walls of Zion to live so near to God, and to be so susceptible to the impressions of His Spirit, that He can work through them to tell sinners of their peril, and point them to the place of safety.[37]

The heart of the true minister is filled with an intense longing to save souls. . . . He watches for souls as one that must give an account. With his eyes fixed on the cross of Calvary, beholding the uplifted Saviour, relying on His grace, believing that He will be with him until the end, as his shield, his strength, his efficiency, he works for God. With invitations and pleadings, mingled with the assurances of God's love, he seeks to win souls to Jesus, and in heaven he is numbered among those who are "called, and chosen, and faithful" (Rev. 17:14).[38]

The Army of the Lord

Take unto you the whole armour of God, that ye may be able to withstand in the evil day, and having done all, to stand. Eph. 6:13.

The strength of an army is measured largely by the efficiency of the men in the ranks. A wise general instructs his officers to train every soldier for active service. He seeks to develop the highest efficiency on the part of all. If he were to depend on his officers alone he could never expect to conduct a successful campaign. He counts on loyal and untiring service from every man in his army. The responsibility rests largely upon the men in the ranks.

And so it is in the army of Prince Immanuel. Our General, who has never lost a battle, expects willing, faithful service from everyone who has enlisted under His banner. In the closing controversy now waging between the forces for good and the hosts of evil He expects all, laymen as well as ministers, to take part. All who have enlisted as His soldiers are to render faithful service as minutemen, with a keen sense of the responsibility resting upon them individually.[39]

All who enter the army are not to be generals, captains, sergeants, or even corporals. All have not the care and responsibility of leaders. There is hard work of other kinds to be done. Some must dig trenches and build fortifications; some are to stand as sentinels, some to carry messages. While there are but few officers, it requires many soldiers to form the rank and file of the army; yet its success depends upon the fidelity of every soldier. One man's cowardice or treachery may bring disaster upon the entire army.

There is earnest work to be done by us individually if we would fight the good fight of faith. Eternal interests are at stake. We must put on the whole armor of righteousness, we must resist the devil, and we have the sure promise that he will be put to flight. The church is to conduct an aggressive warfare, to make conquests for Christ, to rescue souls from the power of the enemy. God and holy angels are engaged in this warfare. Let us please Him who has called us to be soldiers.[40]

A Girdle of Truth

Stand therefore, having your loins girt about with truth. Eph. 6:14.

There is absolutely no safeguard against evil but truth. No man can stand firm for right in whose heart the truth does not abide. There is only one power that can make and keep us steadfast—the power of God, imparted to us through the grace of Christ.[41]

There are many in the church who take it for granted that they understand what they believe; but, until controversy arises, they do not know their own weakness. When separated from those of like faith and compelled to stand singly and alone to explain their belief, they will be surprised to see how confused are their ideas of what they had accepted as truth. . . .

The Lord calls upon all who believe His word to awake out of sleep. Precious light has come, appropriate for this time. It is Bible truth, showing the perils that are right upon us. This light should lead us to a diligent study of the Scriptures and a most critical examination of the positions which we hold. . . . Believers are not to rest in suppositions and ill-defined ideas of what constitutes truth. Their faith must be firmly founded upon the word of God so that when the testing time shall come and they are brought before councils to answer for their faith they may be able to give a reason for the hope that is in them, with meekness and fear. . . .

The erroneous teachings of popular theology have made thousands upon thousands of skeptics and infidels. There are errors and inconsistencies which many denounce as the teaching of the Bible that are really false interpretations of Scripture. . . . Instead of criticizing the Bible, let us seek, by precept and example, to present to the world its sacred, life-giving truths, that we may "show forth the praises of him who hath called you out of darkness into his marvellous light" (1 Peter 2:9).[42]

The truth stands firmly established on the eternal Rock—a foundation that storm and tempest can never move. . . . Do not lower the banner of truth . . . in order to unite with the solemn message for these last days anything that will tend to hide the peculiar features of our faith.[43]

A Breastplate for Safety

And having on the breastplate of righteousness. Eph. 6:14.

We must put on every piece of the armor, and then stand firm. The Lord has honored us by choosing us as His soldiers. Let us fight bravely for Him, maintaining the right in every transaction. . . . Put on as your breastplate that divinely protected righteousness which it is the privilege of all to wear. This will protect your spiritual life.[44]

Ample provisions have been made for all who sincerely, earnestly, and thoughtfully set about the work of perfecting holiness in the fear of God. Strength, grace, and glory have been provided through Christ, to be brought by ministering angels to the heirs of salvation. None are so low, so corrupt and vile, that they cannot find in Jesus, who died for them, strength, purity, and righteousness, if they will put away their sins, cease their course of iniquity, and turn with full purpose of heart to the living God. He is waiting to strip them of their garments, stained and polluted by sin, and to put upon them the white, bright robes of righteousness.[45]

The truly righteous, who sincerely love and fear God, wear the robe of Christís righteousness in prosperity and adversity alike. Self-denial, self-sacrifice, benevolence, kindness, love, patience, fortitude, and Christian trust are the daily fruits borne by those who are truly connected with God. Their acts may not be published to the world, but they themselves are daily wrestling with evil, and gaining precious victories over temptation and wrong.[46]

All who have put on the robe of Christ's righteousness will stand before Him as chosen and faithful and true. Satan has no power to pluck them out of the hand of the Saviour. Not one soul who in penitence and faith has claimed His protection will Christ permit to pass under the enemy's power.[47]

Each one will have a close struggle to overcome sin in his own heart. This is at times a very painful and discouraging work; because, as we see the deformities in our character, we keep looking at them, when we should look to Jesus and put on the robe of His righteousness. Everyone who enters the pearly gates of the city of God will enter there as a conqueror, and his greatest conquest will have been the conquest of self.[48]

Gospel Shoes for a Mission of Peace

And your feet shod with the preparation of the gospel of peace.
Eph. 6:15.

We are living in the midst of an "epidemic of crime," at which thoughtful, God-fearing men everywhere stand aghast. . . . Every day brings its heart-sickening record of violence and lawlessness, of indifference to human suffering, of brutal, fiendish destruction of human life. Every day testifies to the increase of insanity, murder, and suicide. Who can doubt that satanic agencies are at work among men with increasing activity to distract and corrupt the mind, and defile and destroy the body?

And while the world is filled with these evils, the gospel is too often presented in so indifferent a manner as to make but little impression upon the consciences or the lives of men. Everywhere there are hearts crying out for something which they have not. They long for a power that will give them mastery over sin, a power that will deliver them from the bondage of evil, a power that will give health and life and peace.[49]

The gospel is a message of peace. Christianity is a system, which, received and obeyed, would spread peace, harmony, and happiness throughout the earth. The religion of Christ will unite in close brotherhood all who accept its teachings.[50]

The peace of Christ is born of truth. It is harmony with God. The world is at enmity with the law of God; sinners are at enmity with their Maker; and as a result they are at enmity with one another. . . . Men cannot manufacture peace. Human plans for the purification and uplifting of individuals or of society will fail of producing peace, because they do not reach the heart. The only power that can create or perpetuate true peace is the grace of Christ. When this is implanted in the heart, it will cast out the evil passions that cause strife and dissension.[51]

The faces of men and women who walk and work with God express the peace of heaven. They are surrounded with the atmosphere of heaven. For these souls the kingdom of God has begun.[52]

The Lord is soon coming. Talk it, pray it, believe it. Make it a part of the life. . . . Gird on the Christian armor, and be sure that your feet are "shod with the preparation of the gospel of peace."[53]

A Shield for Defense

Above all, taking the shield of faith, wherewith ye shall be able to quench all the fiery darts of the wicked. Eph. 6:16.

Satan watches his opportunity to seize the precious graces when we are unguarded, and we shall have a severe conflict with the powers of darkness to retain them, or to regain a heavenly grace if through lack of watchfulness we lose it. But . . . it is the privilege of Christians to obtain strength from God to hold every precious gift. Fervent and effectual prayer will be regarded in heaven. When the servants of Christ take the shield of faith for their defense, and the sword of the Spirit for war, there is danger in the enemy's camp.[54]

Amidst the snares to which all are exposed, they need strong and trustworthy defenses on which to rely. Many in this corrupt age have so small a supply of the grace of God, that in many instances their defense is broken down by the first assault, and fierce temptations take them captives. The shield of grace can preserve all unconquered by the temptations of the enemy, though surrounded with the most corrupting influences. By firm principle, and unwavering trust in God, their virtue and nobleness of character can shine, and, although surrounded with evil, no taint need be left upon their virtue and integrity.[55]

The work of conquering evil is to be done through faith. Those who go into the battlefield will find that they must put on the whole armor of God. The shield of faith will be their defense and will enable them to be more than conquerors. Nothing else will avail but this—faith in the Lord of hosts, and obedience to His orders. Vast armies furnished with every other facility will avail nothing in the last great conflict. Without faith, an angel host could not help. Living faith alone will make them invincible and enable them to stand in the evil day, steadfast, unmovable, holding the beginning of their confidence firm unto the end.[56]

A Helmet for Protection

And take the helmet of salvation. Eph. 6:17.

God bids us fill the mind with great thoughts, pure thoughts. He desires us to meditate upon His love and mercy, to study His wonderful work in the great plan of redemption. Then clearer and still clearer will be our perception of truth, higher, holier, our desire for purity of heart and clearness of thought. The soul dwelling in the pure atmosphere of holy thought will be transformed by communion with God through the study of the Scriptures.[57]

The mind must be educated and disciplined to love purity. A love for spiritual things should be encouraged; yea, must be encouraged, if you would grow in grace and in the knowledge of the truth. . . . Good purposes are right, but will prove of no avail unless resolutely carried out. Many will be lost while hoping and desiring to be Christians; but they made no earnest effort, therefore they will be weighed in the balances and found wanting. The will must be exercised in the right direction. I *will* be a wholehearted Christian. I *will* know the length and breadth, the height and depth, of perfect love. Listen to the words of Jesus: "Blessed are they which do hunger and thirst after righteousness: for they shall be filled" (Matt. 5:6). Ample provisions are made by Christ to satisfy the soul that hungers and thirsts for righteousness.[58]

We should meditate upon the Scriptures, thinking soberly and candidly upon the things that pertain to our eternal salvation. The infinite mercy and love of Jesus, the sacrifice made in our behalf, call for most serious and solemn reflection. We should dwell upon the character of our dear Redeemer and Intercessor. We should seek to comprehend the meaning of the plan of salvation. We should meditate upon the mission of Him who came to save His people from their sins. By constantly contemplating heavenly themes, our faith and love will grow stronger. Our prayers will be more and more acceptable to God, because they will be more and more mixed with faith and love. They will be more intelligent and fervent. There will be more constant confidence in Jesus, and you will have a daily, living experience in the willingness and power of Christ to save unto the uttermost all that come unto God by Him.[59]

A Sword for Battle

And the sword of the Spirit, which is the word of God. Eph. 6:17.

God has provided abundant means for successful warfare against the evil that is in the world. The Bible is the armory where we may equip for the struggle. Our loins must be girt about with truth. Our breastplate must be righteousness. The shield of faith must be in our hand, the helmet of salvation on our brow; and with the sword of the Spirit, which is the word of God, we are to cut our way through the obstructions and entanglements of sin.[60]

The first Adam fell; the second Adam held fast to God and His Word under the most trying circumstances, and His faith in His Father's goodness, mercy, and love did not waver for one moment. "It is written" was His weapon of resistance, and it is the sword of the Spirit which every human being is to use.[61]

In these days of peril and corruption, the young are exposed to many trials and temptations. Many are sailing in a dangerous harbor. They need a pilot; but they scorn to accept the much needed help, feeling that they are competent to guide their own bark, and not realizing that it is about to strike a hidden rock that may cause them to make shipwreck of faith and happiness. . . . There is a disposition with many to be impetuous and headstrong. They have not heeded the wise counsel of the word of God; they have not battled with self, and obtained precious victories; and their proud, unbending will has driven them from the path of duty and obedience.[62]

There are great things expected from the sons and daughters of God. I look upon the youth of today, and my heart yearns over them. What possibilities are open before them! If they sincerely seek to learn of Christ, He will give them wisdom, as He gave wisdom to Daniel. . . . "The fear of the Lord is the beginning of wisdom." . . . "In all thy ways acknowledge him, and he shall direct thy paths" (Ps. 111:10; Prov. 3:6).

Let the youth try to appreciate the privilege that may be theirs, to be directed by the unerring wisdom of God. Let them take the Word of truth as the man of their counsel, and become skillful in the use of "the sword of the Spirit." Satan is a wise general; but the humble, devoted soldier of Jesus Christ may overcome him.[63]

The Battlefield

We wrestle not against flesh and blood, but against principalities, against powers, against the rulers of the darkness of this world, against spiritual wickedness in high places. Eph. 6:12.

The fallen world is the battlefield for the greatest conflict the heavenly universe and earthly powers have ever witnessed. It was appointed as a theater on which would be fought out the grand struggle between good and evil, between heaven and hell. Every human being acts a part in this conflict. No one can stand on neutral ground. Men must either accept or reject the world's Redeemer. All are witnesses, either for or against Christ. Christ calls upon those who stand under His banner to engage in the conflict with Him as faithful soldiers, that they may inherit the crown of life.[64]

Battles are to be fought every day. A great warfare is going on over every soul, between the prince of darkness and the Prince of life. . . . As God's agents you are to yield yourselves to Him, that He may plan and direct and fight the battle for you, with your cooperation. The Prince of life is at the head of His work. He is to be with you in your daily battle with self, that you may be true to principle; that passion, when warring for the mastery, may be subdued by the grace of Christ; that you come off more than conqueror through Him that hath loved us. Jesus has been over the ground. He knows the power of every temptation. He knows just how to meet every emergency, and how to guide you through every path of danger.[65]

God will have a people zealous of good works, standing firm amid the pollutions of this degenerate age. There will be a people who hold so fast to the divine strength that they will be proof against every temptation. Evil communications in flaming handbills may seek to speak to their senses and corrupt their minds; yet they will be so united to God and angels that they will be as those who see not and hear not. They have a work to do which no one can do for them, which is to fight the good fight of faith, and lay hold on eternal life. . . .

The youth may have principles so firm that the most powerful temptations of Satan will not draw them away from their allegiance.[66]

Loyalty a Must

Thou therefore endure hardness, as a good soldier of Jesus Christ.
2 Tim. 2:3.

We are soldiers of Christ; and those who enlist in His army are expected to do difficult work, work which will tax their energies to the utmost. We must understand that a soldier's life is one of aggressive warfare, of perseverance and endurance. For Christ's sake we are to endure trials. We are not engaged in mimic battles.[67]

Resolve, not in your own strength, but in the strength and grace given of God, that you will consecrate to Him now, just now, every power, every ability. You will then follow Jesus because He bids you, and you will not ask where, or what reward will be given. . . .

When you die to self, when you surrender to God, to do His work, to let the light that He has given you shine forth in good works, you will not labor alone. God's grace stands forth to cooperate with every effort to enlighten the ignorant and those who do not know that the end of all things is at hand. But God will not do your work. Light may shine in abundance, but the grace given will convert your soul only as it arouses you to cooperate with divine agencies. You are called upon to put on the Christian armor and enter the Lord's service as active soldiers. Divine power is to cooperate with human effort to break the spell of worldly enchantment that the enemy has cast upon souls.[68]

The Lord has honored us by choosing us as His soldiers. Let us fight bravely for Him, maintaining the right in every transaction. Rectitude in all things is essential to the warfare of the soul. As you strive for the victory over your own inclinations, He will help you by His Holy Spirit to be circumspect in every action, that you may give no occasion for the enemy to speak evil of the truth.[69]

We are soldiers of Christ. He is the Captain of our salvation, and we are under His orders and rules. We are to wear His armor; we are to be marshaled only under His banner. . . . We are to keep on the whole armor of God, and work as in view of the universe of heaven.[70]

Marching Orders

Speak unto the children of Israel, that they go forward. Ex. 14:15.

The history of the children of Israel is written for the instruction and admonition of all Christians. When the Israelites were overtaken by dangers and difficulties, and their way seemed hedged up, their faith forsook them, and they murmured against the leader whom God had appointed for them. . . . The divine command was: "Go forward." They were not to wait until the way was made plain, and they could comprehend the entire plan of their deliverance. God's cause is onward, and He will open a path before His people. . . .

There are times when the Christian life seems beset by dangers, and duty seems hard to perform. The imagination pictures impending ruin before, and bondage or death behind. Yet the voice of God speaks clearly above all discouragements: "Go forward." We should obey this command, let the result be what it may, even though our eyes cannot penetrate the darkness and though we feel the cold waves about our feet. . . .

Those who think it impossible for them to yield to the will of God and have faith in His promises until all is made clear and plain before them, will never yield at all. Faith is not certainty of knowledge; it "is the substance of things hoped for, the evidence of things not seen" (Heb. 11:1). To obey the commandments of God is the only way to obtain His favor. "Go forward" should be the Christian's watchword.[71]

Continual progress in knowledge and virtue is God's purpose for us. His law is the echo of His own voice, giving to all the invitation, "Come up higher; be holy, holier still." Every day we may advance in perfection of Christian character.[72]

Putting our trust in God, we are to move steadily forward, doing His work with unselfishness, in humble dependence upon Him, committing to His providence ourselves and all that concerns our present and future, holding the beginning of our confidence firm unto the end, remembering that we receive the blessings of heaven, not because of our worthiness, but because of Christ's worthiness and our acceptance, through faith in Him, of God's abounding grace.[73]

The Victory

Thanks be to God, which giveth us the victory through our Lord Jesus Christ. 1 Cor. 15:57.

Victories are not gained by ceremonies or display, but by simple obedience to the highest General, the Lord God of heaven. He who trusts in this Leader will never know defeat.[74]

The largest share of the annoyances of life, its daily corroding cares, its heartaches, its irritation, is the result of a temper uncontrolled. . . . The government of self is the best government in the world. By putting on the ornament of a meek and quiet spirit, ninety-nine out of a hundred of the troubles which so terribly embitter life might be saved. . . . The natural man must die, and the new man, Christ Jesus, take possession of the soul, so that the follower of Jesus may say in verity and truth: "I live; yet not I, but Christ liveth in me" (Gal. 2:20).

Self is difficult to conquer. Human depravity in every form is not easily brought into subjection to the Spirit of Christ. But all should be impressed with the fact that unless this victory is gained through Christ, there is no hope for them. The victory can be gained; for nothing is impossible with God. By His assisting grace, all evil temper, all human depravity, may be overcome. . . . You may be overcomers if you will, in the name of Christ, take hold of the work decidedly.[75]

The temptations of Satan are greater now than ever before, for he knows that his time is short, and that very soon every case will be decided, either for life or for death. It is no time now to sink down beneath discouragement and trial; we must bear up under all our afflictions, and trust wholly in the Almighty God of Jacob. . . . His grace is sufficient for all our trials; and although they are greater than ever before, yet if we trust wholly in God, we can overcome every temptation and through His grace come off victorious. . . .

When temptations and trials rush in upon us, let us go to God and agonize with Him in prayer. He will not turn us away empty, but will give us grace and strength to overcome, and to break the power of the enemy.[76]

Adam and Eve—Rulers in Eden

So God created man in his own image, in the image of God created he him; male and female created he them. And God blessed them and God said unto them, Be fruitful, and multiply, and replenish the earth, and subdue it: and have dominion over . . . every living thing that moveth upon the earth. Gen. 1:27, 28.

Adam was crowned king in Eden. To him was given dominion over every living thing that God had created. The Lord blessed Adam and Eve with intelligence such as He had not given to any other creature. He made Adam the rightful sovereign over all the works of His hands.[1]

Created to be "the image and glory of God," Adam and Eve had received endowments not unworthy of their high destiny. . . . Every faculty of mind and soul reflected the Creator's glory. Endowed with high mental and spiritual gifts, Adam and Eve were made but "little lower than the angels."[2]

Our first parents, though created innocent and holy, were not placed beyond the possibility of wrongdoing. God made them free moral agents, capable of appreciating the wisdom and benevolence of His character and the justice of His requirements, and with full liberty to yield or to withhold obedience. They were to enjoy communion with God and with holy angels; but before they could be rendered eternally secure, their loyalty must be tested. At the very beginning of man's existence a check was placed upon the desire for self-indulgence, the fatal passion that lay at the foundation of Satan's fall. The tree of knowledge, which stood near the tree of life in the midst of the garden, was to be a test of the obedience, faith, and love of our first parents. . . . God placed man under law, as an indispensable condition of his very existence. He was a subject of the divine government, and there can be no government without law. . . .

While they remained true to God, Adam and his companion were to bear rule over the earth. Unlimited control was given them over every living thing. The lion and the lamb sported peacefully around them, or lay . . . together at their feet. The happy birds flitted about them without fear; and as their glad songs ascended to the praise of their Creator, Adam and Eve united with them in thanksgiving to the Father and the Son.[3]

The Rulership Forfeited

The most High ruleth in the kingdom of men, and giveth it to whomsoever he will. Dan. 4:17.

Among the lower creatures Adam had stood as king . . . ; but when he transgressed, this dominion was forfeited. The spirit of rebellion, to which he himself had given entrance, extended throughout the animal creation. Thus not only the life of man, but the nature of the beasts, the trees of the forest, the grass of the field, the very air he breathed, all told the sad lesson of the knowledge of evil.[4]

Not only man but the earth had by sin come under the power of the wicked one. . . . At his creation Adam was placed in dominion over the earth. But by yielding to temptation, he was brought under the power of Satan. "Of whom a man is overcome, of the same is he brought in bondage" (2 Peter 2:19). When man became Satan's captive, the dominion which he held, passed to his conqueror. Thus Satan became "the god of this world" (2 Cor. 4:4). He had usurped that dominion over the earth which had been originally given to Adam.[5]

When Satan declared to Christ, The kingdom and the glory of the world are delivered unto me, and to whomsoever I will I give it, he stated what was true only in part, and he declared it to serve his own purpose of deception. Satan's dominion was that wrested from Adam, but Adam was the vicegerent of the Creator. His was not an independent rule. The earth is God's, and He has committed all things to His Son. Adam was to reign subject to Christ. When Adam betrayed his sovereignty into Satan's hands; Christ still remained the rightful king. . . .

By the one who had revolted in heaven the kingdoms of this world were offered Christ, to buy His homage to the principles of evil; but He would not be bought. . . .

Jesus gained the victory through submission and faith in God, and by the apostle He says to us, "Submit yourselves therefore to God. Resist the devil, and he will flee from you . . ." (James 4:7, 8). We cannot save ourselves from the tempter's power; he has conquered humanity . . . ; but "the name of the Lord is a strong tower: the righteous runneth into it, and is safe" (Prov. 18:10).[6]

Christ the Second Adam

For as in Adam all die, even so in Christ shall all be made alive. 1 Cor. 15:22.

The fall of man filled all heaven with sorrow. . . . The Son of God, heaven's glorious Commander, was touched with pity for the fallen race. His heart was moved with infinite compassion as the woes of the lost world rose up before Him. But divine love had conceived a plan whereby man might be redeemed. The broken law of God demanded the life of the sinner. In all the universe there was but one who could, in behalf of man, satisfy its claims. Since the divine law is as sacred as God Himself, only one equal with God could make atonement for its transgression. None but Christ could redeem fallen man from the curse of the law, and bring him again into harmony with Heaven. Christ would take upon Himself the guilt and shame of sin—sin so offensive to a holy God that it must separate the Father and His Son. Christ would reach to the depths of misery to rescue the ruined race. . . .

The plan of salvation had been laid before the creation of the earth; . . . yet it was a struggle, even with the King of the universe, to yield up His Son to die for the guilty race. . . . Oh, the mystery of redemption! the love of God for a world that did not love Him! . . . Through endless ages immortal minds, seeking to comprehend the mystery of that incomprehensible love, will wonder and adore.[7]

Christ is called the second Adam. In purity and holiness, connected with God and beloved by God, He began where the first Adam began. . . .

Christ was tempted by Satan in a hundredfold severer manner than was Adam, and under circumstances in every way more trying. The deceiver presented himself as an angel of light, but Christ withstood his temptations. He redeemed Adam's disgraceful fall, and saved the world. . . . He lived the law of God, and honored it in a world of transgression, revealing to the heavenly universe, to Satan, and to all the fallen sons and daughters of Adam that through His grace humanity can keep the law of God. . . .

Christ's victory was as complete as had been Adam's failure. So we may resist temptation, and force Satan to depart from us.[8]

Israel's Invisible King

Thou camest down also upon mount Sinai, and spakest with them from heaven, and gavest them right judgments, and true laws, good statutes and commandments. Neh. 9:13.

All through the pages of sacred history, where the dealings of God with His chosen people are recorded, there are burning traces of the great I AM. Never has He given to the sons of men more open manifestations of His power and glory than when He alone was acknowledged as Israel's ruler, and gave the law to His people. Here was a scepter swayed by no human hand; and the stately goings forth of Israel's invisible King were unspeakably grand and awful.

In all these revelations of the divine presence, the glory of God was manifested through Christ. Not alone at the Saviour's advent, but through all the ages after the Fall and the promise of redemption, "God was in Christ, reconciling the world unto himself" (2 Cor. 5:19). Christ was the foundation and center of the sacrificial system in both the patriarchal and the Jewish age. Since the sin of our first parents, there has been no direct communication between God and man. The Father has given the world into the hands of Christ, that through His mediatorial work He may redeem man and vindicate the authority and holiness of the law of God. All the communion between heaven and the fallen race has been through Christ. It was the Son of God that gave to our first parents the promise of redemption. It was He who revealed Himself to the patriarchs. . . . It was He who gave the law to Israel. Amid the awful glory of Sinai, Christ declared in the hearing of all the people the ten precepts of His Father's law. It was He who gave to Moses the law engraved upon the tables of stone. . . .

Jesus was the light of His people—the light of the world—before He came to earth in the form of humanity. The first gleam of light that pierced the gloom in which sin had wrapped the world, came from Christ. And from Him has come every ray of heaven's brightness that has fallen upon the inhabitants of the earth. In the plan of redemption Christ is the Alpha and the Omega—the First and the Last.[9]

Our Ruler in the Heavens

The Lord hath prepared his throne in the heavens; and his kingdom ruleth over all. Ps. 103:19.

The three Hebrews were called upon to confess Christ in the face of the burning fiery furnace. They had been commanded by the king to fall down and worship the golden image which he had set up, and threatened that if they would not, they should be cast alive into the fiery furnace, but they answered, "We are not careful to answer thee in this matter. If it be so, our God whom we serve is able to deliver us from the burning fiery furnace, and he will deliver us out of thine hand, O king. But if not, be it known unto thee, O king, that we will not serve thy gods, nor worship the golden image which thou hast set up" (Dan. 3:16-18).[10]

To bow down when in prayer to God is the proper attitude to occupy. . . . But such an act was homage to be rendered to God alone . . . , the Ruler of the universe; and these three Hebrews refused to give such honor to any idol even though composed of pure gold. In doing so, they would, to all intents and purposes, be bowing to the king of Babylon. . . . They suffered the penalty. . . . But Christ came in person and walked with them through the fire, and they received no harm.[11]

This miracle produced a striking change in the minds of the people. The great golden image, set up with such display, was forgotten. The king published a decree that anyone speaking against the God of these men should be put to death. . . .

These faithful Hebrews possessed great natural ability, they had enjoyed the highest intellectual culture, and now occupied a position of honor; but all this did not lead them to forget God. Their powers were yielded to the sanctifying influence of divine grace. . . . In their wonderful deliverance were displayed, before that vast assembly, the power and majesty of God. Jesus placed Himself by their side in the fiery furnace, and by the glory of His presence convinced the proud king of Babylon that it could be no other than the Son of God. . . . By the deliverance of His faithful servants, the Lord declares that He will take His stand with the oppressed and overthrow all earthly powers that would trample upon the authority of the God of heaven.[12]

God With Us

They shall call his name Emmanuel,
which being interpreted is, God with us. Matt. 1:23.

From the days of eternity the Lord Jesus Christ was one with the Father; He was "the image of God," the image of His greatness and majesty, "the outshining of his glory." It was to manifest this glory that He came to our world. To this sin-darkened earth He came to reveal the light of God's love—to be "God with us.". . .

Our little world is the lesson book of the universe. God's wonderful purpose of grace, the mystery of redeeming love, is the theme into which "angels desire to look," and it will be their study throughout endless ages. Both the redeemed and the unfallen beings will find in the cross of Christ their science and their song. It will be seen that the glory shining in the face of Jesus is the glory of self-sacrificing love. In the light from Calvary it will be seen that the law of self-renouncing love is the law of life for earth and heaven; that the love which "seeketh not her own" has its source in the heart of God. . . .

Jesus might have remained at the Father's side. He might have retained the glory of heaven, and the homage of the angels. But He chose to give back the scepter into the Father's hands, and to step down from the throne of the universe, that He might bring light to the benighted, and life to the perishing. . . .

This great purpose had been shadowed forth in types and symbols. The burning bush, in which Christ appeared to Moses, revealed God. . . . The all-merciful God shrouded His glory in a most humble type, that Moses could look upon it and live. So in the pillar of cloud by day and the pillar of fire by night, God communicated with Israel, revealing to men His will, and imparting to them His grace. God's glory was subdued, and His majesty veiled, that the weak vision of finite men might behold it. So Christ was to come in "the body of our humiliation" (Phil. 3:21, RV), "in the likeness of men.". . . His glory was veiled, His greatness and majesty were hidden, that He might draw near to sorrowful, tempted men.[13]

The Kingdom Threatened

When Jesus therefore perceived that they would come and take him by force, to make him a king, he departed again into a mountain himself alone. John 6:15.

Seated upon the grassy plain, in the twilight of the spring evening, the people ate of the food that Christ had provided. . . . No human power could create from five barley loaves and two small fishes food sufficient to feed thousands of hungry people. And they said one to another, "This is of a truth that Prophet that should come into the world" (John 6:14). . . . He can conquer the nations, and give to Israel the long-sought dominion.

In their enthusiasm the people are ready at once to crown Him king. They see that He makes no effort to attract attention or secure honor to Himself. . . . They fear that He will never urge His claim to David's throne. Consulting together, they agree to take Him by force, and proclaim Him the king of Israel. . . . Jesus sees what is on foot, and understands, as they cannot, what would be the result of such a movement. . . . Violence and insurrection would follow an effort to place Him on the throne, and the work of the spiritual kingdom would be hindered. Without delay the movement must be checked. Calling His disciples, Jesus bids them take the boat and return at once to Capernaum. . . .

Jesus now commands the multitude to disperse; and His manner is so decisive that they dare not disobey. . . . The kingly bearing of Jesus, and His few quiet words of command, quell the tumult, and frustrate their designs. They recognize in Him a power above all earthly authority, and without a question they submit.

When left alone, Jesus "went up into a mountain apart to pray.". . . He prayed for power to reveal to men the divine character of His mission, that Satan might not blind their understanding and pervert their judgment. . . . In travail and conflict of soul He prayed for His disciples. . . . Their long-cherished hopes, based on a popular delusion, were to be disappointed in a most painful and humiliating manner. In the place of His exaltation to the throne of David they were to witness His crucifixion. This was to be indeed His true coronation.[14]

A Kingly Procession

Rejoice greatly, O daughter of Zion; shout, O daughter of Jerusalem: behold, thy King cometh unto thee: he is just, and having salvation; lowly, and riding upon an ass, and upon a colt the foal of an ass. Zech. 9:9.

Five hundred years before the birth of Christ, the prophet Zechariah thus foretold the coming of the King to Israel. . . . Christ was following the Jewish custom for a royal entry. . . . No sooner was He seated upon the colt than a loud shout of triumph rent the air. The multitude hailed Him as Messiah, their King. . . . They could lead the triumphal procession with no royal standards, but they cut down the spreading palm boughs, Nature's emblem of victory, and waved them aloft with loud acclamations and hosannas. . . .

Never before in His earthly life had Christ permitted such a demonstration. He clearly foresaw the result. It would bring Him to the cross. But it was His purpose thus publicly to present Himself as the Redeemer. He desired to call attention to the sacrifice that was to crown His mission. . . .

Never before had the world seen such a triumphal procession. It was not like that of the earth's famous conquerors. No train of mourning captives, as trophies of kingly valor, made a feature of that scene. But about the Saviour were the glorious trophies of His labors of love for sinful man. There were the captives whom He had rescued from Satan's power, praising God for their deliverance. The blind whom He had restored to sight were leading the way. The dumb whose tongues He had loosed shouted the loudest hosannas. The cripples whom He had healed bounded with joy. . . . Lazarus, whose body had seen corruption in the grave, but who now rejoiced in the strength of glorious manhood, led the beast on which the Saviour rode. . . .

That scene of triumph was of God's own appointing. It had been foretold by the prophet, and man was powerless to turn aside God's purpose.[15]

As well might the priests and rulers attempt to deprive the earth of the shining face of the sun, as to shut from the world the beams of glory from the Sun of Righteousness. In spite of all opposition, the kingdom of Christ was confessed by the people.[16]

Jerusalem's King

Beautiful for situation, the joy of the whole earth, is mount Zion, on the sides of the north, the city of the great King. Ps. 48:2.

From the crest of Olivet, Jesus looked upon Jerusalem. Fair and peaceful was the scene spread out before Him. . . . The rays of the setting sun lighted up the snowy whiteness of its marble walls and gleamed from golden gate and tower and pinnacle. "The perfection of beauty" it stood, the pride of the Jewish nation. What child of Israel could gaze upon the scene without a thrill of joy and admiration! But far other thoughts occupied the mind of Jesus. "When he was come near, he beheld the city, and wept over it" (Luke 19:41). Amid the universal rejoicing of the triumphal entry, while palm branches waved, while glad hosannas awoke the echoes of the hills, and thousands of voices declared Him King, the world's Redeemer was overwhelmed with a sudden and mysterious sorrow. He, the Son of God, the Promised One of Israel, whose power had conquered death and called its captives from the grave, was in tears, not of ordinary grief, but of intense, irrepressible agony.

His tears were not for Himself. . . . He wept for the doomed thousands of Jerusalem—because of the blindness and impenitence of those whom He came to bless and to save. . . .

Though rewarded with evil for good, and hatred for His love, He had steadfastly pursued His mission of mercy. Never were those repelled that sought His grace. . . . But Israel had turned from her best Friend and only Helper. The pleadings of His love had been despised, His counsels spurned, His warnings ridiculed. . . .

When Christ should hang upon the cross of Calvary, Israel's day as a nation favored and blessed of God would be ended. . . . As Christ looked upon Jerusalem, the doom of a whole city, a whole nation, was before Him—that city, that nation, which had once been the chosen of God, His peculiar treasure.[17]

The long-suffering of God toward Jerusalem only confirmed the Jews in their stubborn impenitence. . . . Her children had spurned the grace of Christ.[18]

King of Glory

Lift up your heads, O ye gates; and be ye lift up, ye everlasting doors; and the King of glory shall come in. Who is this King of glory? The Lord strong and mighty, the Lord mighty in battle. Ps. 24:7, 8.

Christ came to earth as God in the guise of humanity. He ascended to heaven as the King of saints. His ascension was worthy of His exalted character. He went as One mighty in battle, a conqueror, leading captivity captive. He was attended by the heavenly host, amid shouts and acclamations of praise and celestial song.[19]

The disciples not only saw the Lord ascend, but they had the testimony of the angels that He had gone to occupy His Father's throne in heaven. . . . The brightness of the heavenly escort, and the opening of the glorious gates of God to welcome Him, were not to be discerned by mortal eyes. Had the track of Christ to heaven been revealed to the disciples in all its inexpressible glory, they could not have endured the sight. . . .

Their senses were not to become so infatuated with the glories of heaven that they would lose sight of the character of Christ on earth, which they were to copy in themselves. They were to keep distinctly before their minds the beauty and majesty of His life, the perfect harmony of all His attributes, and the mysterious union of the divine and human in His nature. . . . His visible ascent from the world was in harmony with the meekness and quiet of His life.[20]

What a source of joy to the disciples, to know that they had such a Friend in heaven to plead in their behalf! Through the visible ascension of Christ all their views and contemplation of heaven are changed. . . . They now looked upon it as their future home, where mansions were being prepared for them by their loving Redeemer. Prayer was clothed with a new interest, since it was a communion with their Saviour. . . .

They had a gospel to preach—Christ in human form, a Man of sorrows; Christ in humiliation, taken by wicked hands and crucified; Christ resurrected, and ascended to heaven, into the presence of God, to be man's Advocate; Christ to come again with power and great glory in the clouds of heaven.[21]

Ruler Over All Nations

That men may know that thou, whose name alone is JEHOVAH, art the most high over all the earth. Ps. 83:18.

In the annals of human history the growth of nations, the rise and fall of empires, appear as dependent on the will and prowess of man. The shaping of events seems, to a great degree, to be determined by his power, ambition, or caprice. But in the word of God the curtain is drawn aside, and we behold, behind, above, and through all the play and counterplay of human interests and power and passions, the agencies of the all-merciful One, silently, patiently working out the counsels of His own will. . . .

Every nation that has come upon the stage of action has been permitted to occupy its place on the earth, that it might be seen whether it would fulfill the purpose of "the Watcher and the Holy One." . . . While the nations rejected God's principles, and in this rejection wrought their own ruin, it was still manifest that the divine, overruling purpose was working through all their movements.

This lesson is taught in a wonderful symbolic representation given to the prophet Ezekiel [chapters 1 and 10]. . . . A number of wheels, intersecting one another, were moved by four living beings. . . . The wheels were so complicated in arrangement that at first sight they appeared to be in confusion; but they moved in perfect harmony. Heavenly beings, sustained and guided by the hand beneath the wings of the cherubim, were impelling these wheels; above them upon the sapphire throne, was the Eternal One; and round about the throne a rainbow, the emblem of divine mercy. As the wheellike complications were under the guidance of the hand beneath the wings of the cherubim, so the complicated play of human events is under divine control. Amidst the strife and tumult of nations, He that sitteth above the cherubim still guides the affairs of the earth.

The history of nations that one after another have occupied their allotted time and place, . . . speaks to us. To every nation and to every individual of today God has assigned a place in His great plan. . . . All are by their own choice deciding their destiny, and God is overruling all for the accomplishment of His purposes.[22]

Limits to God's Forbearance

It is time for thee, Lord, to work:
for they have made void thy law. Ps. 119:126.

During a vision of the night, I stood on an eminence, from which I could see houses shaken like a reed in the wind. Buildings, great and small, were falling to the ground. Pleasure resorts, theaters, hotels, and the homes of the wealthy were shaken and shattered. Many lives were blotted out of existence, and the air was filled with the shrieks of the injured and the terrified.

The destroying angels of God were at work. One touch, and buildings, so thoroughly constructed that men regarded them as secure against every danger, quickly became heaps of rubbish. There was no assurance of safety in any place. . . . The awfulness of the scenes that passed before me I cannot find words to describe. It seemed that the forbearance of God was exhausted and that the judgment day had come.

The angel that stood at my side then instructed me that but few have any conception of the wickedness existing in our world today, and especially the wickedness in the large cities. He declared that the Lord has appointed a time when He will visit transgressors in wrath for persistent disregard of His law. . . . God's supreme rulership and the sacredness of His law must be revealed to those who persistently refused to render obedience to the King of kings. Those who choose to remain disloyal must be visited in mercy with judgments, in order that, if possible, they may be aroused to a realization of the sinfulness of their course. . . . While the divine Ruler bears long with perversity, He is not deceived and will not always keep silence. His supremacy, His authority as Ruler of the universe, must finally be acknowledged and the just claims of His law vindicated.[23]

There are limits even to the forbearance of God, and many are exceeding these boundaries. They have overrun the limits of grace, and therefore God must interfere and vindicate His own honor. . . .

When the Lord comes forth as an avenger, He will also come as a protector of all those who have preserved the faith in its purity and kept themselves unspotted from the world.[24]

Qualifying for the Kingdom

Verily I say unto you, Whosoever shall not receive the kingdom of God as a little child, he shall not enter therein. Mark 10:15.

Christ does not acknowledge any caste, color, or grade as necessary to become a subject of His kingdom. Admittance to His kingdom does not depend upon wealth or a superior heredity. But those who are born of the Spirit are the subjects of His kingdom. Spiritual character is that which will be recognized by Christ. His kingdom is not of this world. His subjects are those who are partakers of the divine nature, having escaped the corruption that is in the world through lust. And this grace is given them of God. Christ does not find His subjects fitted for His kingdom, but He qualifies them by His divine power. Those who have been dead in trespasses and sins are quickened to spiritual life. The faculties which God has given them for holy purposes are refined, purified, and exalted, and they are led to form characters after the divine similitude. . . .

Christ draws them to Himself by an unseen power. He is the light of life, and He imbues them with His own Spirit. As they are drawn into the spiritual atmosphere, they see that they have been made the sport of Satan's temptations, and that they have been under his dominion; but they break the yoke of fleshly lusts, and refuse to be the servants of sin. . . . They realize that they have exchanged captains, and they take their directions from the lips of Jesus. As a servant looks to his master, and as a maid looks to her mistress, so these souls, drawn by the cords of love to Christ, constantly look unto Him who is the Author and Finisher of their faith. By beholding Jesus, by obeying His requirements, they increase in the knowledge of God and of Jesus Christ whom He hath sent. Thus they become changed into His image from character to character until they are distinguished from the world, and it can be written of them: "Ye are a chosen generation, a royal priesthood, an holy nation, a peculiar people; that ye should shew forth the praises of him who hath called you out of darkness into his marvellous light: which in time past were not a people, but are now the people of God: which had not obtained mercy, but now have obtained mercy" (1 Peter 2:9, 10).[25]

Sonship

As many as received him, to them gave he the power to become the sons of God, even to them that believe on his name. John 1:12.

When Adam's sin plunged the race into hopeless misery, God might have cut Himself loose from fallen beings. He might have treated them as sinners deserved to be treated. He might have commanded the angels of heaven to pour out upon our world the vials of His wrath. He might have removed this dark blot from His universe. But He did not do this. Instead of banishing them from His presence, He came still nearer to the fallen race. He gave His Son to become bone of our bone and flesh of our flesh. "The Word was made flesh, and dwelt among us, . . . full of grace and truth" (John 1:14). Christ by His human relationship to men drew them close to God. He clothed His divine nature with the garb of humanity, and demonstrated before the heavenly universe, before the unfallen worlds, how much God loves the children of men.

The gift of God to man is beyond all computation. Nothing was withheld. God would not permit it to be said that He could have done more or revealed to humanity a greater measure of love. In the gift of Christ He gave all heaven.[26]

Divine sonship is not something that we gain of ourselves. Only to those who receive Christ as their Saviour is given the power to become sons and daughters of God. The sinner cannot, by any power of his own, rid himself of sin. . . . But the promise of sonship is made to *all* who "believe on His name." Every one who comes to Jesus in faith will receive pardon.[27]

God was to be manifest in Christ, "reconciling the world unto himself" (2 Cor. 5:19). Man had become so degraded by sin that it was impossible for him, in himself, to come into harmony with Him whose nature is purity and goodness. But Christ, after having redeemed man from the condemnation of the law, could impart divine power to unite with human effort. Thus by repentance toward God and faith in Christ the fallen children of Adam might once more become "sons of God."[28]

When a soul receives Christ, he receives power to live the life of Christ.[29]

Adopted Sons and Daughters

Having predestinated us unto the adoption of children by Jesus Christ to himself, according to the good pleasure of his will, to the praise of the glory of his grace, wherein he hath made us accepted in the beloved. Eph. 1:5, 6.

Before the foundations of the earth were laid the covenant was made that all who were obedient, all who should through the abundant grace provided become holy in character and without blame before God by appropriating that grace, should be children of God.[30]

We owe everything to grace, free grace, sovereign grace. Grace in the covenant ordained our adoption. Grace in the Saviour effected our redemption, our regeneration, and our adoption to heirship with Christ.[31]

As we fully believe that we are His by adoption, we may have a foretaste of heaven. . . . We have a nearness to Him, and can hold sweet communion with Him. We obtain distinct views of His tenderness and compassion, and our hearts are broken and melted with contemplation of the love that is given to us. We feel indeed an abiding Christ in the soul. We abide in Him, and feel at home with Jesus. . . . We have a realizing sense of the love of God, and we rest in His love. No language can describe it, it is beyond knowledge. We are one with Christ, our life is hid with Christ in God. We have the assurance that when He who is our life shall appear, then shall we also appear with Him in glory. With strong confidence we can call God our Father.[32]

All who have been born into the heavenly family are in a special sense the brethren of our Lord. The love of Christ binds together the members of His family, and wherever that love is manifest there the divine relationship is revealed. . . .

Love to man is the earthward manifestation of the love of God. It was to implant this love, to make us children of one family, that the King of glory became one with us. And when His parting words are fulfilled, "Love one another, as I have loved you" (John 15:12); when we love the world as He has loved it, then for us His mission is accomplished. We are fitted for heaven; for we have heaven in our hearts.[33]

The Redemption Price

Neither by the blood of goats and calves,
but by his own blood he entered in once into the holy place,
having obtained eternal redemption for us. Heb. 9:12.

Every soul is precious, because it has been purchased by the precious blood of Jesus Christ.[34]

Some speak of the Jewish age as a Christless period, without mercy or grace. To such are applicable the words of Christ to the Sadducees, "Ye know not the Scriptures, neither the power of God" (Mark 12:24). The period of the Jewish economy was one of wonderful manifestations of divine power. . . .

The very system of sacrifices was devised by Christ, and given to Adam as typifying a Saviour to come, who would bear the sins of the world, and die for its redemption. . . .

The blood of the Son of God was symbolized by the blood of the slain victim, and God would have clear and definite ideas preserved between the sacred and the common. Blood was sacred, inasmuch as through the shedding of the blood of the Son of God alone could there be atonement for sin. Blood was also used to cleanse the sanctuary from the sins of the people, thus typifying the blood of Christ which alone can cleanse from sin.[35]

Our Saviour declares that He brought from heaven as a donation eternal life. He was to be lifted up upon the cross of Calvary to draw all men unto Him. How then shall we treat the purchased inheritance of Christ? Tenderness, appreciation, kindness, sympathy, and love should be shown to them. Then we may work to help and bless one another. In this work we have more than human brotherhood. We have the exalted companionship of heavenly angels. They cooperate with us in the work of enlightening high and low. . . .

Christ determined in council with His Father to spare nothing, however costly, to withhold nothing however highly it might be estimated, that would rescue the poor sinner. He would give all heaven to this work of salvation, of restoring the moral image of God in man. . . . To be a child of God is to be one with Christ in God, and to put forth our hands in earnest, self-sacrificing love to stengthen and bless the souls that are perishing in their sins.[36]

Abraham and His Children

If ye be Christ's, then are ye Abraham's seed, and heirs according to the promise. Gal. 3:29.

Of Abraham it is written that "he was called the friend of God," "the father of all them that believe." . . .

It was a high honor to which Abraham was called, that of being the father of the people who for centuries were the guardians and preservers of the truth of God for the world—of that people through whom all the nations of the earth should be blessed in the advent of the promised Messiah.[37]

Abraham was honored by the surrounding nations as a mighty prince and a wise and able chief. He did not shut away his influence from his neighbors. His life and character, in their marked contrast with those of the worshipers of idols, exerted a telling influence in favor of the true faith. His allegiance to God was unswerving, while his affability and benevolence inspired confidence and friendship, and his unaffected greatness commanded respect and honor.

His religion was not held as a precious treasure to be jealously guarded and enjoyed solely by the possessor. True religion cannot be thus held; for such a spirit is contrary to the principles of the gospel. While Christ is dwelling in the heart, it is impossible to conceal the light of His presence, or for that light to grow dim. On the contrary, it will grow brighter and brighter as day by day the mists of selfishness and sin that envelop the soul are dispelled by the bright beams of the Sun of Righteousness.

The people of God are His representatives upon the earth, and He intends that they shall be lights in the moral darkness of this world. Scattered all over the country, in the towns, cities, and villages, they are God's witnesses, the channels through which He will communicate to an unbelieving world the knowledge of His will and the wonders of His grace. It is His plan that all who are partakers of the great salvation shall be missionaries for Him. The piety of the Christian constitutes the standard by which worldlings judge the gospel. Trials patiently borne, blessings gratefully received, meekness, kindness, mercy, and love, habitually exhibited, are the lights that shine forth in the character before the world.[38]

Citizens of Heaven

Now therefore ye are no more strangers and foreigners, but fellow-citizens with the saints, and of the household of God. Eph. 2:19.

The people of God—the true Israel—though scattered throughout all nations, are on earth but sojourners, whose citizenship is in heaven.[39]

The condition of being received into the Lord's family is coming out from the world, separating from all its contaminating influences. The people of God are to have no connection with idolatry in any of its forms. They are to reach a higher standard. We are to be distinguished from the world, and then God says, "I will receive you as members of My royal family, children of the heavenly King." As believers in the truth we are to be distinct in practice from sin and sinners. Our citizenship is in heaven.

We should realize more clearly the value of the promises God has made to us, and appreciate more deeply the honor He has given us. God can bestow no higher honor upon mortals than to adopt them into His family, giving them the privilege of calling Him Father. There is no degradation in becoming children of God.[40]

We are strangers and pilgrims in this world. We are to wait, watch, pray, and work. The whole mind, the whole soul, the whole heart, and the whole strength are purchased by the blood of the Son of God. We are not to feel it our duty to wear a pilgrim's dress of just such a color, just such a shape, but neat, modest apparel, that the word of inspiration teaches us we should wear. If our hearts are united with Christ's heart, we shall have a most intense desire to be clothed with His righteousness. Nothing will be put upon the person to attract attention, or to create controversy.

Christianity—how many there are who do not know what it is! It is not something put on the outside. It is a life inwrought with the life of Jesus. It means that we are wearing the robe of Christ's righteousness.[41]

Citizens of heaven will make the best citizens of earth. A correct view of our duty to God leads to clear perceptions of our duty to our fellow men.[42]

The Test of Loyalty

He that hath my commandments, and keepeth them, he it is that loveth me: and he that loveth me shall be loved of my Father, and I will love him, and will manifest myself to him. John 14:21.

It is essential that every subject of the kingdom of God should be obedient to the law of Jehovah. . . . The fact that the law is holy, just, and good is to be testified before all nations, tongues, and peoples, to worlds unfallen, to angels, seraphim, and cherubim. The principles of the law of God were wrought out in the character of Jesus Christ, and he who cooperates with Christ, becoming a partaker of the divine nature, will develop the divine character, and become an illustration of the divine law. . . .

The more we study the attributes of the character of God as revealed in Christ, the more we see that justice has been sustained in the sacrifice that met the penalty of the law, . . . in order that man might have another probation. . . . Those who are obedient to the law of the government of God while in this brief probation, . . . will be pronounced in heaven loyal children of the Lord of Hosts. . . .

By both creation and redemption we are the Lord's property. We are absolutely His subjects, and amenable to the laws of His kingdom. Let no one foster the delusion that the Lord God of heaven and earth has no law by which to control and govern His subjects. We are dependent upon God for everything we enjoy. The food which we eat, the clothing we wear, the atmosphere we breathe, the life we enjoy from day to day, are received from God. We are under obligation to be governed by His will, to acknowledge Him as our supreme ruler. . . .

We are under a debt of gratitude to God for the revelation of His love in Christ Jesus; and as intelligent human agents, we are to reveal to the world the manner of character that will result from obedience to every specification of the law of God's government. In perfect obedience to His holy will, we are to manifest adoration, love, cheerfulness, and praise, and thus honor and glorify God. It is in this way alone that man may reveal the character of God in Christ to the world, and make manifest to men that happiness, peace, assurance, and grace come from obedience to the law of God.[43]

God's Claims Are First

We ought to obey God rather than men. Acts 5:29.

The message that we have to bear is not one that we need cringe to declare. Its advocates are not to seek to cover it, to conceal its origin and purpose. As those who have made solemn vows to God, and who have been commissioned as the messengers of Christ, as stewards of the mysteries of grace, we are under obligation to declare faithfully the whole counsel of God.

We are not to make less prominent the special truths that have separated us from the world, and made us what we are; for they are fraught with eternal interests. God has given us light in regard to the things that are now taking place, and with pen and voice we are to proclaim the truth to the world.[44]

The Sabbath is the Lord's test, and no man, be he king, priest, or ruler, is authorized to come between God and man. Those who seek to be conscience for their fellow men, place themselves above God. Those who are under the influence of a false religion, who observe a spurious rest day, will set aside the most positive evidence in regard to the true Sabbath. They will try to compel men to obey the laws of their own creation, laws that are directly opposed to the law of God. . . . The law for the observance of the first day of the week is the production of an apostate Christendom. . . . In no case are God's people to pay it homage.[45]

The banner of truth and religious liberty held aloft by the founders of the gospel church and by God's witnesses during the centuries that have passed since then, has, in this last conflict, been committed to our hands. . . . We are to recognize human government as an ordinance of divine appointment, and teach obedience to it as a sacred duty, within its legitimate sphere. But when its claims conflict with the claims of God, we must obey God rather than men. God's word must be recognized as above all human legislation. A "Thus saith the Lord" is not to be set aside for a "Thus saith the church" or a "Thus saith the state." The crown of Christ is to be lifted above the diadems of earthly potentates.[46]

Above Earthly Kingdoms

Whosoever therefore shall break one of these least commandments, and shall teach men so, he shall be called the least in the kingdom of heaven: but whosoever shall do and teach them, the same shall be called great in the kingdom of heaven. Matt. 5:19.

The qualities which shine with greatest luster in the kingdoms of the world, have no place in Christ's spiritual kingdom. That which is highly exalted among men, and brings exaltation to its possessor, such as caste, rank, position, or wealth, is not esteemed in the spiritual kingdom. The Lord says, "Them that honour me, I will honour" (1 Sam. 2:30). In Christ's kingdom men are distinguished according to their piety. . . .

The kingdom of heaven is of a higher order than any earthly kingdom. Whether we shall have a higher position or a lower position, will not be determined by our rank, wealth, or education, but by the character of the obedience rendered to the word of God. Those who have been actuated by selfishness and human ambition, who have been striving to be greatest, who have been self-important, who have felt above confessing mistakes and errors, will have no place in the kingdom of God. Whether men will be honored as members of the royal family of God, will be determined by the manner in which they bear the test and proving of God that is brought to bear upon them in this life. Those who have not been self-denying, who have not manifested sympathy for the woes of others, who have not cultivated the precious attributes of love, who have not manifested forbearance and meekness in this life, will not be changed when Christ comes. . . .

The character which we now manifest is deciding our future destiny. The happiness of heaven will be found by conforming to the will of God, and if men become members of the royal family in heaven, it will be because heaven has begun with them on earth. They have cherished the mind of Christ, and when the call comes, "Child, come up higher," the righteous will take every grace, every precious, sanctified ability, into the courts above, and exchange earth for heaven. God knows who are the loyal and true subjects of His kingdom on earth, and those who do His will upon earth as it is done in heaven, will be made the members of the royal family above.[47]

Blessings Through Obedience

I delight to do thy will, O my God:
yea, thy law is within my heart. Ps. 40:8.

What a God is our God! He rules over His kingdom with diligence and care, and He has built a hedge—the Ten Commandments—about His subjects to preserve them from the results of transgression. In requiring obedience to the laws of His kingdom, God gives His people health and happiness, peace and joy. He teaches them that the perfection of character He requires can be attained only by becoming familiar with His Word.[48]

The true seeker, who is striving to be like Jesus in word, life, and character, will contemplate his Redeemer and, by beholding, become changed into His image, because he longs and prays for the same disposition and mind that was in Christ Jesus. . . . He longs after God. The history of his Redeemer, the immeasurable sacrifice that He made, becomes full of meaning to him. Christ, the Majesty of heaven, became poor, that we through His poverty might become rich; not rich merely in endowments, but rich in attainments.

These are the riches that Christ earnestly longs that His followers shall possess. As the true seeker after the truth reads the Word and opens his mind to receive the Word, he longs after truth with his whole heart. The love, the pity, the tenderness, the courtesy, the Christian politeness, which will be the elements in the heavenly mansions that Christ has gone to prepare for those that love Him, take possession of his soul. His purpose is steadfast. He is determined to stand on the side of righteousness. Truth has found its way into the heart, and is planted there by the Holy Spirit, who is the truth. When truth takes hold of the heart, the man gives sure evidence of this by becoming a steward of the grace of Christ.[49]

Each steward has his own special work to do for the advancement of God's kingdom. . . . The talents of speech, memory, influence, property, are to accumulate for the glory of God and the advancement of His kingdom. He will bless the right use of His gifts.[50]

Stewards of God's Grace

As every man hath received the gift, even so minister the same one to another, as good stewards of the manifold grace of God. 1 Peter 4:10.

The knowledge of God's grace, the truths of His Word, and temporal gifts as well—time and means, talents and influence—are all a trust from God to be employed to His glory and the salvation of men. Nothing can be more offensive to God, who is constantly bestowing His gifts upon man, than to see him selfishly grasping these gifts and making no returns to the Giver. Jesus is today in heaven preparing mansions for those who love Him; yes, more than mansions, a kingdom which is to be ours. But all who shall inherit these blessings must be partakers of the self-denial and self-sacrifice of Christ for the good of others.

Never was there greater need of earnest, self-sacrificing labor in the cause of Christ than now, when the hours of probation are fast closing and the last message of mercy is to be given to the world. . . .

All that men receive of God's bounty still belongs to God. Whatever He has bestowed in the valuable and beautiful things of earth is placed in our hands to test us, to sound the depths of our love for Him and our appreciation of His favors. Whether it be the treasures of wealth or of intellect, they are to be laid, a willing offering, at the feet of Jesus. . . .

Whatever we render to God is, through His mercy and generosity, placed to our account as faithful stewards. . . . Angels of God, whose perceptions are unclouded by sin, recognize the endowments of heaven as bestowed with the intention that they be returned in such a way as to add to the glory of the great Giver. With the sovereignty of God is bound up the well-being of man. The glory of God is the joy and the blessing of all created beings. When we seek to promote His glory we are seeking for ourselves the highest good which it is possible for us to receive. . . . God calls for the consecration to His service of every faculty, of every gift, you have received from Him. He wants you to say, with David: "All things come of thee, and of thine own have we given thee" (1 Chron. 29:14).[51]

Stewards of Truth

Come and hear, all ye that fear God, and I will declare what he hath done for my soul. Ps. 66:16.

Wherever there is life, there is increase and growth; in God's kingdom there is a constant interchange—taking in, and giving out; receiving, and returning to the Lord His own. God works with every true believer, and the light and blessings received are given out again in the work which the believer does. Thus the capacity for receiving is increased. As one imparts of the heavenly gifts, he makes room for fresh currents of grace and truth to flow into the soul from the living fountain. Greater light, increased knowledge and blessing, are his. In this work, which devolves upon every church member, is the life and growth of the church. He whose life consists in ever receiving and never giving, soon loses the blessing. If truth does not flow forth from him to others, he loses his capacity to receive. We must impart the goods of heaven if we desire fresh blessings.[52]

As the knowledge of truth is imparted, it will increase. All who receive the gospel message into the heart will long to proclaim it. The heaven-born love of Christ must find expression. Those who have put on Christ will relate their experience, tracing step by step the leadings of the Holy Spirit—their hungering and thirsting for the knowledge of God and of Jesus Christ whom He has sent, the results of their searching of the Scriptures, their prayers, their soul agony, and the words of Christ to them, "Thy sins be forgiven thee."

It is unnatural for any to keep these things secret, and those who are filled with the love of Christ will not do so. In proportion as the Lord has made them the depositaries of sacred truth will be their desire that others shall receive the same blessing. And as they make known the rich treasures of God's grace, more and still more of the grace of Christ will be imparted to them. They will have the heart of a little child in its simplicity and unreserved obedience. Their souls will pant after holiness and more and more of the treasures of truth and grace will be revealed to them to be given to the world.[53]

Stewards of Strength

Thou shalt love the Lord thy God with all thy heart, and with all thy soul, and with all thy mind, and with all thy strength. Mark 12:30.

To every man is committed individual gifts, termed talents. Some regard these talents as being limited to certain men who possess superior mental endowments and genius. But God has not restricted the bestowal of His talents to a favored few. To every one is committed some special endowment, for which he will be held responsible by the Lord. Time, reason, means, strength, mental powers, tenderness of heart—all are gifts from God, entrusted to be used in the great work of blessing humanity.[54]

In the capital of strength a precious talent has been entrusted to men for labor. This is of more value than any bank deposit, and should be more highly prized. . . . It is a blessing that cannot be purchased with gold or silver, houses or lands; and God requires it to be used wisely. No man has a right to sacrifice this talent to the corroding influence of inaction. All are as accountable for the capital of physical strength as for their capital of means. . . .

The essential lesson of contented industry in the necessary duties of life is yet to be learned by many of Christ's followers. It requires more grace, more stern discipline of character, to work for God in the capacity of mechanic, merchant, lawyer, or farmer, carrying the precepts of Christianity into the ordinary business of life, than to labor as an acknowledged missionary in the open field. It requires a strong spiritual nerve to bring religion into the workshop and the business office, sanctifying the details of everyday life, and ordering every transaction according to the standard of God's word. But this is what the Lord requires.[55]

Religion and business are not two separate things; they are one. Bible religion is to be interwoven with all we do or say. Divine and human agencies are to combine in temporal as well as in spiritual achievements.[56]

We are to love God, not only with all the heart, mind, and soul, but with all the strength. This covers the full, intelligent use of the physical powers.[57]

Stewards of Influence

Lift up the hands which hang down, and the feeble knees; and make straight paths for your feet, lest that which is lame be turned out of the way; but let it rather be healed. Follow peace with all men, and holiness, without which no man shall see the Lord: looking diligently lest any man fail of the grace of God. Heb. 12:12-15.

These words should teach us to be very careful how we snap the thread of our faith by dwelling on our difficulties until they are large in our own eyes, and in the eyes of others, who cannot read our inner, heart life. All should remember that the conversation has a great influence for good or for ill. . . . Do not allow the enemy so to use your tongue. . . . Do not exert an influence that will break the hold of any trembling soul from God. . . .

The graces of Christ's Spirit must be cherished and revealed by the sons and daughters of God. By their humility, their penitence, their desire to be like Jesus, to be conformed to His will by practicing His lessons in their daily life, they honor Him. . . .

"Ye are God's husbandry" (1 Cor. 3:9). As one takes pleasure in the cultivation of a garden, so God takes pleasure in His believing sons and daughters. A garden demands constant labor. The weeds must be removed; new plants must be set out; branches that are making too rapid development must be pruned back. So the Lord works for His garden, so He tends His plants. He cannot take pleasure in any development that does not reveal the graces of the character of Christ. The blood of Christ has made men and women God's precious charge. Then how careful should we be not to manifest too much freedom in pulling up the plants that God has placed in His garden! Some plants are so feeble that they have hardly any life, and for these the Lord has a special care.

In all your transactions with your fellow men, never forget that you are dealing with God's property. Be kind; be pitiful; be courteous. Respect God's purchased possession. Treat one another with tenderness and courtesy. Exert every God-given faculty to become examples to others. . . .

Let Him who knows the heart and all its waywardness be able to deal with you in mercy because you have shown mercy and compassion and love. . . . (Heb. 12:13).[58]

Your Royal Birth

We then, as workers together with him, beseech you also that ye receive not the grace of God in vain. 2 Cor. 6:1.

Many who claim to be Christians are not Christians. . . . God takes none to heaven but those who are first made saints in this world through the grace of Christ, those in whom He can see Christ exemplified. . . .

"The Lord is very pitiful, and of tender mercy" (James 5:11). . . . He looks upon His redeemed heritage with pity. He is ready to pardon their sins if they will surrender and be loyal to Him. In order to be just, and yet the justifier of the sinner, He laid the punishment of sin upon His only begotten Son. . . . For Christ's sake He pardons those that fear Him. He does not see in them the vileness of the sinner; He recognizes in them the likeness of His Son, in whom they believe. In this way only can God take pleasure in any of us. "As many as received him, to them gave he power to become the sons of God, even to them that believe on his name" (John 1:12).

Were it not for Christ's atoning sacrifice, there would be nothing in us in which God could delight. All the natural goodness of man is worthless in God's sight. He does not take pleasure in any man who retains his old nature, and is not so renewed in knowledge and grace that he is a new man in Christ. Our education, our talents, our means, are gifts entrusted to us by God, that He may test us. If we use them for self-glorification, God says, "I cannot delight in them; for Christ has died for them in vain." . . .

To adorn the doctrine of Christ our Saviour, we must have the mind that was in Christ. Our likes and dislikes, our desire to be first, to favor self to the disadvantage of others, must be overcome. The peace of God must rule in our hearts. Christ must be in us a living, working principle. . . .

By your obedience to God, respect yourselves as the purchased possession of His dear Son. Seek to be uplifted in Christ. This work is as lasting as eternity. . . . Shall we, sons and daughters of God, forget our royal birth? Shall we not rather honor our Lord and Saviour Jesus Christ? Shall we not show forth the praises of Him who has called us out of darkness into His marvelous light?[59]

A Share in Christ's Kingdom

I appoint unto you a kingdom, as my Father hath appointed unto me; that ye may eat and drink at my table in my kingdom, and sit on thrones judging the twelve tribes of Israel. Luke 22:29, 30.

What a promise is this! Christ's faithful ones are to be sharers with Him in the kingdom He has received from His Father. This is a spiritual kingdom, in which those who are most active in serving their brethren are the greatest. Christ's servants, under His direction, are to administer the affairs of His kingdom. They are to eat and drink at His table, that is, be admitted to near communion with Him.[60]

Those who search for worldly distinction and glory make a sad mistake. It is the one who denies self, giving to others the preference, who will sit nearest to Christ on His throne. He who reads the heart sees the true merit possessed by His lowly, self-sacrificing disciples, and because they are worthy He places them in positions of distinction, though they do not realize their worthiness and do not seek for honor. . . .

God places no value on outward display or boasting. Many who in this life are looked upon as superior to others, will one day see that God values men according to their compassion and self-denial. . . . Those who follow the example of Him who went about doing good, who help and bless their fellow men, trying always to lift them up, are in God's sight infinitely higher than the selfish ones who exalt themselves.

God does not accept men because of their capabilities, but because they seek His face, desiring His help. God sees not as man sees. He judges not from appearances. He searches the heart, and judges righteously. . . .

He accepts and communes with His lowly, unpretentious followers; for in them He sees the most precious material, which will stand the test of storm and tempest, heat and pressure. Our object in working for the Master should be that His name may be glorified in the conversion of sinners. . . .

Let us rejoice that the Lord does not measure the workers in His vineyard by their learning or by the educational advantages they have had. The tree is judged by its fruit. The Lord will cooperate with those who cooperate with Him.[61]

Heaven's Highest Attraction

Let us therefore come boldly unto the throne of grace, that we may obtain mercy, and find grace to help in time of need. Heb. 4:16.

After pointing to Christ, the compassionate intercessor who is "touched with the feeling of our infirmities," the apostle says: "Let us therefore come boldly unto the throne of grace. . . ." The throne of grace represents the kingdom of grace; for the existence of a throne implies the existence of a kingdom.[1]

God's appointments and grants in our behalf are without limit. The throne of grace is itself the highest attraction because occupied by One who permits us to call Him Father. But God did not deem the principle of salvation complete while invested only with His own love. By His appointment He has placed at His altar an Advocate clothed with our nature. As our Intercessor, His office work is to introduce us to God as His sons and daughters. Christ intercedes in behalf of those who have received Him. To them He gives power, by virtue of His own merits, to become members of the royal family, children of the heavenly King. And the Father demonstrates His infinite love for Christ, who paid our ransom with His blood, by receiving and welcoming Christ's friends as His friends. He is satisfied with the atonement made. He is glorified by the incarnation, the life, death, and mediation of His Son.

No sooner does the child of God approach the mercy seat than he becomes the client of the great Advocate. At his first utterance of penitence and appeal for pardon Christ espouses his case and makes it His own, presenting the supplication before the Father as His own request.

As Christ intercedes in our behalf, the Father lays open all the treasures of His grace for our appropriation, to be enjoyed and to be communicated to others. "Ask in my name," Christ says; "I do not say that I will pray the Father for you; for the Father Himself loveth you, because you have loved Me. Make use of My name. This will give your prayers efficiency, and the Father will give you the riches of His grace; wherefore, 'ask and ye shall receive, that your joy may be full' (John 16:24)."[2]

Christ Is Priest Upon the Throne

Seeing then that we have a great high priest, that is passed into the heavens, Jesus the Son of God, let us hold fast our profession. Heb. 4:14.

In the temple in heaven, the dwelling place of God, His throne is established in righteousness and judgment. In the most holy place is His law, the great rule of right by which all mankind are tested. The ark that enshrines the tables of the law is covered with the mercy seat, before which Christ pleads His blood in the sinner's behalf. Thus is represented the union of justice and mercy in the plan of human redemption. . . .

As a priest, Christ is now set down with the Father in His throne. Upon the throne with the eternal, self-existent One, is He who "hath borne our griefs, and carried our sorrows" (Isa. 53:4), who "was in all points tempted like as we are, yet without sin" (Heb. 4:15). . . . "If any man sin, we have an Advocate with the Father" (1 John 2:1). His intercession is that of a pierced and broken body, of a spotless life. The wounded hands, the pierced side, the marred feet, plead for fallen man, whose redemption was purchased at such infinite cost.[3]

The intercession of Christ in man's behalf in the sanctuary above is as essential to the plan of salvation as was His death upon the cross. . . . Through defects in the character, Satan works to gain control of the whole mind, and he knows that if these defects are cherished, he will succeed. Therefore he is constantly seeking to deceive the followers of Christ with his fatal sophistry that it is impossible for them to overcome. But Jesus pleads in their behalf His wounded hands, His bruised body; and He declares to all who would follow Him: "My grace is sufficient for thee" (2 Cor. 12:9). . . . Let none, then, regard their defects as incurable. God will give faith and grace to overcome them.

We are now living in the great day of atonement. . . . All who would have their names retained in the book of life should now, in the few remaining days of their probation, afflict their souls before God by sorrow for sin and true repentance. There must be deep, faithful searching of heart.[4]

Encircled by a Rainbow

Behold, a throne was set in heaven, and one sat on the throne . . . and there was a rainbow round about the throne. Rev. 4:2, 3.

The rainbow of promise encircling the throne on high is an everlasting testimony that "God so loved the world, that he gave his only begotten son, that whosoever believeth in him should not perish, but have everlasting life" (John 3:16). It testifies to the universe that God will never forsake His people in their struggle with evil. It is an assurance to us of strength and protection as long as the throne itself shall endure.[5]

As the bow in the cloud is formed by the union of the sunlight and the shower, so the rainbow encircling the throne represents the combined power of mercy and justice. It is not justice alone that is to be maintained; for this would eclipse the glory of the rainbow of promise above the throne; man could see only the penalty of the law. Were there no justice, no penalty, there would be no stability to the government of God.

It is the mingling of judgment and mercy that makes salvation full and complete. It is the blending of the two that leads us, as we view the world's Redeemer and the law of Jehovah, to exclaim, "Thy gentleness hath made me great" (2 Sam. 22:36). We know that the gospel is a perfect and complete system, revealing the immutability of the law of God. . . . Mercy invites us to enter through the gates into the city of God, and justice is sacrificed to accord to every obedient soul full privileges as a member of the royal family, a child of the heavenly King.[6]

By faith let us look upon the rainbow round about the throne, the cloud of sins confessed behind it. The rainbow of promise is an assurance to every humble, contrite, believing soul, that his life is one with Christ, and that Christ is one with God. The wrath of God will not fall upon one soul that seeks refuge in Him. God Himself has declared, "When I see the blood, I will pass over you." "The bow shall be in the cloud; and I will look upon it, that I may remember the everlasting covenant" (Ex. 12:13; Gen. 9:16).[7]

In the Most Holy Place

The Lord is in his holy temple:
let all the earth keep silence before him. Hab. 2:20.

I saw a throne, and on it sat the Father and the Son. I gazed on Jesus' countenance and admired His lovely person. The Father's person I could not behold, for a cloud of glorious light covered Him. I asked Jesus if His Father had a form like Himself. He said He had, but I could not behold it, for said He, "If you should once behold the glory of His person, you would cease to exist." . . .

I saw the Father rise from the throne, and in a flaming chariot go into the holy of holies within the veil, and sit down. . . . Then a cloudy chariot, with wheels like flaming fire, surrounded by angels, came to where Jesus was. He stepped into the chariot and was borne to the holiest, where the Father sat. There I beheld Jesus, a great High Priest, standing before the Father.[8]

Two lovely cherubs, one on each side of the ark, stood with their wings outstretched above it, and touching each other above the head of Jesus as He stood before the mercy seat. Their faces were turned toward each other, and they looked downward to the ark, representing all the angelic host looking with interest at the law of God. Between the cherubim was a golden censer, and as the prayers of the saints, offered in faith, came up to Jesus, and He presented them to His Father, a cloud of fragrance arose from the incense, looking like smoke of most beautiful colors. Above the place where Jesus stood, before the ark, was exceedingly bright glory that I could not look upon; it appeared like the throne of God.[9]

Our crucified Lord is pleading for us in the presence of the Father at the throne of grace. His atoning sacrifice we may plead for our pardon, our justification, and our sanctification. The lamb slain is our only hope. Our faith looks up to Him, grasps Him as the One who can save to the uttermost, and the fragrance of the all-sufficient offering is accepted of the Father. . . . Christ's glory is concerned in our success. He has a common interest in all humanity. He is our sympathizing Saviour.[10]

Guarded by Seraphim

I saw also the Lord sitting upon a throne, high and lifted up, and his train filled the temple. Isa. 6:1.

When God was about to send Isaiah with a message to His people, He first permitted the prophet to look in vision into the holy of holies within the sanctuary. Suddenly the gate and the inner veil of the temple seemed to be uplifted or withdrawn, and he was permitted to gaze within, upon the holy of holies, where even the prophet's feet might not enter. There rose before him a vision of Jehovah sitting upon a throne high and lifted up, while the train of His glory filled the temple. Around the throne were seraphim, as guards about the great King, and they reflected the glory that surrounded them. As their songs of praise resounded in deep notes of adoration, the pillars of the gate trembled, as if shaken by an earthquake. With lips unpolluted by sin, these angels poured forth the praises of God. "Holy, holy, holy, is the Lord of hosts," they cried: "the whole earth is full of his glory" (Isa. 6:3).

The seraphim around the throne are so filled with reverential awe as they behold the glory of God, that they do not for an instant look upon themselves with admiration. Their praise is for the Lord of hosts. As they look into the future, when the whole earth shall be filled with His glory, the triumphant song is echoed from one to another in melodious chant, "Holy, holy, holy, is the Lord of hosts." They are fully satisfied to glorify God; abiding in His presence, beneath His smile of approbation, they wish for nothing more.[11]

The world that Satan has claimed and has ruled over with cruel tyranny, the Son of God has, by one vast achievement, encircled in His love and connected again with the throne of Jehovah. Cherubim and seraphim, and the unnumbered hosts of all the unfallen worlds, sang anthems of praise to God and the Lamb when this triumph was assured. They rejoiced that the way of salvation had been opened to the fallen race and that the earth would be redeemed from the curse of sin. How much more should those rejoice who are the objects of such amazing love! How can we ever be in doubt and uncertainty, and feel that we are orphans?[12]

Founded on Righteousness

Righteousness and justice are the foundation of his throne.
Ps. 97:2, NEB.

In all His dealings with His creatures God has maintained the principles of righteousness by revealing sin in its true character—by demonstrating that its sure result is misery and death. The unconditional pardon of sin never has been, and never will be. Such pardon would show the abandonment of the principles of righteousness, which are the very foundation of the government of God. It would fill the unfallen universe with consternation. God has faithfully pointed out the results of sin, and if these warnings were not true, how could we be sure that His promises would be fulfilled? That so-called benevolence which would set aside justice, is not benevolence, but weakness.

God is the life-giver. From the beginning, all His laws were ordained to life. But sin broke in upon the order that God had established, and discord followed. So long as sin exists, suffering and death are inevitable. It is only because the Redeemer has borne the curse of sin in our behalf, that man can hope to escape, in his own person, its dire results.[13]

We are to accept of Christ as our personal Saviour, and He imputes unto us the righteousness of God in Christ. "Herein is love, not that we loved God, but that he loved us, and sent his Son to be the propitiation for our sins" (1 John 4:10).

In the love of God has been opened the most marvelous vein of precious truth, and the treasures of the grace of Christ are laid open before the church and the world. . . . What love is this, what marvelous, unfathomable love that would lead Christ to die for us while we were yet sinners. What a loss it is to the soul who understands the strong claims of the law, and who yet fails to understand the grace of Christ which doth much more abound. . . . Look at the cross of Calvary. It is a standing pledge of the boundless love, the measureless mercy of the heavenly Father.[14]

There is a God in Israel, with whom is deliverance for all that are oppressed. Righteousness is the habitation of His throne.[15]

Established in Justice and Judgment

Justice and judgment are the habitation of thy throne:
mercy and truth shall go before thy face. Ps. 89:14.

Through Jesus, God's mercy was manifested to men; but mercy does not set aside justice. The law reveals the attributes of God's character, and not a jot or tittle of it could be changed to meet man in his fallen condition. God did not change His law, but He sacrificed Himself, in Christ, for man's redemption. "God was in Christ, reconciling the world unto himself" (2 Cor. 5:19). . . .

God's love has been expressed in His justice no less than in His mercy. Justice is the foundation of His throne, and the fruit of His love. It had been Satan's purpose to divorce mercy from truth and justice. He sought to prove that the righteousness of God's law is an enemy to peace. But Christ shows that in God's plan they are indissolubly joined together; the one cannot exist without the other. "Mercy and truth are met together; righteousness and peace have kissed each other" (Ps. 85:10).

By His life and His death, Christ proved that God's justice did not destroy His mercy, but that sin could be forgiven, and that the law is righteous, and can be perfectly obeyed. Satan's charges were refuted.[16]

The grace of Christ and the law of God are inseparable. In Jesus mercy and truth are met together. . . . He was the representative of God and the exemplar of humanity. He presented to the world what humanity might become when united by faith with divinity. The only-begotten Son of God took upon Him the nature of man, and established His cross between earth and heaven. Through the cross, man was drawn to God, and God to man. Justice moved from its high and awful position, and the heavenly hosts, the armies of holiness, drew near to the cross, bowing with reverence; for at the cross justice was satisfied. Through the cross the sinner was drawn from the stronghold of sin, from the confederacy of evil, and at every approach to the cross his heart relents and in penitence he cries, "It was my sins that crucified the Son of God." At the cross he leaves his sins, and through the grace of Christ his character is transformed.[17]

Fountain of Life and Power

Every creature which is in heaven, and on the earth, and under the earth, and such as are in the sea, and all that are in them, heard I saying, Blessing, and honour, and glory, and power, be unto him that sitteth upon the throne, and unto the Lamb for ever and ever. Rev. 5:13.

God desires His obedient children to claim His blessing and to come before Him with praise and thanksgiving. God is the Fountain of life and power. . . . He has done for His chosen people that which should inspire every heart with thanksgiving, and it grieves Him that so little praise is offered. He desires to have a stronger expression from His people, showing that they know they have reason for joy and gladness.

The dealings of God with His people should be often repeated. How frequently were the waymarks set up by the Lord in His dealings with ancient Israel! Lest they should forget the history of the past, He commanded Moses to frame these events into song, that parents might teach them to their children. . . . For His people in this generation the Lord has wrought as a wonder-working God. The past history of the cause of God needs to be often brought before the people, young and old. We need often to recount God's goodness and to praise Him for His wonderful works. . . .

The church of God below is one with the church of God above. Believers on the earth and the beings in heaven who have never fallen constitute one church. Every heavenly intelligence is interested in the assemblies of the saints who on earth meet to worship God. In the inner court of heaven they listen to the testimony of the witnesses for Christ in the outer court on earth, and the praise and thanksgiving from the worshipers below is taken up in the heavenly anthem, and praise and rejoicing sound through the heavenly courts because Christ has not died in vain for the fallen sons of Adam. While angels drink from the fountainhead, the saints on earth drink of the pure streams flowing from the throne, the streams that make glad the city of our God. Oh, that we could all realize the nearness of heaven to earth! . . . In every assembly of the saints below are angels of God, listening to the testimonies, songs, and prayers. Let us remember that our praises are supplemented by the choirs of the angelic host above.[18]

Center of Worship

I will worship toward thy holy temple, and praise thy name for thy lovingkindness and for thy truth. Ps. 138:2.

The bright and cheerful side of our religion will be represented by all who are daily consecrated to God. . . . While we review, not the dark chapters in our experience, but the manifestations of God's great mercy and unfailing love, we shall praise far more than complain. We shall talk of the loving faithfulness of God as the true, tender, compassionate shepherd of His flock, which He has declared that none shall pluck out of His hand. The language of the heart will not be selfish murmuring and repining. Praise, like clear-flowing streams, will come from God's truly believing ones. . . .

The temple of God is opened in heaven, and the threshold is flushed with the glory of God which is for every church that will love God and keep His commandments. We need to study, to meditate, and to pray. Then we shall have spiritual eyesight to discern the inner courts of the celestial temple. We shall catch the themes of song and thanksgiving of the heavenly choir round about the throne. When Zion shall arise and shine, her light will be most penetrating, and precious songs of praise and thanksgiving will be heard in the assemblies of the saints. Murmuring and complaining over little disappointments and difficulties will cease. . . . We shall see our Advocate offering up the incense of His own merits in our behalf. . . .

God teaches that we should assemble in His house to cultivate the attributes of perfect love. This will fit the dwellers of earth for the mansions that Christ has gone to prepare for all who love Him. There they will assemble in the sanctuary from Sabbath to Sabbath, from one new moon to another, to unite in loftiest strains of song, in praise and thanksgiving to Him who sits upon the throne, and to the Lamb for ever and ever.[19]

Our God, the Creator of the heavens and the earth, declares: "Whoso offereth praise glorifieth me" (Ps. 50:23). All heaven unite in praising God. Let us learn the song of the angels now, that we may sing it when we join their shining ranks. Let us say with the psalmist: "While I live will I praise the Lord: I will sing praises unto my God while I have any being" (Ps. 146:2).[20]

Source of Compassion and Mercy

Thy throne, O God, is for ever and ever: the sceptre of thy kingdom is a right sceptre. Ps. 45:6.

Though now He has ascended to the presence of God, and shares the throne of the universe, Jesus has lost none of His compassionate nature. Today, the same tender, sympathizing heart is open to all the woes of humanity. Today the hand that was pierced is reached forth to bless more abundantly His people that are in the world. . . .

Through all our trials we have a never-failing Helper. He does not leave us alone to struggle with temptation, to battle with evil, and be finally crushed with burdens and sorrow. Though now He is hidden from mortal sight, the ear of faith can hear His voice saying, Fear not; I am with you. "I am he that liveth, and was dead; and, behold, I am alive forevermore" (Rev. 1:18).[21]

Those who put away iniquity from their hearts and stretch out their hands in earnest supplication unto God will have that help which God alone can give them. A ransom has been paid for the souls of men, that they may have an opportunity to escape from the thralldom of sin and obtain pardon, purity, and heaven. . . . Those who frequent the throne of grace, offering up sincere, earnest petitions for divine wisdom and power, will not fail to become active, useful servants of Christ. They may not possess great talents, but with humility of heart and firm reliance upon Jesus they may do a good work in bringing souls to Christ. . . .

Thousands have a false conception of God and His attributes. . . . God is a God of truth. Justice and mercy are the attributes of His throne. He is a God of love, of pity and tender compassion. Thus He is represented in His Son, our Saviour. He is a God of patience and long-suffering. If such is the being whom we adore and to whose character we are seeking to assimilate, we are worshiping the true God.

If we are following Christ, His merits, imputed to us, come up before the Father as sweet odor. And the graces of our Saviour's character, implanted in our hearts, will shed around us a precious fragrance.[22]

A Symphathizing High Priest

Thou hast maintained my right and my cause;
thou satest in the throne judging right. Ps. 9:4.

We do not understand the greatness and majesty of God nor remember the immeasurable distance between the Creator and the creatures formed by His hand. He who sitteth in the heavens, swaying the scepter of the universe, does not judge according to our finite standard, nor reckon according to our computation. We are in error if we think that that which is great to us must be great to God, and that that which is small to us must be small to Him. . . .

No sin is small in the sight of God. The sins which man is disposed to look upon as small may be the very ones which God accounts as great crimes. The drunkard is despised and is told that his sin will exclude him from heaven, while pride, selfishness, and covetousness go unrebuked. But these are sins that are especially offensive to God. . . . We need clear discernment, that we may measure sin by the Lord's standard.[23]

Now, while probation lingers, it does not become one to pronounce sentence upon others and look to himself as a model man. Christ is our model; imitate Him, plant your feet in His steps. You may professedly believe every point of present truth, but unless you practice these truths it will avail you nothing. We are not to condemn others; this is not our work; but we should love one another and pray for one another. When we see one err from the truth, then we may weep over him as Christ wept over Jerusalem. Let us see what our heavenly Father in His word says about the erring: "If a man be overtaken in a fault, ye which are spiritual, restore such an one in the spirit of meekness; considering thyself, lest thou also be tempted" (Gal. 6:1). . . .

Jesus cares for each one as though there were not another individual on the face of the earth. As Deity He exerts mighty power in our behalf, while as our Elder Brother He feels for all our woes. The Majesty of heaven held not Himself aloof from degraded, sinful humanity. We have not a high priest who is so high, so lifted up, that He cannot notice us or sympathize with us, but one who was in all points tempted like as we are, yet without sin.[24]

Christ Shares His Father's Throne

The Lord said unto my Lord, Sit thou at my right hand, until I make thine enemies thy footstool. Ps. 110:1.

The love of the Father toward a fallen race is unfathomable, indescribable, without a parallel. This love led Him to consent to give His only begotten Son to die, that rebellious man might be brought into harmony with the government of Heaven, and be saved from the penalty of his transgression. The Son of God stepped down from His royal throne, and for our sakes became poor, that we through His poverty might be rich. He became "a Man of sorrows," that we might be made partakers of everlasting joy. . . . God permitted His beloved Son, full of grace and truth, to come from a world of indescribable glory to a world marred and blighted with sin, shadowed with the shadow of death and the curse.[25]

Since Jesus came to dwell with us, we know that God is acquainted with our trials, and sympathizes with our griefs. Every son and daughter of Adam may understand that our Creator is the friend of sinners. For in every doctrine of grace, every promise of joy, every deed of love, every divine attraction presented in the Saviour's life on earth, we see "God with us" (Matt. 1:23). . . .

By His humanity, Christ touched humanity; by His divinity, He lays hold upon the throne of God. As the Son of man, He gave us an example of obedience; as the Son of God, He gives us power to obey. . . . The Child of Bethlehem, the meek and lowly Saviour, is God "manifest in the flesh" (1 Tim. 3:16). . . . "God with us" is the surety of our deliverance from sin, the assurance of our power to obey the law of heaven. . . .

In taking our nature, the Saviour has bound Himself to humanity by a tie that is never to be broken. Through the eternal ages He is linked with us. . . . "Unto *us* a child is born, unto *us* a son is given: . . ." (Isa. 9:6). God has adopted human nature in the person of His Son, and has carried the same into the highest heaven. It is the "Son of man" who shares the throne of the universe. . . . In Christ the family of earth and the family of heaven are bound together. Christ glorified is our brother. Heaven is enshrined in humanity, and humanity is enfolded in the bosom of Infinite Love.[26]

God's Law Is Linked With His Throne

Open thou mine eyes, that I may behold wondrous things out of thy law. Ps. 119:18.

God has given His holy law to man as His measure of character. By this law you may see and overcome every defect in your character. You may sever yourself from every idol, and link yourself to the throne of God by the golden chain of grace and truth.[27]

The moral law was never a type or a shadow. It existed before man's creation, and will endure as long as God's throne remains. God could not change nor alter one precept of His law in order to save man; for the law is the foundation of His government. It is unchangeable, unalterable, infinite, and eternal. In order for man to be saved, and for the honor of the law to be maintained, it was necessary for the Son of God to offer Himself as a sacrifice for sin. He who knew no sin became sin for us, He died for us on Calvary. His death shows the wonderful love of God for man, and the immutability of His law. . . .

The glory of Christ is revealed in the law, which is a transcript of His character, and His transforming efficacy is felt upon the soul until men become changed to His likeness. They are made partakers of the divine nature, and grow more and more like their Saviour, advancing step by step in conformity to the will of God, till they reach perfection.[28]

The law of God was not given to the Jews alone. It is of world-wide and perpetual obligation. . . . Its ten precepts are like a chain of ten links. If one is broken, the chain becomes worthless. Not a single precept can be revoked or changed to save the transgressor.[29]

Christ designs that heaven's order, heaven's plan of government, heaven's divine harmony, shall be represented in His church on earth. Thus in His people He is glorified. Through them the Sun of Righteousness will shine in undimmed luster to the world. . . . The church, endowed with the righteousness of Christ, is His depositary, in which the riches of His mercy, His grace, and His love, are to appear in full and final display. Christ looks upon His people in their purity and perfection, as the reward of His humiliation, and the supplement of His glory—Christ, the great Center, from whom radiates all glory.[30]

Help in Resisting Temptation

Because thou hast kept the word of my patience, I also will keep thee from the hour of temptation, which shall come upon all the world, to try them that dwell upon the earth. Rev. 3:10.

All heaven is interested in the work going on in this world, which is to prepare men and women for the future, immortal life. It is God's plan that human agencies shall have the high honor of acting as co-workers with Jesus Christ in the salvation of souls. . . . They should look upon the work of God as sacred and holy, and should bring to Him, every day, offerings of joy and gratitude, in return for the power of His grace, by which they are enabled to make advancement in the divine life. . . .

It is not necessary that anyone should yield to the temptations of Satan and thus violate his conscience and grieve the Holy Spirit. Every provision has been made in the Word of God whereby all may have divine help in their endeavors to overcome.[31]

In the religious life of every soul who is finally victorious there will be scenes of terrible perplexity and trial; but his knowledge of the Scriptures will enable him to bring to mind the encouraging promises of God, which will comfort his heart and strengthen his faith in the power of the Mighty One. He reads: . . . "that the trial of your faith, being much more precious than of gold that perisheth, though it be tried with fire, might be found unto praise and honour and glory at the appearing of Jesus Christ . . ." (1 Peter 1:7). The trial of faith is more precious than gold. All should learn that this is a part of the discipline in the school of Christ, which is essential to purify and refine them from the dross of earthliness. . . .

Summon all your powers to look up, not down at your difficulties; then you will never faint by the way. You will soon see Jesus behind the cloud, reaching out His hand to help you; and all you have to do is to give Him your hand in simple faith and let Him lead you. . . . A great name among men is as letters traced in sand, but a spotless character will endure to all eternity. God gives you intelligence and a reasoning mind, whereby you may grasp His promises; and Jesus is ready to help you in forming a strong, symmetrical character.[32]

Where Sins May Be Blotted Out

I, even I, am he that blotteth out thy transgressions for mine own sake, and will not remember thy sins. Isa. 43:25.

Some seem to feel that they must be on probation, and must prove to the Lord that they are reformed, before they can claim His blessing. But they may claim the blessing of God even now. They must have His grace, the spirit of Christ, to help their infirmities, or they cannot resist evil. Jesus loves to have us come to Him just as we are, sinful, helpless, dependent. We may come with all our weakness, our folly, our sinfulness, and fall at His feet in penitence. It is His glory to encircle us in the arms of His love and to bind up our wounds, to cleanse us from all impurity.

Here is where thousands fail; they do not believe that Jesus pardons them personally, individually. They do not take God at His word. It is the privilege of all who comply with the conditions to know for themselves that pardon is freely extended for every sin. Put away the suspicion that God's promises are not meant for you. They are for every repentant transgressor. Strength and grace have been provided through Christ to be brought by ministering angels to every believing soul. None are so sinful that they cannot find strength, purity, and righteousness in Jesus, who died for them. He is waiting to strip them of their garments stained and polluted with sin, and to put upon them the white robes of righteousness; He bids them live and not die. . . .

With the rich promises of the Bible before you, can you give place to doubt? Can you believe that when the poor sinner longs to return, longs to forsake his sins, the Lord sternly withholds him from coming to His feet in repentance? Away with such thoughts! Nothing can hurt your own soul more than to entertain such a conception of our heavenly Father. He hates sin, but He loves the sinner. . . . As you read the promises, remember they are the expression of unutterable love and pity. The great heart of Infinite Love is drawn toward the sinner with boundless compassion. . . . He wants to restore His moral image in man. As you draw near to Him with confession and repentance, He will draw near to you with mercy and forgiveness.[33]

Where We Find Deliverance From Sin

Who hath delivered us from the power of darkness, and hath translated us into the kingdom of his dear Son: in whom we have redemption through his blood, even the forgiveness of sins. Col. 1:13, 14.

The Prince of heaven has placed man in an exalted position. His life has been valued at the cost of Calvary's cross. . . . From the depths of sin's degradation, we may be exalted to become heirs with Christ, the sons of God, and kings and priests unto the Most High. . . .

When Christ bowed on the banks of Jordan, after His baptism, the heavens were opened, and the Spirit descended in the form of a dove, like burnished gold, and encircled Him with its glory; and the voice of God from the highest heaven was heard, saying, "This is my beloved Son, in whom I am well pleased" (Matt. 3:17). The prayer of Christ in man's behalf opened the gates of heaven, and the Father had responded, accepting the petition for the fallen race. Jesus prayed as our substitute and surety, and now the human family may find access to the Father through the merits of His well-beloved Son. . . . Jesus is "the way, the truth, and the life" (John 14:6). The gate of heaven has been left ajar, and the radiance from the throne of God shines into the hearts of those who love Him.[34]

The word that was spoken to Jesus at the Jordan . . . embraces humanity. God spoke to Jesus as our representative. With all our sins and weaknesses, we are not cast aside as worthless. . . . The glory that rested upon Christ is a pledge of the love of God for us. It tells us of the power of prayer—how the human voice may reach the ear of God, and our petition find acceptance in the courts of heaven. By sin, earth was cut off from heaven, and alienated from its communion; but Jesus has connected it again with the sphere of glory. His love has encircled man, and reached the highest heaven. The light which fell from the open portals upon the head of our Saviour will fall upon us as we pray for help to resist temptation. The voice which spoke to Jesus says to every believing soul, This is My beloved child, in whom I am well pleased. . . . Our Redeemer has opened the way so that the most sinful, the most needy, . . . may find access to the Father. All may have a home in the mansions which Jesus has gone to prepare.[35]

Accessible to All

In whom we have boldness and access with confidence by the faith of him. Eph. 3:12.

Many who are sincerely seeking for holiness of heart and purity of life seem perplexed and discouraged. . . . Darkness and discouragement will sometimes come upon the soul and threaten to overwhelm us, but we should not cast away our confidence. We must keep the eye fixed on Jesus, feeling or no feeling. We should seek to faithfully perform every known duty, and then calmly rest in the promises of God.

At times a deep sense of our unworthiness will send a thrill of terror through the soul, but this is no evidence that God has changed toward us, or we toward God. No effort should be made to rein the mind up to a certain intensity of emotion. We may not feel today the peace and joy which we felt yesterday; but we should by faith grasp the hand of Christ, and trust Him as fully in the darkness as in the light.

Satan may whisper, "You are too great a sinner for Christ to save." While you acknowledge that you are indeed sinful and unworthy, you may meet the tempter with the cry, "By virtue of the atonement, I claim Christ as my Saviour. I trust not to my own merits, but to the precious blood of Jesus, which cleanses me. This moment I hang my helpless soul on Christ." . . .

Be not discouraged because your heart seems hard. Every obstacle, every internal foe, only increases your need of Christ. He came to take away the heart of stone, and give you a heart of flesh. Look to Him for special grace to overcome your peculiar faults. When assailed by temptation, steadfastly resist the evil promptings. . . . Cry to the dear Saviour for help to sacrifice every idol and to put away every darling sin. Let the eye of faith see Jesus standing before the Father's throne, presenting His wounded hands as He pleads for you. Believe that strength comes to you through your precious Saviour. . . .

If we would permit our minds to dwell more upon Christ and the heavenly world, we should find a powerful stimulus and support in fighting the battles of the Lord. . . . Beside the loveliness of Christ, all earthly attractions will seem of little worth.[36]

Christ's Name Our Password

Whatsoever ye shall ask in my name, that will I do, that the Father may be glorified in the Son. John 14:13.

Through Christ we may present our petitions at the throne of grace. Through Him, unworthy as we are, we may obtain all spiritual blessings.[37]

Make your requests known to your Maker. Never is one repulsed who comes to Him with a contrite heart. Not one sincere prayer is lost. Amid the anthems of the celestial choir, God hears the cries of the weakest human being. We pour out our heart's desire in our closets, we breathe a prayer as we walk by the way, and our words reach the throne of the Monarch of the universe. They may be inaudible to any human ear, but they cannot die away into silence, nor can they be lost through the activities of business that are going on. Nothing can drown the soul's desire. It rises above the din of the street, above the confusion of the multitude, to the heavenly courts. It is God to whom we are speaking, and our prayer is heard.[38]

"Ask in my name," Christ says. . . . Christ is the connecting link between God and man. He has promised His personal intercession. He places the whole virtue of His righteousness on the side of the suppliant. He pleads for man, and man, in need of divine help, pleads for himself in the presence of God, using the influence of the One who gave His life for the life of the world. As we acknowledge before God our appreciation of Christ's merits, fragrance is given to our intercessions. As we approach God through the virtue of the Redeemer's merits, Christ places us close by His side, encircling us with His human arm, while with His divine arm He grasps the throne of the Infinite. . . .

Yes, Christ has become the medium of prayer between man and God. He has also become the medium of blessing between God and man. He has united divinity with humanity. . . .

Pray, yes, pray with unshaken faith and trust. The Angel of the covenant, even our Lord Jesus Christ, is the Mediator who secures the acceptance of the prayers of His believing ones.[39]

Prayers Like Fragrant Incense

Another angel came and stood at the altar, having a golden censer; and there was given unto him much incense, that he should offer it with the prayers of all the saints upon the golden altar which was before the throne. Rev. 8:3.

True prayer takes hold upon Omnipotence and gives us the victory. Upon his knees the Christian obtains strength to resist temptation. . . . The silent, fervent prayer of the soul will rise like holy incense to the throne of grace and will be as acceptable to God as if offered in the sanctuary. To all who thus seek Him, Christ becomes a present help in time of need. They will be strong in the day of trial.[40]

It is a wonderful favor for any man in this life to be commended of God as was Cornelius. And what was the ground of this approval? "Thy prayers and thine alms are come up for a memorial before God" (Acts 10:4).

Neither prayer nor almsgiving has any virtue in itself to recommend the sinner to God; the grace of Christ, through His atoning sacrifice, can alone renew the heart and make our service acceptable to God. This grace had moved upon the heart of Cornelius. The Spirit of Christ had spoken to his soul; Jesus had drawn him, and he had yielded to the drawing. His prayers and alms were not urged or extorted from him; they were not a price he was seeking to pay in order to secure heaven; but they were the fruit of love and gratitude to God.

Such prayer from a sincere heart ascends as incense before the Lord; and offerings to His cause and gifts to the needy and suffering are a sacrifice well pleasing to Him. . . .

Prayer and almsgiving are closely linked together—the expression of love to God and to our fellow men. They are the outworking of the two great principles of the divine law, "Thou shalt love the Lord thy God with all thy heart, and with all thy soul, and with all thy mind, and with all thy strength"; and, "Thou shalt love thy neighbour as thyself" (Mark 12:30, 31). Thus while our gifts cannot recommend us to God or earn His favor, they are an evidence that we have received the grace of Christ. They are a test of the sincerity of our profession of love.[41]

Press Your Case

I will heal their backsliding, I will love them freely.
Hosea 14:4.

I hope that none will obtain the idea that they are earning the favor of God by confession of sins or that there is special virtue in confessing to human beings. . . . The Lord would have us come to Him daily with all our troubles and confessions of sin, and He can give us rest. . . .

Confess your secret sins alone before your God. Acknowledge your heart wanderings to Him who knows perfectly how to treat your case. If you have wronged your neighbor, acknowledge to him your sin and show fruit of the same by making restitution. Then claim the blessing. Come to God just as you are, and let Him heal all your infirmities. Press your case to the throne of grace; let the work be thorough. Be sincere in dealing with God and your own soul. If you come to Him with a heart truly contrite, He will give you the victory. . . . He will not misapprehend or misjudge you.

Your fellow men cannot absolve you from sin or cleanse you from iniquity. Jesus is the only One who can give you peace. He loved you and gave Himself for you. His great heart of love is "touched with the feeling of our infirmities" (Heb. 4:15). What sins are too great for Him to pardon? what soul too dark and sin-oppressed for Him to save? He is gracious, not looking for merit in us, but of His own boundless goodness healing our backslidings and loving us freely, while we are yet sinners. He is "slow to anger, and of great kindness" (Neh. 9:17).[42]

There is a remedy for the sin-sick soul. That remedy is in Jesus. Precious Saviour! His grace is sufficient for the weakest; and the strongest must also have His grace or perish.

I saw how this grace could be obtained. Go to your closet and there alone plead with God. "Create in me a clean heart, O God; and renew a right spirit within me" (Ps. 51:10). Be in earnest, be sincere. Fervent prayer availeth much. Jacob-like, wrestle in prayer. Agonize. Jesus in the garden sweat great drops of blood; you must make an effort. Do not leave your closet until you feel strong in God; then watch, and just as long as you watch and pray, you can keep these evil besetments under, and the grace of God can, and will, appear in you.[43]

Elijah's Example

Elias was a man subject to like passions as we are, and he prayed earnestly that it might not rain: and it rained not on the earth by the space of three years and six months. And he prayed again, and the heaven gave rain, and the earth brought forth her fruit. James 5:17, 18.

When upon Mount Carmel he [Elijah] offered the prayer for rain (1 Kings 18:41-45), his faith was tested, but he persevered in making known his request unto God. Six times he prayed earnestly, and yet there was no sign that his petition was granted, but with a strong faith he urged his plea to the throne of grace. Had he given up in discouragement at the sixth time, his prayer would not have been answered, but he persevered till the answer came. We have a God whose ear is not closed to our petitions; and if we prove His Word, He will honor our faith. He wants us to have all our interests interwoven with His interests, and then He can safely bless us; for we shall not then take glory to self when the blessing is ours, but shall render all the praise to God. God does not always answer our prayers the first time we call upon Him; for should He do this, we might take it for granted that we had a right to all the blessings and favors He bestowed upon us. Instead of searching our hearts to see if any evil was entertained by us, any sin indulged, we should become careless, and fail to recognize our dependence upon Him, and our need of His help.[44]

The servant watched while Elijah prayed. Six times he returned from the watch, saying, There is nothing, no cloud, no sign of rain. But the prophet did not give up in discouragement. . . . As he searched his heart, he seemed to be less and less, both in his own estimation and in the sight of God. . . . And when he reached the point of renouncing self, while he clung to the Saviour as his only strength and righteousness, the answer came. The servant appeared, and said, "Behold, there ariseth a little cloud out of the sea, like a man's hand."[45]

Elijah did not wait for the heavens to gather blackness. In that small cloud, he beheld by faith an abundance of rain; and he acted in harmony with his faith. . . . Faith such as this is needed in the world today—faith that will lay hold on the promises of God's word, and refuse to let go until Heaven hears.[46]

When Affliction Comes

When he was in affliction, he besought the Lord his God, and humbled himself greatly before the God of his fathers.
2 Chron. 33:12.

"In the world ye shall have tribulation" (John 16:33), says Christ; but in Me ye shall have peace. The trials to which Christians are subjected in sorrow, adversity, and reproach are the means appointed of God to separate the chaff from the wheat. Our pride, selfishness, evil passions, and love of worldly pleasure must all be overcome; therefore God sends us afflictions to test and prove us, and show us that these evils exist in our characters. We must overcome through His strength and grace, that we may be partakers of the divine nature, having escaped the corruption that is in the world through lust. "For our light affliction," says Paul, "which is but for a moment, worketh for us a far more exceeding and eternal weight of glory; while we look not at the things which are seen, but at the things which are not seen: for the things which are seen are temporal; but the things which are not seen are eternal" (2 Cor. 4:17, 18). Afflictions, crosses, temptations, adversity, and our varied trials are God's workmen to refine us, sanctify us, and fit us for the heavenly garner.[47]

Many of your afflictions have been visited upon you, in the wisdom of God, to bring you closer to the throne of grace. He softens and subdues His children by sorrows and trials. This world is God's workshop, where He fashions us for the courts of heaven. He uses the planing knife upon our quivering hearts until the roughness and irregularities are removed and we are fitted for our proper places in the heavenly building. Through tribulation and distress the Christian becomes purified and strengthened, and develops a character after the model that Christ has given.[48]

Let the afflictions which pain us so grievously become instructive lessons, teaching us to press forward toward the mark of the prize of our high calling in Christ. Let us be encouraged by the thought that the Lord is soon to come. Let this hope gladden our hearts.[49]

Sharing Christ's Suffering

Rejoice, inasmuch as ye are partakers of Christ's sufferings;
that, when his glory shall be revealed,
ye may be glad also with exceeding joy. 1 Peter 4:13.

To have strength we must have exercise. To have strong faith, we must be placed in circumstances where our faith will be exercised. . . . It is through much tribulation that we are to enter the kingdom of God. Our Saviour was tried in every possible way, and yet He triumphed in God continually. It is our privilege to be strong in the strength of God under all circumstances and to glory in the cross of Christ.[50]

In this life we must meet fiery trials and make costly sacrifices, but the peace of Christ is the reward. There has been so little self-denial, so little suffering for Christ's sake, that the cross is almost entirely forgotten. We must be partakers with Christ of His sufferings if we would sit down in triumph with Him on His throne.[51]

Heaven is very near those who suffer for righteousness' sake. Christ identifies His interests with the interests of His faithful people; He suffers in the person of His saints, and whoever touches His chosen ones touches Him. The power that is near to deliver from physical harm or distress is also near to save from the greater evil, making it possible for the servant of God to maintain his integrity under all circumstances, and to triumph through divine grace.[52]

Persecution should bring joy to the disciples of Christ, for it is an evidence that they are following in the steps of their Master.

While the Lord has not promised His people exemption from trials, He has promised that which is far better. He has said, "As thy days, so shall thy strength be" (Deut. 33:25). "My grace is sufficient for thee: for my strength is made perfect in weakness" (2 Cor. 12:9). If you are called to go through the fiery furnace for His sake, Jesus will be by your side even as He was with the faithful three in Babylon. Those who love their Redeemer will rejoice at every opportunity of sharing with Him humiliation and reproach. The love they bear their Lord makes suffering for His sake sweet.[53]

Come With Reverence

Let us have grace, whereby we may serve God acceptably with reverence and godly fear. Heb. 12:28.

There should be an intelligent knowledge of how to come to God in reverence and godly fear with devotional love. There is a growing lack of reverence for our Maker, a growing disregard of His greatness and His majesty. But God is speaking to us in these last days. We hear His voice in the storm, in the rolling thunder. We hear of calamities He permits in the earthquakes, the breaking forth of waters, and the destructive elements sweeping all before them.[54]

In these perilous times, those who profess to be God's commandment-keeping people should guard against the tendency to lose the spirit of reverence and godly fear. The Scriptures teach men how to approach their Maker—with humility and awe, through faith in a divine Mediator. Let man come on bended knee, as a subject of grace, a suppliant at the footstool of mercy. Thus he is to testify that the whole soul, body, and spirit are in subjection to his Creator.

Both in public and in private worship, it is our duty* to bow upon our knees before God when we offer our petitions to Him. Jesus, our example, "kneeled down, and prayed." And of His disciples it is recorded that they, too, "kneeled down, and prayed." Stephen "kneeled." Paul declared: "I bow my knees unto the Father of our Lord Jesus Christ" (Eph. 3:14). In confessing before God the sins of Israel, Ezra knelt. Daniel "kneeled upon his knees three times a day, and prayed, and gave thanks before his God" (Dan. 6:10). And the invitation of the psalmist is: "O come, let us worship and bow down: let us kneel before the Lord our Maker" (Ps. 95:6).

"What doth the Lord thy God require of thee, but to fear the Lord thy God, to walk in all his ways, and to love him, and to serve the Lord thy God with all thy heart and with all thy soul?" (Deut. 10:12). . . . "The eye of the Lord is upon them that fear him, upon them that hope in his mercy" (Ps. 33:18). "By humility and the fear of the Lord are riches, and honour, and life" (Prov. 22:4).[55]

---

* There are instances where Ellen White stood at the desk while offering prayers of consecration during church services.

Come in Humility and Holy Fear

God is greatly to be feared in the assembly of the saints, and to be had in reverence of all them that are about him. Ps. 89:7.

Humility and reverence should characterize the deportment of all who come into the presence of God. In the name of Jesus we may come before Him with confidence, but we must not approach Him with the boldness of presumption, as though He were on a level with ourselves. There are those who address the great and all-powerful and holy God, who dwelleth in light unapproachable, as they would address an equal, or even an inferior. There are those who conduct themselves in His house as they would not presume to do in the audience-chamber of an earthly ruler. These should remember that they are in His sight whom seraphim adore, before whom angels veil their faces. God is greatly to be reverenced; all who truly realize His presence will bow in humility before Him.[56]

Some think it a mark of humility to pray to God in a common manner, as if talking with a human being. They profane His name by needlessly and irreverently mingling with their prayers the words, "God Almighty"—awful, sacred words, which should never pass the lips except in subdued tones and with a feeling of awe. . . .

It is the heartfelt prayer of faith that is heard in heaven and answered on earth. God understands the needs of humanity. He knows what we desire before we ask Him. He sees the soul's conflict with doubt and temptation. He marks the sincerity of the suppliant. He will accept the humiliation and affliction of the soul. "To this man will I look," He declares, "even to him that is poor and of a contrite spirit, and trembleth at my word."

It is our privilege to pray with confidence, the Spirit inditing our petitions. With simplicity we should state our needs to the Lord, and claim His promise. . . .

Our prayers should be full of tenderness and love. When we yearn for a deeper, broader realization of the Saviour's love, we shall cry to God for more wisdom. If ever there was a need of soul-stirring prayers and sermons, it is now. The end of all things is at hand. O that we could see as we should the necessity of seeking the Lord with all the heart! Then we should find Him. May God teach His people how to pray.[57]

A Sacred Experience

Let all the earth fear the Lord: let all the inhabitants of the world stand in awe of him. Ps. 33:8.

Holy angels have been displeased and disgusted with the irreverent manner in which many have used the name of God, the great Jehovah. Angels mention that sacred name with the greatest awe, ever veiling their faces when they speak the name of God; and the name of Christ is so sacred to them that they speak it with the greatest reverence.[58]

True reverence for God is inspired by a sense of His infinite greatness and a realization of His presence. With this sense of the Unseen, every heart should be deeply impressed. The hour and place of prayer are sacred, because God is there. And as reverence is manifested in attitude and demeanor, the feeling that inspires it will be deepened. "Holy and reverend is his name," the psalmist declares. Angels, when they speak that name, veil their faces. With what reverence, then, should we, who are fallen and sinful, take it upon our lips![59]

Well would it be for young and old to study and ponder and often repeat those words of Holy Writ that show how the place marked by God's special presence should be regarded. "Put off thy shoes from off thy feet," He commanded Moses at the burning bush; "for the place whereon thou standest is holy ground" (Ex. 3:5). Jacob, after beholding the vision of the angels, exclaimed, "The Lord is in this place; and I knew it not. . . . This is none other but the house of God, and this is the gate of heaven" (Gen. 28:16, 17). "The Lord is in his holy temple: let all the earth keep silence before him" (Hab. 2:20).

"The Lord is a great God,
And a great King above all gods. . . .
O come, let us worship and bow down:
Let us kneel before the Lord our Maker."
"It is he that hath made us, and not we ourselves;
We are his people, and the sheep of his pasture.
Enter into his gates with thanksgiving,
And into his courts with praise:
Be thankful unto him, and bless his name."
(Ps. 95:3-6; 100:3, 4).[60]

A Hallowed Name

Our Father which art in heaven, Hallowed be thy name. Matt. 6:9.

To hallow the name of the Lord requires that the words in which we speak of the Supreme Being be uttered with reverence. "Holy and reverend is his name" (Ps. 111:9). We are never in any manner to treat lightly the titles or appellations of the Deity. In prayer we enter the audience chamber of the Most High; and we should come before Him with holy awe. The angels veil their faces in His presence. The cherubim and the bright and holy seraphim approach His throne with solemn reverence. How much more should we, finite, sinful beings, come in a reverent manner before the Lord, our Maker!

But to hallow the name of the Lord means much more than this. We may, like the Jews in Christ's day, manifest the greatest outward reverence for God, and yet profane His name continually. "The name of the Lord" is "merciful and gracious, longsuffering, and abundant in goodness and truth, . . . forgiving iniquity and transgression and sin" (Ex. 34:5-7). Of the church of Christ it is written, "This is the name wherewith she shall be called, The Lord our Righteousness" (Jer. 33:16). This name is put upon every follower of Christ. It is the heritage of the child of God. The family are called after the Father. The prophet Jeremiah, in the time of Israel's sore distress and tribulation, prayed, "We are called by thy name; leave us not" (Jer. 14:9).

This name is hallowed by the angels of heaven, by the inhabitants of unfallen worlds. When you pray, "Hallowed be thy name," you ask that it may be hallowed in this world, hallowed in you. God has acknowledged you before men and angels as His child; pray that you may do no dishonor to the "worthy name by which ye are called" (James 2:7). God sends you into the world as His representatives. In every act of life you are to make manifest the name of God. This petition calls upon you to possess His character. You cannot hallow His name, you cannot represent Him to the world, unless in life and character you represent the very life and character of God. This you can do only through the acceptance of the grace and righteousness of Christ.[61]

Our Continual Dependence

The Lord sitteth King for ever. The Lord will give strength unto his people. Ps. 29:10, 11.

The throne of grace is to be our continual dependence. . . . There is strength for us in Christ. He is our Advocate before the Father. He dispatches His messengers to every part of His dominion to communicate His will to His people. He walks in the midst of His churches. He desires to sanctify, elevate, and ennoble His followers. The influence of those who truly believe in Him will be a savor of life in the world. He holds the stars in His right hand, and it is His purpose to let His light shine through these to the world. Thus He desires to prepare His people for higher service in the church above. He has given us a great work to do. Let us do it with accuracy and determination. Let us show in our lives what the truth has done for us.

"Who walketh in the midst of the seven golden candlesticks" (Rev. 2:1). This Scripture shows Christ's relation to the churches. He walks in the midst of His churches throughout the length and breadth of the earth. He watches them with intense interest to see whether they are in such a condition spiritually that they can advance His kingdom. Christ is present in every assembly of the church. He is acquainted with everyone connected with His service. He knows those whose hearts He can fill with the holy oil, that they may impart it to others. Those who faithfully carry forward the work of Christ in our world, representing in word and works the character of God, fulfilling the Lord's purpose for them, are in His sight very precious. Christ takes pleasure in them as a man takes pleasure in a well-kept garden and the fragrance of the flowers he has planted.[62]

No candlestick, no church, shines of itself. From Christ emanates all its light. The church in heaven today is only the complement of the church on earth; but it is higher, grander—perfect. The same divine illumination is to continue through eternal ages. The Lord God Almighty and the Lamb are the light thereof. No church can have light if it fails to diffuse the glory it receives from the throne of God.[63]

A Throne in Every Heart

That Christ may dwell in your hearts by faith. Eph. 3:17.

God has bought us, and He claims a throne in each heart. Our minds and bodies must be subordinated to Him, and the natural habits and appetites must be made subservient to the higher wants of the soul. But we can place no dependence upon ourselves in this work. We cannot with safety follow our own guidance. The Holy Spirit must renew and sanctify us. In God's service there must be no halfway work.[64]

When the heart is cleansed from sin, Christ is placed on the throne that self-indulgence and love of earthly treasure once occupied. The image of Christ is seen in the expression of the countenance. The work of sanctification is carried forward in the soul. Self-righteousness is banished. There is seen the putting on of the new man, which after Christ is created in righteousness and true holiness.[65]

"But we all, with open face beholding as in a glass the glory of the Lord, are changed into the same image from glory to glory even as by the Spirit of the Lord" (2 Cor. 3:18). Beholding Christ means studying His life as given in His Word. We are to dig for truth as for hidden treasure. We are to fix our eyes upon Christ. When we take Him as our personal Saviour, this gives us boldness to approach the throne of grace. By beholding we become changed, morally assimilated to the One who is perfect in character. By receiving His imputed righteousness, through the transforming power of the Holy Spirit, we become like Him. The image of Christ is cherished, and it captivates the whole being.[66]

The upward progress of the soul indicates that Jesus bears rule in the heart. That heart through which He diffuses His peace and joy, and the blessed fruits of His love, becomes His temple and His throne. "Ye are my friends," says Christ, "if ye do whatsoever I command you" (John 15:14).[67]

Give to God the most precious offering that it is possible for you to make; give Him your heart.[68]

Undivided Occupancy

They that are Christ's have crucified the flesh with the affections and lusts. Gal. 5:24.

We are commanded to crucify the flesh, with the affections and lusts. How shall we do it? Shall we inflict pain on the body? No; but put to death the temptation to sin. The corrupt thought is to be expelled. Every thought is to be brought into captivity to Jesus Christ. . . . The love of God must reign supreme; Christ must occupy an undivided throne. Our bodies are to be regarded as His purchased possession. The members of the body are to become the instruments of righteousness.[69]

There are two kingdoms in this world, the kingdom of Christ and the kingdom of Satan. To one of these kingdoms each one of us belongs. In His wonderful prayer for His disciples, Christ said, "I pray not that thou shouldest take them out of the world, but that thou shouldest keep them from the evil. They are not of the world, even as I am not of the world. Sanctify them through thy truth: thy word is truth. As thou hast sent me into the world, even so have I also sent them into the world" (John 17:15-18).

It is not God's will that we should seclude ourselves from the world. But while in the world we should sanctify ourselves to God. We should not pattern after the world. We are to be in the world, as a corrective influence, as salt that retains its savor. Among an unholy, impure, idolatrous generation, we are to be pure and holy, showing that the grace of Christ has power to restore in man the divine likeness. We are to exert a saving influence upon the world. . . .

The world has become a lazar house of sin, a mass of corruption. . . . We are not to practice its ways or follow its customs. Continually we are to resist its lax principles. . . .

The blessing of grace is given to men that the heavenly universe and the fallen world may see as they could not otherwise, the perfection of Christ's character. The Great Physician came to our world to show men and women that through His grace they may so live that in the great day of God they can receive the precious testimony, "Ye are complete in him" (Col. 2:10).[70]

Even for Ever

Of the increase of his government and peace there shall be no end, upon the throne of David, and upon his kingdom, to order it, and to establish it with judgment and with justice from henceforth even for ever. Isa. 9:7.

In this life we can only begin to understand the wonderful theme of redemption. With our finite comprehension we may consider most earnestly the shame and the glory, the life and the death, the justice and the mercy, that meet in the cross; yet with the utmost stretch of our mental powers we fail to grasp its full significance. The length and the breadth, the depth and the height, of redeeming love are but dimly comprehended. The plan of redemption will not be fully understood, even when the ransomed see as they are seen and know as they are known; but through the eternal ages, new truth will continually unfold to the wondering and delighted mind. Though the griefs and pains and temptations of earth are ended, and the cause removed, the people of God will ever have a distinct, intelligent knowledge of what their salvation has cost.

The cross of Christ will be the science and the song of the redeemed through all eternity. In Christ glorified they will behold Christ crucified. Never will it be forgotten that He whose power created and upheld the unnumbered worlds through the vast realms of space—the Beloved of God, the Majesty of heaven, He whom cherub and shining seraph delighted to adore—humbled Himself to uplift fallen man; that He bore the guilt and shame of sin, and the hiding of His Father's face, till the woes of a lost world broke His heart, and crushed out His life on Calvary's cross. That the Maker of all worlds, the Arbiter of all destinies, should lay aside His glory and humiliate Himself from love to man will ever excite the wonder and adoration of the universe. As the nations of the saved look upon their Redeemer and behold the eternal glory of the Father shining in His countenance; as they behold His throne, which is from everlasting to everlasting, and know that His kingdom is to have no end, they break forth in rapturous song: "Worthy, worthy, is the Lamb that was slain, and hath redeemed us to God, by His own most precious blood!"[71]

To Draw Us to God

I have loved thee with an everlasting love: therefore with lovingkindness have I drawn thee. Jer. 31:3.

The Lord of life and glory clothed His divinity with humanity to demonstrate to man that God through the gift of Christ would connect us with Him. Without a connection with God no one can possibly be happy. Fallen man is to learn that our Heavenly Father cannot be satisfied until His love embraces the repentant sinner, transformed through the merits of the spotless Lamb of God.

The work of all the heavenly intelligences is to this end. Under the command of their General they are to work for the reclaiming of those who by transgression have separated themselves from their Heavenly Father. A plan has been devised whereby the wondrous grace and love of Christ shall stand revealed to the world. In the infinite price paid by the Son of God to ransom man, the love of God is revealed. This glorious plan of redemption is ample in its provisions to save the whole world. Sinful and fallen man may be made complete in Jesus through the forgiveness of sin and the imputed righteousness of Christ.[1]

In all the gracious deeds that Jesus did, He sought to impress upon men the parental, benevolent attributes of God. . . . Jesus would have us understand the love of the Father, and He seeks to draw us to Him by presenting His parental grace. He would have the whole field of our vision filled with the perfection of God's character. . . . It was only by living among men that He could reveal the mercy, compassion, and love of His heavenly Father; for it was only by actions of benevolence that He could set forth the grace of God.[2]

Christ came to manifest the love of God to the world, to draw the hearts of all men to Himself. . . . The first step toward salvation is to respond to the drawing of the love of Christ. . . . It is that men may understand the joy of forgiveness, the peace of God, that Christ draws them through the manifestation of His love. If they respond to His drawing, yielding their hearts to His grace, He will lead them on step by step, to a full knowledge of Himself, and this is life eternal.[3]

To Change the Heart

A new heart also will I give you, and a new spirit will I put within you: and I will take away the stony heart out of your flesh, and I will give you an heart of flesh. Eze. 36:26.

When Jesus speaks of the new heart, He means the mind, the life, the whole being. To have a change of heart is to withdraw the affections from the world, and fasten them upon Christ. To have a new heart is to have a new mind, new purposes, new motives. What is the sign of a new heart?—a changed life. There is a daily, hourly dying to selfishness and pride.[4]

The appetites and passions, clamoring for indulgence, trample reason and conscience underfoot. This is the cruel work of Satan, and he is constantly putting forth the most determined efforts to strengthen the chains by which he has bound his victims. Those who have been all their lives indulging wrong habits do not always realize the necessity of a change. . . . Let the conscience be aroused and much is gained. Nothing but the grace of God can convict and convert the heart; here alone can the slaves of custom obtain power to break the shackles which bind them. The self-indulgent must be led to see and feel that a great moral renovation is necessary if they would meet the claims of the divine law; the soul-temple has been defiled, and God calls upon them to arouse and strive with all their might to win back the God-given manhood which has been sacrificed through sinful indulgences.[5]

Oh, what rays of softness and beauty shone forth in the daily life of our Saviour! What sweetness flowed from His very presence! The same spirit will be revealed in His children. Those with whom Christ dwells will be surrounded with a divine atmosphere. Their white robes of purity will be fragrant with perfume from the garden of the Lord. Their faces will reflect light from His, brightening the path for stumbling and weary feet.

No man who has the true ideal of what constitutes a perfect character will fail to manifest the sympathy and tenderness of Christ. The influence of grace is to soften the heart, to refine and purify the feelings, giving a heaven-born delicacy and sense of propriety.[6]

Brings Peace and Rest

The wicked are like the troubled sea, when it cannot rest. . . . There is no peace, saith my God, to the wicked. Isa. 57:20, 21.

Sin has destroyed our peace. While self is unsubdued, we can find no rest. The masterful passions of the heart no human power can control. We are as helpless here as were the disciples to quiet the raging storm [Matt. 8:23-27]. But He who spoke peace to the billows of Galilee, has spoken the word of peace for every soul. However fierce the tempest, those who turn to Jesus . . . will find deliverance. His grace . . . quiets the strife of human passion, and in His love the heart is at rest.[7]

For every soul struggling to rise from a life of sin to a life of purity, the great element of power abides in the only "name under heaven given among men, whereby we must be saved" (Acts 4:12). . . . The only remedy for vice is the grace and power of Christ. The good resolutions made in one's own strength avail nothing.[8]

Every unholy passion must be kept under the control of sanctified reason through the grace abundantly bestowed of God. We are living in an atmosphere of satanic witchery. The enemy will weave a spell of licentiousness around every soul that is not barricaded by the grace of Christ. Temptations will come; but if we watch against the enemy, and maintain the balance of self-control and purity, the seducing spirits will have no influence over us. Those who do nothing to encourage temptation will have strength to withstand it when it comes; but those who keep themselves in an atmosphere of evil will have only themselves to blame if they are overcome and fall from their steadfastness. . . .

Men and women are to watch themselves; they are to be constantly on guard, allowing no word or act that would cause their good to be evil spoken of. He who professes to be a follower of Christ is to watch himself, keeping himself pure and undefiled in thought, word, and deed. His influence upon others is to be uplifting. His life is to reflect the bright beams of the Sun of Righteousness. . . . Eternal vigilance is the price of safety.[9]

Exalts God's Law

Receive, I pray thee, the law from his mouth, and lay up his words in thine heart. Job 22:22.

Everything in nature, from the mote in the sunbeam to the worlds on high, is under law. And upon obedience to these laws the order and harmony of the natural world depend. So there are great principles of righteousness to control the life of all intelligent beings, and upon conformity to these principles the well-being of the universe depends. Before this earth was called into being, God's law existed. Angels are governed by its principles, and in order for earth to be in harmony with heaven, man also must obey the divine statutes. To man in Eden Christ made known the precepts of the law "when the morning stars sang together, and all the sons of God shouted for joy" (Job 38:7). The mission of Christ on earth was not to destroy the law, but by His grace to bring man back to obedience to its precepts. . . .

His mission was to "magnify the law, and make it honourable" (Isa. 42:21). He was to show the spiritual nature of the law, to present its far-reaching principles, and to make plain its eternal obligation.

The divine beauty of the character of Christ, of whom the noblest and most gentle among men are but a faint reflection; . . . Jesus, the express image of the Father's person, the effulgence of His glory; the self-denying Redeemer, throughout His pilgrimage of love on earth was a living representative of the character of the law of God. In His life it is made manifest that heaven-born love, Christlike principles, underlie the laws of eternal rectitude.[10]

The Bible is God's will expressed to man. It is the only perfect standard of character, and marks out the duty of man in every circumstance of life.[11]

We must so conduct our life work that we can go to God in confidence and open our hearts before Him, telling Him our necessities and believing that He hears and will give us grace and strength to carry out the principles of the Word of God.[12]

Gives Power to Obey

For as by one man's disobedience many were made sinners, so by the obedience of one shall many be made righteous. Rom. 5:19.

One honored of all heaven came to this world to stand in human nature at the head of humanity, testifying to the fallen angels and to the inhabitants of the unfallen worlds that through the divine help which has been provided, every one may walk in the path of obedience to God's commands. . . .

No one less holy than the Only Begotten of the Father, could have offered a sacrifice that would be efficacious to cleanse all—even the most sinful and degraded—who accept the Saviour as their atonement and become obedient to Heaven's law. Nothing less could have reinstated man in God's favor.[13]

Christ gave His life to make it possible for man to be restored to the image of God. It is the power of His grace that draws men together in obedience to the truth.[14]

God desires us to reach the standard of perfection made possible for us by the gift of Christ. He calls upon us to make our choice on the right side, to connect with heavenly agencies, to adopt principles that will restore in us the divine image. In His written Word and in the great book of nature He has revealed the principles of life. It is our work to obtain a knowledge of these principles, and by obedience to cooperate with Him in restoring health to the body as well as to the soul.

Men need to learn that the blessings of obedience, in their fullness, can be theirs only as they receive the grace of Christ. It is His grace that gives men power to obey the laws of God. It is this that enables him to break the bondage of evil habit. This is the only power that can make him and keep him steadfast in the right path.[15]

To the heart that has become purified, all is changed. . . . The Spirit of God produces a new life in the soul, bringing the thoughts and desires into obedience to the will of Christ; and the inward man is renewed in the image of God. Weak and erring men and women show to the world that the redeeming power of grace can cause the faulty character to develop into symmetry and abundant fruitfulness.[16]

Breaks the Hold of Evil

Where sin abounded, grace did much more abound. Rom. 5:20.

The gifts of Jesus are ever fresh and new. . . . Each new gift increases the capacity of the receiver to appreciate and enjoy the blessings of the Lord. He gives grace for grace. There can be no failure of supply. If you abide in Him, the fact that you receive a rich gift today insures the reception of a richer gift tomorrow. . . .

The gift of Christ to the marriage feast was a symbol [John 2:1-11]. The water represented baptism into His death; the wine, the shedding of His blood for the sins of the world. The water to fill the jars was brought by human hands, but the word of Christ alone could impart to it life-giving virtue. . . .

The word of Christ supplied ample provision for the feast. So abundant is the provision of His grace to blot out the iniquities of men, and to renew and sustain the soul.[17]

Our condition through sin is unnatural, and the power that restores us must be supernatural, else it has no value. There is but one power that can break the hold of evil from the hearts of men, and that is the power of God in Jesus Christ. Only through the blood of the Crucified One is there cleansing from sin. His grace alone can enable us to resist and subdue the tendencies of our fallen nature.[18]

Satan is determined that men shall not see the love of God, which led Him to give His only-begotten Son to save the lost race; for it is the goodness of God that leads men to repentance. Oh, how shall we succeed in setting forth before the world the deep, precious love of God? In no other way can we compass it than by exclaiming, "Behold, what manner of love the Father hath bestowed upon us, that we should be called the sons of God" (1 John 3:1)! Let us say to sinners, "Behold the Lamb of God, which taketh away the sin of the world" (John 1:29)! . . .

Look at the cross of Calvary. It is a standing pledge of the boundless love, the measureless mercy, of the heavenly Father.[19]

Magnifies the Lord

*Let such as love thy salvation say continually,
The Lord be magnified. Ps.40:16.*

As witnesses for Christ, we are to tell what we know, what we ourselves have seen and heard and felt. If we have been following Jesus step by step, we shall have something right to the point to tell concerning the way in which He has led us. We can tell how we have tested His promise, and found the promise true. We can bear witness to what we have known of the grace of Christ. This is the witness for which our Lord calls, and for want of which the world is perishing.[20]

God would have every family that He is preparing to inhabit the eternal mansions above, give glory to Him for the rich treasures of His grace. Were children, in the home life, educated and trained to be grateful to the Giver of all good things we would see an element of heavenly grace manifest in our families. Cheerfulness would be seen in the home life, and coming from such homes, the youth would bring a spirit of respect and reverence with them into the schoolroom, and into the church. . . .

Every temporal blessing would be received with gratitude, and every spiritual blessing become doubly precious because the perception of each member of the household had become sanctified by the Word of truth. The Lord Jesus is very near to those who thus appreciate His gracious gifts, tracing all their good things back to the benevolent, loving, caretaking God, and recognizing Him as the great Fountain of all comfort and consolation, the inexhaustible Source of grace.[21]

The true Christian will make God first and last and best in everything. No ambitious motives will chill his love for God; steadily, perseveringly, will he cause honor to redound to his heavenly Father. It is when we are faithful in exalting the name of God that our impulses are under divine supervision, and we are enabled to develop spiritual and intellectual power.

Jesus, the divine Master, ever exalted the name of His heavenly Father. He taught His disciples to pray, "Our Father who art in heaven, hallowed be thy name" (Matt. 6:9, ARV). And they were not to forget to acknowledge, "Thine is . . . the glory" (verse 13).[22]

To Uproot Selfishness

Beware ye of the leaven of the Pharisees,
which is hypocrisy. Luke 12:1.

The hypocrisy of the Pharisees was the product of self-seeking. The glorification of themselves was the object of their lives. . . . Even the disciples, though outwardly they had left all for Jesus' sake, had not in heart ceased to seek great things for themselves. . . . As leaven, if left to complete its work, will cause corruption and decay, so does the self-seeking spirit, cherished, work the defilement and ruin of the soul. Among the followers of our Lord today, as of old, how widespread is this subtle, deceptive sin! How often our service to Christ, our communion with one another, is marred by the secret desire to exalt self! . . . To His own disciples the warning words of Christ are spoken, "Take heed and beware of the leaven of the Pharisees." . . . Only the power of God can banish self-seeking and hypocrisy.[23]

When Judas joined the disciples, he was not insensible to the beauty of the character of Christ. He felt the influence of that divine power which was drawing souls to the Saviour. . . . The Saviour read the heart of Judas; He knew the depths of iniquity to which, unless delivered by the grace of God, Judas would sink. In connecting this man with Himself, He placed him where he might, day by day, be brought in contact with the outflowing of His own unselfish love. If he would open his heart to Christ, divine grace would banish the demon of selfishness, and even Judas might become a subject of the kingdom of God.[24]

No one was so exalted as Christ, and yet He stooped to the humblest duty. . . . Christ Himself set the example of humility. He would not leave this great subject in man's charge. Of so much consequence did He regard it, that He Himself, One equal with God, acted as servant to His disciples. While they were contending for the highest place, He to whom every knee shall bow, He whom the angels of glory count it honor to serve, bowed down to wash the feet of those who called Him Lord. He washed the feet of His betrayer. . . . His whole life was under a law of service. He served all, ministered to all. Thus He lived the law of God, and by His example showed how we are to obey it.[25]

To Break Bad Habits

If any man be in Christ, he is a new creature: old things are passed away; behold, all things are become new. 2 Cor. 5:17.

Through the power of Christ, men and women have broken the chains of sinful habit. They have renounced selfishness. The profane have become reverent, the drunken sober, the profligate pure. Souls that have borne the likeness of Satan have become transformed into the image of God. This change is in itself the miracle of miracles. A change wrought by the Word, it is one of the deepest mysteries of the Word. We cannot understand it; we can only believe, as declared by the Scriptures, it is "Christ in you, the hope of glory" (Col. 1:27). . . .

Renouncing all that would hinder him from making progress in the upward way or that would turn the feet of another from the narrow path, the believer will reveal in his daily life mercy, kindness, humility, meekness, forbearance, and the love of Christ.

The power of a higher, purer, nobler life is our great need. The world has too much of our thought, and the kingdom of heaven too little.

In his efforts to reach God's ideal for him, the Christian is to despair of nothing. Moral and spiritual perfection, through the grace and power of Christ, is promised to all. Jesus is the source of power, the fountain of life.[26]

Let us make God's holy word our study, bringing its holy principles into our lives. Let us walk before God in meekness and humility, daily correcting our faults. . . . Peace and rest will come to you as you bring your will into subjection to the will of Christ. Then the love of Christ will rule in the heart, bringing into captivity to the Saviour the secret springs of action. The hasty, easily roused temper will be soothed and subdued by the oil of Christ's grace. . . .

In humble, grateful dependence he who has been given a new heart relies upon the help of Christ. He reveals in his life the fruit of righteousness. He once loved himself. Worldly pleasure was his delight. Now his idol is dethroned, and God reigns supreme. The sins he once loved he now hates. Firmly and resolutely he follows in the path of holiness.[27]

Creates Hatred for Satan

Give no opportunity to the devil. Eph. 4:27, RSV.

Satan's enmity against the human race is kindled because, through Christ, they are the objects of God's love and mercy. He desires to thwart the divine plan for man's redemption, to cast dishonor upon God, by defacing and defiling His handiwork; he would cause grief in heaven and fill the earth with woe and desolation. And he points to all this evil as the result of God's work in creating man.

It is the grace that Christ implants in the soul which creates in man enmity against Satan. Without this converting grace and renewing power, man would continue the captive of Satan, a servant ever ready to do his bidding. But the new principle in the soul creates conflict where hitherto had been peace. The power which Christ imparts, enables man to resist the tyrant and usurper. Whoever is seen to abhor sin instead of loving it, whoever resists and conquers those passions that have held sway within, displays the operation of a principle wholly from above.[28]

Like a roaring lion, Satan is seeking for his prey. He tries his wiles upon every unsuspecting youth; there is safety only in Christ. It is through His grace alone that Satan can be successfully repulsed. Satan tells the young that there is time enough yet, that they may indulge in sin and vice this once and never again; but that one indulgence will poison their whole life. Do not once venture on forbidden ground. In this perilous day of evil, when allurements to vice and corruption are on every hand, let the earnest, heartfelt cry of the young be raised to heaven: "Wherewithal shall a young man cleanse his way?" And may his ears be open and his heart inclined to obey the instruction given in the answer: "By taking heed thereto according to thy word" (Ps. 119:9). The only safety for the youth in this age of pollution is to make God their trust. Without divine help they will be unable to control human passions and appetites. In Christ is the very help needed. . . . You can say with the apostle: "Nay, in all these things we are more than conquerors through him that loved us" (Rom. 8:37). Again; "But I keep under my body, and bring it into subjection" (1 Cor. 9:27).[29]

To Banish Unrest and Doubt

O thou of little faith, wherefore didst thou doubt? Matt. 14:31.

Christ came to this world to show that by receiving power from on high, man can live an unsullied life. With unwearying patience and sympathetic helpfulness He met men in their necessities. By the gentle touch of grace He banished from the soul unrest and doubt, changing enmity to love, and unbelief to confidence.[30]

It is not wise to look to ourselves and study our emotions. If we do this, the enemy will present difficulties and temptations that weaken faith and destroy courage. Closely to study our emotions and give way to our feelings is to entertain doubt and entangle ourselves in perplexity. We are to look away from self to Jesus.

When temptations assail you, when care, perplexity, and darkness seem to surround your soul, look to the place where you last saw the light. Rest in Christ's love and under His protecting care. When sin struggles for the mastery in the heart, when guilt oppresses the soul and burdens the conscience, when unbelief clouds the mind, remember that Christ's grace is sufficient to subdue sin and banish the darkness.[31]

He will give you grace to be patient, He will give you grace to be trustful, He will give you grace to overcome restlessness, He will warm your heart with His own sweet Spirit, He will revive your soul in its weakness. . . . Then stay your soul in confidence upon God. Roll all your burdens upon Him.[32]

The soul that loves God, rises above the fog of doubt; he gains a bright, broad, deep, living experience, and becomes meek and Christlike. His soul is committed to God, hid with Christ in God. He will be able to stand the test of neglect, of abuse and contempt, because his Saviour has suffered all this. He will not become fretful and discouraged when difficulties press him, because Jesus did not fail or become discouraged. Every true Christian will be strong, not in the strength and merit of his good works, but in the righteousness of Christ, which through faith is imputed unto him. It is a great thing to be meek and lowly in heart, to be pure and undefiled, as was the Prince of heaven when He walked among men.[33]

To Unify the Church

Be not carried about with divers and strange doctrines.
For it is a good thing that the heart be established with grace.
Heb. 13:9.

The Lord in His wisdom has arranged that by means of the close relationship that should be maintained by all believers, Christian shall be united to Christian and church to church. Thus the human instrumentality will be enabled to cooperate with the divine. Every agency will be subordinate to the Holy Spirit, and all the believers will be united in an organized and well-directed effort to give to the world the glad tidings of the grace of God.[34]

God deals with men as individuals, giving to everyone his work. All are to be taught of God. Through the grace of Christ every soul must work out his own righteousness, maintaining a living connection with the Father and the Son. . . .

While it is true that the Lord guides individuals, it is also true that He is leading out a people, not a few separate individuals here and there, one believing this thing, another that. Angels of God are doing the work committed to their trust. The third angel is leading out and purifying a people, and they should move with him unitedly. . . .

Some have advanced the thought that as we near the close of time, every child of God will act independently of any religious organization. But I have been instructed by the Lord that in this work there is no such thing as every man's being independent. . . . In order that the Lord's work may advance healthfully and solidly, His people must draw together.[35]

Each member of the church should feel under sacred obligations to guard strictly the interests of the cause of God. . . . Jesus has opened to everyone a way by which wisdom, grace, and power may be obtained. He is our example in all things, and nothing should divert the mind from the main object in life, which is to have Christ in the soul, melting and subduing the heart. When this is the case, every member of the church, every professor of the truth, will be Christlike in character, in words, in actions.[36]

ABC HOLIDAY OPEN HOUSE

Sunday, November 18
10 A.M. – 4 P.M.

Come in for the best prices of Spring!!
10% off Most Books
Sales on most Worthington, Loma Linda, Morningstar Farms Food
15% off Most EGWhite
10% off all Childrens
15% off many Bibles

34 Sawyer Street South Lancaster, MA
11 Gerry Street Stoneham, MA
NEW ENGLAND ADVENTIST BOOK CENTER

That We Might Be Overcomers

They overcame him by the blood of the Lamb, and by the word of their testimony. Rev. 12:11.

Christ has made it possible for every member of the human family to resist temptation. All who would live godly lives may overcome as Christ overcame.[37]

To make God's grace our own, we must act our part. The Lord does not propose to perform for us either the willing or the doing. His grace is given to work in us to will and to do, but never as a substitute for our effort. Our souls are to be aroused to cooperate. The Holy Spirit works in us, that we may work out our own salvation. . . . Fine mental qualities and a high tone of moral character are not the result of accident. God gives opportunities; success depends upon the use made of them. The openings of Providence must be quickly discerned and eagerly entered. There are many who might become mighty men, if, like Daniel, they would depend upon God for grace to be overcomers, and for strength and efficiency to do their work.[38]

It is necessary to maintain a living connection with heaven, seeking as often as did Daniel—three times a day—for divine grace to resist appetite and passion. Wrestling with appetite and passion unaided by divine power will be unsuccessful; but make Christ your stronghold, and the language of your soul will be, "In all these things we are more than conquerors through him that loved us" (Rom. 8:37). Said the apostle Paul, "I keep under my body, and bring it into subjection: lest that by any means, when I have preached to others, I myself should be a castaway" (1 Cor. 9:27).

Let no one think he can overcome without the help of God. You must have the energy, the strength, the power, of an inner life developed within you. You will then bear fruit unto godliness, and will have an intense loathing of vice. You need to constantly strive to work away from earthliness, from cheap conversation, from everything sensual, and aim for nobility of soul and a pure and unspotted character. Your name may be kept so pure that it cannot justly be connected with anything dishonest or unrighteous, but will be respected by all the good and pure, and it may be written in the Lamb's book of life, to be immortalized among the holy angels.[39]

To Build Noble Characters

And from his fulness have we all received, grace upon grace.
John 1:16, RSV.

God expects us to build characters in accordance with the Pattern set before us. We are to lay brick by brick, adding grace to grace, finding our weak points and correcting them in accordance with the directions given. When a crack is seen in the walls of a mansion, we know that something about the building is wrong. In our character building, cracks are often seen. Unless these defects are remedied, the house will fall when the tempest of trial beats upon it.

God gives us strength, reasoning power, time, in order that we may build characters on which He can place His stamp of approval. He desires each child of His to build a noble character, by the doing of pure, noble deeds, that in the end He may present a symmetrical structure, a fair temple, honored by man and God.[40]

A noble all-round character is not inherited. It does not come to us by accident. A noble character is earned by individual effort through the merits and grace of Christ. God gives the talents, the powers of the mind; we form the character. It is formed by hard, stern battles with self. Conflict after conflict must be waged against hereditary tendencies. We shall have to criticize ourselves closely, and allow not one unfavorable trait to remain uncorrected.[41]

By the life we live through the grace of Christ the character is formed. The original loveliness begins to be restored to the soul. The attributes of the character of Christ are imparted, and the image of the Divine begins to shine forth. The faces of men and women who walk and work with God express the peace of heaven. They are surrounded with the atmosphere of heaven. For these souls the kingdom of God has begun. They have Christ's joy, the joy of being a blessing to humanity. They have the honor of being accepted for the Master's use; they are trusted to do His work in His name.[42]

As God is pure in His sphere, so man is to be pure in his. And he will be pure if Christ is formed within, the hope of glory; for he will imitate Christ's life and reflect His character.[43]

To Strengthen and Encourage

I can do all things through Christ which strengtheneth me. Phil. 4:13.

The Lord has in readiness the most precious exhibitions of His grace to strengthen and encourage the sincere, humble worker.[44]

The disciples of Christ had a deep sense of their own inefficiency, and with humiliation and prayer they joined their weakness to His strength, their ignorance to His wisdom, their unworthiness to His righteousness, their poverty to His exhaustless wealth. Thus strengthened and equipped, they hesitated not to press forward in the service of the Master.[45]

All that man has, God has given him, and he who improves his abilities to God's glory will be an instrument to do good; but we can no more live a religious life without constant prayer and the performance of religious duties than we can have physical strength without partaking of temporal food. We must daily sit down at God's table. We must receive strength from the living Vine, if we are nourished. . . .

I entreat you to move with an eye single to the glory of God. Let His power be your dependence, His grace your strength. By study of the Scriptures and earnest prayer seek to obtain clear conceptions of your duty, and then faithfully perform it. It is essential that you cultivate faithfulness in little things, and in so doing you will acquire habits of integrity in greater responsibilities. . . . Every event of life is great for good or for evil. The mind needs to be trained by daily tests, that it may acquire power to stand in any difficult position. In the days of trial and of peril you will need to be fortified to stand firmly for the right, independent of every opposing influence.[46]

Jesus consents to bear our burdens only when we trust Him. He is saying: "Come unto me, all ye weary and heavyladen; give Me your load; trust Me to do the work that it is impossible for the human agent to do." Let us trust Him. Worry is blind and cannot discern the future. But Jesus sees the end from the beginning, and in every difficulty He has His way prepared to bring relief. Abiding in Christ, we can do all things through Him who strengthens us.[47]

For Times of Trial

Blessed is the man that endureth temptation: for when he is tried, he shall receive the crown of life, which the Lord hath promised to them that love him. James 1:12.

The powers of darkness gather about the soul and shut Jesus from our sight, and at times we can only wait in sorrow and amazement until the cloud passes over. These seasons are sometimes terrible. Hope seems to fail, and despair seizes upon us. In these dreadful hours we must learn to trust, to depend solely upon the merits of the atonement, and in all our helpless unworthiness cast ourselves upon the merits of the crucified and risen Saviour. We shall never perish while we do this—*never!* When light shines on our pathway, it is no great thing to be strong in the strength of grace. But to wait patiently in hope when clouds envelop us and all is dark, requires faith and submission which causes our will to be swallowed up in the will of God. We are too quickly discouraged, and earnestly cry for the trial to be removed from us, when we should plead for patience to endure and grace to overcome.[48]

Those who turn to God with heart and soul and mind will find in Him peaceful security. . . . He knows just what we need, just what we can bear, and He will give us grace to endure every trial and test that He brings upon us. My constant prayer is for a greater nearness to God.[49]

God in His great love is seeking to develop in us the precious graces of His Spirit. He permits us to encounter obstacles, persecution, and hardships, not as a curse, but as the greatest blessing of our lives. Every temptation resisted, every trial bravely borne, gives us a new experience and advances us in the work of character building. The soul that through divine power resists temptation reveals to the world and to the heavenly universe the efficiency of the grace of Christ.[50]

Those who surrender their lives to His guidance and to His service will never be placed in a position for which He has not made provision. Whatever our situation, if we are doers of His word, we have a Guide to direct our way; whatever our perplexity, we have a sure Counselor; whatever our sorrow, bereavement, or loneliness, we have a sympathizing Friend.[51]

To Establish the Home

Through wisdom is an house builded;
and by understanding it is established. Prov. 24:3.

He who gave Eve to Adam as a helpmeet performed His first miracle at a marriage festival. . . . Thus He sanctioned marriage, recognizing it as an institution that He Himself had established. He ordained that men and women should be united in holy wedlock, to rear families whose members, crowned with honor, should be recognized as members of the family above.[52]

Like every other one of God's good gifts . . . , marriage has been perverted by sin; but it is the purpose of the gospel to restore its purity and beauty. . . .

The grace of Christ, and this alone, can make this institution what God designed it should be—an agent for the blessing and uplifting of humanity. And thus the families of earth, in their unity and peace and love, may represent the family of heaven. The condition of society presents a sad comment upon Heaven's ideal of this sacred relation. Yet even for those who have found bitterness and disappointment where they had hoped for companionship and joy, the gospel of Christ offers a solace. The patience and gentleness which His Spirit can impart, will sweeten the bitter lot. The heart in which Christ dwells will be so filled, so satisfied, with His love that it will not be consumed with longing to attract sympathy and attention to itself. And through the surrender of the soul to God, His wisdom can accomplish what human wisdom fails to do. Through the revelation of His grace, hearts that were once indifferent or estranged may be united. . . .

Men and women can reach God's ideal for them if they will take Christ as their helper. What human wisdom cannot do, His grace will accomplish for those who give themselves to Him in loving trust. His providence can unite hearts in bonds that are of heavenly origin. Love will not be a mere exchange of soft and flattering words. The loom of heaven weaves with warp and woof finer, yet more firm, than can be woven by the looms of earth. The result is not a tissue fabric, but a texture that will bear wear and test and trial. Heart will be bound to heart in the golden bonds of a love that is enduring.[53]

To Sustain the Burden Bearer

Cast thy burden upon the Lord, and he shall sustain thee. Ps. 55:22.

In the humble round of toil, the very weakest, the most obscure, may be workers together with God and may have the comfort of His presence and sustaining grace. They are not to weary themselves with busy anxieties and needless cares. Let them work on from day to day, accomplishing faithfully the task that God's providence assigns, and He will care for them. . . .

The Lord's care is over all His creatures. He loves them all, and makes no difference, except that He has the most tender pity for those who are called to bear life's heaviest burdens.[54]

Keep your wants, your joys, your sorrows, your cares, and your fears, before God. You cannot burden Him; you cannot weary Him. He who numbers the hairs of your head is not indifferent to the wants of His children. . . . Take to Him everything that perplexes the mind. Nothing is too great for Him to bear, for He holds up worlds, He rules over all the affairs of the universe. Nothing that in any way concerns our peace is too small for Him to notice. There is no chapter in our experience too dark for Him to read; there is no perplexity too difficult for Him to unravel. No calamity can befall the least of His children, no anxiety harass the soul, no joy cheer, no sincere prayer escape the lips, of which our heavenly Father is unobservant, or in which He takes no immediate interest. "He healeth the broken in heart, and bindeth up their wounds" (Ps. 147:3). The relations between God and each soul are as distinct and full as though there were not another soul upon earth to share His watchcare, not another soul for whom He gave His beloved Son.[55]

The Lord does not press on anyone burdens too heavy to be borne. He estimates every weight before He allows it to rest upon the hearts of those who are laborers together with Him. To every one of His workers our loving heavenly Father says: "Cast thy burden upon the Lord, and he shall sustain thee" (Ps. 55:22). Let the burden bearers believe that He will carry every load, great or small.[56]

For Each Day's Need

My God shall supply all your need according to his riches in glory by Christ Jesus. Phil. 4:19.

All blessings are bestowed upon those who have a vital connection with Jesus Christ. Jesus calls them to Himself not simply to refresh us with His grace and presence for a few hours, and then to send us forth from His light to walk apart from Him in sadness and gloom. No, no. He tells us that we must abide with Him and He with us. . . . Trust in Him continually, and doubt not His love. He knows all our weakness and that which we need. He will give us grace sufficient for our days.[57]

Those only who are constantly receiving fresh supplies of grace, will have power proportionate to their daily need and their ability to use that power. Instead of looking forward to some future time when, through a special endowment of spiritual power, they will receive a miraculous fitting up for soul winning, they are yielding themselves daily to God, that He may make them vessels meet for His use. Daily they are improving the opportunities for service that lie within their reach. Daily they are witnessing for the Master wherever they may be, whether in some humble sphere of labor in the home, or in a public field of usefulness.

To the consecrated worker there is wonderful consolation in the knowledge that even Christ during His life on earth sought His Father daily for fresh supplies of needed grace; and from this communion with God He went forth to strengthen and bless others. . . .

Every worker who follows the example of Christ will be prepared to receive and use the power that God has promised to His church for the ripening of earth's harvest. Morning by morning, as the heralds of the gospel kneel before the Lord and renew their vows of consecration to Him, He will grant them the presence of His Spirit, with its reviving, sanctifying power. As they go forth to the day's duties, they have the assurance that the unseen agency of the Holy Spirit enables them to be "laborers together with God" (1 Cor. 3:9).[58]

To Lift the Most Sinful

But he giveth more grace. Wherefore he saith, God resisteth the proud, but giveth grace unto the humble. James 4:6.

Mary had been looked upon as a great sinner, but Christ knew the circumstances that had shaped her life. He might have extinguished every spark of hope in her soul, but He did not. It was He who had lifted her from despair and ruin. Seven times she had heard His rebuke of the demons that controlled her heart and mind. She had heard His strong cries to the Father in her behalf. She knew how offensive is sin to His unsullied purity, and in His strength she had overcome.

When to human eyes her case appeared hopeless, Christ saw in Mary capabilities for good. He saw the better traits of her character. The plan of redemption has invested humanity with great possibilities, and in Mary these possibilities were to be realized. Through His grace she became a partaker of the divine nature. The one who had fallen, and whose mind had been a habitation of demons, was brought very near to the Saviour in fellowship and ministry. It was Mary who sat at His feet and learned of Him. It was Mary who poured upon His head the precious anointing oil, and bathed His feet with her tears. Mary stood beside the cross, and followed Him to the sepulcher. Mary was first at the tomb after His resurrection. It was Mary who first proclaimed a risen Saviour.

Jesus knows the circumstances of every soul. You may say, I am sinful, very sinful. You may be; but the worse you are, the more you need Jesus. He turns no weeping, contrite one away. . . . He bids every trembling soul take courage. Freely will He pardon all who come to Him for forgiveness and restoration. . . .

The souls that turn to Him for refuge, Jesus lifts above the accusing and the strife of tongues. No man or evil angel can impeach these souls. Christ unites them to His own divine-human nature.[59]

To those who with steadfast perseverance strive to reveal the attributes of Christ, angels are commissioned to give enlarged views of His character and work, His power and grace and love. Thus they become partakers of His nature.[60]

Gives Life to the Soul

Whosoever drinketh of the water that I shall give him shall never thirst; but the water that I shall give him shall be in him a well of water springing up into everlasting life. John 4:14.

He who seeks to quench his thirst at the fountains of this world will drink to thirst again. Everywhere men are unsatisfied. They long for something to supply the need of the soul. Only One can meet that want. The need of the world, "the Desire of all nations," is Christ. The divine grace which He alone can impart, is as living water, purifying, refreshing, and invigorating the soul.

Jesus did not convey the idea that merely one draught of the water of life would suffice the receiver. He who tastes of the love of Christ will continually long for more; but he seeks for nothing else. The riches, honors, and pleasures of the world do not attract him. The constant cry of his heart is, More of Thee. And He who reveals to the soul its necessity is waiting to satisfy its hunger and thirst. Every human resource and dependence will fail. The cisterns will be emptied, the pools become dry; but our Redeemer is an inexhaustible fountain. We may drink, and drink again, and ever find a fresh supply. He in whom Christ dwells has within himself the fountain of blessing. . . . From this source he may draw strength and grace sufficient for all his needs.[61]

He who drinks of the living water becomes a fountain of life. The receiver becomes a giver. The grace of Christ in the soul is like a spring in the desert, welling up to refresh all, and making those who are ready to perish eager to drink of the water of life.[62]

The water that Christ referred to was the revelation of His grace in His Word. . . . Christ's gracious presence in His Word is ever speaking to the soul, representing Him as the well of living water to refresh the thirsting. It is our privilege to have a living, abiding Saviour. He is the source of spiritual power implanted within us, and His influence will flow forth in words and actions, refreshing all within the sphere of our influence, begetting in them desires and aspirations for strength and purity, for holiness and peace, and for that joy which brings with it no sorrow. This is the result of an indwelling Saviour.[63]

To Make Us Holy

Ye shall be holy: for I the Lord your God am holy. Lev. 19:2.

Holiness is not rapture: it is an entire surrender of the will to God; it is living by every word that proceeds from the mouth of God; it is doing the will of our heavenly Father; it is trusting God in trial, in darkness as well as in the light; it is walking by faith and not by sight; it is relying on God with unquestioning confidence, and resting in His love.[64]

Our hearts are evil, and we cannot change them. . . . Education, culture, the exercise of the will, human effort, all have their proper sphere, but here they are powerless. They may produce an outward correctness of behavior, but they cannot change the heart; they cannot purify the springs of life. There must be a power working from within, a new life from above, before men can be changed from sin to holiness. That power is Christ. His grace alone can quicken the lifeless faculties of the soul, and attract it to God, to holiness.[65]

No man receives holiness as a birthright, or as a gift from any other human being. Holiness is the gift of God through Christ. Those who receive the Saviour become sons of God. They are His spiritual children, born again, renewed in righteousness and true holiness. Their minds are changed. With clearer vision they behold eternal realities. They are adopted into God's family, and they become conformed to His likeness, changed by His Spirit from glory to glory. From cherishing supreme love for self, they come to cherish supreme love for God and for Christ. . . . Accepting Christ as a personal Saviour, and following His example of self-denial—this is the secret of holiness.[66]

Forgetting the things that are behind, let us press forward in the heavenward way. Let us neglect no opportunity that, if improved, will make us more useful in God's service. Then like threads of gold, holiness will run through our lives, and the angels, beholding our consecration, will repeat the promise, "I will make a man more precious than fine gold; even a man than the golden wedge of Ophir" (Isa. 13:12). All heaven rejoices when weak, faulty human beings give themselves to Jesus, to live His life.[67]

To Adorn the Christian

Whose adorning, let it not be that outward adorning of plaiting the hair, and of wearing of gold, or of putting on of apparel; but let it be the hidden man of the heart, in that which is not corruptible, even the ornament of a meek and quiet spirit, which is in the sight of God of great price. 1 Peter 3:3, 4.

God, who created everything lovely and beautiful that the eye rests upon, is a lover of the beautiful. He shows you how He estimates true beauty. The ornament of a meek and quiet spirit is in His sight of *great price.*[68]

Of how little value are gold or pearls or costly array in comparison with the loveliness of Christ. Natural loveliness consists in symmetry, or the harmonious proportion of parts, each with the other; but spiritual loveliness consists in the harmony or likeness of our souls to Jesus. This will make its possessor more precious than fine gold, even the golden wedge of Ophir. The grace of Christ is indeed a priceless adornment. It elevates and ennobles its possessor and reflects beams of glory upon others, attracting them also to the Source of light and blessing.[69]

Our appearance in every respect should be characterized by neatness, modesty, and purity. But the Word of God gives no sanction to the making of changes in apparel merely for the sake of fashion, that we may appear like the world. Christians are not to decorate the person with costly array or expensive ornaments. . . .

All who are in earnest in seeking for the grace of Christ will heed the precious words of instruction inspired by God. Even the style of the apparel will express the truth of the gospel.[70]

It is right to love beauty and to desire it; but God desires us to love and seek first the highest beauty, that which is imperishable. No outward adorning can compare in value or loveliness with that "meek and quiet spirit," the "fine linen, white and clean" (Rev. 19:14), which all the holy ones of earth will wear. This apparel will make them beautiful and beloved here, and will hereafter be their badge of admission to the palace of the King.[71]

To Bring Comfort

Who comforteth us in all our tribulation, that we may be able to comfort them which are in any trouble, by the comfort wherewith we ourselves are comforted. 2 Cor. 1:4.

The Lord has special grace for the mourner, and its power is to melt hearts, to win souls. His love opens a channel into the wounded and bruised soul, and becomes a healing balsam to those who sorrow.[72]

Those who have borne the greatest sorrows are frequently the ones who carry the greatest comfort to others, bringing sunshine wherever they go. Such ones have been chastened and sweetened by their afflictions; they did not lose confidence in God when trouble assailed them, but clung closer to His protecting love. Such ones are living proof of the tender care of God, who makes the darkness as well as the light and chastens us for our good. Christ is the light of the world; in Him is no darkness. Precious light! Let us live in that light! Bid adieu to sadness and repining. Rejoice in the Lord always.[73]

It is your privilege to receive grace from Christ that will enable you to comfort others with the same comfort wherewith you yourselves are comforted of God. . . . Let each try to help the next one. Thus you may have a little heaven here below, and angels of God will work through you to make right impressions. . . . Seek to help wherever you can. Cultivate the best dispositions that the grace of God may rest richly upon you.

Young and old may learn to look to God as the One who will heal, as One who sympathizes, who understands their necessities and who will never make a mistake.[74]

Find time to comfort some other heart, to bless with a kind, cheering word someone who is battling with temptation and maybe with affliction. In thus blessing another with cheering, hopeful words, pointing him to the Burden Bearer, you may unexpectedly find peace, happiness, and consolation yourself.[75]

A consecrated Christian life is ever shedding light and comfort and peace. It is characterized by purity, tact, simplicity, and usefulness. It is controlled by that unselfish love that sanctifies the influence. It is full of Christ, and leaves a track of light wherever its possessor may go.[76]

Makes Our Foundation Sure

Therefore thus saith the Lord God, Behold, I lay in Zion for a foundation a stone, a tried stone, a precious corner stone, a sure foundation. Isa. 28:16.

In the Scriptures the figure of the erection of a temple is frequently used to illustrate the building of the church. . . . Writing of the building of this temple, Peter says, "To whom coming, as unto a living stone, disallowed indeed of men, but chosen of God, and precious, ye also, as lively stones, are built up a spiritual house, an holy priesthood . . ." (1 Peter 2:4, 5). . . .

The apostles built upon a sure foundation, even the Rock of Ages. To this foundation they brought the stones that they quarried from the world. Not without hindrance did the builders labor. Their work was made exceedingly difficult by the opposition of the enemies of Christ. They had to contend against the bigotry, prejudice, and hatred of those who were building upon a false foundation. . . . But in the face of imprisonment, torture, and death, faithful men carried the work forward; and the structure grew, beautiful and symmetrical. . . .

Through the ages that have passed since the days of the apostles, the building of God's temple has never ceased. We may look back through the centuries and see the living stones of which it is composed gleaming like jets of light through the darkness of error and superstition. Throughout eternity these precious jewels will shine with increasing luster. . . .

But the structure is not yet complete. We who are living in this age have a work to do, a part to act. We are to bring to the foundation material that will stand the test of fire—gold, silver, and precious stones. . . . The Christian who faithfully presents the word of life, leading men and women into the way of holiness and peace, is bringing to the foundation material that will endure, and in the kingdom of God he will be honored as a wise builder.[77]

Divine power will unite with our efforts, and as we cling to God with the hand of faith, Christ will impart to us His wisdom and His righteousness. Thus, by His grace, we shall be enabled to build upon the sure foundation.[78]

A Preserving Power

Ye are the salt of the earth. Matt. 5:13.

By these words of Christ we gain some idea of what constitutes the value of human influence. It is to work with the influence of Christ, to lift where Christ lifts, to impart correct principles, and stay the progress of the world's corruption. It is to diffuse that grace which Christ alone can impart. It is to uplift, to sweeten, the lives and characters of others by the power of a pure example united with earnest faith and love. God's people are to exercise a reforming, preserving power in the world. They are to counterwork the destroying, corrupting influence of evil. . . .

The work of the people of God in the world is to restrain evil, to elevate, to purify, and to ennoble mankind. The principles of kindness and love and benevolence are to uproot every fiber of the selfishness that has permeated all society and corrupted the church. . . . If men and women will open their hearts to the heavenly influence of truth and love, these principles will flow forth again, like streams in the desert, refreshing all, and causing freshness to appear where now are barrenness and dearth. The influence of those who keep the way of the Lord will be as far-reaching as eternity. They will carry with them the cheerfulness of heavenly peace as an abiding, refreshing, enlightening power.

Again, there is to be an open influence. Christ says, "Let your light so shine before men, that they may see your good works, and glorify your Father which is in heaven." . . .

The light that shines from those who receive Jesus Christ is not self-originated. It is all from the Light and Life of the world. . . . Christ is the light, the life, the holiness, the sanctification, of all who believe, and His light is to be received and imparted in all good works. In many different ways His grace is also acting as the salt of the earth; whithersoever this salt finds its way, to homes or communities, it becomes a preserving power to save all that is good, and to destroy all that is evil. True religion is the light of the world, the salt of the earth. . . .

The fountain of grace and knowledge is ever flowing. It is inexhaustible. It is from this abundant fulness that we are supplied.[79]

A Light to Shine

Arise, shine; for thy light is come, and the glory of the Lord is risen upon thee. Isa. 60:1.

Through the social relations, Christianity comes in contact with the world. Everyone who has received the divine illumination is to brighten the pathway of those who know not the Light of life. . . . Social power, sanctified by the grace of Christ, must be improved in winning souls to the Saviour. Let the world see that we are not selfishly absorbed in our own interests, but that we desire others to share our blessings and privileges. Let them see that our religion does not make us unsympathetic or exacting. Let all who profess to have found Christ, minister as He did for the benefit of men.

We should never give to the world the false impression that Christians are a gloomy, unhappy people. If our eyes are fixed on Jesus, we shall see a compassionate Redeemer, and shall catch light from His countenance. Wherever His Spirit reigns, there peace abides. And there will be joy also, for there is a calm, holy trust in God.

Christ is pleased with His followers when they show that, though human, they are partakers of the divine nature. They are not statues, but living men and women. Their hearts, refreshed by the dews of divine grace, open and expand to the Sun of Righteousness. The light that shines upon them they reflect upon others in works that are luminous with the love of Christ.[80]

The confession of faith made by saints and martyrs was recorded for the benefit of succeeding generations. Those living examples of holiness and steadfast integrity have come down to inspire courage in those who are now called to stand as witnesses for God. They received grace and truth, not for themselves alone, but that, through them, the knowledge of God might enlighten the earth. Has God given light to His servants in this generation? Then they should let it shine forth to the world.[81]

We are to be channels through which the Lord can send light and grace to the world. . . . The entire church, acting as one, blending in perfect union, is to be a living, active missionary agency, moved and controlled by the Holy Spirit.[82]

Workers With God

For we are laborers together with God. 1 Cor. 3:9.

God will honor and uphold every true-hearted, earnest soul who is seeking to walk before Him in the perfection of Christ's grace. He will never leave nor forsake one humble, trembling soul. Shall we believe that He will work in our hearts? that if we allow Him to do so, He will make us pure and holy, by His rich grace qualifying us to be laborers together with Him? Can we with keen, sanctified perception appreciate the strength of His promises, and appropriate them, not because we are worthy, but because by living faith we claim the righteousness of Christ?[83]

In giving light to His people anciently, God did not work exclusively through any one class. Daniel was a prince of Judah. Isaiah also was of the royal line. David was a shepherd boy, Amos a herdsman, Zechariah a captive from Babylon, Elisha a tiller of the soil. The Lord raised up as His representatives prophets and princes, the noble and the lowly, and taught them the truths to be given to the world. To every one who becomes a partaker of His grace, the Lord appoints a work for others. . . .

Let all cultivate their physical and mental powers to the utmost of their ability, that they may work for God where His providence shall call them. The same grace that came from Christ to Paul and Apollos, that distinguished them for spiritual excellencies, will today be imparted to devoted Christian missionaries. God desires His children to have intelligence and knowledge, that with unmistakable clearness and power His glory may be revealed in our world. . . .

Men deficient in school education, lowly in social position, have, through the grace of Christ, sometimes been wonderfully successful in winning souls for Him. The secret of their success was their confidence in God. They learned daily of Him who is wonderful in counsel and mighty in power.[84]

Everyone in whose heart Christ abides, everyone who will show forth His love to the world, is a worker together with God for the blessing of humanity. As he receives from the Saviour grace to impart to others, from his whole being flows forth the tide of spiritual life.[85]

Fishers of Men

And he saith unto them, Follow me,
and I will make you fishers of men. Matt. 4:19.

Divine grace in the newly converted soul is progressive. It gives an increase of grace, which is received, not to be hidden under a bushel, but to be imparted, that others may be benefited. He who is truly converted will work to save others who are in darkness.[86]

When a crisis comes in the life of any soul, and you attempt to give counsel or admonition, your words will have only the weight of influence for good that your own example and spirit have gained for you. You must *be* good before you can *do* good. You cannot exert an influence that will transform others until your own heart has been humbled and refined and made tender by the grace of Christ. When this change has been wrought in you, it will be as natural for you to live to bless others as it is for the rosebush to yield its fragrant bloom.[87]

He whose heart is filled with the grace of God and love for his perishing fellow men will find opportunity, wherever he may be placed, to speak a word in season to those who are weary. Christians are to work for their Master in meekness and lowliness, holding fast to their integrity amid the noise and bustle of life.[88]

We should strive to understand the weakness of others. We know little of the heart trials of those who have been bound in chains of darkness and who lack resolution and moral power. . . .

We become too easily discouraged over the souls who do not at once respond to our efforts. Never should we cease to labor for a soul while there is one gleam of hope. Precious souls cost our self-sacrificing Redeemer too dear a price to be lightly given up to the tempter's power. . . . Without a helping hand many would never recover themselves, but by patient, persistent effort they may be uplifted. Such need tender words, kind consideration, tangible help. . . . Christ is able to uplift the most sinful and place them where they will be acknowledged as children of God, joint heirs with Christ to the immortal inheritance. By the miracle of divine grace many may be fitted for lives of usefulness.[89]

A Completed Work

He shall bring forth the headstone thereof with shoutings, crying, Grace, grace unto it. Zech. 4:7.

Human power did not establish the work of God, neither can human power destroy it. To those who carry forward His work in face of difficulty and opposition, God will give the constant guidance and guardianship of His holy angels. His work on earth will never cease. The building of His spiritual temple will be carried forward until it shall stand complete, and the headstone shall be brought forth with shoutings: "Grace, grace unto it."[90]

Christ has given to the church a sacred charge. Every member should be a channel through which God can communicate to the world the treasures of His grace, the unsearchable riches of Christ. There is nothing that the Saviour desires so much as agents who will represent to the world His Spirit and His character. There is nothing that the world needs so much as the manifestation through humanity of the Saviour's love. . . .

The church is God's agency for the proclamation of truth, empowered by Him to do a special work; and if she is loyal to Him, obedient to all His commandments, there will dwell within her the excellency of divine grace. If she will be true to her allegiance, if she will honor the Lord God of Israel, there is no power that can stand against her.[91]

Christ desires by the fullness of His power so to strengthen His people that through them the whole world shall be encircled with an atmosphere of grace. When His people shall make a whole-hearted surrender of themselves to God, this purpose will be accomplished. . . . Christ will abide in humanity, and humanity will abide in Christ. In all the work will appear, not the character of finite man, but the character of the infinite God. . . .

The goodly fabric of character wrought out through divine power will receive light and glory from heaven, and will stand before the world as a witness pointing to the throne of the living God. Then the work will move forward with solidity and redoubled strength.[92]

Before Creation

Who hath saved us, and called us with an holy calling, not according to our works, but according to his own purpose and grace, which was given us in Christ Jesus before the world began. 2 Tim. 1:9.

The purpose and plan of grace existed from all eternity. Before the foundation of the world it was according to the determinate counsel of God that man should be created, endowed with power to do the divine will. But the defection of man, with all its consequences, was not hidden from the Omnipotent, and yet it did not deter Him from carrying out His eternal purpose; for the Lord would establish His throne in righteousness. God knows the end from the beginning. . . . Therefore redemption was not an afterthought . . . but an eternal purpose to be wrought out for the blessing not only of this atom of a world but for the good of all the worlds which God has created.

The creation of the worlds, the mystery of the gospel, are for one purpose, to make manifest to all created intelligences, through nature and through Christ, the glories of the divine character. By the marvelous display of His love in giving "his only-begotten Son, that whosoever believeth in him should not perish, but have everlasting life," the glory of God is revealed to lost humanity and to the intelligences of other worlds.[1]

Jesus encircles the race with His human arm, while with His divine arm He lays hold upon infinity. He is the "daysman" between a holy God and our sinful humanity—one who can "lay his hand on us both" (Job 9:33).

The terms of this oneness between God and man in the great covenant of redemption were arranged with Christ from all eternity. The covenant of grace was revealed to the patriarchs. The covenant made with Abraham . . . was a covenant confirmed by God in Christ, the very same gospel which is preached to us. . . . Paul speaks of the gospel, the preaching of Jesus Christ, as "the revelation of the mystery, which hath been kept in silence through times eternal, but now is manifested, and by the Scriptures of the prophets, according to the commandment of the eternal God, is made known unto all the nations unto obedience of faith" (Rom. 16:25, 26, RV).[2]

Everlasting

Incline your ear, and come unto me: hear, and your soul shall live; and I will make an everlasting covenant with you, even the sure mercies of David. Isa. 55:3.

The salvation of the human race has ever been the object of the councils of heaven. The covenant of mercy was made before the foundation of the world. It has existed from all eternity, and is called the everlasting covenant. So surely as there never was a time when God was not, so surely there never was a moment when it was not the delight of the eternal mind to manifest His grace to humanity.[3]

From the opening of the great controversy it has been Satan's purpose to misrepresent God's character, and to excite rebellion against His law. . . . But amid the working of evil, God's purposes move steadily forward to their accomplishment; to all created intelligences He is making manifest His justice and benevolence. Through Satan's temptations the whole human race have become transgressors of God's law, but by the sacrifice of His Son a way is opened whereby they may return to God. Through the grace of Christ they may be enabled to render obedience to the Father's law. Thus in every age, from the midst of apostasy and rebellion, God gathers out a people that are true to Him—a people "in whose heart is his law."[4]

God's work is the same in all time, although there are different degrees of development and different manifestations of His power, to meet the wants of men in the different ages. Beginning with the first gospel promise, and coming down through the patriarchal and Jewish ages, and even to the present time, there has been a gradual unfolding of the purposes of God in the plan of redemption. . . . He who proclaimed the law from Sinai, and delivered to Moses the precepts of the ritual law, is the same that spoke the sermon on the mount. . . . The Teacher is the same in both dispensations. God's claims are the same. The principles of His government are the same.[5]

In the closing work of God in the earth, the standard of His law will be again exalted. . . . God will not break His covenant, nor alter the thing that has gone out of His lips. His word will stand fast forever as unalterable as His throne.[6]

In Eden

I will put enmity between thee and the woman,
and between thy seed and her seed; it shall bruise thy head,
and thou shalt bruise his heel. Gen. 3:15.

The covenant of grace was first made with man in Eden, when after the fall, there was given a divine promise that the seed of the woman should bruise the serpent's head. To all men this covenant offered pardon, and the assisting grace of God for future obedience through faith in Christ. It also promised them eternal life on condition of fidelity to God's law. Thus the patriarchs received the hope of salvation.[7]

Adam and Eve, at their creation, had a knowledge of the law of God. It was printed on their hearts, and they understood its claims upon them.[8]

The law of God existed before man was created. It was adapted to the condition of holy beings; even angels were governed by it. After the fall, the principles of righteousness were unchanged. Nothing was taken from the law; not one of its holy precepts could be improved. And as it has existed from the beginning, so will it continue to exist throughout the ceaseless ages of eternity.[9]

After the transgression of Adam the principles of the law were . . . definitely arranged and expressed to meet man in his fallen condition. Christ, in counsel with His Father, instituted the system of sacrificial offerings; that death, instead of being immediately visited upon the transgressor, should be transferred to a victim which should prefigure the great and perfect offering of the Son of God. . . . Through the blood of this victim, man looked forward by faith to the blood of Christ which would atone for the sins of the world.[10]

The mission of Christ on earth was not to destroy the law, but by His grace to bring man back to obedience to its precepts. . . . By His own obedience to the law, Christ testified to its immutable character and proved that through His grace it could be perfectly obeyed by every son and daughter of Adam.[11]

Shared With Noah

And God spake unto Noah, . . . saying, And I, behold, I establish my covenant with you, and with your seed after you. Gen. 9:8, 9.

Wickedness was so widespread that God said, "I will destroy man whom I have created from the face of the earth. . . . But Noah found grace in the eyes of the Lord. . . . Noah was a just man and perfect in his generations, and Noah walked with God" (Gen. 6:7-9).[12]

Noah was to preach to the people, and also to prepare an ark as God should direct him for the saving of himself and family. He was not only to preach, but his example in building the ark was to convince all that he believed what he preached.[13]

Noah did not forget God who had so graciously preserved them, but immediately [on coming out of the ark] erected an altar and . . . offered burnt offerings on the altar, showing his faith in Christ the great sacrifice, and manifesting his gratitude to God for their wonderful preservation. The offering of Noah came up before God like a sweet savor. He accepted the offering, and blessed Noah and his family. . . .

And lest man should be terrified with gathering clouds, and falling rains, . . . God graciously encourages the family of Noah by a promise. "And I will establish my covenant with you; neither shall all flesh be cut off any more by the waters of a flood. . . . And God said, This is the token of the covenant which I make between me and you and every living creature that is with you, for perpetual generations. I do set my bow in the cloud, and it shall be for a token of a covenant between me and the earth. . . . And the bow shall be seen in the cloud; and I will look upon it, that I may remember the everlasting covenant between God and every living creature of all flesh that is upon the earth" (Gen. 9:11-16).[14]

With the assurance given to Noah concerning the flood, God Himself has linked one of the most precious promises of His grace; "As I have sworn that the waters of Noah should no more go over the earth, so have I sworn that I would not be wroth with thee, nor rebuke thee. For the mountains shall depart, and the hills be removed; but my kindness shall not depart from thee, neither shall the covenant of my peace be removed, saith Jehovah that hath mercy on thee" (Isa. 54:9, 10).[15]

Renewed to Abraham

I will establish my covenant between me and thee and thy seed after thee in their generations for an everlasting covenant, to be a God unto thee, and to thy seed after thee. Gen. 17:7.

After the Flood the people once more increased on the earth, and wickedness also increased. . . . The Lord finally left the hardened transgressors to follow their evil ways, while He chose Abraham, of the line of Shem, and made him the keeper of His law for future generations.[16]

This same covenant [the covenant of grace] was renewed to Abraham in the promise "In thy seed shall all the nations of the earth be blessed" (Gen. 22:18). This promise pointed to Christ. So Abraham understood it, and he trusted in Christ for the forgiveness of sins. It was this faith that was accounted to him for righteousness. The covenant with Abraham also maintained the authority of God's law. The Lord appeared unto Abraham, and said, "I am the Almighty God; walk before me, and be thou perfect" (Gen. 17:1). The testimony of God concerning His faithful servant was, "Abraham obeyed my voice, and kept my charge, my commandments, my statutes, and my laws" (Gen. 26:5). . . .

Though this covenant was made with Adam and renewed to Abraham, it could not be ratified until the death of Christ. It had existed by the promise of God since the first intimation of redemption had been given; it had been accepted by faith; yet when ratified by Christ, it is called a new covenant. The law of God was the basis of this covenant, which was simply an arrangement for bringing men again into harmony with the divine will, placing them where they could obey God's law.[17]

If it were not possible for human beings under the Abrahamic covenant to keep the commandments of God, every soul of us is lost. The Abrahamic covenant is the covenant of grace. "By grace are ye saved" (Eph. 2:8). Disobedient children? No, obedient to all His commandments.[18]

Abraham's unquestioning obedience was one of the most striking instances of faith and reliance upon God to be found in the Sacred Record. . . . Just such faith and confidence as Abraham had the messengers of God need today.[19]

Terms of the Covenant

If ye will obey my voice indeed, and keep my covenant, then ye shall be a peculiar treasure unto me above all people. Ex. 19:5.

In the beginning, God gave His law to mankind as a means of attaining happiness and eternal life.[20]

The ten commandments, Thou shalt, and Thou shalt not, are ten promises, assured to us if we render obedience to the law governing the universe. "If ye love me, keep my commandments" (John 14:15). Here is the sum and substance of the law of God. The terms of salvation for every son and daughter of Adam are here outlined. . . .

That law of ten precepts of the greatest love that can be presented to man is the voice of God from heaven speaking to the soul in promise, "This do, and you will not come under the dominion and control of Satan." There is not a negative in that law, although it may appear thus. It is DO and Live.[21]

The condition of eternal life is now just what it always has been—just what it was in Paradise before the fall of our first parents—perfect obedience to the law of God, perfect righteousness. If eternal life were granted on any condition short of this, then the happiness of the whole universe would be imperiled. The way would be open for sin, with all its train of woe and misery, to be immortalized.[22]

Christ does not lessen the claims of the law. In unmistakable language He presents obedience to it as the condition of eternal life—the same condition that was required of Adam before his fall. . . . The requirement under the covenant of grace is just as broad as the requirement made in Eden—harmony with God's law, which is holy, just, and good.[23]

The standard of character presented in the Old Testament is the same that is presented in the New Testament. This standard is not one to which we cannot attain. In every command or injunction that God gives there is a promise, the most positive, underlying the command. God has made provision that we may become like unto Him, and He will accomplish this for all who do not interpose a perverse will and thus frustrate His grace.[24]

The Promises of Men

All the people answered together, and said, All that the Lord hath spoken we will do. And Moses returned the words of the people unto the Lord. Ex. 19:8.

Another compact [other than the Abrahamic covenant]—called in Scripture the "old" covenant—was formed between God and Israel at Sinai, and was then ratified by the blood of a sacrifice. The Abrahamic covenant was ratified by the blood of Christ, and it is called the "second," or "new" covenant, because the blood by which it was sealed was shed after the blood of the first covenant.[25]

Soon after the encampment at Sinai, Moses was called up into the mountain to meet with God. . . . Israel was now to be taken into a close and peculiar relation to the Most High—to be incorporated as a church and a nation under the government of God. The message to Moses for the people was: ". . . if ye will obey my voice indeed, and keep my covenant, then ye shall be a peculiar treasure unto me above all people; for all the earth is mine. And ye shall be unto me a kingdom of priests, and an holy nation" (Ex. 19:4-6).

Moses returned to the camp, and having summoned the elders of Israel, he repeated to them the divine message. Their answer was, "All that the Lord hath spoken we will do." Thus they entered into a solemn covenant with God, pledging themselves to accept Him as their Ruler, by which they became, in a special sense, the subjects of His authority.[26]

In their bondage the people had to a great extent lost the knowledge of God and of the principles of the Abrahamic covenant. . . . Living in the midst of idolatry and corruption, they had no true conception of the holiness of God, of the exceeding sinfulness of their own hearts, their utter inability, in themselves, to render obedience to God's law, and their need of a Saviour. . . . God brought them to Sinai; He manifested His glory; He gave them His law, with the promise of great blessings on condition of obedience. . . . The people did not realize . . . that without Christ it was impossible for them to keep God's law. . . . Feeling that they were able to establish their own righteousness, they declared, "All that the Lord hath said will we do, and be obedient" (Ex. 24:7).[27]

Better Promises

He is the mediator of a better covenant which was established upon better promises. Heb. 8:6.

The Israelites had been specially charged not to lose sight of the commandments of God, in obedience to which they would find strength and blessing.[28]

They had witnessed the proclamation of the law in awful majesty, and had trembled with terror before the mount; and yet only a few weeks passed before they broke their covenant with God, and bowed down to worship a graven image. They could not hope for the favor of God through a covenant which they had broken; and now, seeing their sinfulness and their need of pardon, they were brought to feel their need of the Saviour revealed in the Abrahamic covenant and shadowed forth in the sacrificial offerings. Now by faith and love they were bound to God as their deliverer from the bondage of sin. Now they were prepared to appreciate the blessings of the new covenant.

The terms of the "old covenant" were, Obey and live: "If a man do, he shall even live in them" (Eze. 20:11; Lev. 18:5); but "cursed be he that confirmeth not all the words of this law to do them" (Deut. 27:26). The "new covenant" was established upon "better promises"—the promise of forgiveness of sins and of the grace of God to renew the heart and bring it into harmony with the principles of God's law.[29]

The blessings of the new covenant are grounded purely on mercy in forgiving unrighteousness and sins. . . . All who humble their hearts, confessing their sins, will find mercy and grace and assurance. Has God, in showing mercy to the sinner, ceased to be just? Has He dishonored His holy law, and will He henceforth pass over the violation of it? God is true. He changes not. The conditions of salvation are ever the same. Life, eternal life, is for all who will obey God's law. . . .

Under the new covenant, the conditions by which eternal life may be gained are the same as under the old—perfect obedience. . . . In the new and better covenant, Christ has fulfilled the law for the transgressors of law, if they receive Him by faith as a personal Saviour. . . . In the better covenant we are cleansed from sin by the blood of Christ.[30]

Written on the Heart

After those days, saith the Lord, I will put my law in their inward parts, and write it in their hearts. . . . I will forgive their iniquity, and I will remember their sin no more. Jer. 31:33, 34.

The same law that was engraved upon the tables of stone, is written by the Holy Spirit upon the tables of the heart. Instead of going about to establish our own righteousness we accept the righteousness of Christ. His blood atones for our sins. His obedience is accepted for us. Then the heart renewed by the Holy Spirit will bring forth "the fruits of the Spirit." Through the grace of Christ we shall live in obedience to the law of God written upon our hearts. Having the Spirit of Christ, we shall walk even as He walked.[31]

There are two errors against which the children of God—particularly those who have just come to trust in His grace—especially need to guard. The first . . . is that of looking to their own works, trusting to anything they can do, to bring themselves into harmony with God. He who is trying to become holy by his own works in keeping the law, is attempting an impossibility. . . .

The opposite and no less dangerous error is, that belief in Christ releases men from keeping the law of God; that since by faith alone we become partakers of the grace of Christ, our works have nothing to do with our redemption. . . . If the law is written in the heart, will it not shape the life? . . . Instead of releasing man from obedience, it is faith, and faith only, that makes us partakers of the grace of Christ, which enables us to render obedience. . . .

Where there is not only a belief in God's Word, but a submission of the will to Him; where the heart is yielded to Him, the affections fixed upon Him, there is faith—faith that works by love, and purifies the soul. Through this faith the heart is renewed in the image of God. And the heart that in its unrenewed state is not subject to the law of God, neither indeed can be, now delights in its holy precepts, exclaiming with the psalmist, "O how love I thy law! it is my meditation all the day" (Ps. 119:97). And the righteousness of the law is fulfilled in us, "who walk not after the flesh, but after the Spirit" (Rom. 8:1).[32]

The Gift of Repentance

Him hath God exalted with his right hand to be a Prince and a Saviour, for to give repentance to Israel, and forgiveness of sins. Acts 5:31.

Repentance is one of the first fruits of saving grace. Our great Teacher, in His lessons to erring, fallen man, presents the life-giving power of His grace, declaring that through this grace men and women may live the new life of holiness and purity. He who lives this life works out the principles of the kingdom of heaven. Taught of God, he leads others in straight paths. He will not lead the lame into paths of uncertainty. The working of the Holy Spirit in his life shows that he is a partaker of the divine nature. Every soul thus worked by the Spirit of Christ receives so abundant a supply of the rich grace that, beholding his good works, the unbelieving world acknowledges that he is controlled and sustained by divine power, and is led to glorify God. . . .

Read and study the thirty-fourth chapter of Ezekiel. In it we are given most precious encouragement. "I will save my flock, and they shall be no more a prey," the Lord declares. ". . . And I will make with them a covenant of peace. . . ."

The most striking feature of this covenant of peace is the exceeding richness of the pardoning mercy expressed to the sinner if he repents and turns from his sin. The Holy Spirit describes the gospel as salvation through the tender mercies of our God. "I will be merciful to their unrighteousness," the Lord declares of those who repent, "and their sins and their iniquities will I remember no more" (Heb. 8:12). Does God turn from justice in showing mercy to the sinner? No; God cannot dishonor His law by suffering it to be transgressed with impunity. Under the new covenant, perfect obedience is the condition of life. If the sinner repents and confesses his sins, he will find pardon. By Christ's sacrifice in his behalf, forgiveness is secured for him. Christ has satisfied the demands of the law for every repentant, believing sinner. . . .

The atonement that has been made for us by Christ is wholly and abundantly satisfactory to the Father. God can be just, and yet the justifier of those who believe.[33]

The Gift of Pardon

Thou art a God ready to pardon, gracious and merciful, slow to anger, and of great kindness, and forsookest them not. Neh. 9:17.

Justice demands that sin be not merely pardoned, but the death penalty must be executed. God, in the gift of His only-begotten Son, met both these requirements. By dying in man's stead, Christ exhausted the penalty and provided a pardon.[34]

God requires that we confess our sins, and humble our hearts before Him; but at the same time we should have confidence in Him as a tender Father, who will not forsake those who put their trust in Him. . . . God does not give us up because of our sins. We may make mistakes, and grieve His Spirit; but when we repent, and come to Him with contrite hearts, He will not turn us away. There are hindrances to be removed. Wrong feelings have been cherished, and there have been pride, self-sufficiency, impatience, and murmurings. All these separate us from God. Sins must be confessed; there must be a deeper work of grace in the heart. . . .

We must learn in the school of Christ. Nothing but His righteousness can entitle us to one of the blessings of the covenant of grace. . . . We look to self, as though we had power to save ourselves; but Jesus died for us because we are helpless to do this. In Him is our hope, our justification, our righteousness. . . .

Jesus is our only Saviour; and although millions who need to be healed will reject His offered mercy, not one who trusts in His merits will be left to perish. . . .

You may see that you are sinful and undone; but it is just on this account that you need a Saviour. If you have sins to confess, lose no time. These moments are golden. "If we confess our sins, he is faithful and just to forgive us our sins, and to cleanse us from all unrighteousness" (1 John 1:9). Those who hunger and thirst after righteousness will be filled; for Jesus has promised it. Precious Saviour! His arms are open to receive us, and His great heart of love is waiting to bless us.[35]

Accepted by Faith

For ye are all the children of God by faith in Christ Jesus. Gal. 3:26.

To talk of religion in a casual way, to pray without soul hunger and living faith, avails nothing. A nominal faith in Christ, which accepts Him merely as the Saviour of the world, can never bring healing to the soul. The faith that is unto salvation is not a mere intellectual assent to the truth. He who waits for entire knowledge before he will exercise faith cannot receive blessing from God. It is not enough to believe *about* Christ; we must believe *in* Him. The only faith that will benefit us is that which embraces Him as a personal Saviour; which appropriates His merits to ourselves. Many hold faith as an opinion. Saving faith is a transaction by which those who receive Christ join themselves in covenant relation with God. Genuine faith is life. A living faith means an increase of vigor, a confiding trust, by which the soul becomes a conquering power.[36]

True faith is that which receives Christ as a personal Saviour. God gave His only-begotten Son, that I, by believing in Him, "should not perish, but have everlasting life" (John 3:16). When I come to Christ, according to His word, I am to believe that I receive His saving grace. The life that I now live, I am to "live by the faith of the Son of God, who loved *me*, and gave himself for *me*" (Gal. 2:20).[37]

The apostle Paul clearly presents the relation between faith and the law under the new covenant. He says: "Being *justified by faith,* we have peace with God through our Lord Jesus Christ." "Do we then make void the law through faith? God forbid; yea, we establish the law." "For what the law could not do, in that it was weak through the flesh"—it could not justify man, because in his sinful nature he could not keep the law—"God sending his own Son in the likeness of sinful flesh, and for sin, condemned sin in the flesh; that *the righteousness of the law* might be fulfilled in us, who walk not after the flesh, but after the Spirit" (Rom. 5:1; 3:31; 8:3, 4).[38]

God's Law Is Its Standard

Let us hear the conclusion of the whole matter: Fear God, and keep his commandments: for this is the whole duty of man. Eccl. 12:13.

Before the foundations of the earth were laid, the covenant was made that all who were obedient, all who should through the abundant grace provided, become holy in character, and without blame before God, by appropriating that grace, should be children of God. This covenant, made from eternity, was given to Abraham hundreds of years before Christ came. With what interest and what intensity did Christ in humanity study the human race to see if they would avail themselves of the provision offered.[39]

In His teachings, Christ showed how far-reaching are the principles of the law spoken from Sinai. He made a living application of that law whose principles remain forever the great standard of righteousness—the standard by which all shall be judged in that great day when the judgment shall sit, and the books shall be opened. He came to fulfill all righteousness, and, as the head of humanity, to show man that he can do the same work, meeting every specification of the requirements of God. Through the measure of His grace furnished to the human agent, not one need miss heaven. Perfection of character is attainable by every one who strives for it. This is made the very foundation of the new covenant of the gospel. The law of Jehovah is the tree; the gospel is the fragrant blossoms and fruit which it bears.[40]

God's law is the transcript of His character. It embodies the principles of His kingdom. He who refuses to accept these principles is placing himself outside the channel where God's blessings flow.

The glorious possibilities set before Israel could be realized only through obedience to God's commandments. The same elevation of character, the same fulness of blessing—blessing on mind and soul and body, blessing on house and field, blessing for this life and for the life to come—is possible for us only through obedience.[41]

Let us not lower the standard, but keep it lifted high, looking to Him who is the Author and the Finisher of our faith.[42]

The Pledge of Obedience

He took the book of the covenant, and read in the audience of the people: and they said, All that the Lord hath said will we do, and be obedient. Ex. 24:7.

The covenant that God made with His people at Sinai is to be our refuge and defense. . . . This covenant is of just as much force today as it was when the Lord made it with ancient Israel. . . .

This is the pledge that God's people are to make in these last days. Their acceptance with God depends on a faithful fulfillment of the terms of their agreement with Him. God includes in His covenant all who will obey Him. To all who will do justice and judgment, keeping their hand from doing any evil, the promise is, "Even unto them will I give in mine house and within my walls a place and a name better than of sons and of daughters: I will give them an everlasting name, that shall not be cut off" (Isa. 56:5).[43]

The Father sets His love upon His elect people who live in the midst of men. These are the people whom Christ has redeemed by the price of His own blood; and because they respond to the drawing of Christ, through the sovereign mercy of God, they are elected to be saved as His obedient children. Upon them is manifested the free grace of God, the love wherewith He hath loved them. Everyone who will humble himself as a little child, who will receive and obey the Word of God with a child's simplicity will be among the elect of God.[44]

To make God's grace our own, we must act our part. The Lord does not propose to perform for us either the willing or the doing. His grace is given to work in us to will and to do, but never as a substitute for our effort.[45]

Let the human agent compare his life with the life of Christ. . . . Let him imitate the example of Him who lived out the law of Jehovah, who said, "I have kept my father's commandments." Those who follow Christ will be continually looking into the perfect law of liberty, and through the grace given them by Christ, will fashion the character according to the divine requirements.[46]

The Role of Baptism

We are buried with him by baptism into death; that like as Christ was raised up from the dead by the glory of the Father, even so we also should walk in newness of life. Rom. 6:4.

Christ made baptism the entrance to His spiritual kingdom. He made this a positive condition with which all must comply who wish to be acknowledged as under the authority of the Father, the Son, and the Holy Ghost. Those who receive the ordinance of baptism thereby make a public declaration that they have renounced the world, and have become members of the royal family, children of the heavenly King. . . .

Christ enjoins those who receive this ordinance to remember that they are bound by a solemn covenant to live to the Lord. They are to use for Him all their entrusted capabilities, never losing the realization that they bear God's sign of obedience to the Sabbath of the fourth commandment, that they are subjects of Christ's kingdom, partakers of the divine nature. They are to surrender all they have and are to God, employing all their gifts to God's glory.

Those who are baptized in the threefold name of the Father, the Son, and the Holy Ghost, at the very entrance of their Christian life declare publicly that they have accepted the invitation, "Come out from among them, and be ye separate, saith the Lord, and touch not the unclean thing; and I will receive you, and will be a Father unto you, and ye shall be my sons and daughters, saith the Lord Almighty" (2 Cor. 6:17, 18). "Having therefore these promises, dearly beloved, let us cleanse ourselves from all filthiness of the flesh and spirit, perfecting holiness in the fear of God" (2 Cor. 7:1). . . .

Let those who received the imprint of God by baptism heed these words, remembering that upon them the Lord has placed His signature, declaring them to be His sons and daughters. The Father, the Son, and the Holy Ghost, powers infinite and omniscient, receive those who truly enter into covenant relation with God. They are present at every baptism, to receive the candidates who have renounced the world and have received Christ into the soul temple. These candidates have entered into the family of God, and their names are inscribed in the Lamb's book of life.[47]

Not a Substitute for the Law

What then? shall we sin, because we are not under the law, but under grace? God forbid. Rom. 6:15.

It is the sophistry of Satan that the death of Christ brought in grace to take the place of the law. The death of Jesus did not change or annul, or lessen in the slightest degree, the law of ten commandments. That precious grace offered to men through a Saviour's blood, establishes the law of God. Since the fall of man, God's moral government and His grace are inseparable. They go hand in hand through all dispensations.[48]

The gospel of the New Testament is not the Old Testament standard lowered to meet the sinner and save him in his sins. God requires of all His subjects obedience, entire obedience to all His commandments.[49]

Jesus was tempted in all points like as we are, that He might know how to succor those who should be tempted. His life is our example. He shows by His willing obedience that man may keep the law of God and that transgression of the law, not obedience to it, brings him into bondage. . . .

Man, who has defaced the image of God in his soul by a corrupt life, cannot, by mere human effort, effect a radical change in himself. He must accept the provisions of the gospel; he must be reconciled to God through obedience to His law and faith in Jesus Christ. His life from thenceforth must be governed by a new principle. . . . He must face the mirror, God's law, discern the defects in his moral character, and put away his sins, washing his robe of character in the blood of the Lamb. . . .

The influence of a gospel hope will not lead the sinner to look upon the salvation of Christ as a matter of free grace, while he continues to live in transgression of the law of God. When the light of truth dawns upon his mind and he fully understands the requirements of God and realizes the extent of his transgressions, he will reform his ways, become loyal to God through the strength obtained from His Saviour, and lead a new and purer life.[50]

It is not the work of the gospel to weaken the claims of God's holy law, but to bring men up where they can keep its precepts.[51]

Includes Love to God and Man

Jesus said unto him, Thou shalt love the Lord thy God with all thy heart, and with all thy soul, and with all thy mind. . . . And . . . thou shalt love thy neighbour as thyself. Matt. 22:37-39.

The whole work of grace is one continual service of love, of self-denying, self-sacrificing effort. During every hour of Christ's sojourn upon the earth, the love of God was flowing from Him in irrepressible streams. All who are imbued with His Spirit will love as He loved. The very principle that actuated Christ will actuate them in all their dealing one with another.

This love is the evidence of their discipleship. . . . When men are bound together, not by force or self-interest, but by love, they show the working of an influence that is above every human influence. Where this oneness exists, it is evidence that the image of God is being restored in humanity, that a new principle of life has been implanted. It shows that there is power in the divine nature to withstand the supernatural agencies of evil, and that the grace of God subdues the selfishness inherent in the natural heart.[52]

When self is merged in Christ, love springs forth spontaneously. The completeness of Christian character is attained when the impulse to help and bless others springs constantly from within—when the sunshine of heaven fills the heart and is revealed in the countenance.

It is not possible for the heart in which Christ abides to be destitute of love. If we love God because He first loved us, we shall love all for whom Christ died. We cannot come in touch with divinity without coming in touch with humanity; for in Him who sits upon the throne of the universe, divinity and humanity are combined. Connected with Christ, we are connected with our fellow men by the golden links of the chain of love. Then the pity and compassion of Christ will be manifest in our life. . . . It will be as natural for us to minister to the needy and suffering as it was for Christ to go about doing good.[53]

The law of God requires that man shall love God supremely, and his neighbor as himself. When through the grace of our Lord Jesus Christ, this is perfectly done, we shall be complete in Christ.[54]

Involves Character Building

Ye are a chosen generation, a royal priesthood, an holy nation, a peculiar people; that ye should shew forth the praises of him who hath called you out of darkness into his marvellous light. 1 Peter 2:9.

Obedience to the laws of God develops in man a beautiful character that is in harmony with all that is pure and holy and undefiled. In the life of such a man the message of the gospel of Christ is made clear. Accepting the mercy of Christ and His healing from the power of sin, he is brought into right relation with God. His life, cleansed from vanity and selfishness, is filled with the love of God. His daily obedience to the law of God obtains for him a character that assures him eternal life in the kingdom of God.[55]

But Christ has given us no assurance that to attain perfection of character is an easy matter. A noble, all-round character is not inherited. It does not come to us by accident. A noble character is earned by individual effort through the merits and grace of Christ. God gives the talents, the powers of the mind; we form the character. It is formed by hard, stern battles with self. Conflict after conflict must be waged against hereditary tendencies. We shall have to criticize ourselves closely, and allow not one unfavorable trait to remain uncorrected.[56]

The truth is no truth to the one who does not reveal, by his elevated spiritual character, a power beyond that which the world can give, and influence corresponding in its sacred, peculiar character to the truth itself. He who is sanctified by the truth will exert a saving, vital influence upon all with whom he comes in contact. This is Bible religion.[57]

We need constantly a fresh revelation of Christ, a daily experience that harmonizes with His teachings. High and holy attainments are within our reach. Continual progress in knowledge and virtue is God's purpose for us. His law is the echo of His own voice, giving to all the invitation, "Come up higher. Be holy, holier still." Every day we may advance in perfection of Christian character.[58]

Demands Purity

For God hath not called us unto uncleanness, but unto holiness. 1 Thess. 4:7.

Life is a gift of God. Our bodies have been given us to use in God's service, and He desires that we shall care for and appreciate them. We are possessed of physical as well as mental faculties. Our impulses and passions have their seat in the body, and therefore we must do nothing that would defile this entrusted possession. Our bodies must be kept in the best possible condition physically, and under the most spiritual influences, in order that we may make the best use of our talents. Read 1 Cor. 6:13.[59]

Our bodies belong to God. He paid the price of redemption for the body as well as the soul. . . . God is the great caretaker of the human machinery. In the care of our bodies we must cooperate with Him. Love for God is essential for life and health. In order to have perfect health our hearts must be filled with hope, and love, and joy.

The lower passions are to be strictly guarded. The perceptive faculties are abused, terribly abused, when the passions are allowed to run riot. When the passions are indulged, the blood, instead of circulating to all parts of the body, thereby relieving the heart and clearing the mind, is called in undue amount to the internal organs. Disease comes as the result. The man cannot be healthy until the evil is seen and remedied.

"He that is joined unto the Lord"—bound up with Christ in the covenant of grace—"is one spirit. Flee fornication" (1 Cor. 6:17, 18). Do not stop for one moment to reason. Satan would rejoice to see you overthrown by temptation. Do not stop to argue the case with your weak conscience. Turn away from the first step of transgression.

Would that the example of Joseph might be followed by all who claim to be wise, who feel competent in their own strength to discharge the duties of life. A wise man will not be governed and controlled by his appetites and passions, but will control and govern them. He will draw nigh to God, striving to prepare mind and body to discharge aright the duties of life. . . . Satan is the destroyer; Christ the restorer.[60]

Encourages Christlikeness

He that saith he abideth in him ought himself also so to walk, even as he walked. 1 John 2:6.

The gospel is to be presented, not as a lifeless theory, but as a living force to change the life. God desires that the receivers of His grace shall be witnesses to its power. . . . He would have His servants bear testimony to the fact that through His grace men may possess Christlikeness of character, and may rejoice in the assurance of His great love. He would have us bear testimony to the fact that He cannot be satisfied until the human race are reclaimed and reinstated in their holy privileges as His sons and daughters.[61]

God's people are to be distinguished as a people who serve Him fully, wholeheartedly, taking no honor to themselves, and remembering that by a most solemn covenant they have bound themselves to serve the Lord and Him only.[62]

God requires perfection of His children. His law is a transcript of His own character, and it is the standard of all character. This infinite standard is presented to all that there may be no mistake in regard to the kind of people whom God will have to compose His kingdom. The life of Christ on earth was a perfect expression of God's law, and when those who claim to be children of God become Christlike in character, they will be obedient to God's commandments. Then the Lord can trust them to be of the number who shall compose the family of heaven. Clothed in the glorious apparel of Christ's righteousness, they have a place at the King's feast. They have a right to join the blood-washed throng.[63]

Everything must be viewed in the light of the example of Christ. He is the truth. He is the true Light that lighteth every man who cometh into the world. Listen to His words, copy His example in self-denial and self-sacrifice, and look to the merits of Christ for the glory in character which He possesses to be bestowed on you. Those who follow Christ live not to please themselves. Human standards are like feeble reeds. The Lord's standard is perfection of character.[64]

With All the Heart

This day the Lord thy God hath commanded thee to do these statutes and judgments: thou shalt therefore keep and do them with all thine heart, and with all thy soul. Deut. 26:16.

In God's covenant with His people in ancient times, directions were given for the faithful recognition of the gracious and marvelous works which He had done for them. God delivered His people Israel from bondage in Egypt. He brought them into their own land, and gave them goodly heritage and sure dwelling places. And He asked of them a recognition of His marvelous works. The first fruits of the earth were to be consecrated to God, and given back to Him as an offering of gratitude, an acknowledgment of His goodness to them. . . .

These directions, which the Lord has given to His people, express the principles of the law of the kingdom of God, and they are made specific, so that the minds of the people may not be left in ignorance and uncertainty. These scriptures present the never-ceasing obligation of all whom God has blessed with life and health and advantages in temporal and spiritual things. The message has not grown weak because of age. God's claims are just as binding now, just as fresh in their importance, as God's gifts are fresh and continual.

Lest any should forget these important directions, Christ has repeated them with His own voice. He calls His followers to a life of consecration and self-denial. He says: "If any man will come after me, let him deny himself, and take up his cross, and follow me" (Matt. 16:24). This means what it says. Only by self-denial and self-sacrifice can we show that we are true disciples of Christ.

Christ counted it essential to remind His people that obedience to the commandments of God is for their present and future good. Obedience brings a blessing, disobedience a curse. Besides, when the Lord in a special manner favors His people, He exhorts them publicly to acknowledge His goodness. In this way His name will be glorified; for such an acknowledgment is a testimony that His words are faithful and true. "Thou shalt rejoice in every good thing which the Lord thy God hath given unto thee" (Deut. 26:11).[65]

A Mutual Pact

You have recognized the Lord this day as your God; you are to conform to his ways, to keep his statutes, his commandments, and his laws, and to obey him. The Lord has recognized you this day as his special possession, as he promised you, and to keep his commandments. Deut. 26:17, 18, NEB.

There must be no withholding on our part, of our service or our means, if we would fulfill our covenant with God. . . . The purpose of all God's commandments is to reveal man's duty not only to God, but to his fellow man. In this late age of the world's history, we are not, because of the selfishness of our hearts, to question or dispute the right of God to make these requirements, or we will deceive ourselves, and rob our souls of the richest blessings of the grace of God. Heart and mind and soul are to be merged in the will of God. Then the covenant, framed from the dictates of infinite wisdom, and made binding by the power and authority of the King of kings and Lord of lords, will be our pleasure. . . . It is enough that He has said that obedience to His statutes and laws is the life and prosperity of His people.

The blessings of God's covenant are mutual. . . . God accepts those who will work for His name's glory, to make His name a praise in a world of apostasy and idolatry. He will be exalted by His commandment-keeping people that He may make them "high above all nations which he hath made, in praise, and in name, and in honour" (Deut. 26:19).

By our baptismal pledge we avouched and solemnly confessed the Lord Jehovah as our Ruler. We virtually took a solemn oath, in the name of the Father, and of the Son, and of the Holy Ghost, that henceforth our lives would be merged into the life of these three great agencies, that the life we should live in the flesh would be lived in faithful obedience to God's sacred law. We declared ourselves dead, and our life hid with Christ in God, that henceforth we should walk with Him in newness of life, as men and women having experienced the new birth. We acknowledge God's covenant with us, and pledge ourselves to seek those things which are above, where Christ sitteth on the right hand of God. By our profession of faith we acknowledged the Lord as our God, and yielded ourselves to obey His commandments.[66]

Blessings of the Covenant

Give, and it shall be given unto you; good measure, pressed down, and shaken together, and running over, shall men give into your bosom. For with the same measure that ye mete withal it shall be measured to you again. Luke 6:38.

God blesses the work of men's hands, that they may return to Him His portion. He gives them the sunshine and the rain; He causes vegetation to flourish; He gives health and ability to acquire means. Every blessing comes from His bountiful hand, and He desires men and women to show their gratitude by returning Him a portion in tithes and offerings—in thank offerings, in freewill offerings, in trespass offerings. . . . They are to reveal an unselfish interest in the building up of His work in all parts of the world.[67]

In the great work of warning the world, those who have the truth in the heart, and are sanctified through the truth, will act their assigned part. They will be faithful in the payment of tithes and offerings. Every church member is bound by covenant relation with God to deny himself of every extravagant outlay of means. Let not the want of economy in the home life render us unable to act our part in strengthening the work already established, and in entering new territory. . . .

I entreat my brethren and sisters throughout the world to awaken to the responsibility that rests upon them to pay a faithful tithe. . . . Keep a faithful account with your Creator. . . .

He who gave His only-begotten Son to die for you, has made a covenant with you. He gives you His blessings, and in return He requires you to bring Him your tithes and offerings. . . . God calls upon His human agents to be true to the contract He has made with them. "Bring ye all the tithes into the storehouse," He says, "that there may be meat in mine house" (Mal. 3:10).[68]

How great was the gift of God to man, and how like our God to make it! With a liberality that can never be exceeded He gave, that He might save the rebellious sons of men and bring them to see His purpose and discern His love. Will you, by your gifts and offerings, show that you think nothing too good for Him who "gave his only begotten Son"?[69]

Ratified by Christ's Blood

For as often as ye eat this bread, and drink this cup, ye do shew forth the Lord's death till he come. 1 Cor. 11:26.

In instituting the sacramental service to take the place of the Passover, Christ left for His church a memorial of His great sacrifice for man. "This do," He said, "in remembrance of me." This was the point of transition between two economies and their two great festivals. The one was to close forever; the other, which He had just established, was to take its place, and to continue through all time as the memorial of His death. . . .

In this last act of Christ in partaking with His disciples of the bread and wine, He pledged Himself to them as their Redeemer by a new covenant, in which it was written and sealed that upon all who will receive Christ by faith will be bestowed all the blessings that heaven can supply, both in this life and in the future immortal life. This covenant deed was to be ratified by Christ's own blood, which it had been the office of the old sacrificial offerings to keep before the minds of His chosen people. Christ designed that this supper should be often commemorated in order to bring to our remembrance His sacrifice in giving His life for the remission of the sins of all who will believe on Him and receive Him.[70]

In the Saviour's death the powers of darkness seemed to prevail, and they exulted in their victory. But from the rent sepulcher of Joseph, Jesus came forth a conqueror.[71]

Jesus refused to receive the homage of His people until He had the assurance that His sacrifice was accepted by the Father. He ascended to the heavenly courts, and from God Himself heard the assurance that His atonement for the sins of men had been ample, that through His blood all might gain eternal life. The Father ratified the covenant made with Christ, that He would receive repentant and obedient men, and would love them even as He loves His Son. Christ was to complete His work, and fulfill His pledge to "make a man more precious than fine gold; even a man than the golden wedge of Ophir" (Isa. 13:12).[72]

Sealed by Christ's Atonement

In whom we have redemption through his blood, the forgiveness of sins, according to the riches of his grace. Eph. 1:7.

Christ on the cross not only draws men to repentance toward God for the transgression of His law—for whom God pardons He first makes penitent—but Christ has satisfied justice; He has proffered Himself as an atonement. His gushing blood, His broken body, satisfy the claims of the broken law, and thus He bridges the gulf which sin has made. He suffered in the flesh, that with His bruised and broken body He might cover the defenseless sinner. The victory gained at His death on Calvary broke forever the accusing power of Satan over the universe and silenced his charges that self-denial was impossible with God and therefore not essential in the human family.[73]

Christ was without sin, else His life in human flesh and His death on the cross would have been of no more value in procuring grace for the sinner than the death of any other man. While He took upon Him humanity, it was a life taken into union with Deity. He could lay down His life as priest and also victim. . . . He offered Himself without spot to God.

The atonement of Christ sealed forever the everlasting covenant of grace. It was the fulfilling of every condition upon which God suspended the free communication of grace to the human family. Every barrier was then broken down which intercepted the freest exercise of grace, mercy, peace, and love to the most guilty of Adam's race.[74]

In the courts above, Christ is pleading for His church—pleading for those for whom He has paid the redemption price of His blood. Centuries, ages, can never lessen the efficacy of His atoning sacrifice. Neither life nor death, height nor depth, can separate us from the love of God which is in Christ Jesus; not because we hold Him so firmly, but because He holds us so fast. If our salvation depended on our own efforts, we could not be saved; but it depends on the One who is behind all the promises. Our grasp on Him may seem feeble, but His love is that of an elder brother; so long as we maintain our union with Him, no one can pluck us out of His hand.[75]

Christ the Mediator

For Christ is not entered into the holy places made with hands, which are the figures of the true, but into heaven itself, now to appear in the presence of God for us. Heb. 9:24.

The sin of Adam and Eve caused a fearful separation between God and man. And Christ steps in between fallen man and God, and says to man: "You may yet come to the Father; there is a plan devised through which God can be reconciled to man, and man to God; through a mediator you can approach God." And now He stands to mediate for you. He is the great High Priest who is pleading in your behalf; and you are to come and present your case to the Father through Jesus Christ. Thus you can find access to God.[76]

Christ Jesus is represented as continually standing at the altar, momentarily offering up the sacrifice for the sins of the world. He is a minister of the true tabernacle which the Lord pitched and not man. The typical shadows of the Jewish tabernacle no longer possess any virtue. A daily and yearly typical atonement is no longer to be made, but the atoning sacrifice through a mediator is essential because of the constant commission of sin. Jesus is officiating in the presence of God, offering up His shed blood, as it had been a lamb slain. . . .

The religious services, the prayers, the praise, the penitent confession of sin, ascend from true believers as incense to the heavenly sanctuary: but passing through the corrupt channels of humanity, they are so defiled that unless purified by blood, they can never be of value with God. . . . All incense from earthly tabernacles must be moist with the cleansing drops of the blood of Christ. He holds before the Father the censer of His own merits, in which there is no taint of earthly corruption. He gathers into this censer the prayers, the praise, and the confessions of His people, and with these He puts His own spotless righteousness. Then, perfumed with the merits of Christ's propitiation, the incense comes up before God wholly and entirely acceptable. . . .

O, that all may see that everything in obedience, in penitence, in praise and thanksgiving must be placed upon the glowing fire of the righteousness of Christ.[77]

The Blood of the Covenant

Now the God of peace, that brought again from the dead our Lord Jesus, that great shepherd of the sheep, through the blood of the everlasting covenant, make you perfect in every good work to do his will. Heb. 13:20, 21.

To many it has been a mystery why so many sacrificial offerings were required in the old dispensation, why so many bleeding victims were led to the altar. But the great truth that was kept before men, and imprinted upon mind and heart, was this, "Without shedding of blood is no remission" (Heb. 9:22). In every bleeding sacrifice was typified "the Lamb of God, which taketh away the sin of the world" (John 1:29).

Christ Himself was the originator of the Jewish system of worship, in which, by types and symbols, were shadowed forth spiritual and heavenly things. Many forgot the true significance of these offerings; and the great truth that through Christ alone there is forgiveness of sin, was lost to them. The multiplying of sacrificial offerings, the blood of bulls and goats, could not take away sin. . . .

A lesson was embodied in every sacrifice, impressed in every ceremony, solemnly preached by the priest in his holy office, and inculcated by God Himself—that through the blood of Christ alone is there forgiveness of sins.[78]

Anciently believers were saved by the same Saviour as now, but it was a God veiled. They saw God's mercy in figures. . . . Christ's sacrifice is the glorious fulfillment of the whole Jewish economy. . . . When as a sinless offering Christ bowed His head and died, when by the Almighty's unseen hand the veil of the temple was rent in twain, a new and living way was opened. All can now approach God through the merits of Christ. It is because the veil has been rent that men can draw nigh to God. They need not depend on priest or ceremonial sacrifice. Liberty is given to all to go directly to God through a personal Saviour.[79]

The whole mind, the whole soul, the whole heart, and the whole strength are purchased by the blood of the Son of God.[80]

The Covenant and the Sabbath

Wherefore the children of Israel shall keep the sabbath, to observe the sabbath throughout their generations, for a perpetual covenant. It is a sign between me and the children of Israel for ever. Ex. 31:16, 17.

When the Lord delivered His people Israel from Egypt and committed to them His law, He taught them that by the observance of the Sabbath they were to be distinguished from idolaters. . . .

As the Sabbath was the sign that distinguished Israel when they came out of Egypt to enter the earthly Canaan, so it is the sign that now distinguishes God's people as they come out from the world to enter the heavenly rest. The Sabbath is a sign of a relationship existing between God and His people, a sign that they honor His law. It distinguishes between His loyal subjects and transgressors. . . . The Sabbath given to the world as the sign of God as the Creator is also the sign of Him as the Sanctifier. The power that created all things is the power that recreates the soul in His own likeness. To those who keep holy the Sabbath day it is the sign of sanctification. True sanctification is harmony with God, oneness with Him in character. It is received through obedience to those principles that are the transcript of His character. And the Sabbath is the sign of obedience. He who from the heart obeys the fourth commandment will obey the whole law. He is sanctified through obedience.

To us as to Israel the Sabbath is given "for a perpetual covenant." To those who reverence His holy day the Sabbath is a sign that God recognizes them as His chosen people. It is a pledge that He will fulfill to them His covenant. Every soul who accepts the sign of God's government places himself under the divine, everlasting covenant. He fastens himself to the golden chain of obedience, every link of which is a promise.

The fourth commandment alone of all the ten contains the seal of the great Lawgiver, the Creator of the heavens and the earth. Those who obey this commandment take upon themselves His name, and all the blessings it involves are theirs.[81]

The Sabbath has lost none of its meaning. It is still a sign between God and His people, and it will be so forever.[82]

God's Eternal Pledge

He hath remembered his covenant forever,
the word which he commanded to a thousand generations.
Ps. 105:8.

God stands back of every promise He has made. With your Bibles in your hands, say: "I have done as Thou hast said. I present Thy promise, 'Ask, and it shall be given you; seek, and ye shall find; knock, and it shall be opened unto you' (Matt. 7:7)." . . .

The rainbow about the throne is an assurance that God is true; that in Him is no variableness, neither shadow of turning. We have sinned against Him and are undeserving of His favor; yet He Himself has put into our lips that most wonderful of pleas: "Do not abhor us, for thy name's sake, do not disgrace the throne of thy glory: remember, break not thy covenant with us" (Jer. 14:21). He has pledged Himself to give heed to our cry when we come to Him confessing our unworthiness and sin. The honor of His throne is staked for the fulfillment of His word to us.[83]

To everyone who offers himself to the Lord for service, withholding nothing, is given power for the attainment of measureless results. The Lord God is bound by an eternal pledge to supply power and grace to everyone who is sanctified through obedience to the truth.[84]

Nehemiah pressed into the presence of the King of kings and won to his side a power that can turn hearts as rivers of waters are turned. [See Nehemiah 1 and 2.]

To pray as Nehemiah prayed in his hour of need is a resource at the command of the Christian under circumstances when other forms of prayer may be impossible. Toilers in the busy walks of life, crowded and almost overwhelmed with perplexity, can send up a petition to God for divine guidance. . . . In times of sudden difficulty or peril the heart may send up its cry for help to One who has pledged Himself to come to the aid of His faithful, believing ones whenever they call upon Him. In every circumstance, under every condition, the soul weighed down with grief and care, or fiercely assailed by temptation, may find assurance, support, and succor in the unfailing love and power of a covenant-keeping God.[85]

Perpetual and Unalterable

Come, and let us join ourselves to the Lord,
in a perpetual covenant that shall not be forgotten. Jer. 50:5.

A covenant is an agreement by which parties bind themselves and each other to the fulfillment of certain conditions. Thus the human agent enters into agreement with God to comply with the conditions specified in His Word. His conduct shows whether or not he respects these conditions.

Man gains everything by obeying the covenant-keeping God. God's attributes are imparted to man, enabling him to exercise mercy and compassion. God's covenant assures us of His unchangeable character. . . . We must know for ourselves what His requirements and our obligations are. The terms of God's covenant are, "Thou shalt love the Lord thy God with all thy heart, and with all thy soul, and with all thy strength, and with all thy mind; and thy neighbour as thyself." These are the conditions of life. "This do," Christ said, "and thou shalt live" (Luke 10:27, 28).[86]

The law of God was written with His own finger on tables of stone, thus showing that it could never be changed or abrogated. It is to be preserved through the eternal ages, immutable as the principles of His government. . . . Christ gave His life to make it possible for man to be restored to the image of God. It is the power of His grace that draws men together in obedience to the truth.[87]

My brethren, bind up with the Lord God of hosts. Let Him be your fear, and let Him be your dread. . . . Troublous times are before us, but if we stand together in Christian fellowship, none striving for supremacy, God will work mightily for us. . . .

He knows our every necessity. He has all power. He can bestow upon His servants the measure of efficiency that their need demands. His infinite love and compassion never weary. With the majesty of omnipotence He unites the gentleness and care of a tender shepherd. We need have no fear that He will not fulfill His promises. He is eternal truth. Never will He change the covenant that He has made with those that love Him. His promises to His church stand fast forever. He will make her an eternal excellence, a joy of many generations.[88]

The Symbol of the Covenant

And God said, This is the token of the covenant which I make between me and you and every living creature that is with you, for perpetual generations: I do set my bow in the cloud, and it shall be for a token of a covenant between me and the earth. Gen. 9:12, 13.

What compassion for erring man, to place the beautiful, variegated rainbow in the clouds, a token of the covenant of the great God with man! . . . It was His design that as the children of after generations should see the bow in the cloud, . . . their parents could explain to them the destruction of the old world by a flood, because the people gave themselves up to all manner of wickedness, and that the hands of the Most High had bended the bow, and placed it in the clouds, as a token that He would never bring again a flood of waters on the earth. This symbol in the clouds was to confirm the belief of all, and establish their confidence in God, for it was a token of divine mercy and goodness to man. . . .

A rainbow is represented in Heaven round about the throne, also above the head of Christ, as a symbol of God's mercy encompassing the earth. When man by his great wickedness provokes the wrath of God, Christ, man's intercessor, pleads for him, and points to the rainbow in the cloud, as evidence of God's great mercy and compassion for erring man.[89]

Angels rejoice as they gaze upon this precious token of God's love to man. The world's Redeemer looks upon it; for it was through His instrumentality that this bow was made to appear in the heavens, as a token or covenant of promise to man. God Himself looks upon the bow in the clouds, and remembers His everlasting covenant between Himself and man. . . . As we gaze upon the beautiful sight, we may be joyful in God, assured that He Himself is looking upon this token of His covenant, and that as He looks upon it He remembers the children of earth, to whom it was given. Their afflictions, perils, and trials are not hidden from Him. We may rejoice in hope, for the bow of God's covenant is over us. He never will forget the children of His care.[90]

Exile From Heaven's Throne

Who, being in the form of God, . . . was made in the likeness of men: and . . . humbled himself, and became obedient unto death, even the death of the cross. Phil. 2:6-8.

In order to fully realize the value of salvation, it is necessary to understand what it cost. In consequence of limited ideas of the sufferings of Christ, many place a low estimate upon the great work of the atonement. The glorious plan of man's salvation was brought about through the infinite love of God the Father. In this divine plan is seen the most marvelous manifestation of the love of God to the fallen race. Such love as is manifested in the gift of God's beloved Son amazed the holy angels. "God so loved the world, that he gave his only begotten Son, that whosoever believeth in him should not perish, but have everlasting life" (John 3:16). This Saviour was the brightness of His Father's glory and the express image of His person. He possessed divine majesty, perfection, and excellence. He was equal with God. "It pleased the Father that in him should all fulness dwell" (Col. 1:19). . . .

Christ consented to die in the sinner's stead, that man, by a life of obedience, might escape the penalty of the law of God.[1]

Jesus was the majesty of heaven, the beloved commander of the angels, who delighted to do His pleasure. He was one with God, "in the bosom of the Father" (John 1:18), yet He thought it not a thing to be desired to be equal with God while man was lost in sin and misery. He stepped down from His throne, He left His crown and royal scepter, and clothed His divinity with humanity. He humbled Himself even to the death of the cross, that man might be exalted to a seat with Him upon His throne. In Him we have a complete offering, an infinite sacrifice, a mighty Saviour, who is able to save unto the uttermost all that come unto God by Him. In love He comes to reveal the Father, to reconcile man to God, to make him a new creature renewed after the image of Him who created him.[2]

Our heavenly Father made an infinite sacrifice in giving His Son to die for fallen man. The price paid for our redemption should give us exalted views of what we may become through Christ.[3]

Matchless Condescension

Forasmuch then as the children are partakers of flesh and blood, he also himself likewise took part of the same; that through death he might destroy him that had the power of death, that is, the devil.
Heb. 2:14.

Satan accomplished the fall of man, and since that time it has been his work to efface in man the image of God, and to stamp upon human hearts his own image. . . . He intercepts every ray of light that comes from God to man, and appropriates the worship that is due to God. . . .

But the only begotten Son of God has looked upon the scene, has beheld human suffering and misery. . . . He looked upon the schemes by which Satan works to blot from the human soul every trace of likeness to God; how he led them into intemperance so as to destroy the moral powers which God gave to man as a most precious, priceless endowment. He saw how, through indulgence in appetite, brain power was destroyed, and the temple of God was in ruins. . . . The senses, the nerves, the passions, the organs of man, were worked by supernatural agencies in the indulgence of the grossest, vilest lust. The very stamp of demons was impressed upon the countenances of men, and human faces reflected the expression of the legions of evil with which they were possessed. Such was the prospect upon which the world's Redeemer looked. What a horrible spectacle for the eyes of infinite purity to behold! . . .

The great condescension on the part of God is a mystery beyond our fathoming. The greatness of the plan cannot be fully comprehended, nor could infinite wisdom devise a plan that would surpass it. It could be successful only by . . . Christ becoming man, and suffering the wrath which sin has made because of the transgression of God's law. Through this plan the great, the dreadful God can be just, and yet be the justifier of all who believe in Jesus, and who receive Him as their personal Saviour. This is the heavenly science of redemption, of saving men from eternal ruin. . . .

God so loved the world that He gave Himself in Christ to the world to bear the penalty of man's transgression. God suffered with His Son, as the divine Being alone could suffer, in order that the world might become reconciled to Him.[4]

Incomparable Temptations

The prince of this world cometh, and hath nothing in me. John 14:30.

From the moment that Christ entered the world, the whole confederacy of Satanic agencies was set at work to deceive and overthrow Him as Adam had been deceived and overthrown. . . .

When Christ was born in Bethlehem, the angels of God appeared to the shepherds, who were watching their flocks by night, and gave divine credentials of the authority of the newborn babe. Satan knew that One had come to the earth with a divine commission to dispute his authority. He heard the angel declare: ". . . Unto you is born this day in the city of David a Saviour, which is Christ the Lord . . ." (Luke 2:10, 11).

The heavenly heralds aroused all the wrath of the synagogue of Satan. He followed the steps of those who had charge of the infant Jesus. He heard the prophecy of Simeon in the temple courts. . . . "Lord, now lettest thou thy servant depart in peace, according to thy word: for mine eyes have seen thy salvation, . . ." (Luke 2:29-32). Satan was filled with frenzy as he saw that the aged Simeon recognized the divinity of Christ.

The Commander of heaven was assailed by the tempter. . . . From the time that He was a helpless babe in Bethlehem, when the agencies of hell sought to destroy Him in His infancy through the jealousy of Herod, until He came to Calvary's cross, He was continually assailed by the evil one. In the councils of Satan it was determined that He must be overcome. No human being had come into the world and escaped the power of the deceiver. The whole forces of the confederacy of evil were set upon His track. . . . Satan knew that he must either conquer or himself be conquered. Success or failure involved too much for him to leave the work with any one of his agents of evil. The prince of evil himself must personally conduct the warfare. . . .

The life of Christ was a perpetual warfare against Satanic agencies. Satan rallied the whole energies of apostasy against the Son of God.[5]

On not one occasion was there a response to his manifold temptations. Not once did Christ step on Satan's ground, to give him any advantage.[6]

Unutterable Loneliness

I have trodden the winepress alone;
and of the people there was none with me. Isa. 63:3.

Through childhood, youth, and manhood, Jesus walked alone. In His purity and His faithfulness, He trod the winepress alone, and of the people there was none with Him. He carried the awful weight of responsibility for the salvation of men. He knew that unless there was a decided change in the principles and purposes of the human race, all would be lost. This was the burden of His soul, and none could appreciate the weight that rested upon Him.[7]

Throughout His life His mother and His brothers did not comprehend His mission. Even His disciples did not understand Him. He had dwelt in eternal light, as one with God, but His life on earth must be spent in solitude. As one with us, He must bear the burden of our guilt and woe. The Sinless One must feel the shame of sin. The peace lover must dwell with strife, the truth must abide with falsehood, purity with vileness. Every sin, every discord, every defiling lust that transgression had brought, was torture to His spirit.

Alone He must tread the path; alone He must bear the burden. Upon Him who had laid off His glory and accepted the weakness of humanity the redemption of the world must rest. He saw and felt it all, but His purpose remained steadfast. Upon His arm depended the salvation of the fallen race, and He reached out His hand to grasp the hand of Omnipotent love.[8]

The loneliness of Christ, separated from the heavenly courts, living the life of humanity, was never understood or appreciated by the disciples as it should have been. . . . When Jesus was no longer with them, . . . they began to see how they might have shown Him attentions that would have brought gladness to His heart. . . .

The same want is evident in our world today. But few appreciate all that Christ is to them. If they did, the great love of Mary [Matt. 26:6-13] would be expressed, the anointing would be freely bestowed. . . . Nothing would be thought too costly to give for Christ, no self-denial or self-sacrifice too great to be endured for His sake.[9]

Unequaled Test

For we have not an high priest which cannot be touched with the feeling of our infirmities; but was in all points tempted like as we are, yet without sin. Heb. 4:15.

After His baptism, the Son of God entered the dreary wilderness, there to be tempted by the devil. . . . For forty days He ate and drank nothing. . . . He realized the power of appetite upon man; and in behalf of sinful man, He bore the closest test possible upon that point. Here a victory was gained which few can appreciate. The controlling power of depraved appetite, and the grievous sin of indulging it, can only be understood by the length of the fast which our Saviour endured that He might break its power. . . . He came to earth to unite His divine power with our human efforts, that through the strength and moral power which He imparts, we might overcome in our own behalf.

Oh! what matchless condescension for the King of glory to come down to this world to endure the pangs of hunger and the fierce temptations of a wily foe, that He might gain an infinite victory for man. Here is love without a parallel. . . .

It was not the gnawing pangs of hunger alone which made the sufferings of our Redeemer so inexpressibly severe. It was the sense of guilt which had resulted from the indulgence of appetite that had brought such terrible woe into the world, which pressed so heavily upon His divine soul. . . .

With man's nature, and the terrible weight of his sins pressing upon Him, our Redeemer withstood the power of Satan upon this great leading temptation, which imperils the souls of men. If man should overcome this temptation, he could conquer on every other point.

Intemperance lies at the foundation of all the moral evils known to man. Christ began the work of redemption just where the ruin began. The fall of our first parents was caused by the indulgence of appetite. In redemption, the denial of appetite is the first work of Christ. What amazing love has Christ manifested in coming into the world to bear our sins and infirmities, and to tread the path of suffering, that He might show us by His life of spotless merit how we should walk, and overcome as He had overcome.[10]

Infinite Suffering

For in that he himself hath suffered being tempted, he is able to succour them that are tempted. Heb. 2:18.

Would that we could comprehend the significance of the words, Christ "suffered being tempted." While He was free from the taint of sin, the refined sensibilities of His holy nature rendered contact with evil unspeakably painful to Him. Yet with human nature upon Him, He met the archapostate face to face, and single-handed withstood the foe of His throne. Not even by a thought could Christ be brought to yield to the power of temptation.[11]

What a sight was this for Heaven to look upon! Christ, who knew not the least taint of sin or defilement, took our nature in its deteriorated condition. This was humiliation greater than finite man can comprehend. God was manifest in the flesh. He humbled Himself. What a subject for thought, for deep, earnest contemplation! So infinitely great that He was the Majesty of heaven, and yet He stooped so low, without losing one atom of His dignity and glory! He stooped to poverty and to the deepest abasement among men. For our sake He became poor, that we through His poverty might be made rich.[12]

The world had lost the original pattern of goodness and had sunk into universal apostasy and moral corruption; and the life of Jesus was one of laborious, self-denying effort to bring man back to his first estate by imbuing him with the spirit of divine benevolence and unselfish love. While in the world, He was not of the world. It was a continual pain to Him to be brought in contact with the enmity, depravity, and impurity which Satan had brought in; but He had a work to do to bring man into harmony with the divine plan, and earth in connection with heaven, and He counted no sacrifice too great for the accomplishment of the object. He "was in all points tempted like as we are" (Heb. 4:15). Satan stood ready to assail Him at every step, hurling at Him his fiercest temptations; yet He "did no sin, neither was guile found in his mouth" (1 Peter 2:22). "He . . . suffered being tempted," suffered in proportion to the perfection of His holiness. But the prince of darkness found nothing in Him; not a single thought or feeling responded to temptation.[13]

Agonizing Prayer

Who in the days of his flesh . . . offered up prayers and supplications with strong crying and tears unto him that was able to save him from death.
Heb. 5:7.

While you pray, dear youth, that you may not be led into temptation, remember that your work does not end with the prayer. You must then answer your own prayer as far as possible by resisting temptation, and leave that which you cannot do for yourselves for Jesus to do for you. . . .

I would remind the youth who ornament their persons . . . that, because of their sins, the Saviour's head wore the shameful crown of thorns. When you devote precious time to trimming your apparel, remember that the King of glory wore a plain, seamless coat. You who weary yourselves in decorating your persons, please bear in mind that Jesus was often weary from incessant toil and self-denial and self-sacrifice to bless the suffering and needy. He spent whole nights in prayer upon the lonely mountains, not because of His weakness and His necessities, but because He saw, He felt, the weakness of your natures to resist the temptations of the enemy upon the very points where you are now overcome. He knew that you would be indifferent in regard to your dangers and would not feel your need of prayer. It was on our account that He poured out His prayers to His Father with strong cries and tears. It was to save us from the very pride and love of vanity and pleasure which we now indulge, and which crowds out the love of Jesus, that those tears were shed. . . .

Will you, young friends, arise and shake off this dreadful indifference and stupor which has conformed you to the world? Will you heed the voice of warning which tells you that destruction lies in the path of those who are at ease in this hour of danger?[14]

Many of our youth, by their careless disregard of the warnings and reproofs given them, open the door wide for Satan to enter. With God's word for our guide and Jesus as our heavenly Teacher we need not be ignorant of His requirements or of Satan's devices. . . . It will be no unpleasant task to be obedient to the will of God when we yield ourselves fully to be directed by His Spirit.[15]

Whole Nights of Prayer

And it came to pass in those days, that he went out into a mountain to pray, and continued all night in prayer to God. Luke 6:12.

The Majesty of heaven, while engaged in His earthly ministry, prayed much to His Father. He was frequently bowed all night in prayer. . . . The Mount of Olives was the favorite resort of the Son of God for His devotions. Frequently after the multitude had left Him for the retirement of the night, He rested not, though weary with the labors of the day. . . . While the city was hushed in silence, and the disciples had returned to their homes to obtain refreshment in sleep, Jesus slept not. His divine pleadings were ascending to His Father from the Mount of Olives that His disciples might be kept from the evil influences which they would daily encounter in the world, and that His own soul might be strengthened and braced for the duties and trials of the coming day. All night, while His followers were sleeping, was their divine Teacher praying. The dew and the frost of night fell upon His head bowed in prayer. His example is left for His followers. . . .

He chose the stillness of night, when there would be no interruption. Jesus could heal the sick and raise the dead. He was Himself a source of blessing and strength. He commanded even the tempests, and they obeyed Him. He was unsullied with corruption, a stranger to sin; yet He prayed, and that often with strong crying and tears. He prayed for His disciples and for Himself, thus identifying Himself with our needs, our weaknesses, and our failings, which are so common with humanity. He was a mighty petitioner, not possessing the passions of our human, fallen natures, but compassed with like infirmities, tempted in all points even as we are. Jesus endured agony which required help and support from His Father.

Christ is our example. Are the ministers of Christ tempted and fiercely buffeted by Satan? so also was He who knew no sin. He turned to His Father in these hours of distress. He came to earth that He might provide a way whereby we could find grace and strength to help in every time of need, by following His example in frequent, earnest prayer.[16]

Gethsemane's Anguish

O my Father, if it be possible, let this cup pass from me: nevertheless not as I will, but as thou wilt. Matt. 26:39.

In the Garden of Gethsemane Christ suffered in man's stead, and the human nature of the Son of God staggered under the terrible horror of the guilt of sin, until from His pale and quivering lips was forced the agonizing cry, "O my Father, if it be possible, let this cup pass from me." . . . Human nature would then and there have died under the horror of the sense of sin, had not an angel from heaven strengthened Him to bear the agony. . . . Christ was suffering the death that was pronounced upon the transgressors of God's law.

It is a fearful thing for the unrepenting sinner to fall into the hands of the living God. This is proved by the history of the destruction of the old world by a flood, by the record of the fire which fell from heaven and destroyed the inhabitants of Sodom. But never was this proved to so great an extent as in the agony of Christ, the Son of the infinite God, when He bore the wrath of God for a sinful world. It was in consequence of sin, the transgression of God's law, that the Garden of Gethsemane has become pre-eminently the place of suffering to a sinful world. No sorrow, no agony, can measure with that which was endured by the Son of God.

Man has not been made a sin-bearer, and he will never know the horror of the curse of sin which the Saviour bore. No sorrow can bear any comparison with the sorrow of Him upon whom the wrath of God fell with overwhelming force. Human nature can endure but a limited amount of test and trial. The finite can only endure the finite measure, and human nature succumbs; but the nature of Christ had a greater capacity for suffering. . . . The agony which Christ endured, broadens, deepens, and gives a more extended conception of the character of sin, and the character of the retribution which God will bring upon those who continue in sin. The wages of sin is death, but the gift of God is eternal life through Jesus Christ to the repenting, believing sinner.[17]

The sword of justice was unsheathed, and the wrath of God against iniquity rested upon man's substitute, Jesus Christ, the only begotten of the Father.[18]

The Father's Frown

This is your hour, and the power of darkness. Luke 22:53.

As the Son of God bowed in the attitude of prayer in the Garden of Gethsemane, the agony of His spirit forced from His pores sweat like great drops of blood. It was here that the horror of great darkness surrounded Him. The sins of the world were upon Him. He was suffering in man's stead as a transgressor of His Father's law. Here was the scene of temptation. The divine light of God was receding from His vision, and He was passing into the hands of the powers of darkness. In His soul anguish He lay prostrate on the cold earth. He was realizing His Father's frown. He had taken the cup of suffering from the lips of guilty man, and proposed to drink it Himself, and in its place give to man the cup of blessing. The wrath that would have fallen upon man was now falling upon Christ. It was here that the mysterious cup trembled in His hand.

Jesus had often resorted to Gethsemane with His disciples for meditation and prayer. . . . Never before had the Saviour visited the spot with a heart so full of sorrow. It was not bodily suffering from which the Son of God shrank. . . . The sins of a lost world were upon Him and overwhelming Him. It was a sense of His Father's frown, in consequence of sin, which rent His heart with such piercing agony and forced from His brow great drops of blood. . . .

We can have but faint conceptions of the inexpressible anguish of God's dear Son in Gethsemane, as He realized His separation from His Father in consequence of bearing man's sin. He became sin for the fallen race. The sense of the withdrawal of His Father's love pressed from His anguished soul these mournful words: "My soul is exceeding sorrowful, even unto death" (Matt. 26:38). . . .

The divine Son of God was fainting, dying. The Father sent a messenger from His presence to strengthen the divine Sufferer and brace Him to tread the bloodstained path. Could mortals have viewed the amazement and the sorrow of the angelic host as they watched in silent grief the Father separating His beams of light, love, and glory from the beloved Son of His bosom, they would better understand how offensive sin is in His sight.[19]

Forsaken by His Father

My God, my God, why has thou forsaken me? Matt. 27:46.

He [Jesus] was betrayed by a kiss into the hands of His enemies, and hurried to the judgment hall of an earthly court. . . . The angelic host beheld with wonder and with grief Him who had been the Majesty of heaven, and who had worn the crown of glory, now wearing the crown of thorns, a bleeding victim to the rage of an infuriated mob, fired to insane madness by the wrath of Satan. Behold the patient Sufferer! Upon His head is the thorny crown. His lifeblood flows from every lacerated vein. . . .

Behold the oppressor and the oppressed! A vast multitude enclose the Saviour of the world. Mockings and jeerings are mingled with the coarse oaths of blasphemy. . . . Christ, the precious Son of God, was led forth, and the cross was laid upon His shoulders. . . . Thronged by an immense crowd of bitter enemies and unfeeling spectators, He is led away to the crucifixion. . . . He is nailed to the cross, and hangs suspended between the heavens and the earth. . . . The glorious Redeemer of a lost world was suffering the penalty of man's transgression of the Father's law. He was about to ransom His people with His own blood. . . .

Oh, was there ever suffering and sorrow like that endured by the dying Saviour! It was the sense of His Father's displeasure which made His cup so bitter. It was not bodily suffering which so quickly ended the life of Christ upon the cross. It was the crushing weight of the sins of the world, and a sense of His Father's wrath. . . . The fierce temptation that His own Father had forever left Him caused that piercing cry from the cross: "My God, my God, why hast thou forsaken me?" . . .

In His dying agony, as He yields up His precious life, He has by faith alone to trust in Him whom it has ever been His joy to obey. . . . Denied even bright hope and confidence in the triumph which will be His in the future, He cries with a loud voice: "Father, into thy hands I commend my spirit" (Luke 23:46). He is acquainted with the character of His Father, with His justice, His mercy, and His great love, and in submission He drops into His hands.[20]

The Sins of the World

He was wounded for our transgressions, he was bruised for our iniquities: the chastisement of our peace was upon him; and with his stripes we are healed. Isa. 53:5.

Some have limited views of the atonement. They think that Christ suffered only a small portion of the penalty of the law of God; they suppose that, while the wrath of God was felt by His dear Son, He had, through all His painful sufferings, the evidence of His Father's love and acceptance; that the portals of the tomb before Him were illuminated with bright hope, and that He had the abiding evidence of His future glory. Here is a great mistake. Christ's keenest anguish was a sense of His Father's displeasure. His mental agony because of this was of such intensity that man can have but faint conception of it.

With many the story of the condescension, humiliation, and sacrifice of our divine Lord awakens no deeper interest . . . than does the history of the death of the martyrs of Jesus. Many have suffered death by slow tortures; others have suffered death by crucifixion. In what does the death of God's dear Son differ from these? . . . If the sufferings of Christ consisted in physical pain alone, then His death was no more painful than that of some of the martyrs. But bodily pain was but a small part of the agony of God's dear Son. The sins of the world were upon Him, also the sense of His Father's wrath as He suffered the penalty of the law transgressed. It was these that crushed His divine soul. . . . The separation that sin makes between God and man was fully realized and keenly felt by the innocent, suffering Man of Calvary. He was oppressed by the powers of darkness. He had not one ray of light to brighten the future. . . . It was in this terrible hour of darkness, the face of His Father hidden, legions of evil angels enshrouding Him, the sins of the world upon Him, that the words were wrenched from His lips: "My God, my God, why hast thou forsaken me?" . . .

In comparison with the enterprise of everlasting life, every other sinks into insignificance.[21]

What a Price!

Ye know that ye were not redeemed with corruptible things, as silver and gold, . . . but with the precious blood of Christ, as of a lamb without blemish and without spot. 1 Peter 1:18, 19.

Ye know," says Peter, "that ye were not redeemed with corruptible things, as silver and gold." Oh, had these been sufficient to purchase the salvation of man, how easily it might have been accomplished by Him who says: "The silver is mine, and the gold is mine" (Haggai 2:8). But the transgressor of God's holy law could be redeemed only by the precious blood of the Son of God.[22]

It was through infinite sacrifice and inexpressible suffering that our Redeemer placed redemption within our reach. He was in this world unhonored and unknown, that, through His wonderful condescension and humiliation, He might exalt man to receive eternal honors and immortal joys in the heavenly courts. During His thirty years of life on earth His heart was wrung with inconceivable anguish. The path from the manger to Calvary was shadowed by grief and sorrow. He was a man of sorrows, and acquainted with grief, enduring such heartache as no human language can portray. He could have said in truth, "Behold, and see if there be any sorrow like unto my sorrow" (Lam. 1:12). Hating sin with a perfect hatred, He yet gathered to His soul the sins of the whole world. Guiltless, He bore the punishment of the guilty. Innocent, yet offering Himself as a substitute for the transgressor. The guilt of every sin pressed its weight upon the divine soul of the world's Redeemer. The evil thoughts, the evil words, the evil deeds of every son and daughter of Adam, called for retribution upon Himself; for He had become man's substitute. Though the guilt of sin was not His, His spirit was torn and bruised by the transgressions of men, and He who knew no sin became sin for us, that we might be made the righteousness of God in Him.[23]

What a price has been paid for us! Behold the cross, and the Victim uplifted upon it. Look at those hands, pierced with the cruel nails. Look at His feet, fastened with spikes to the tree. Christ bore our sins in His own body. That suffering, that agony, is the price of your redemption.[24]

The Worth of One Soul

Know ye not that . . . ye are not your own? For ye are bought with a price. 1 Cor. 6:19, 20.

All men have been bought with this infinite price. By pouring the whole treasury of heaven into this world, by giving us in Christ all heaven, God has purchased the will, the affections, the mind, the soul, of every human being. Whether believers or unbelievers, all men are the Lord's property.[25]

We are His by creation and by redemption. Our very bodies are not our own, to treat as we please, to cripple by habits that lead to decay, making it impossible to render to God perfect service. Our lives and all our faculties belong to Him. He is caring for us every moment; He keeps the living machinery in action; if we were left to run it for one moment, we should die. We are absolutely dependent upon God.

A great lesson is to be learned when we understand our relation to God, and His relation to us. The words, "Ye are not your own, for ye are bought with a price," should be hung in memory's hall, that we may ever recognize God's right to our talents, our property, our influence, our individual selves. We are to learn how to treat this gift of God, in mind, in soul, in body, that as Christ's purchased possession, we may do Him healthful, savory service.[26]

The wealth of earth dwindles into insignificance when compared with the worth of a single soul for whom our Lord and Master died. He who weigheth the hills in scales and the mountains in a balance regards a human soul as of infinite value.[27]

Let the youth be impressed with the thought that they are not their own. They belong to Christ. They are the purchase of His blood, the claim of His love. They live because He keeps them by His power. Their time, their strength, their capabilities are His, to be developed, to be trained, to be used for Him.[28]

Christ has bought you at a dear price, and offers you grace and glory if you will receive it.[29]

The Sacrifice of Love

And walk in love, as Christ also hath loved us, and hath given himself for us an offering and a sacrifice to God for a sweetsmelling savour. Eph. 5:2.

This is the oblation of a life-gift in our behalf, that we may be all that He desires us to be—representatives of Him, expressing the fragrance of His character, His own pure thoughts, His divine attributes as manifested in His sanctified human life, in order that others may behold Him in His human form, and . . . be led to desire to be like Christ—pure, undefiled, wholly acceptable to God, without spot, or wrinkle, or any such thing.[30]

How earnestly Christ prosecuted the work of our salvation! What devotion His life revealed as He sought to give value to fallen man by imputing to every repenting, believing sinner the merits of His spotless righteousness! How untiringly He worked! In the Temple and in the synagogue, in the streets of the cities, in the market place, in the workshop, by the seaside, among the hills, He preached the gospel and healed the sick. He gave all there was of Himself, that He might work out the plan of redeeming grace.[31]

Christ offered up His broken body to purchase back God's heritage, to give man another trial. "Wherefore he is able also to save them to the uttermost that come unto God by him, seeing he ever liveth to make intercession for them" (Heb. 7:25). By His spotless life, His obedience, His death on the cross of Calvary, Christ interceded for the lost race. And now, not as a mere petitioner does the Captain of our salvation intercede for us, but as a Conqueror claiming His victory. His offering is complete, and as our Intercessor He executes His self-appointed work, holding before God the censer containing His own spotless merits and the prayers, confessions, and thanksgiving of His people. Perfumed with the fragrance of His righteousness, these ascend to God as a sweet savor. The offering is wholly acceptable, and pardon covers all transgression.[32]

Heaven Itself Imperiled

I will make a man more precious than fine gold; even a man than the golden wedge of Ophir. Isa. 13:12.

The value of a soul, who can estimate? Would you know its worth, go to Gethsemane, and there watch with Christ through those hours of anguish, when He sweat as it were great drops of blood. Look upon the Saviour uplifted on the cross. Hear that despairing cry, "My God, my God, why hast thou forsaken me?" (Mark 15:34). Look upon the wounded head, the pierced side, the marred feet. Remember that Christ risked all. For our redemption, heaven itself was imperiled. At the foot of the cross, remembering that for one sinner Christ would have laid down His life, you may estimate the value of a soul.

If you are in communion with Christ you will place His estimate upon every human being. You will feel for others the same deep love that Christ has felt for you. Then you will be able to win, not drive, to attract, not repulse, those for whom He died. . . . The greater their sin and the deeper their misery, the more earnest and tender will be your efforts for their recovery. You will discern the need of those who are suffering, who have been sinning against God, and who are oppressed with a burden of guilt. Your heart will go out in sympathy for them, and you will reach out to them a helping hand.[33]

Christ and Him crucified should become the theme of our thoughts and stir the deepest emotions of our souls. . . . It is through the cross alone that we can estimate the worth of the human soul. Such is the value of men for whom Christ died that the Father is satisfied with the infinite price which He pays for the salvation of man in yielding up His own Son to die for their redemption. What wisdom, mercy, and love in its fullness are here manifested! The worth of man is known only by going to Calvary. In the mystery of the cross of Christ we can place an estimate upon man.[34]

How glorious are the possibilities set before the fallen race! Through His Son, God has revealed the excellency to which man is capable of attaining. Through the merits of Christ man is lifted from his depraved state, purified, and made more precious than the golden wedge of Ophir.[35]

The Father's Immeasurable Sacrifice

Herein is love, not that we loved God, but that he loved us, and sent his Son to be the propitiation for our sins. 1 John 4:10.

Love is the underlying principle of God's government in heaven and earth, and it must be the foundation of the Christian's character. . . . And love will be revealed in sacrifice.

The plan of redemption was laid in sacrifice—a sacrifice so broad and deep and high that it is immeasurable. Christ gave all for us, and those who receive Christ will be ready to sacrifice all for the sake of their Redeemer.[36]

When Adam's sin plunged the race into hopeless misery, God might have cut Himself loose from fallen beings. He might have treated them as sinners deserve to be treated. He might have commanded the angels of heaven to pour out upon our world the vials of His wrath. He might have removed this dark blot from His universe. But He did not do this. Instead of banishing them from His presence, He came still nearer to the fallen race. He gave His Son to become bone of our bone and flesh of our flesh. . . .

The gift of God to man is beyond all computation. Nothing was withheld. God would not permit it to be said that He could have done more or revealed to humanity a greater measure of love. In the gift of Christ He gave all heaven.[37]

Those who have professed to love Christ, have not comprehended the relation which exists between them and God, and it is still but dimly outlined to their understanding. They but vaguely comprehend the amazing grace of God in giving His only-begotten Son for the salvation of the world.[38]

In order to secure man to Himself and ensure his eternal salvation, Christ left the royal courts of heaven and came to this earth, endured the agonies of sin and shame in man's stead, and died to make him free. In view of the infinite price paid for man's redemption, how dare any professing the name of Christ treat with indifference one of His little ones? . . . How patiently, kindly, and affectionately should they deal with the purchase of the blood of Christ![39]

The Only Acceptable Ransom

For there is one God, and one Mediator between God and men, the man Christ Jesus; who gave himself a ransom for all. 1 Tim. 2:5, 6.

Through Christ, restoration as well as reconciliation is provided for man. The gulf that was made by sin has been spanned by the cross of Calvary. A full, complete ransom has been paid by Jesus, by virtue of which the sinner is pardoned, and the justice of the law is maintained. All who believe that Christ is the atoning sacrifice may come and receive pardon for their sins; for through the merit of Christ, communication has been opened between God and man. God can accept me as His child, and I can claim Him and rejoice in Him as my loving Father. We must center our hopes of heaven upon Christ alone, because He is our substitute and surety. . . .

The best efforts that man in his own strength can make, are valueless to meet the holy and just law that he has transgressed; but through faith in Christ he may claim the righteousness of the Son of God as all-sufficient. Christ satisfied the demands of the law in His human nature. He bore the curse of the law for the sinner, made an atonement for him, that whosoever believeth in Him should not perish. . . . Genuine faith appropriates the righteousness of Christ, and the sinner is made an overcomer with Christ; for he is made a partaker of the divine nature, and thus divinity and humanity are combined.

He who is trying to reach heaven by his own works in keeping the law, is attempting an impossibility. Man cannot be saved without obedience, but his works should not be of himself; Christ should work in him to will and to do of His good pleasure. . . . All that man can do without Christ is polluted with selfishness and sin; but that which is wrought through faith is acceptable to God. When we seek to gain heaven through the merits of Christ, the soul makes progress. Looking unto Jesus, the author and finisher of our faith, we may go on from strength to strength, from victory to victory; for through Christ the grace of God has worked out our complete salvation.[40]

We cannot estimate the precious ransom paid to redeem fallen man. The heart's best and holiest affections should be given in return for such wondrous love.[41]

God's Unspeakable Gift

Thanks be unto God for his unspeakable gift. 2 Cor. 9:15.

The revelation of God's love to man centers in the cross. Its full significance tongue cannot utter; pen cannot portray; the mind of man cannot comprehend. . . . Christ crucified for our sins, Christ risen from the dead, Christ ascended on high, is the science of salvation that we are to learn and to teach.

"Who, being in the form of God, counted it not a thing to be grasped to be on an equality with God, but emptied himself, taking the form of a servant, being made in the likeness of men; and being found in fashion as a man, he humbled himself, becoming obedient even unto death, yea, the death of the cross" (Phil. 2:6-8, RV, margin). "It is Christ that died, yea rather, that is risen again, who is even at the right hand of God." "Wherefore he is able also to save them to the uttermost that come unto God by him, seeing he ever liveth to make intercession for them" (Rom. 8:34; Heb. 7:25). . . .

Here are infinite wisdom, infinite love, infinite justice, infinite mercy—"the depth of the riches both of the wisdom and knowledge of God" (Rom. 11:33).

It is through the gift of Christ that we receive every blessing. Through that gift there comes to us day by day the unfailing flow of Jehovah's goodness. Every flower, with its delicate tints and sweet fragrance, is given for our enjoyment through that one Gift. The sun and moon were made by Him; there is not a star that beautifies the heavens which He did not make. There is not an article of food upon our tables that He has not provided for our sustenance. The superscription of Christ is upon it all. Everything is supplied to man through the one unspeakable Gift, the only-begotten Son of God. He was nailed to the cross that all these bounties might flow to God's workmanship.[42]

"Eye hath not seen, nor ear heard, neither have entered into the heart of man, the things which God hath prepared for them that love him" (1 Cor. 2:9). Surely there are none that, beholding the riches of His grace, can forbear to exclaim with the apostle: "Thanks be unto God for his unspeakable gift."[43]

So Costly—And Yet So Free

By the righteousness of one the free gift came upon all men unto justification of life. Rom. 5:18.

Money cannot buy it, intellect cannot grasp it, power cannot command it; but to all who will accept it, God's glorious grace is freely given. But men may feel their need, and, renouncing all self-dependence, accept salvation as a gift. Those who enter heaven will not scale its walls by their own righteousness, nor will its gates be opened to them for costly offerings of gold or silver, but they will gain an entrance to the many mansions of the Father's house through the merits of the cross of Christ.

For sinful men, the highest consolation, the greatest cause of rejoicing, is that Heaven has given Jesus to be the sinner's Saviour. . . . He offered to go over the ground where Adam stumbled and fell; to meet the tempter on the field of battle, and conquer him in man's behalf. Behold Him in the wilderness of temptation. Forty days and forty nights He fasted, enduring the fiercest assaults of the powers of darkness. He trod the "winepress alone; and of the people there was none with" Him (Isa. 63:3). It was not for Himself, but that He might break the chain that held the human race in slavery to Satan.[44]

As Christ in His humanity sought strength from His Father, that He might be enabled to endure trial and temptation, so are we to do. We are to follow the example of the sinless Son of God. Daily we need help and grace and power from the Source of all power. We are to cast our helpless souls upon the One who is ready to help us in every time of need. Too often we forget the Lord. Self gives way to impulse, and we lose the victories that we should gain.

If we are overcome let us not delay to repent, and to accept the pardon that will place us on vantage ground. If we repent and believe, the cleansing power from God will be ours. His saving grace is freely offered. His pardon is given to all who will receive it. . . . Over every sinner that repents the angels of God rejoice with songs of joy. Not one sinner need be lost. Full and free is the gift of saving grace.[45]

Bought Without Money

I thank my God always on your behalf, for the grace of God which is given you by Jesus Christ. 1 Cor. 1:4.

There are many who hope by their own works to merit God's favor. They do not realize their helplessness. They do not accept the grace of God as a free gift, but are trying to build themselves up in self-righteousness.[46]

The blessings of redeeming love our Saviour compared to a precious pearl [Matt. 13:45, 46]. . . .

In the parable the pearl is not represented as a gift. The merchantman bought it at the price of all that he had. Many question the meaning of this, since Christ is represented in the Scriptures as a gift. He is a gift, but only to those who give themselves soul, body, and spirit, to Him without reserve. We are to give ourselves to Christ, to live a life of willing obedience to all His requirements. All that we are, all the talents and capabilities we possess, are the Lord's, to be consecrated to His service. When we thus give ourselves wholly to Him, Christ, with all the treasures of heaven, gives Himself to us. We obtain the pearl of great price.

Salvation is a free gift, and yet it is to be bought and sold. In the market of which divine mercy has the management, the precious pearl is represented as being bought without money and without price. . . .

The gospel of Christ is a blessing that all may possess. The poorest are as well able as the richest to purchase salvation; for no amount of worldly wealth can secure it. It is obtained by willing obedience, by giving ourselves to Christ as His own purchased possession. . . .

We are to seek for the pearl of great price, but not in worldly marts or in worldly ways. The price we are required to pay is not gold or silver, for this belongs to God. Abandon the idea that temporal or spiritual advantages will win for you salvation. God calls for your willing obedience.[47]

All His gifts are promised on condition of obedience. God has a heaven full of blessings for those who will cooperate with Him.[48]

Grace Enough for All

For if by one man's offence death reigned by one; much more they which receive abundance of grace and of the gift of righteousness shall reign in life by one, Jesus Christ. Rom. 5:17.

God has an abundance of grace and power awaiting our demand. But the reason we do not feel our great need of it is because we look to ourselves and not to Jesus. We do not exalt Jesus and rely wholly upon His merits.[49]

The provision made is complete, and the eternal righteousness of Christ is placed to the account of every believing soul. The costly, spotless robe, woven in the loom of heaven, has been provided for the repenting, believing sinner, and he may say: "I will greatly rejoice in the Lord, my soul shall be joyful in my God; for he hath clothed me with the garments of salvation, he hath covered me with the robe of righteousness" (Isa. 61:10).

Abundant grace has been provided that the believing soul may be kept free from sin; for all heaven, with its limitless resources, has been placed at our command. We are to draw from the well of salvation. . . . In ourselves we are sinners; but in Christ we are righteous. Having made us righteous through the imputed righteousness of Christ, God pronounces us just, and treats us as just. He looks upon us as His dear children. Christ works against the power of sin, and where sin abounded, grace much more abounds.[50]

We may make daily progress in the upward path to holiness and yet we find still greater heights to be reached; but every stretch of the spiritual muscles, every taxation of heart and brain, brings to light the abundance of the supply of grace essential for us as we advance.

The more we contemplate these riches, the more we will come into possession of them, and the more we shall reveal the merits of Christ's sacrifice, the protection of His righteousness, His inexpressible love, the fullness of His wisdom, and His power to present us before the Father without spot or wrinkle or any such thing.[51]

We are living in the day of preparation. We must obtain a full supply of grace from the divine storehouse. The Lord has made provision for every day's demand.[52]

Unmerited Favor

Remember me, O Lord, with the favour that thou bearest unto thy people: O visit me with thy salvation. Ps. 106:4.

Grace is unmerited favor, and the believer is justified without any merit of his own, without any claim to offer to God. He is justified through the redemption that is in Christ Jesus, who stands in the courts of heaven as the sinner's substitute and surety. But while he is justified because of the merit of Christ, he is not free to work unrighteousness. Faith works by love and purifies the soul. Faith buds and blossoms and bears a harvest of precious fruit. Where faith is, good works appear. The sick are visited, the poor are cared for, the fatherless and the widows are not neglected, the naked are clothed, the destitute are fed.

Christ went about doing good, and when men are united with Him, they love the children of God, and meekness and truth guide their footsteps. The expression of the countenance reveals their experience, and men take knowledge of them that they have been with Jesus and learned of Him. Christ and the believer become one, and His beauty of character is revealed in those who are vitally connected with the Source of power and love. Christ is the great depositary of justifying righteousness and sanctifying grace.

All may come to Him and receive of His fullness. He says, "Come unto me, all ye that labour and are heavy laden, and I will give you rest" (Matt. 11:28). . . . Have you been looking unto Jesus, who is the author and finisher of your faith? Have you been beholding Him who is full of truth and grace? Have you accepted the peace which Christ alone can give? If you have not, then yield to Him, and through His grace seek for a character that will be noble and elevated. Seek for a constant, resolute, cheerful spirit. Feed on Christ who is the Bread of life, and you will manifest His loveliness of character and spirit.[53]

The very best you can do will not merit the favor of God. It is Jesus' worthiness that will save you, His blood that will cleanse you.[54]

Christ Our Righteousness

Whom God hath set forth to be a propitiation through faith in his blood, to declare his righteousness for the remission of sins that are past, through the forbearance of God. Rom. 3:25.

Christ is called "the Lord our righteousness," and through faith each one should say, "The Lord my righteousness." When faith lays hold upon this gift of God, the praise of God will be upon our lips, and we shall be able to say to others, "Behold the Lamb of God, which taketh away the sin of the world" (John 1:29). We shall then be able to tell the lost concerning the plan of salvation, that while the world was lying under the curse of sin, the Lord presented terms of mercy to the fallen and hopeless sinner, and revealed the value and meaning of His grace. Grace is unmerited favor. . . . It was grace that sent our Saviour to seek us as wanderers and bring us back to the fold. . . .

No man can look within himself and find anything in his character that will recommend him to God, or make his acceptance sure. It is only through Jesus, whom the Father gave for the life of the world, that the sinner may find access to God. Jesus alone is our Redeemer, our Advocate and Mediator; in Him is our only hope for pardon, peace, and righteousness. It is by virtue of the blood of Christ that the sin-stricken soul can be restored to soundness. . . .

Apart from Christ we have no merit, no righteousness. Our sinfulness, our weakness, our human imperfection make it impossible that we should appear before God unless we are clothed in Christ's spotless righteousness. . . .

When you respond to the drawing of Christ, and join yourself to Him, you manifest saving faith. . . . Faith familiarizes the soul with the existence and presence of God, and, living with an eye single to the glory of God, more and more we discern the beauty of His character, the excellence of His grace. Our souls become strong in spiritual power; for we are breathing the atmosphere of heaven. . . . We are rising above the world, beholding Him who is the Chief among ten thousand, the One altogether lovely, and by beholding we are to become changed into His image.[55]

The Bright Side of Religion

I will rejoice in the Lord, I will joy in the God of my salvation. Hab. 3:18.

Every one who loves God is to testify of the preciousness of His grace and truth. Those who receive the light of truth are to have lesson upon lesson to educate them not to keep silent, but to speak often one to another. They are to keep in mind the Sabbath meeting, when those who love and fear God, and who think upon His name, can have opportunity to express their thoughts in speaking one to another. . . .

The Majesty of heaven identifies His interests with those of the believers, however humble may be their circumstances. And whenever they are privileged to meet together, it is appropriate that they speak often one to another, giving utterance to the gratitude and love that is a result of thinking upon the name of the Lord. Thus shall God be glorified as He hearkens and hears, and the testimony meeting will be considered the most precious of all meetings; for the words spoken are recorded in the book of remembrance. . . .

Do not gratify the enemy by dwelling upon the dark side of your experience; trust Jesus more fully for help to resist temptation. If we thought and talked more of Jesus, and less of ourselves, we should have much more of His presence. If we abide in Him, we shall be so filled with peace, faith, and courage, and shall have so victorious an experience to relate when we come to meeting, that others will be refreshed by our clear, strong testimony for God. These precious acknowledgements to the praise of the glory of His grace, when supported by a Christlike life, have an irresistible power, which works for the salvation of souls. The bright and cheerful side of religion will be represented by all who are daily consecrated to God. We should not dishonor our Lord by a mournful relation of trials that appear grievous. All trials that are received as educators will produce joy. The whole religious life will be uplifting, elevating, ennobling, fragrant with good words and works.[56]

"Worthy Is the Lamb!"

Worthy is the Lamb that was slain to receive power, and riches, and wisdom, and strength, and honour, and glory, and blessing. Rev. 5:12.

We are not worthy of God's love, but Christ, our surety, is worthy, and is abundantly able to save all who shall come unto Him.[57]

Christ delights to take apparently hopeless material, those whom Satan has debased and through whom he has worked, and make them the subjects of His grace. He rejoices to deliver them from suffering and from the wrath that is to fall upon the disobedient.[58]

If the enemy can lead the desponding to take their eyes off from Jesus, and look to themselves, and dwell upon their own unworthiness, instead of dwelling upon the worthiness of Jesus, His love, His merits, and His great mercy, he will get away their shield of faith and gain his object; they will be exposed to his fiery temptations. The weak should therefore look to Jesus, and believe in Him; they then exercise faith.[59]

The Son of God gave all—life and love and suffering—for our redemption. And can it be that we, the unworthy objects of so great love, will withhold our hearts from Him? Every moment of our lives we have been partakers of the blessings of His grace, and for this very reason we cannot fully realize the depths of ignorance and misery from which we have been saved.[60]

Many make a serious mistake in their religious life by keeping the attention fixed upon their feelings and thus judging of their advancement or decline. Feelings are not a safe criterion. We are not to look within for evidence of our acceptance with God. We shall find there nothing but that which will discourage us. Our only hope is in "looking unto Jesus the author and finisher of our faith" (Heb. 12:2). There is everything in Him to inspire with hope, with faith, and with courage. He is our righteousness, our consolation and rejoicing. . . .

A sense of our weakness and unworthiness should lead us with humility of heart to plead the atoning sacrifice of Christ. As we rely upon His merits we shall find rest and peace and joy. He saves to the uttermost all who come unto God by Him.[61]

Mystery of Mysteries

Without controversy great is the mystery of godliness: God was manifest in the flesh, justified in the Spirit, seen of angels, preached unto the Gentiles, believed on in the world, received up into glory. 1 Tim. 3:16.

What a mystery of mysteries! It is difficult for the reason to grasp the majesty of Christ, the mystery of redemption. The shameful cross has been upraised, the nails have been driven through His hands and feet, and the cruel spear has pierced to His heart, and the redemption price has been paid for the human race. . . .

Redemption is an inexhaustible theme, worthy of our closest contemplation. It passes the comprehension of the deepest thought, the stretch of the most vivid imagination. . . .

Were Jesus with us today, He would say to us as He did to His disciples, "I have yet many things to say unto you, but ye cannot bear them now" (John 16:12). Jesus longed to open before the minds of His disciples deep and living truths, but their earthliness, their clouded, deficient comprehension made it impossible. . . . The want of spiritual growth closes the door to the rich rays of light that shine from Christ. . . .

Those who have been diligently working in the mines of God's Word, and have discovered the precious ore in the rich veins of truth, in the divine mysteries that have been hidden for ages, will exalt the Lord Jesus, the Source of all truth, by revealing in their characters the sanctifying power of what they believe. Jesus and His grace must be enshrined in the inner sanctuary of the soul. Then He will be revealed in words, in prayer, in exhortation, in the presentation of sacred truth.[62]

The mystery of the cross explains all other mysteries. In the light that streams from Calvary, the attributes of God which had filled us with fear and awe appear beautiful and attractive. Mercy, tenderness, and parental love are seen to blend with holiness, justice, and power. While we behold the majesty of His throne, high and lifted up, we see His character in His gracious manifestations, and comprehend, as never before, the significance of that endearing title, "Our Father."[63]

Unsearchable Riches

Unto me, who am less than the least of all saints, is this grace given, that I should preach among the Gentiles the unsearchable riches of Christ. Eph. 3:8.

It is not because of any restriction on the part of God that the riches of His grace do not flow earthward to men. If all were willing to receive, all would become filled with His Spirit.

It is the privilege of every soul to be a living channel through which God can communicate to the world the treasures of His grace, the unsearchable riches of Christ. There is nothing that Christ desires so much as agents who will represent to the world His Spirit and character. There is nothing that the world needs so much as the manifestation through humanity of the Saviour's love. All heaven is waiting for channels through which can be poured the holy oil to be a joy and blessing to human hearts.[64]

"God, who is rich in mercy, for his great love wherewith he loved us, even when we were dead in sins, hath quickened us together with Christ, . . . and hath raised us up together, and made us sit together in heavenly places in Christ Jesus: that in ages to come He might show the *exceeding riches* of his grace in his kindness toward us through Christ Jesus" (Eph. 2:4-7).

Such are the words in which "Paul the aged," "a prisoner of Jesus Christ," writing from his prison house at Rome, endeavored to set before his brethren that which he found language inadequate to express in its fulness—"the unsearchable riches of Christ," the treasure of grace freely offered to the fallen sons of men.[65]

As your soul yearns after God, you will find more and still more of the unsearchable riches of His grace. As you contemplate these riches, you will come into possession of them, and will reveal the merits of the Saviour's sacrifice, the protection of His righteousness, the fulness of His wisdom, and His power to present you before the Father "without spot, and blameless" (2 Peter 3:14).[66]

"Behold, What Manner of Love"

Behold, what manner of love the Father hath bestowed upon us, that we should be called the sons of God. 1 John 3:1.

It is from the Father's heart that the streams of divine compassion, manifest in Christ, flow out to the children of men. . . . God permitted His beloved Son, full of grace and truth, to come from a world of indescribable glory, to a world marred and blighted with sin, darkened with the shadow of death and the curse. He permitted Him to leave the bosom of His love, the adoration of the angels, to suffer shame, insult, humiliation, hatred, and death. . . . It was the burden of sin, the sense of its terrible enormity, of its separation of the soul from God—it was this that broke the heart of the Son of God. . . .

God suffered with His Son. In the agony of Gethsemane, the death of Calvary, the heart of Infinite Love paid the price of our redemption. . . . Nothing less than the infinite sacrifice made by Christ in behalf of fallen man could express the Father's love to lost humanity. . . .

The price paid for our redemption, the infinite sacrifice of our heavenly Father in giving His Son to die for us, should give us exalted conceptions of what we may become through Christ. As the inspired apostle John beheld the height, the depth, the breadth of the Father's love toward the perishing race, he was filled with adoration and reverence; and, failing to find suitable language in which to express the greatness and tenderness of this love, he called upon the world to behold it. . . . What a value this places upon man! Through transgression, the sons of man become subjects of Satan. Through faith in the atoning sacrifice of Christ, the sons of Adam may become the sons of God. By assuming human nature, Christ elevates humanity. Fallen men are placed where, through connection with Christ, they may indeed become worthy of the name, "sons of God."

Such love is without a parallel. Children of the heavenly King! Precious promise! Theme of the most profound meditation! The matchless love of God for a world that did not love Him![67]

How Long Must Heaven Suffer?

I and my Father are one. John 10:30.

God Himself was crucified with Christ; for Christ was one with the Father.[68]

Few give thought to the suffering that sin has caused our Creator. All heaven suffered in Christ's agony; but that suffering did not begin or end with His manifestation in humanity. The cross is a revelation to our dull senses of the pain that, from its very inception, sin has brought to the heart of God. Every departure from the right, every deed of cruelty, every failure of humanity to reach His ideal, brings grief to Him. When there came upon Israel the calamities that were the sure result of separation from God—subjugation by their enemies, cruelty, and death—it is said that "his soul was grieved for the misery of Israel." "In all their affliction he was afflicted: . . . and he bare them, and carried them all the days of old" (Judges 10:16; Isa. 63:9).

His Spirit "maketh intercession for us with groanings which cannot be uttered." As the "whole creation groaneth and travaileth in pain together" (Rom. 8:26, 22), the heart of the infinite Father is pained in sympathy. Our world is a vast lazar house, a scene of misery that we dare not allow our thoughts to dwell upon. Did we realize it as it is, the burden would be too terrible. Yet God feels it all.[69]

Not a sigh is breathed, not a pain felt, not a grief pierces the soul, but the throb vibrates to the Father's heart.[70]

He who knows the depths of the world's misery and despair, knows by what means to bring relief. . . . Although human beings have abused their mercies, wasted their talents, and lost the dignity of godlike manhood, the Creator is to be glorified in their redemption.[71]

In order to destroy sin and its results He gave His best Beloved, and He has put it in our power, through cooperation with Him, to bring this scene of misery to an end.[72]

With such an army of workers as our youth, rightly trained, might furnish, how soon the message of a crucified, risen, and soon-coming Saviour might be carried to the whole world! How soon might the end come—the end of suffering and sorrow and sin![73]

From the Beginning

The prophecy came not in old time by the will of man: but holy men of God spake as they were moved by the Holy Ghost. 2 Peter 1:21.

It is the glory of the gospel that it is founded upon the principle of restoring in the fallen race the divine image by a constant manifestation of benevolence. This work began in the heavenly courts. . . . The Godhead was stirred with pity for the race, and the Father, the Son, and the Holy Spirit gave themselves to the working out of the plan of redemption.[1]

Before the entrance of sin, Adam enjoyed open communion with his Maker; but since man separated himself from God by transgression, the human race has been cut off from this high privilege. By the plan of redemption, however, a way has been opened whereby the inhabitants of the earth may still have connection with heaven. God has communicated with men by His Spirit, and divine light has been imparted to the world by revelations to His chosen servants.[2]

From the beginning, God has been working by His Holy Spirit through human instrumentalities for the accomplishment of His purpose in behalf of the fallen race. This was manifest in the lives of the patriarchs. To the church in the wilderness also, in the time of Moses, God gave His "good Spirit to instruct them" (Neh. 9:20). And in the days of the apostles He wrought mightily for His church through the agency of the Holy Spirit. The same power that sustained the patriarchs . . . and that made the work of the apostolic church effective, has upheld God's faithful children in every succeeding age. It was through the power of the Holy Spirit that during the Dark Ages the Waldensian Christians helped to prepare the way for the Reformation. It was the same power that made successful the efforts of the noble men and women who pioneered the way for the establishment of modern missions. . . .

Today the heralds of the cross are . . . preparing the way for the second advent of Christ. . . . And as they continue to let their light shine, as did those who were baptized with the Spirit on the day of Pentecost, they receive more and still more of the Spirit's power. Thus the earth is to be lightened with the glory of God.[3]

Christ's Promise of the Spirit

I will pray the Father, and he shall give you another Comforter, that he may abide with you for ever; even the Spirit of truth. John 14:16, 17.

Before offering Himself as the sacrificial victim, Christ sought for the most essential and complete gift to bestow upon His followers, a gift that would bring within their reach the boundless resources of grace. "I will pray the Father," He said, "and he shall give you another Comforter, that he may abide with you for ever; even the Spirit of truth; whom the world cannot receive, because it seeth him not, neither knoweth him: but ye know him; for he dwelleth with you, and shall be in you. I will not leave you orphans: I will come to you" (John 14:16-18, margin).

Before this the Spirit had been in the world; from the very beginning of the work of redemption He had been moving upon men's hearts. But while Christ was on earth, the disciples had desired no other helper. Not until they were deprived of His presence would they feel their need of the Spirit, and then He would come.

The Holy Spirit is Christ's representative, but divested of the personality of humanity, and independent thereof. Cumbered with humanity, Christ could not be in every place personally. Therefore it was for their interest that He should go to the Father, and send the Spirit to be His successor on earth. No one could then have any advantage because of his location or his personal contact with Christ. By the Spirit the Saviour would be accessible to all. In this sense He would be nearer to them than if He had not ascended on high.[4]

This promise belongs to us now as surely as it belonged to the disciples. . . . Let every church member kneel before God, and pray earnestly for the impartation of the Spirit. Cry, "Lord, increase my faith. Make me to understand Thy word; for the entrance of Thy word giveth light. Refresh me by Thy presence. Fill my heart with Thy Spirit."[5]

At all times and in all places, in all sorrows and in all afflictions, when the outlook seems dark and the future perplexing, and we feel helpless and alone, the Comforter will be sent in answer to the prayer of faith.[6]

The Spirit's Power

Behold, I send the promise of my Father upon you: but tarry ye in the city of Jerusalem, until ye be endued with power from on high. Luke 24:49.

Christ's visible presence was about to be withdrawn from the disciples, but a new endowment of power was to be theirs. The Holy Spirit was to be given them in its fullness, sealing them for their work.[7]

In obedience to Christ's command, they waited in Jerusalem for the promise of the Father—the outpouring of the Spirit. They did not wait in idleness. The record says that they were "continually in the temple, praising and blessing God" (Luke 24:53). They also met together to present their requests to the Father in the name of Jesus. . . . Higher and still higher they extended the hand of faith, with the mighty argument, "It is Christ that died, yea rather, that is risen again, who is even at the right hand of God, who also maketh intercession for us" (Rom. 8:34). . . .

The disciples prayed with intense earnestness for a fitness to meet men and in their daily intercourse to speak words that would lead sinners to Christ. Putting away all differences, all desire for the supremacy, they came close together in Christian fellowship. They drew nearer and nearer to God. . . .

These days of preparation were days of deep heart searching. The disciples felt their spiritual need, and cried to the Lord for the holy unction that was to fit them for the work of soul saving. They did not ask for a blessing for themselves merely. They were weighted with the burden of the salvation of souls. They realized that the gospel was to be carried to the world, and they claimed the power that Christ had promised.

During the patriarchal age the influence of the Holy Spirit had often been revealed in a marked manner, but never in its fullness. Now, in obedience to the word of the Saviour, the disciples offered their supplications for this gift, and in heaven Christ added His intercession. He claimed the gift of the Spirit, that He might pour it upon His people.[8]

Pentecost

And when the day of Pentecost was fully come, they were all with one accord in one place. And suddenly there came a sound from heaven as of a rushing mighty wind, and it filled all the house where they were sitting.
Acts 2:1, 2.

The Spirit came upon the waiting, praying disciples with a fullness that reached every heart. The Infinite One revealed Himself in power to His church. It was as if for ages this influence had been held in restraint, and now Heaven rejoiced in being able to pour out upon the church the riches of the Spirit's grace. And under the influence of the Spirit, words of penitence and confession mingled with songs of praise for sins forgiven. Words of thanksgiving and of prophecy were heard. All heaven bent low to behold and to adore the wisdom of matchless, incomprehensible love. Lost in wonder, the apostles exclaimed, "Herein is love." They grasped the imparted gift. And what followed? The sword of the Spirit, newly edged with power and bathed in the lightnings of heaven, cut its way through unbelief. Thousands were converted in a day. . . .

Christ's ascension to heaven was the signal that His followers were to receive the promised blessing. For this they were to wait before they entered upon their work. When Christ passed within the heavenly gates, He was enthroned amidst the adoration of the angels. As soon as this ceremony was completed, the Holy Spirit descended upon the disciples in rich currents, and Christ was indeed glorified, even with the glory which He had with the Father from all eternity. The Pentecostal outpouring was Heaven's communication that the Redeemer's inauguration was accomplished. According to His promise He had sent the Holy Spirit from heaven to His followers, as a token that He had, as Priest and King, received all authority in heaven and on earth, and was the Anointed One over His people.[9]

God is willing to give us a similar blessing, when we seek for it as earnestly. The Lord did not lock the reservoir of heaven after pouring His Spirit upon the early disciples. We also may receive of the fullness of His blessing. Heaven is full of the treasures of His grace, and those who come to God in faith may claim all that He has promised.[10]

The Office of the Spirit

When he is come, he will reprove the world of sin, and of righteousness, and of judgment. John 16:8.

The Spirit was to be given as a regenerating agent, and without this the sacrifice of Christ would have been of no avail. The power of evil had been strengthening for centuries, and the submission of men to this satanic captivity was amazing. Sin could be resisted and overcome only through the mighty agency of the Third Person of the Godhead, who would come with no modified energy, but in the fullness of divine power. It is the Spirit that makes effectual what has been wrought out by the world's Redeemer. It is by the Spirit that the heart is made pure. Through the Spirit the believer becomes a partaker of the divine nature. Christ has given His Spirit as a divine power to overcome all hereditary and cultivated tendencies to evil, and to impress His own character upon His church.[11]

While we yield ourselves as instruments for the Holy Spirit's working, the grace of God works in us to deny old inclinations, to overcome powerful propensities, and to form new habits.[12]

The Spirit of God, received into the soul, quickens all its faculties. Under the guidance of the Holy Spirit, the mind that is devoted unreservedly to God, develops harmoniously, and is strengthened to comprehend and fulfill the requirements of God. The weak, vacillating character becomes changed to one of strength and steadfastness. . . .

It is the Spirit that causes to shine into darkened minds the bright beams of the Sun of Righteousness; that makes men's hearts burn within them with an awakened realization of the truths of eternity; that presents before the mind the great standard of righteousness, and convinces of sin; that inspires faith in Him who alone can save from sin; that works to transform character by withdrawing the affections of men from those things which are temporal and perishable, and fixing them upon the eternal inheritance. The Spirit recreates, refines, and sanctifies human beings, fitting them to become members of the royal family, children of the heavenly King.[13]

A Comforter Like Christ

Nevertheless I tell you the truth; it is expedient for you that I go away: for if I go not away, the Comforter will not come unto you; but if I depart, I will send him unto you. John 16:7.

The Comforter that Christ promised to send after He ascended to heaven, is the Spirit in all the fullness of the Godhead, making manifest the power of divine grace to all who receive and believe in Christ as a personal Saviour.[14]

With the consecrated worker for God, in whatever place he may be, the Holy Spirit abides. The words spoken to the disciples are spoken also to us. The Comforter is ours as well as theirs.[15]

There is no comforter like Christ, so tender and so true. He is touched with the feeling of our infirmities. His Spirit speaks to the heart. Circumstances may separate us from our friends; the broad, restless ocean may roll between us and them. Though their sincere friendship may still exist, they may be unable to demonstrate it. . . . But no circumstances, no distance, can separate us from the heavenly Comforter. Wherever we are, wherever we may go, He is always there, one given in Christ's place, to act in His stead. He is always at our right hand, to speak soothing, gentle words; to support, sustain, uphold, and cheer. The influence of the Holy Spirit is the life of Christ in the soul. This Spirit works in and through every one who receives Christ. Those who know the indwelling of this Spirit reveal its fruit—love, joy, peace, long-suffering, gentleness, goodness, faith.[16]

The Holy Spirit ever abides with him who is seeking for perfection of Christian character. The Holy Spirit furnishes the pure motive, the living, active principle, that sustains striving, wrestling, believing souls in every emergency and under every temptation. The Holy Spirit sustains the believer amid the world's hatred, amid the unfriendliness of relatives, amid disappointment, amid the realization of imperfection, and amid the mistakes of life. Depending upon the matchless purity and perfection of Christ, the victory is sure to him who looks unto the Author and Finisher of our faith. . . . He has borne our sins, in order that through Him we might have moral excellence, and attain unto the perfection of Christian character.[17]

Christ's Representative

Lo, I am with you alway, even unto the end of the world. Matt. 28:20.

When Christ ascended to the Father, He did not leave His followers without help. The Holy Spirit, as His representative, and the heavenly angels, as ministering spirits, are sent forth to aid those who against great odds are fighting the good fight of faith. Ever remember that Jesus is your helper. No one understands as well as He your peculiarities of character. He is watching over you, and if you are willing to be guided by Him, He will throw around you influences for good that will enable you to accomplish all His will for you.[18]

The Christian life is a warfare. But "we wrestle not against flesh and blood, but against principalities, against powers, against the rulers of the darkness of this world, against spiritual wickedness in high places" (Eph. 6:12). In this conflict of righteousness against unrighteousness we can be successful only by divine aid. Our finite will must be brought into submission to the will of the Infinite; the human will must be blended with the divine. This will bring the Holy Spirit to our aid. . . .

The Lord Jesus acts through the Holy Spirit; for it is His representative. Through it He infuses spiritual life into the soul, quickening its energies for good, cleansing it from moral defilement, and giving it a fitness for His kingdom. Jesus has large blessings to bestow, rich gifts to distribute among men. He is the wonderful Counselor, infinite in wisdom and strength; and if we will acknowledge the power of His Spirit, and submit to be molded by it, we shall stand complete in Him. What a thought is this! In Christ "dwelleth all the fulness of the Godhead bodily. And ye are complete in him" (Col. 2:9, 10). Never will the human heart know happiness until it is submitted to be molded by the Spirit of God. The Spirit conforms the renewed soul to the model, Jesus Christ. Through the influence of the Spirit, enmity against God is changed into faith and love, and pride into humility. The soul perceives the beauty of truth, and Christ is honored in excellence and perfection of character. As these changes are effected, angels break out in rapturous song, and God and Christ rejoice over souls fashioned after the divine similitude.[19]

Like Dew, Rain, and Sunshine

I will be as the dew unto Israel: he shall grow as the lily, and cast forth his roots as Lebanon. Hosea 14:5.

Of the almost innumerable lessons taught in the varied processes of growth, some of the most precious are conveyed in the Saviour's parable of the growing seed. . . .

The seed has in itself a germinating principle, a principle that God Himself has implanted; yet if left to itself the seed would have no power to spring up. Man has his part to act in promoting the growth of the grain; but there is a point beyond which he can accomplish nothing. He must depend upon One who has connected the sowing and the reaping by wonderful links of His own omnipotent power.

There is life in the seed, there is power in the soil; but unless infinite power is exercised day and night, the seed will yield no return. The showers of rain must refresh the thirsty fields; the sun must impart warmth; electricity must be conveyed to the buried seed. The life which the Creator has implanted, He alone can call forth. Every seed grows, every plant develops, by the power of God. . . .

The germination of the seed represents the beginning of spiritual life, and the development of the plant is a figure of the development of character. There can be no life without growth.

The plant must either grow or die. As its growth is silent and imperceptible, but continuous, so is the growth of character. At every stage of development our life may be perfect; yet if God's purpose for us is fulfilled, there will be constant advancement.

The plant grows by receiving that which God has provided to sustain its life. So spiritual growth is attained through cooperation with divine agencies. As the plant takes root in the soil, so we are to take root in Christ. As the plant receives the sunshine, the dew, and the rain, so we are to receive the Holy Spirit. If our hearts are stayed upon Christ, He will come unto us "as the rain, as the latter and former rain unto the earth." As the Sun of righteousness, He will arise upon us "with healing in His wings." We shall "grow as the lily." We shall "revive as the corn, and grow as the vine" (Hosea 6:3; Mal. 4:2; Hosea 14:5, 7).[20]

Illuminates the Scriptures

But God hath revealed them unto us by his Spirit: for the Spirit searcheth all things, yea, the deep things of God. 1 Cor. 2:10.

God has been pleased to communicate His truth to the world by human agencies, and He Himself, by His Holy Spirit, qualified men and enabled them to do this work. He guided the mind in the selection of what to speak and what to write. The treasure was intrusted to earthen vessels, yet it is, none the less, from Heaven. The testimony is conveyed through the imperfect expression of human language, yet it is the testimony of God; and the obedient, believing child of God beholds in it the glory of a divine power, full of grace and truth.

In His Word, God has committed to men the knowledge necessary for salvation. The Holy Scriptures are to be accepted as an authoritative, infallible revelation of His will. They are the standard of character, the revealer of doctrines, and the test of experience. . . . Yet the fact that God has revealed His will to men through His Word, has not rendered needless the continued presence and guiding of the Holy Spirit. On the contrary, the Spirit was promised by our Saviour, to open the Word to His servants, to illuminate and apply its teachings.[21]

Those who dig beneath the surface discover the hidden gems of truth. The Holy Spirit is present with the earnest searcher. Its illumination shines upon the Word, stamping the truth upon the mind with a new, fresh importance. The searcher is filled with a sense of peace and joy never before felt. The preciousness of truth is realized as never before. A new, heavenly light shines upon the Word, illuminating it as though every letter were tinged with gold. God Himself has spoken to the mind and heart, making the Word spirit and life.[22]

The Holy Spirit is implanting the grace of Christ in the heart of many a noble seeker after truth, quickening his sympathies contrary to his nature, contrary to his former education. "The light, which lighteth every man that cometh into the world" (John 1:9), is shining in his soul; and this Light, if heeded, will guide his feet to the kingdom of God.[23]

Teacher of Truth

When he, the Spirit of truth is come, he will guide you into all truth.
John 16:13.

The Comforter is called "the Spirit of truth." His work is to define and maintain the truth. He first dwells in the heart as the Spirit of truth, and thus He becomes the Comforter. There is comfort and peace in the truth, but no real peace or comfort can be found in falsehood. It is through false theories and traditions that Satan gains his power over the mind. By directing men to false standards, he misshapes the character. Through the Scriptures the Holy Spirit speaks to the mind, and impresses truth upon the heart. Thus He exposes error, and expels it from the soul. It is by the Spirit of truth, working through the Word of God, that Christ subdues His chosen people to Himself.[24]

God intends that even in this life the truths of His Word shall be ever unfolding to His people. There is only one way in which this knowledge can be obtained. We can attain to an understanding of God's Word only through the illumination of that Spirit by which the Word was given. "The things of God knoweth no man, but the Spirit of God;" "for the Spirit searcheth all things, yea, the deep things of God" (1 Cor. 2:11, 10).[25]

From God, the fountain of wisdom, proceeds all the knowledge that is of value to man, all that the intellect can grasp or retain. The fruit of the tree representing good and evil is not to be eagerly plucked because it is recommended by one who was once a bright angel in glory. He has said that if men eat thereof, they shall know good and evil; but let it alone. The true knowledge comes not from infidels or wicked men. The word of God is light and truth. The true light shines from Jesus Christ, who "lighteth every man that cometh into the world" (John 1:9). From the Holy Spirit proceeds divine knowledge. He knows what humanity needs to promote peace, happiness, and restfulness here in this world, and to secure eternal rest in the kingdom of God.[26]

Never should the Bible be studied without prayer. Before opening its pages we should ask for the enlightenment of the Holy Spirit, and it will be given. . . . The Spirit of truth is the only effectual teacher of divine truth.[27]

A Faithful Guide

For this God is our God for ever and ever:
he will be our guide even unto death. Ps. 48:14.

No truth is more clearly taught in the Bible than that God by His Holy Spirit especially directs His servants on earth in the great movements for the carrying forward of the work of salvation. Men are instruments in the hands of God, employed by Him to accomplish His purposes of grace and mercy.[28]

I am encouraged and blessed as I realize that the God of Israel is still guiding His people, and that He will continue to be with them, even to the end. . . .

If ever there was a time when we needed the special guidance of the Holy Spirit, it is now. We need a thorough consecration. It is fully time that we gave to the world a demonstration of the power of God in our own lives and in our ministry.

The Lord desires to see the work of proclaiming the third angel's message carried forward with increasing efficiency. As He has worked in all ages to give victories to His people, so in this age He longs to carry to a triumphant fulfillment His purposes for His church. He bids His believing saints to advance unitedly, going from strength to greater strength, from faith to increased assurance and confidence in the truth and righteousness of His cause.

We are to stand firm as a rock to the principles of the Word of God, remembering that God is with us to give us strength to meet each new experience. . . . We are to hold as very sacred the faith that has been substantiated by the instruction and approval of the Spirit of God from our earliest experience until the present time. We are to cherish as very precious the work that the Lord has been carrying forward through His commandment-keeping people, and which, through the power of His grace will grow stronger and more efficient as time advances. The enemy is seeking to becloud the discernment of God's people, and to weaken their efficiency, but if they will labor as the Spirit of God shall direct, He will open doors of opportunity before them. . . . Their experience will be one of constant growth, until the Lord shall descend from heaven with power and great glory to set His seal of final triumph upon His faithful ones.[29]

Our Personal Guide

Thine ears shall hear a word behind thee, saying, This is the way, walk ye in it, when ye turn to the right hand, and when ye turn to the left. Isa. 30:21.

I have no higher wish than to see our youth imbued with that spirit of pure religion which will lead them to take up the cross and follow Jesus. Go forth, young disciples of Christ, controlled by principle, clad in the robes of purity and righteousness. Your Saviour will guide you into the position best suited to your talents and where you can be most useful.[30]

"If any of you lack wisdom, let him ask of God, that giveth to all men liberally, and upbraideth not; and it shall be given him" (James 1:5). Such a promise is of more value than gold or silver. If with a humble heart you seek divine guidance in every trouble and perplexity, His word is pledged that a gracious answer will be given you. And His word can never fail.[31]

As we near the end of time, falsehood will be so mingled with truth, that only those who have the guidance of the Holy Spirit will be able to distinguish truth from error. We need to make every effort to keep the way of the Lord. We must in no case turn from His guidance to put our trust in man. The Lord's angels are appointed to keep strict watch over those who put their faith in the Lord, and these angels are to be our special help in every time of need. Every day we are to come to the Lord with full assurance of faith, and to look to Him for wisdom. . . . Those who are guided by the Word of the Lord will discern with certainty between falsehood and truth, between sin and righteousness.[32]

"Emmanuel, God with us." This means everything to us. What a broad foundation does it lay for our faith! What a hope big with immortality does it place before the believing soul! God with us in Christ Jesus to accompany us every step of the journey to heaven! The Holy Spirit with us as a Comforter, a Guide in our perplexities, to soothe our sorrows, and shield us in temptation![33]

He who does the will of God, who walks in the path that God has marked out, cannot stumble and fall. The light of God's guiding Spirit gives him a clear perception of his duty, and leads him aright till the close of his work.[34]

That Still Small Voice

To day if ye will hear his voice, harden not your hearts. Heb. 3:7, 8.

Conscience is the voice of God, heard amid the conflict of human passions; when it is resisted, the Spirit of God is grieved.[35]

Men have the power to quench the Spirit of God; the power of choosing is left with them. They are allowed freedom of action. They may be obedient through the name and grace of our Redeemer, or they may be disobedient, and realize the consequences.[36]

The Lord requires us to obey the voice of duty, when there are other voices all around us urging us to pursue an opposite course. It requires earnest attention from us to distinguish the voice which speaks from God. We must resist and conquer inclination, and obey the voice of conscience without parleying or compromise, lest its promptings cease and will and impulse control. The word of the Lord comes to us all who have not resisted His Spirit by determining not to hear and obey. This voice is heard in warnings, in counsels, in reproof. It is the Lord's message of light to His people. If we wait for louder calls or better opportunities, the light may be withdrawn, and we left in darkness. . . .

The pleadings of the Spirit, neglected today because pleasure or inclination leads in an opposite direction, may be powerless to convince, or even impress, tomorrow. To improve the opportunities of the present, with prompt and willing hearts, is the only way to grow in grace and the knowledge of the truth. We should ever cherish a sense that, individually, we are standing before the Lord of hosts; no word, no act, no thought, even, should be indulged to offend the eye of the Eternal One. . . . If we would feel that in every place we are the servants of the Most High, we would be more circumspect; our whole life would possess to us a meaning and a sacredness which earthly honors can never give.

The thoughts of the heart, the words of the lips, and every act of the life, will make our character more worthy, if the presence of God is continually felt. Let the language of the heart be: "Lo, God is here." Then the life will be pure, the character unspotted, the soul continually uplifted to the Lord.[37]

A Refining and Sanctifying Force

I the Lord do sanctify them. Lev. 22:9.

None but He who has created man can effect a change in the human heart. . . . The human judgment and ideas of the most experienced are liable to be imperfect and faulty, and the frail instrument, subject to his own hereditary traits of character, has need to submit to the sanctification of the Holy Spirit every day, else self will gather the reins and want to drive.[38]

A mind trained only in worldly science fails to understand the things of God; but the same mind, converted and sanctified, will see the divine power in the word. Only the mind and heart cleansed by the sanctification of the Spirit can discern heavenly things.[39]

An earthly parent cannot give his child a sanctified character. He cannot transfer his character to his child. God alone can transform us. Christ breathed on His disciples, and said, "Receive ye the Holy Ghost" (John 20:22). This is the great gift of heaven. Christ imparted to them through the Spirit His own sanctification. He imbued them with His power, that they might win souls to the gospel. Henceforth Christ would live through their faculties, and speak through their words. . . . They must cherish His principles and be controlled by His Spirit. They were no longer to follow their own way, to speak their own words. The words they spoke were to proceed from a sanctified heart, and fall from sanctified lips.[40]

We need the softening, subduing, refining influence of the Holy Spirit, to mold our characters, and to bring every thought into captivity to Christ. It is the Holy Spirit that will enable us to overcome, that will lead us to sit at the feet of Jesus, as did Mary, and learn His meekness and lowliness of heart. We need to be sanctified by the Holy Spirit every hour of the day, lest we be ensnared by the enemy, and our souls be imperiled.[41]

The light of truth is to shine to the ends of the earth. Greater and still greater light is beaming with celestial brightness from the Redeemer's face upon His representatives, to be diffused through the darkness of a benighted world. As laborers together with Him, let us pray for the sanctification of His Spirit, that we may shine more and more brightly.[42]

Molds Into the Divine Likeness

*And hereby we know that he abideth in us,
by the Spirit which he hath given us. 1 John 3:24.*

The promise of the Holy Spirit is not limited to any age or to any race. Christ declared that the divine influence of His Spirit was to be with His followers unto the end. From the Day of Pentecost to the present time, the Comforter has been sent to all who have yielded themselves fully to the Lord and to His service. To all who have accepted Christ as a personal Saviour, the Holy Spirit has come as a counselor, sanctifier, guide, and witness. The more closely believers have walked with God, the more clearly and powerfully they have testified of their Redeemer's love and of His saving grace. The men and women who through the long centuries of persecution and trial enjoyed a large measure of the presence of the Spirit in their lives, have stood as signs and wonders in the world. Before angels and men they have revealed the transforming power of redeeming love.

Those who at Pentecost were endued with power from on high, were not thereby freed from further temptation and trial. As they witnessed for truth and righteousness, they were repeatedly assailed by the enemy of all truth, who sought to rob them of their Christian experience. They were compelled to strive with all their God-given powers to reach the measure of the stature of grace, that they might reach higher and still higher toward perfection. Under the Holy Spirit's working, even the weakest, by experiencing faith in God, learned to improve their entrusted powers and to become sanctified, refined, and ennobled. As in humility they submitted to the moulding influence of the Holy Spirit, they received of the fullness of the Godhead and were fashioned in the likeness of the divine. . . .

The Holy Spirit withdraws the affections from the things of this earth and fills the soul with a desire for holiness. . . . If men are willing to be moulded, there will be brought about a sanctification of the whole being. The Spirit will take the things of God and stamp them on the soul.[43]

Brings Refreshing

Repent ye therefore, and be converted, that your sins may be blotted out, when the times of refreshing shall come from the presence of the Lord. Acts 3:19.

The third angel's message is swelling into a loud cry, and you must not feel at liberty to neglect the present duty, and still entertain the idea that at some future time you will be the recipients of great blessing, when without any effort on your part a wonderful revival will take place. Today you are to give yourselves to God, that He may make of you vessels unto honor, and meet for His service. Today you are to give yourself to God, that you may be emptied of self, emptied of envy, jealousy, evil surmising, strife, everything that shall be dishonoring to God. Today you are to have your vessel purified that it may be ready for the heavenly dew, ready for the showers of the latter rain; for the latter rain will come, and the blessing of God will fill every soul that is purified from every defilement. It is our work today to yield our souls to Christ, that we may be fitted for the time of refreshing from the presence of the Lord—fitted for the baptism of the Holy Spirit. . . .

God has not revealed to us the time when this message will close, or when probation will have an end. . . . It is our duty to watch and work and wait, to labor every moment for the souls of men that are ready to perish. We are to keep walking continually in the footsteps of Jesus, working in His lines, dispensing His gifts as good stewards of the manifold grace of God. . . .

The Word of the Lord reveals the fact that the end of all things is at hand, and its testimony is most decided that it is necessary for every soul to have the truth planted in the heart so that it will control the life and sanctify the character. The Spirit of the Lord is working to take the truth of the inspired Word and stamp it upon the soul so that professed followers of Christ will have a holy, sacred joy that they will be able to impart to others.

Our only safety is in being ready for the heavenly refreshing, having our lamps trimmed and burning. . . . Day by day we are to seek the enlightenment of the Spirit of God, that it may do its office work upon the soul and character.[44]

Purifying, Vitalizing Power

*Create in me a clean heart, O God;
and renew a right spirit within me. Ps. 51:10.*

The Lord purifies the heart very much as we air a room. We do not close the doors and windows, and throw in some purifying substance; but we open the doors and throw wide the windows, and let heaven's purifying atmosphere flow in. . . . The windows of impulse, of feeling must be opened up toward heaven, and the dust of selfishness and earthliness must be expelled. The grace of God must sweep through the chambers of the mind, the imagination must have heavenly themes for contemplation, and every element of the nature must be purified and vitalized by the Spirit of God.[45]

He who lives the principles of Bible religion, will not be found weak in moral power. Under the ennobling influence of the Holy Sprit, the tastes and inclinations become pure and holy. Nothing takes so strong a hold upon the affections, nothing reaches so fully down to the deepest motives of action, nothing exerts so potent an influence upon the life, and gives so great firmness and stability to the character, as the religion of Christ. It leads its possessor ever upward, inspiring him with noble purposes, teaching him propriety of deportment, and imparting a becoming dignity to every action.[46]

The church is the object of God's tenderest love and care. If the members will allow Him, He will reveal His character through them. He says to them, "Ye are the light of the world" (Matt. 5:14). Those who walk and talk with God practice the gentleness of Christ. In their lives, forbearance, meekness, and self-restraint are united with holy earnestness and diligence. As they advance heavenward, the sharp, rough edges of character are worn off, and godliness is seen. The Holy Spirit, full of grace and power, works upon mind and heart.[47]

The heart in which Jesus makes His abode will be quickened, purified, guided, and ruled by the Holy Spirit, and the human agent will make strenuous efforts to bring his character into harmony with God. He will avoid everything that is contrary to the revealed will and mind of God.[48]

Received by Naked Faith

The just shall live by his faith. Hab. 2:4.

Many do not exercise that faith which it is their privilege and duty to exercise, often waiting for that feeling which faith alone can bring. Feeling is not faith; the two are distinct. Faith is ours to exercise, but joyful feeling and the blessing are God's to give. The grace of God comes to us through the channel of living faith, and that faith it is in our power to exercise.

True faith lays hold of and claims the promised blessing before it is realized and felt. We must send up our petitions in faith within the second vail, and let our faith take hold of the promised blessing, and claim it as ours. We are then to believe that we receive the blessing, because our faith has hold of it, and according to the Word it is ours. "What things soever ye desire when ye pray, believe that ye receive them, and ye shall have them" (Mark 11:24). Here is faith, naked faith, to believe that we receive the blessing, even before we realize it. . . . But many suppose . . . that they cannot have faith unless they feel the power of the Spirit. Such confound faith with the blessing that comes through faith. The very time to exercise faith is when we feel destitute of the Spirit. When thick clouds of darkness seem to hover over the mind, then is the time to let living faith pierce the darkness and scatter the clouds. True faith rests on the promises contained in the Word of God, and those only who obey that Word can claim its glorious promises.[49]

Should anyone dishonor God by imagining that He would not respond to the appeals of His children? . . . The Holy Spirit, the representative of Himself, is the greatest of all gifts. All "good things" are comprised in this. The Creator Himself can give us nothing greater, nothing better. When we beseech the Lord to pity us in our distress, and to guide us by His Holy Spirit, He will never turn away our prayer.[50]

The measure of the Holy Spirit we receive will be proportioned to the measure of our desire and the faith exercised for it. . . . We can be assured that we shall receive the Holy Spirit if we individually try the experiment of testing God's word.[51]

For All Who Believe

God hath from the beginning chosen you to salvation through sanctification of the Spirit and belief of the truth. 2 Thess. 2:13.

In this text the two agencies in the work of salvation are revealed—the divine influence, and the strong, living faith of those who follow Christ. It is through the sanctification of the Spirit and belief of the truth that we become laborers together with God. Christ waits for the cooperation of His church. . . . The blood of Jesus Christ, the Holy Spirit, the divine Word, are ours. The object of all this provision of heaven is before us—the salvation of the souls for whom Christ died; and it depends upon us to lay hold on the promises God has given, and become laborers together with Him. Divine and human agencies must cooperate in the work. . . .

Christ crucified for our sins; Christ risen from the dead; Christ ascended on high as our intercessor—this is the science of salvation that we need to learn and to teach.[52]

It is God's purpose that His people shall be a sanctified, purified, holy people, communicating light to all around them. It is His purpose that, by exemplifying the truth in their lives, they shall be a praise in the earth. The grace of Christ is sufficient to bring this about.[53]

There is no limit to the usefulness of one who, putting self aside, makes room for the working of the Holy Spirit upon his heart and lives a life wholly consecrated to God. All who consecrate body, soul, and spirit to His service will be constantly receiving a new endowment of physical, mental, and spiritual power. The inexhaustible supplies of heaven are at their command. Christ gives them the breath of His own Spirit, the life of His own life. The Holy Spirit puts forth its highest energies to work in mind and heart. Through the grace given us we may achieve victories that because of our own erroneous and preconceived opinions, our defects of character, our smallness of faith, have seemed impossible.

To everyone who offers himself to the Lord for service, withholding nothing, is given power for the attainment of measureless results.[54]

More Than Mortal Power

When the enemy shall come in like a flood, the Spirit of the Lord shall lift up a standard against him. Isa. 59:19.

God has provided divine assistance for all the emergencies to which our human resources are unequal. He gives the Holy Spirit to help in every strait, to strengthen our hope and assurance, to illuminate our minds and purify our hearts.[55]

Your part is to put your will on the side of Christ. When you yield your will to His, He immediately takes possession of you, and works in you to will and to do of His good pleasure. Your nature is brought under the control of His Spirit. Even your thoughts are subject to Him. If you cannot control your impulses, your emotions, as you may desire, you can control the will, and thus an entire change will be wrought in your life. When you yield up your will to Christ, your life is hid with Christ in God. It is allied to the power which is above all principalities and powers. You have a strength from God that holds you fast to His strength; and a new life, even the life of faith, is possible to you.

You can never be successful in elevating yourself, unless your will is on the side of Christ, cooperating with the Spirit of God. Do not feel that you cannot; but say, "I can, I will." And God has pledged His Holy Spirit to help you in every decided effort.[56]

The lifework given us is that of preparation for the life eternal. If we accomplish this work as God designs we shall, every temptation may work for our advancement; for as we resist its allurements, we make progress in the divine life. In the heat of the conflict, unseen agencies will be by our side, commanded of heaven to aid us in our wrestlings; and in the crisis, strength and firmness and energy will be imparted to us, and we shall have more than mortal power. . . .

Those who would be conquerors must engage in conflict with unseen agencies. . . . The Holy Spirit is ever at work, seeking to purify, refine, and discipline the souls of men, in order that they may become fitted for the society of saints and angels.[57]

Brings Harmony

Neither pray I for these alone, but for them also which shall believe on me through their word; that they all may be one; as thou, Father, art in me, and I in thee, that they also may be one in us: that the world may believe that thou hast sent me. John 17:20, 21.

After the descent of the Holy Spirit the disciples went forth to proclaim a risen Saviour, their one desire the salvation of souls. They rejoiced in the sweetness of the communion with saints. They were tender, thoughtful, self-denying, willing to make any sacrifice for the truth's sake. In their daily association with one another they revealed the love that Christ had commanded them to reveal. . . .

Harmony and union existing among men of varied dispositions is the strongest witness that can be borne that God has sent His Son into the world to save sinners. It is our privilege to bear this witness. But, in order to do this, we must place ourselves under Christ's command. Our characters must be molded in harmony with His character, our wills must be surrendered to His will.[58]

We are of the same faith, members of one family, all children of the same heavenly Father, with the same blessed hope of immortality. How close and tender should be the tie that binds us together. The people of the world are watching us to see if our faith is exerting a sanctifying influence upon our hearts. They are quick to discern every defect in our lives, every inconsistency in our actions. Let us give them no occasion to reproach our faith. . . .

Little differences dwelt upon lead to actions that destroy Christian fellowship. Let us not allow the enemy thus to gain the advantage over us. Let us keep drawing nearer to God and to one another. . . . The heart of the Saviour is set upon His followers' fulfilling God's purpose in all its height and depth. They are to be one in Him, even though they are scattered the world over. . . . When Christ's prayer is fully believed . . . unity of action will be seen in our ranks. Brother will be bound to brother by the golden bonds of the love of Christ. The Spirit of God alone can bring about this oneness. He who sanctified Himself can sanctify His disciples. United with Him, they will be united with one another in the most holy faith.[59]

Creates Unity in Diversity

I . . . beseech you that ye walk worthy of the vocation wherewith ye are called, with all lowliness and meekness, with longsuffering, forbearing one another in love; endeavoring to keep the unity of the Spirit in the bond of peace. Eph. 4:1-3.

Paul urges the Ephesians to preserve unity and love. . . . Divisions in the church dishonor the religion of Christ before the world and give occasion to the enemies of truth to justify their course.[60]

A union of believers with Christ will as a natural result lead to a union with one another, which bond of union is the most enduring upon earth. We are one in Christ, as Christ is one with the Father. . . . It is only by personal union with Christ, by communion with Him daily, hourly, that we can bear the fruits of the Holy Spirit. . . . Our growth in grace, our joy, our usefulness, all depend on our union with Christ and the degree of faith we exercise in Him.[61]

The word and Spirit of truth, dwelling in our hearts, will separate us from the world. The immutable principles of truth and love will bind heart to heart, and the strength of the union will be according to the measure of grace and truth enjoyed.[62]

The vine has many branches, but though all the branches are different, they do not quarrel. In diversity there is unity. All the branches obtain their nourishment from one source. This is an illustration of the unity that is to exist among Christ's followers. In their different lines of work they all have but one Head. The same Spirit, in different ways, works through them. There is harmonious action, though the gifts differ. . . . God calls for each one . . . to do his appointed work according to the ability which has been given him.[63]

We have a character to maintain, but it is the character of Christ. Having the character of Christ, we can carry on the work of God together. The Christ in us will meet the Christ in our brethren, and the Holy Spirit will give that union of heart and action which testifies to the world that we are children of God. . . .

The world needs to see worked out before it the miracle that binds the hearts of God's people together in Christian love.[64]

Given on Condition

For they that are after the flesh do mind the things of the flesh; but they that are after the Spirit the things of the Spirit. Rom. 8:5.

Christ promised the gift of the Holy Spirit to His church, and the promise belongs as much to us as to the first disciples. But like every other promise, it is given on conditions. There are many who profess to believe and claim the Lord's promises; they talk about Christ and the Holy Spirit; yet they receive no benefit, because they do not surrender their souls to the guidance and control of divine agencies.

We cannot use the Holy Spirit; the Spirit is to use us. Through the Spirit, God works in His people "to will and to do of his good pleasure" (Phil. 2:13). But many will not submit to be led. They want to manage themselves. This is why they do not receive the heavenly gift. Only to those who wait humbly upon God, who watch for His guidance and grace, is the Spirit given. The promised blessing, claimed by faith, brings all other blessings in its train. It is given according to the riches of the grace of Christ, and He is ready to supply every soul according to the capacity to receive.

The impartation of the Spirit is the impartation of the life of Christ. Those only who are thus taught of God, those only who possess the inward working of the Spirit, and in whose life the Christ-life is manifested, can stand as true representatives of the Saviour. . . .

Christ promised that the Holy Spirit should abide with those who wrestle for victory over sin, to demonstrate the power of divine might by endowing the human agent with supernatural strength and instructing the ignorant in the mysteries of the kingdom of God. . . .

When one is fully emptied of self, when every false god is cast out of the soul, the vacuum is filled by the inflowing of the Spirit of Christ. Such a one has the faith that purifies the soul from defilement. He is conformed to the Spirit, and he minds the things of the Spirit. He has no confidence in self. Christ is all and in all.[65]

Giving and Receiving

Freely ye have received, freely give. Matt. 10:8.

Jesus said, "The water that I shall give him shall be in him a well of water springing up into everlasting life" (John 4:14). As the Holy Spirit opens to you the truth you will treasure up the most precious experiences and will long to speak to others of the comforting things that have been revealed to you. When brought into association with them you will communicate some fresh thought in regard to the character or the work of Christ. You will have some fresh revelation of His pitying love to impart to those who love Him and to those who love Him not. . . .

The heart that has once tasted the love of Christ, cries out continually for a deeper draft, and as you impart you will receive in richer and more abundant measure. Every revelation of God to the soul increases the capacity to know and to love. The continual cry of the heart is, "More of Thee," and ever the Spirit's answer is, "Much more." . . . To Jesus, who emptied Himself for the salvation of lost humanity, the Holy Spirit was given without measure. So it will be given to every follower of Christ when the whole heart is surrendered for His indwelling. Our Lord Himself has given the command, "Be filled with the Spirit" (Eph. 5:18), and this command is also a promise of its fulfillment. It was the good pleasure of the Father that in Christ should "all the fullness dwell," and "in him ye are made full" (Col. 1:19, RV; 2:10, RV).[66]

The more of the Spirit of God, the more of His grace, is brought into our daily experience, the less friction there will be, the more happiness we shall have, and the more we shall impart to others.[67]

Christ is the great center, the source of all strength. . . . The most intelligent, the most spiritually minded, can bestow only as they receive. Of themselves they can supply nothing for the needs of the soul. We can impart only that which we receive from Christ; and we can receive only as we impart to others. As we continue imparting, we continue to receive; and the more we impart, the more we shall receive. Thus we may be constantly believing, trusting, receiving, and imparting.[68]

Oil for Our Lamps

The wise took oil in their vessels with their lamps. Matt. 25:4.

The two classes of watchers [in the parable of the ten virgins] represent the two classes who profess to be waiting for their Lord. They are called virgins because they profess a pure faith. By the lamps is represented the Word of God. . . . The oil is a symbol of the Holy Spirit. . . .

In the parable, all the ten virgins went out to meet the bridegroom. All had lamps and vessels for oil. For a time there was seen no difference between them. So with the church that lives just before Christ's second coming. All have a knowledge of the Scriptures. All have heard the message of Christ's near approach, and confidently expect His appearing. But as in the parable, so it is now. A time of waiting intervenes, faith is tried; and when the cry is heard, "Behold, the Bridegroom cometh; go ye out to meet him," many are unready. . . . They are destitute of the Holy Spirit. Without the Spirit of God a knowledge of His Word is of no avail. The theory of truth, unaccompanied by the Holy Spirit, cannot quicken the soul or sanctify the heart. . . . Without the enlightenment of the Spirit, men will not be able to distinguish truth from error, and they will fall under the masterful temptations of Satan. . . .

The grace of God has been freely offered to every soul. . . . But character is not transferable. No man can believe for another. . . . No man can impart to another the character which is the fruit of the Spirit's working. . . .

We cannot be ready to meet the Lord by waking when the cry is heard, "Behold, the Bridegroom!" and then gathering up our empty lamps to have them replenished. . . . In the parable the wise virgins had oil in their vessels with their lamps. Their light burned with undimmed flame through the night of watching. . . . So the followers of Christ are to shed light into the darkness of the world. Through the Holy Spirit, God's word is a light as it becomes a transforming power in the life of the receiver. By implanting in their hearts the principles of His word, the Holy Spirit develops in men the attributes of God. The light of His glory—His character—is to shine forth in His followers.[69]

Ask God to give you much of the oil of His grace.[70]

The Sin God Cannot Forgive

Wherefore I say unto you, All manner of sin and blasphemy shall be forgiven unto men: but the blasphemy against the Holy Ghost shall not be forgiven unto men. Matt. 12:31.

Whatever the sin, if the soul repents and believes, the guilt is washed away in the blood of Christ; but he who rejects the work of the Holy Spirit is placing himself where repentance and faith cannot come to him. It is by the Spirit that God works upon the heart; when men willfully reject the Spirit, and declare it to be from Satan, they cut off the channel by which God can communicate with them. When the Spirit is finally rejected, there is no more that God can do for the soul. . . .

It is not God that blinds the eyes of men or hardens their hearts. He sends them light to correct their errors, and to lead them in safe paths; it is by the rejection of this light that the eyes are blinded and the heart hardened. Often the process is gradual, and almost imperceptible. Light comes to the soul through God's word, through His servants, or by the direct agency of His Spirit; but when one ray of light is disregarded, there is a partial benumbing of the spiritual perceptions, and the second revealing of light is less clearly discerned. So the darkness increases, until it is night in the soul. . . .

It is not necessary for us deliberately to choose the service of the kingdom of darkness in order to come under its dominion. We have only to neglect to ally ourselves with the kingdom of light. . . . The most common manifestation of the sin against the Holy Spirit is in persistently slighting Heaven's invitation to repent. Every step in the rejection of Christ is a step toward the rejection of salvation, and toward the sin against the Holy Spirit.[71]

When the soul surrenders itself to Christ, a new power takes possession of the new heart. A change is wrought which man can never accomplish for himself. It is a supernatural work, bringing a supernatural element into human nature. The soul that is yielded to Christ becomes His own fortress, which He holds in a revolted world, and He intends that no authority shall be known in it but His own. A soul thus kept in possession by the heavenly agencies is impregnable to the assaults of Satan.[72]

Grieved by Our Doubts

*And grieve not the holy Spirit of God,
whereby ye are sealed unto the day of redemption. Eph. 4:30.*

When we seem to doubt God's love and distrust His promises we dishonor Him and grieve His Holy Spirit. . . . How can our heavenly Father regard us when we distrust His love, which has led Him to give His only-begotten Son that we might have life? The apostle writes, "He that spared not his own Son, but delivered him up for us all, how shall he not with him also freely give us all things" (Rom. 8:32)? And yet how many, by their actions, if not in word, are saying, "The Lord does not mean this for me. Perhaps He loves others, but He does not love me."[73]

Faith takes God at His word, not asking to understand the meaning of the trying experiences that come. But there are many who have little faith. . . . And the difficulties they encounter, instead of driving them to God, separate them from Him, by arousing unrest and repining. Do they well to be thus unbelieving? Jesus is their friend. All heaven is interested in their welfare, and their fear and repining grieve the Holy Spirit. Not because we see or feel that God hears us are we to believe. We are to trust His promises. . . . When we have asked for His blessing, we should believe that we receive it, and thank Him that we have it. Then we are to go about our duties, assured that the blessing will be sent when we need it most.[74]

It is a serious thing to grieve the Holy Spirit; and it is grieved when the human agent seeks to work himself, and refuses to enter the service of the Lord because the cross is too heavy, or the self-denial too great. The Holy Spirit seeks to abide in each soul. If it is welcomed as an honored guest, those who receive it will be made complete in Christ.[75]

Are we striving with all our power to attain to the stature of men and women in Christ? Are we seeking for His fullness, ever pressing toward the mark set before us—the perfection of His character? When the Lord's people reach this mark, they will be sealed in their foreheads. Filled with the Spirit, they will be complete in Christ, and the recording angel will declare, "It is finished."[76]

For Those Who Seek

I am the Lord your God; ye shall therefore sanctify yourselves, and ye shall be holy; for I am holy. Lev. 11:44.

It is the glory of God to give His virtue to His children. He desires to see men and women reaching the highest standard; and when by faith they lay hold of the power of Christ, when they plead His unfailing promises, and claim them as their own, when with an importunity that will not be denied they seek for the power of the Holy Spirit, they will be made complete in Him. . . .

Before the believer is held out the wonderful possibility of being like Christ, obedient to all the principles of the law. But of himself man is utterly unable to reach this condition. The holiness that God's Word declares he must have before he can be saved is the result of the working of divine grace as he bows in submission to the discipline and restraining influences of the Spirit of truth. Man's obedience can be made perfect only by the incense of Christ's righteousness, which fills with divine fragrance every act of obedience. The part of the Christian is to persevere in overcoming every fault. Constantly he is to pray to the Saviour to heal the disorders of his sin-sick soul. He has not the wisdom or the strength to overcome; these belong to the Lord, and He bestows them on those who in humiliation and contrition seek Him for help.[77]

The Holy Spirit will be given to those who seek for its power and grace and will help our infirmities when we would have an audience with God. Heaven is open to our petitions, and we are invited to come "boldly unto the throne of grace, that we may obtain mercy, and find grace to help in time of need" (Heb. 4:16). We are to come in faith, believing that we shall obtain the very things we ask of Him.[78]

If you have a sense of need in your soul, if you hunger and thirst after righteousness, this is an evidence that Christ has wrought upon your heart, in order that He may be sought unto to do for you, through the endowment of the Holy Spirit, those things which it is impossible for you to do for yourself.[79]

If we will empty the soul of self, He will supply all our necessities.[80]

Pentecostal Power

And with great power gave the apostles witness of the resurrection of the Lord Jesus: and great grace was upon them all. Acts 4:33.

What was the result of the outpouring of the Spirit on the Day of Pentecost? The glad tidings of a risen Saviour were carried to the uttermost parts of the inhabited world. As the disciples proclaimed the message of redeeming grace, hearts yielded to the power of this message. The Church beheld converts flocking to her from all directions. Backsliders were reconverted. Sinners united with believers in seeking the pearl of great price. Some who had been the bitterest opponents of the gospel became its champions. . . . Every Christian saw in his brother a revelation of divine love and benevolence. One interest prevailed; one subject of emulation swallowed up all others. The ambition of the believers was to reveal the likeness of Christ's character, and to labor for the enlargement of His kingdom.

"With great power gave the apostles witness. . . ." Under their labors were added to the church chosen men, who, receiving the word of truth, consecrated their lives to the work of giving to others the hope that filled their hearts with peace and joy. They could not be restrained or intimidated by threatenings. The Lord spoke through them, and as they went from place to place, the poor had the gospel preached to them, and miracles of divine grace were wrought. So mightily can God work when men give themselves up to the control of His Spirit.[81]

To us today, as verily as to the first disciples, the promise of the Spirit belongs. God will today endow men and women with power from above, as He endowed those who on the Day of Pentecost heard the word of salvation. At this very hour His Spirit and His grace are for all who need them and will take Him at His word. . . .

Zeal for God moved the disciples to bear witness to the truth with mighty power. Should not this zeal fire our hearts with a determination to tell the story of redeeming love, of Christ and Him crucified? Is not the Spirit of God to come today, in answer to earnest, persevering prayer, and fill men with power for service?[82]

Ask for It

If ye then, being evil, know how to give good gifts unto your children: how much more shall your heavenly Father give the Holy Spirit to them that ask him? Luke 11:13.

Our Lord is rich in grace, mighty in power; He will abundantly bestow these gifts upon all who come to Him in faith. . . . We should pray as earnestly for the descent of the Holy Spirit as the disciples prayed on the day of Pentecost. If they needed it at that time, we need it more today. Moral darkness, like a funeral pall, covers the earth. All manner of false doctrines, heresies, and satanic deceptions are misleading the minds of men. Without the Spirit and power of God it will be in vain that we labor to present the truth.[83]

By the grace of Christ the apostles were made what they were. It was sincere devotion and humble, earnest prayer that brought them into close communion with Him. They sat together with Him in heavenly places. They realized the greatness of their debt to Him. By earnest, persevering prayer they obtained the endowment of the Holy Spirit, and then they went forth, weighted with the burden of saving souls. . . . Shall we be less earnest than were the apostles?[84]

Since this is the means by which we are to receive power, why do we not hunger and thirst for the gift of the Spirit? Why do we not talk of it, pray for it, and preach concerning it? . . . For the daily baptism of the Spirit, every worker should offer his petition to God. Companies of Christian workers should gather to ask for special help for heavenly wisdom, that they may know how to plan and execute wisely.[85]

Day after day is passing into eternity, bringing us nearer to the close of probation. As never before we must pray for the Holy Spirit to be more abundantly bestowed upon us, and we must look for its sanctifying influence to come upon the workers. . . .

Those who are under the influence of the Spirit of God will not be fanatical, but calm and steadfast, free from extravagance in thought, word, or deed. Amid the confusion of delusive doctrines, the Spirit of God will be a guide and a shield to those who have not resisted the evidences of truth, silencing every other voice but that which comes from Him who is the truth.[86]

The Latter Rain

*Ask ye of the Lord rain in the time of the latter rain;
so the Lord shall make bright clouds, and give them showers of rain,
to every one grass in the field. Zech. 10:1.*

Under the figure of the early and the latter rain, that falls in Eastern lands at seedtime and harvest, the Hebrew prophets foretold the bestowal of spiritual grace in extraordinary measure upon God's church. The outpouring of the Spirit in the days of the apostles was the beginning of the early, or former rain, and glorious was the result. . . . But near the close of earth's harvest, a special bestowal of spiritual grace is promised to prepare the church for the coming of the Son of man. This outpouring of the Spirit is likened to the falling of the latter rain; and it is for this added power that Christians are to send their petitions to the Lord of the harvest "in the time of the latter rain."[87]

As Christ was glorified on the day of Pentecost so will He again be glorified in the closing work of the gospel, when He shall prepare a people to stand the final test, in the closing conflict of the great controversy.[88]

Many . . . will be seen hurrying hither and thither, constrained by the Spirit of God to bring the light to others. The truth, the Word of God, is as a fire in their bones, filling them with a burning desire to enlighten those who sit in darkness. Many, even among the uneducated, now proclaim the words of the Lord. Children are impelled by the Spirit to go forth and declare the message from heaven. The Spirit is poured out upon all who will yield to its promptings, and . . . they will declare the truth with the might of the Spirit's power.[89]

But unless the members of God's church today have a living connection with the Source of all spiritual growth, they will not be ready for the time of reaping. Unless they keep their lamps trimmed and burning, they will fail of receiving added grace in times of special need.[90]

Divine grace is needed at the beginning, divine grace at every step of advance, and divine grace alone can complete the work. There is no place for us to rest in a careless attitude. . . . By prayer and faith we are continually to seek more of the Spirit.[91]

A Miracle

God also bearing them witness, both with signs and wonders, and with divers miracles, and gifts of the Holy Ghost. Heb. 2:4.

Christ wrought no miracle at the demand of the Pharisees. He wrought no miracle in the wilderness in answer to Satan's insinuations. He does not impart to us power to vindicate ourselves or to satisfy the demands of unbelief and pride. But the gospel is not without a sign of its divine origin. Is it not a miracle that we can break from the bondage of Satan? Enmity against Satan is not natural to the human heart; it is implanted by the grace of God. When one who has been controlled by a stubborn, wayward will is set free, and yields himself wholeheartedly to the drawing of God's heavenly agencies, a miracle is wrought; so also when a man who has been under strong delusion comes to understand moral truth. Every time a soul is converted, and learns to love God and keep His commandments, the promise of God is fulfilled, "A new heart also will I give you, and a new spirit will I put within you" (Eze. 36:26). The change in human hearts, the transformation of human characters, is a miracle that reveals an ever-living Saviour, working to rescue souls. A consistent life in Christ is a great miracle. In the preaching of the Word of God, the sign that should be manifest now and always is the presence of the Holy Spirit, to make the Word a regenerating power to those that hear. This is God's witness before the world to the divine mission of His Son.[1]

Many are utterly discouraged. . . . They are looked upon as unable to comprehend or to receive the gospel of Christ. Yet by the miracle of divine grace they may be changed. Under the ministration of the Holy Spirit the stupidity that makes their uplifting appear so hopeless will pass away. . . . Vice will disappear, and ignorance will be overcome.[2]

The chain that has been let down from the throne of God is long enough to reach to the lowest depths. Christ is able to lift the most sinful out of the pit of degradation, and to place them where they will be acknowledged as children of God, heirs with Christ to an immortal inheritance.[3]

Amazing Transformations

For we are made a spectacle unto the world, and to angels, and to men. 1 Cor. 4:9.

The Lord Jesus is making experiments on human hearts through the exhibition of His mercy and abundant grace. He is effecting transformations so amazing that Satan, with all his triumphant boasting, with all his confederacy of evil united against God and the laws of His government, stands viewing them as a fortress impregnable to his sophistries and delusions. They are to him an incomprehensible mystery. The angels of God, seraphim and cherubim, the powers commissioned to cooperate with human agencies, look on with astonishment and joy, that fallen men, once children of wrath, are through the training of Christ developing characters after the divine similitude, to be sons and daughters of God, to act an important part in the occupations and pleasure of heaven.

To His church, Christ has given ample facilities, that He may receive a large revenue of glory from His redeemed, purchased possession. The church, being endowed with the righteousness of Christ, is His depository, in which the wealth of His mercy, His love, His grace, is to appear in full and final display. The declaration in His intercessory prayer, that the Father's love is as great toward us as toward Himself, the only-begotten Son, and that we shall be with Him where He is, forever one with Christ and the Father, is a marvel to the heavenly host, and it is their great joy. The gift of His Holy Spirit, rich, full, and abundant, is to be to His church as an encompassing wall of fire, which the powers of hell shall not prevail against. In their untainted purity and spotless perfection, Christ looks upon His people as the reward of all His suffering, His humiliation, and His love, and the supplement of His glory—Christ, the great center from which radiates all glory.[4]

All heaven is watching those agencies that are as the hand to work out the purpose of God in the earth, thus doing the will of God in heaven. Such co-operation accomplishes a work that brings honor and glory and majesty to God. Oh, if all would love as Christ has loved, that perishing men might be saved from ruin, what a change would come to our world![5]

Heart Renewal

And be renewed in the spirit of your mind; and that ye put on the new man, which after God is created in righteousness and true holiness.
Eph. 4:23, 24.

Christ was a faithful reprover. . . . To all things untrue and base His very presence was a rebuke. In the light of His purity, men saw themselves unclean, their life's aims mean and false. Yet He drew them. He who had created man, understood the value of humanity. . . .

In every human being He discerned infinite possibilities. He saw men as they might be, transfigured by His grace—in "the beauty of the Lord our God" (Ps. 90:17).[6]

All defects of character originate in the heart. Pride, vanity, evil temper, and covetousness proceed from the carnal heart unrenewed by the grace of Christ.[7]

It is by the renewing of the heart that the grace of God works to transform the life. No mere external change is sufficient to bring us into harmony with God. There are many who try to reform by correcting this bad habit or that bad habit and they hope in this way to become Christians, but they are beginning in the wrong place. Our first work is with the heart. . . .

The Scriptures are the great agency in this transformation of character. Christ prayed, "Sanctify them through thy truth: Thy Word is truth" (John 17:17). If studied and obeyed, the Word of God works in the heart, subduing every unholy attribute. The Holy Spirit comes to convict of sin, and the faith that springs up in the heart works by love to Christ, conforming us, body, soul, and spirit, to His will. . . .

Let us not spare ourselves, but carry forward in earnest the work of reform that must be done in our lives. Let us crucify self. Unholy habits will clamor for the mastery, but in the name and through the power of Jesus we may conquer. To him who daily seeks to keep his heart with all diligence, the promise is given, "Neither death, nor life, nor angels, nor principalities, nor powers, nor things present, nor things to come, nor height, nor depth, nor any other creature, shall be able to separate us from the love of God, which is in Christ Jesus our Lord" (Rom. 8:38, 39).[8]

It Takes Time

I the Lord do keep it; I will water it every moment: lest any hurt it, I will keep it night and day. Isa. 27:3.

The mind of a man or a woman does not come down in a moment from purity and holiness to depravity, corruption, and crime. It takes time to transform the human to the divine, or to degrade those formed in the image of God to the brutal or the satanic. By beholding we become changed. Though formed in the image of his Maker, man can so educate his mind that sin which he once loathed will become pleasant to him. As he ceases to watch and pray, he ceases to guard the citadel, the heart. . . . Constant war against the carnal mind must be maintained; and we must be aided by the refining influence of the grace of God, which will attract the mind upward and habituate it to meditate upon pure and holy things.[9]

Character does not come by chance. It is not determined by one outburst of temper, one step in the wrong direction. It is the repetition of the act that causes it to become habit, and molds the character either for good or for evil. Right characters can be formed only by persevering, untiring effort, by improving every entrusted talent and capability to the glory of God.[10]

God expects us to build characters in accordance with the pattern set before us. We are to lay brick by brick, adding grace to grace, finding our weak points and correcting them in accordance with the directions given.[11]

God gives us strength, reasoning power, time, in order that we may build characters on which He can place His stamp of approval. He desires each child of His to build a noble character, by the doing of pure, noble deeds, that in the end he may present a symmetrical structure, a fair temple, honored by man and God. . . .

He who would grow into a beautiful building for the Lord must cultivate every power of the being. It is only by the right use of the talents that the character can be developed harmoniously. Thus we bring to the foundation that which is represented in the Word as gold, silver, precious stones—material that will stand the test of God's purifying fires.[12]

Determination the Key

For I am determined not to know any thing among you, save Jesus Christ, and him crucified. 1 Cor. 2:2.

Many are attracted by the beauty of Christ and the glory of heaven, who yet shrink from the conditions by which alone these can become their own. . . . To renounce their own will, their chosen objects of affection or pursuit, requires a sacrifice at which they hesitate and falter and turn back. . . . They desire the good, they make some effort to obtain it; but they do not choose it; they have not a settled purpose to secure it at the cost of all things.

The only hope for us if we would overcome is to unite our will to God's will, and work in cooperation with Him, hour by hour and day by day. We cannot retain self and yet enter the kingdom of God. If we ever attain unto holiness, it will be through the renunciation of self and the reception of the mind of Christ. Pride and self-sufficiency must be crucified. Are we willing to pay the price required of us? Are we willing to have our will brought into perfect conformity to the will of God? Until we are willing the transforming grace of God cannot be manifest upon us.[13]

By becoming thoroughly acquainted with ourselves, and then combining with the grace of God a firm determination on our part, we may be conquerors, and become perfect in all things, wanting in nothing.[14]

Opposing circumstances should create a firm determination to overcome them. The breaking down of one barrier will give greater ability and courage to go forward. Press with determination in the right direction, and circumstances will be your helpers, not your hindrances.[15]

True Christian character is marked by a singleness of purpose, an indomitable determination, which refuses to yield to worldly influences, which will aim at nothing short of the Bible standard. . . . The consecration of Christ's follower must be complete. . . . He must be willing to bear patiently, cheerfully, joyfully, whatever in God's providence he may be called to suffer. His final reward will be to share with Christ the throne of immortal glory.[16]

Felt in the Home

Believe on the Lord Jesus Christ, and thou shalt be saved, and thy house. Acts 16:31.

Missionary work is to be done in the home. Here those who have received Christ are to show what grace has done for them. A divine influence controls the true believer in Christ, and this influence makes itself felt throughout the home and is favorable for the perfection of the characters of all in the home. . . .

The church needs all the cultivated spiritual force which can be obtained, that all, and especially the younger members of the Lord's family, may be carefully guarded. The truth lived at home makes itself felt in disinterested labor abroad. He who lives Christianity in the home will be a bright and shining light everywhere.[17]

God wants the children and youth to join the Lord's army. . . . They must be trained to resist temptation and to fight the good fight of faith. Direct their minds to Jesus as soon as they can comprehend your lessons in simple words, easy to be understood. Teach them self-control. Teach them to begin the work of overcoming when young, and they will receive the precious help that Jesus can and will give, connected with prayerful efforts of parents. Cheer them with encouraging words for the battles they fight in resisting temptation and coming off conquerors through grace given them of Jesus Christ.[18]

The harmony of the domestic circle is often broken by a hasty word and abusive language. How much better were it left unsaid. One smile of pleasure, one peaceful, approving word spoken in the spirit of meekness, would be a power to soothe, to comfort, and to bless. . . . Many excuse their hasty words and passionate tempers by saying: "I am sensitive; I have a hasty temper." This will never heal the wounds made by hasty, passionate words. . . . The natural man must die, and the new man, Christ Jesus, take possession of the soul. . . . You may show by your life what the power and grace of God can do in transforming the natural man into a spiritual man in Christ Jesus.[19]

That the World May Know

Ye are my witnesses, saith the Lord, that I am God. Isa. 43:12.

A living Christian will have a living testimony to bear. If you have been following Jesus step by step, you will have something right to the point to relate of the way He has led you. You can tell how you tested His promise, and found the promise true. You can point to the living spots in your experience, without going back for years into the past. Would that we could oftener hear the simple, earnest testimony of heart conflicts and victories. . . .

Every true Christian will have a battle to fight to practice the principles of truth as well as to assent to them. . . . The Captain of our salvation calls for witnesses fresh from the field of action. Those who have been fiercely assaulted by the enemies of truth and the adversary of souls, and who have conducted themselves as did Jesus in His hour of trial, will have a testimony to bear which will thrill the hearts of the hearers. They will indeed be witnesses for Jesus.[20]

We do not always realize the power of example. We are brought in contact with others. We meet persons who are erring, who do wrong in various ways; they may be disagreeable, quick, passionate, dictatorial. While dealing with these we must be patient, forbearing, kind, and gentle. . . . There are trials and perplexities for us all to encounter; for we are in a world of cares, anxieties, and disappointments. But these continual annoyances must be met in the spirit of Christ. Through grace we may rise superior to our surroundings, and keep our spirits calm and unruffled amid the frets and worries of everyday life. We shall thus represent Christ to the world.[21]

Christ sought to save the world, not by conformity to it, but by revealing to the world the transforming power of the grace of God to mold and fashion the human character after the likeness of the character of Christ.[22]

The grace of Christ is to work a wonderful transformation in the life and character of its receiver; and if we are truly the disciples of Christ, the world will see that divine power has done something for us; for while we are in the world, we shall not be of it.[23]

Sustaining the Spiritual Life

Jesus said unto them, I am the bread of life: he that cometh to me shall never hunger; and he that believeth on me shall never thirst. John 6:35.

God speaks to us in His Word. Here we have in clearer lines the revelation of His character, of His dealings with men, and the great work of redemption. Here is open before us the history of patriarchs and prophets and other holy men of old. They were men "subject to like passions as we are" (James 5:17). We see how they struggled through discouragements like our own, how they fell under temptation as we have done, and yet took heart again and conquered through the grace of God: and beholding, we are encouraged in our striving after righteousness. As we read of the precious experiences granted them, of the light and love and blessing it was theirs to enjoy, and of the work they wrought through the grace given them, the spirit that inspired them kindles a flame of holy emulation in our hearts and a desire to be like them in character—like them to walk with God.

Jesus said of the Old Testament Scriptures—and how much more it is true of the New—"They are they which testify of me" (John 5:39). . . . If you would become acquainted with the Saviour, study the Holy Scriptures. Fill the whole heart with the words of God. They are the living water, quenching your burning thirst. They are the living bread from heaven. . . . Our bodies are built up from what we eat and drink; and as in the natural economy, so in the spiritual economy: it is what we meditate upon that will give tone and strength to our spiritual nature.[24]

Spiritual life must be sustained by communion with Christ through His Word. The mind must dwell upon it, the heart must be filled with it. The Word of God laid up in the heart and sacredly cherished and obeyed, through the power of the grace of Christ can make man right, and keep him right.[25]

When His words of instruction have been received, and have taken possession of us, Jesus is to us an abiding presence, controlling our thoughts and ideas and actions. . . . Jesus Christ is everything to us—the first, the last, the best in everything.[26]

Reveals God's Character

The Lord, The Lord God, merciful and gracious, longsuffering, and abundant in goodness and truth. Ex. 34:6.

All the light of the past, all the light which shines in the present and reaches forth into the future, as revealed in the Word of God, is for every soul who will receive it. The glory of this light, which is the very glory of the character of Christ, is to be manifested in the individual Christian, in the family, in the church, in the ministry of the Word, and in every institution established by God's people. All these the Lord designs shall be symbols of what can be done for the world. They are to be types of the saving power of the truths of the gospel. . . .

By beholding the goodness, the mercy, the justice, and the love of God revealed in the church, the world is to have a representation of His character. . . .

In order to manifest the character of God . . . we must become personally acquainted with God. If we have fellowship with God, we are His ministers, though we may never preach to a congregation. We are workers together with God in presenting the perfection of His character in humanity.[27]

God has enjoined the duty upon His human agents to communicate the character of God, testifying to His grace, His wisdom, and His benevolence, by manifesting His refined, tender, merciful love. . . .

Our work is to restore the moral image of God in man through the abundant grace given us of God by Jesus Christ. . . . Oh, how much we need to know Jesus and our heavenly Father that we may represent Him in character![28]

The soul that is transformed by the grace of Christ will admire His divine character. . . . The less we see to esteem in ourselves, the more we shall see to esteem in the infinite purity and loveliness of our Saviour. A view of our sinfulness drives us to Him who can pardon; and when the soul, realizing its helplessness, reaches out after Christ, He will reveal Himself in power. The more our sense of need drives us to Him and to the Word of God, the more exalted views we shall have of His character, and the more fully we shall reflect His image.[29]

Perfection Now?

Be ye therefore perfect, even as your Father which is in heaven is perfect. Matt. 5:48.

When God gave His Son to the world, He made it possible for men and women to be perfect by the use of every capability of their beings to the glory of God. In Christ He gave to them the riches of His grace, and a knowledge of His will. As they would empty themselves of self, and learn to walk in humility, leaning on God for guidance, men would be enabled to fulfill God's high purpose for them.[30]

Perfection of character is based upon that which Christ is to us. If we have constant dependence on the merits of our Saviour, and walk in His footsteps, we shall be like Him, pure and undefiled.

Our Saviour does not require impossibilities of any soul. He expects nothing of His disciples that He is not willing to give them grace and strength to perform. He would not call upon them to be perfect if He had not at His command every perfection of grace to bestow on the ones upon whom He would confer so high and holy a privilege. . . .

Our work is to strive to attain in our sphere of action the perfection that Christ in His life on the earth attained in every phase of character. He is our example. In all things we are to strive to honor God in character. . . . We are to be wholly dependent on the power that He has promised to give us.[31]

Jesus revealed no qualities, and exercised no powers, that men may not have through faith in Him. His perfect humanity is that which all His followers may possess, if they will be in subjection to God as He was.[32]

Our Saviour is a Saviour for the perfection of the whole man. He is not the God of part of the being only. The grace of Christ works to the disciplining of the whole human fabric. He made all. He has redeemed all. He has made the mind, the strength, the body as well as the soul, partaker of the divine nature, and all is His purchased possession. He must be served with the whole mind, heart, soul, and strength. Then the Lord will be glorified in His saints in even the common, temporal things with which they are connected. "Holiness unto the Lord" will be in the inscription placed upon them.[33]

Ever-widening Influence

In all things shewing thyself a pattern of good works; in doctrine shewing uncorruptness, gravity, sincerity, sound speech, that cannot be condemned. Titus 2:7, 8.

The life of Christ was an ever-widening, shoreless influence, an influence that bound Him to God and to the whole human family. Through Christ, God has invested man with an influence that makes it impossible for him to live to himself. Individually we are connected with our fellow men, a part of God's great whole, and we stand under mutual obligations. No man can be independent of his fellow men; for the well-being of each affects others. It is God's purpose that each shall feel himself necessary to others' welfare, and seek to promote their happiness. . . .

By the atmosphere surrounding us, every person with whom we come in contact is consciously or unconsciously affected. . . .

Our words, our acts, our dress, our deportment, even the expression of the countenance, has an influence. . . . If by our example we aid others in the development of good principles, we give them power to do good. In their turn they exert the same influence upon others, and they upon still others. Thus by our unconscious influence thousands may be blessed. . . .

Character is power. The silent witness of a true, unselfish, godly life carries an almost irresistible influence. By revealing in our own life the character of Christ we co-operate with Him in the work of saving souls. It is only by revealing in our life His character that we can co-operate with Him. And the wider the sphere of our influence, the more good we may do. When those who profess to serve God follow Christ's example, practicing the principles of the law in their daily life; when every act bears witness that they love God supremely and their neighbor as themselves, then will the church have power to move the world.

But never should it be forgotten that influence is no less a power for evil. To lose one's own soul is a terrible thing; but to cause the loss of other souls is still more terrible. . . . It is only through the grace of God that we can make a right use of this endowment.[34]

Hearts Made Pure

And every man that hath this hope in him purifieth himself, even as he is pure. 1 John 3:3.

Here is a work for man to do. He must face the mirror, God's law, discern the defects in his moral character, and put away his sins, washing his robe of character in the blood of the Lamb. Envy, pride, malice, deceit, strife, and crime will be cleansed from the heart that is a recipient of the love of Christ and that cherishes the hope of being made like Him when we shall see Him as He is. The religion of Christ refines and dignifies its possessor, whatever his associations or station in life may be. Men who become enlightened Christians rise above the level of their former character into greater mental and moral strength. Those fallen and degraded by sin and crime may, through the merits of the Saviour, be exalted to a position but little lower than that of the angels.

But the influence of a gospel hope will not lead the sinner to look upon the salvation of Christ as a matter of free grace, while he continues to live in transgression of the law of God. When the light of truth dawns upon his mind and he fully understands the requirements of God and realizes the extent of his transgressions, he will reform his ways, become loyal to God through the strength obtained from his Saviour, and lead a new and purer life.[35]

We have a work to do to fashion the character after the divine Model. All wrong habits must be given up. The impure must become pure in heart; the selfish man must put away his selfishness; the proud man must get rid of his pride; the self-sufficient man must overcome his self-confidence, and realize that he is nothing without Christ. . . . We must have a living connection with God.[36]

A stubborn and rebellious heart can close its doors to all the sweet influences of the grace of God and all the joy in the Holy Ghost; but the ways of wisdom are ways of pleasantness, and all her paths are peace. The more closely we are connected with Christ, the more will our words and actions show the subduing, transforming power of His grace.[37]

Changed by Beholding

We all, with open face beholding as in a glass the glory of the Lord, are changed into the same image from glory to glory even as by the Spirit of the Lord. 2 Cor. 3:18.

The work of transformation from unholiness is a continuous one. Day by day God labors for man's sanctification, and man is to co-operate with Him, putting forth persevering efforts in the cultivation of right habits. He is to add grace to grace; and as he thus works on the plan of addition, God works for him on the plan of multiplication. Our Saviour is always ready to hear and answer the prayer of the contrite heart, and grace and peace are multiplied to His faithful ones. Gladly He grants them the blessings they need in their struggle against the evils that beset them.[38]

John and Judas are representatives of those who profess to be Christ's followers. Both these disciples had the same opportunities to study and follow the divine Pattern. Both were closely associated with Jesus and were privileged to listen to His teaching. Each possessed serious defects of character; and each had access to the divine grace that transforms character. But while one in humility was learning of Jesus, the other revealed that he was not a doer of the Word, but a hearer only. One, daily dying to self and overcoming sin, was sanctified through the truth; the other, resisting the transforming power of grace and indulging selfish desires, was brought into bondage to Satan.

Such transformation of character as is seen in the life of John is ever the result of communion with Christ. There may be marked defects in the character of an individual, yet when he becomes a true disciple of Christ, the power of divine grace transforms and sanctifies him. Beholding as in a glass the glory of the Lord, he is changed from glory to glory, until he is like Him whom he adores. . . .

God can be honored by those who profess to believe in Him, only as they are conformed to His image and controlled by His Spirit. Then, as witnesses for the Saviour, they may make known what divine grace has done for them.[39]

For the Most Hopeless

Finally, be ye all of one mind, having compassion one of another, love as brethren, be pitiful, be courteous. 1 Peter 3:8.

Christ came to bring salvation within the reach of all. Upon the cross of Calvary He paid the infinite redemption price for a lost world. . . . His mission was to sinners, sinners of every grade, of every tongue and nation. . . . The most erring, the most sinful, were not passed by; His labors were especially for those who most needed the salvation He came to bring. The greater their need of reform, the deeper was His interest, the greater His sympathy, and the more earnest His labors. His great heart of love was stirred to its depths for the ones whose condition was most hopeless and who most needed His transforming grace. . . .

We should cultivate the spirit with which Christ labored to save the erring. They are as dear to Him as we are. They are equally capable of being trophies of His grace and heirs of the kingdom. But they are exposed to the snares of a wily foe, exposed to danger and defilement, and without the saving grace of Christ, to certain ruin. Did we view the matter in the right light, how would our zeal be quickened and our earnest, self-sacrificing efforts be multiplied, that we might come close to those who need our help, our prayers, our sympathy, and our love! . . . If our hearts are softened and subdued by the grace of Christ, and glowing with a sense of God's goodness and love, there will be a natural outflow of love, sympathy, and tenderness to others.[40]

Come close to the great heart of pitying love, and let the current of that divine compassion flow into your heart and from you to the hearts of others. Let the tenderness and mercy that Jesus has revealed in His own precious life be an example to us of the manner in which we should treat our fellow beings, especially those who are our brethren in Christ. . . . Never, never become heartless, cold, unsympathetic, and censorious. Never lose an opportunity to say a word to encourage and inspire hope. We cannot tell how far-reaching may be our tender words of kindness, our Christlike efforts to lighten some burden. The erring can be restored in no other way than in the spirit of meekness, gentleness, and tender love.[41]

Partakers of Christ's Nature

Whereby are given unto us exceeding great and precious promises: that by these ye might be partakers of the divine nature, having escaped the corruption that is in the world through lust. 2 Peter 1:4.

What beauty of character shone forth in the daily life of Christ! He is to be our pattern. There is a great work to be done in fashioning the character after the divine similitude. The grace of Christ must mold the entire being, and its triumph will not be complete until the heavenly universe shall witness habitual tenderness of feeling, Christlike love, and holy deeds in the deportment of the children of God.[42]

Each person must obtain an experience for himself. No one can depend for salvation on the experience or practice of any other man. We must each become acquainted with Christ in order properly to represent Him to the world. "His divine power hath given unto us all things that pertain unto life and godliness, through the knowledge of him that hath called us to glory and virtue" (2 Peter 1:3). None of us need excuse our hasty temper, our misshapen characters, our selfishness, envy, jealousy, or any impurity of soul, body, or spirit. . . .

We must learn of Christ. We must know what He is to those He has ransomed. We must realize that through belief in Him it is our privilege to be partakers of the divine nature, and so escape the corruption that is in the world through lust. Then we are cleansed from all sin, all defects of character. We need not retain one sinful propensity. . . .

As we partake of the divine nature, hereditary and cultivated tendencies to wrong are cut away from the character, and we are made a living power for good. Ever learning of the divine Teacher, daily partaking of His nature, we cooperate with God in overcoming Satan's temptations. God works, and man works, that man may be one with Christ as Christ is one with God. Then we sit together with Christ in heavenly places. The mind rests with peace and assurance in Jesus. . . . In Him there is inexhaustible fullness. . . .

God has given us every facility, every grace. He has provided the riches of heaven's treasure, and it is our privilege to draw continually from this capital.[43]

Fashions the Character

As obedient children, not fashioning yourselves according to the former lusts in your ignorance: but as he which hath called you is holy, so be ye holy. 1 Peter 1:14, 15.

The transforming power of Christ's grace molds the one who gives himself to God's service. Imbued with the Spirit of the Redeemer, he is ready to deny self, ready to take up the cross, ready to make any sacrifice for the Master. No longer can he be indifferent to the souls perishing around him. He is lifted above self-serving. He has been created anew in Christ, and self-serving has no place in his life. He realizes that every part of his being belongs to Christ, who has redeemed him from the slavery of sin; that every moment of his future has been bought with the precious lifeblood of God's only-begotten Son.[44]

Christ is our pattern, and those who follow Christ will not walk in darkness, for they will not seek their own pleasure. To glorify God will be the continual aim of their life. Christ represented the character of God to the world. The Lord Jesus so conducted His life that men were compelled to acknowledge that He had done all things well. The world's Redeemer was the light of the world, for His character was without fault. Though He was the only begotten Son of God, and the heir of all things in heaven and earth, He did not leave an example of indolence and self-indulgence. . . .

Christ never flattered any one. He never deceived or defrauded, never changed His course of straightforward uprightness to obtain favor or applause. He ever expressed the truth. The law of kindness was in His lips, and there was no guile in His mouth. Let the human agent compare his life with the life of Christ, and through the grace which Jesus imparts to those who make Him their personal Saviour, reach the standard of righteousness. . . . Those who follow Christ will be continually looking into the perfect law of liberty, and through the grace given them by Christ, will fashion the character according to the divine requirements.[45]

Revealed by Love

A new commandment I give unto you, That ye love one another; as I have loved you, that ye also love one another. By this shall all men know that ye are my disciples, if ye have love one to another. John 13:34, 35.

The golden chain of love, binding the hearts of the believers in unity, in bonds of fellowship and love, and in oneness with Christ and the Father, makes the connection perfect, and bears to the world a testimony of the power of Christianity that cannot be controverted. . . .

Satan understands the power of such a testimony as a witness to the world of what grace can do in transforming character. . . . He will work every conceivable device to break this golden chain which links heart to heart of those who believe the truth and binds them up in close connection with the Father and the Son.[46]

Those who have never experienced the tender, winning love of Christ cannot lead others to the fountain of life. His love in the heart is a constraining power, which leads men to reveal Him in the conversation, in the tender, pitiful spirit, in the uplifting of the lives of those with whom they associate. . . .

In the heart renewed by divine grace, love is the ruling principle of action. It modifies the character, governs the impulses, controls the passions, and ennobles the affections. This love, cherished in the soul, sweetens the life, and sheds a refining influence on all around.[47]

He who loves God supremely and his neighbor as himself will work with the constant realization that he is a spectacle to the world, to angels, and to men. Making God's will his will, he will reveal in his life the transforming power of the grace of Christ. In all the circumstances of life, he will take Christ's example as his guide.

Every true, self-sacrificing worker for God is willing to spend and be spent for the sake of others. . . . By earnest, thoughtful efforts to help where help is needed, the true Christian shows his love for God and for his fellow beings. He may lose his life in service. But when Christ comes to gather His jewels to Himself, he will find it again.[48]

A Life-giving Atmosphere

Now thanks be unto God, which always causeth us to triumph in Christ, and maketh manifest the savour of his knowledge by us in every place. For we are unto God a sweet savour of Christ, in them that are saved, and in them that perish. 2 Cor. 2:14, 15.

In the matchless gift of His Son, God has encircled the whole world with an atmosphere of grace as real as the air which circulates around the globe. All who choose to breathe this life-giving atmosphere will live, and grow up to the stature of men and women in Christ Jesus.[49]

Not all the beauty of art can bear comparison with the beauty of temper and character to be revealed in those who are Christ's representatives. It is the atmosphere of grace which surrounds the soul of the believer, the Holy Spirit working upon mind and heart, that makes him a savor of life unto life, and enables God to bless his work.[50]

Transformation of character is to be the testimony to the world of the indwelling love of Christ. The Lord expects His people to show that the redeeming power of grace can work upon the faulty character and cause it to develop in symmetry and abundant fruitfulness. . . .

When the grace of God reigns within, the soul will be surrounded with an atmosphere of faith and courage and Christlike love, an atmosphere invigorating to the spiritual life of all who inhale it. . . . Those who are humble in heart the Lord will use to reach souls whom the ordained ministers cannot approach. They will be moved to speak words which reveal the saving grace of Christ.

And in blessing others they will themselves be blessed. God gives us the opportunity to impart grace, that He may refill us with increased grace. Hope and faith will strengthen as the agent for God works with the talents and facilities that God has provided. He will have a divine agency to work with him.[51]

A holy influence is to go forth to the world from those who are sanctified through the truth. The earth is to be encircled with an atmosphere of grace. The Holy Spirit is to work on human hearts, taking the things of God and showing them to men.[52]

Awaiting Our Demand

Ask, and ye shall receive, that your joy may be full. John 16:24.

Prayer is heaven's ordained means of success in the conflict with sin and the development of Christian character. The divine influences that come in answer to the prayer of faith will accomplish in the soul of the suppliant all for which he pleads. For the pardon of sin, for the Holy Spirit, for a Christlike temper, for wisdom and strength to do His work, for any gift He has promised, we may ask; and the promise is, "Ye shall receive."[53]

Jesus is our helper; in Him and through Him we must conquer. . . . The grace of Christ is waiting your demand upon it. He will give you grace and strength as you need it if you ask Him. . . . The religion of Christ will bind and restrain every unholy passion, will stimulate to energy, to self-discipline, and industry, even in the matters of homely, everyday life, leading us to learn economy, tact, and self-denial, and to endure even privation without a murmur. The Spirit of Christ in the heart will be revealed in the character, will develop noble qualities and powers. "My grace is sufficient" (2 Cor. 12:9) says Christ.[54]

Make every effort to keep open the communion between Jesus and your own soul. . . . We should pray in the family circle, and above all we must not neglect secret prayer; for this is the life of the soul. It is impossible for the soul to flourish while prayer is neglected. Family or public prayer alone is not sufficient. In solitude let the soul be laid open to the inspecting eye of God. Secret prayer is to be heard only by the prayer-hearing God. No curious ear is to receive the burden of such petitions. In secret prayer the soul is free from surrounding influences, free from excitement. . . . By calm, simple faith, the soul holds communion with God, and gathers to itself rays of divine light to strengthen and sustain it in the conflict with Satan. . . .

Pray in your closet, and as you go about your daily labor, let your heart be often uplifted to God. It was thus that Enoch walked with God. These silent prayers rise like precious incense before the throne of grace. Satan cannot overcome him whose heart is thus stayed upon God.[55]

Disciplines and Refines

Behold, happy is the man whom God correcteth: therefore despise not thou the chastening of the Almighty. Job 5:17.

Trials and obstacles are the Lord's chosen methods of discipline and His appointed conditions of success. . . . He sees that some have powers and susceptibilities which, rightly directed, might be used in the advancement of His work. In His providence He brings these persons into different positions and varied circumstances that they may discover in their character the defects which have been concealed from their own knowledge. He gives them opportunity to correct these defects and to fit themselves for His service. . . .

The fact that we are called upon to endure trial shows that the Lord Jesus sees in us something precious which He desires to develop. If He saw in us nothing whereby He might glorify His name, He would not spend time in refining us. He does not cast worthless stones into His furnace. It is valuable ore that He refines. The blacksmith puts the iron and steel into the fire that he may know what manner of metal they are. The Lord allows His chosen ones to be placed in the furnace of affliction to prove what temper they are of and whether they can be fashioned for His work.[56]

It may seem that we are to study our own hearts, and square our own actions by some standard of our own; but this is not the case. This would but work deform instead of reform. The work must begin in the heart, and then the spirit, the words, the expression of the countenance, and the actions of the life, will make manifest that a change has taken place. In knowing Christ through the grace that He has shed forth abundantly, we become changed. . . . In humility we shall correct every fault and defect of character; because Christ is abiding in the heart, we shall be fitted up for the heavenly family above.[57]

The Christian is not to retain his sinful habits and cherish his defects of character. . . . Whatever may be the nature of your defects, the Spirit of the Lord will enable you to discern them, and grace will be given you whereby they may be overcome.[58]

Ever Upward

As ye have therefore received Christ Jesus the Lord, so walk ye in him. Col. 2:6.

This means that you are to study the life of Christ. You are to study it with as much more earnestness than you study secular lines of knowledge, as eternal interests are more important than temporal, earthly pursuits. If you appreciate the value and sacredness of eternal things, you will bring your sharpest thoughts, your best energies, to the solving of the problem that involves your eternal well-being; for every other interest sinks into nothingness in comparison with that.

You have the Pattern, Christ Jesus; walk in His footsteps.[59]

"*Add* to your faith virtue" (2 Peter 1:5). There is no promise given to the one who is retrograding. The apostle, in his testimony, is aiming to excite the believers to advancement in grace and holiness. They already profess to be living the truth, they have a knowledge of the precious faith, they have been made partakers of the divine nature. But if they stop here they will lose the grace they have received. . . .

Truth is an active, working principle, molding heart and life so that there is a constant upward movement. . . . In every step of climbing, the will is obtaining a new spring of action. The moral tone is becoming more like the mind and character of Christ. The progressive Christian has grace and love which passes knowledge, for divine insight into the character of Christ takes a deep hold upon his affections. The glory of the Lord revealed above the ladder can only be appreciated by the progressive climber, who is ever attracted higher, to nobler aims which Christ reveals.[60]

The steps upward to heaven must be taken one at a time; every advance step strengthens us for the next. The transforming power of the grace of God upon the human heart is a work which but few comprehend because they are too indolent to make the necessary effort. . . .

It is beyond the power of man to conceive the high and noble attainments that are within his reach if he will combine human effort with the grace of God, who is the Source of all wisdom and power. And there is an eternal weight of glory beyond.[61]

Grace Sufficient

And he said unto me, My grace is sufficient for thee:
for my strength is made perfect in weakness. 2 Cor. 12:9.

When thou wast little in thine own sight, wast thou not made the head of the tribes of Israel" (1 Sam. 15:17)? Here Samuel points out the reason for Saul's appointment to the throne of Israel. He had a humble opinion of his own capabilities, and was willing to be instructed. When the divine choice fell upon him, he was deficient in knowledge and experience, and had, with many good qualities, serious defects of character. . . . But if he would remain humble, seeking constantly to be guided by divine wisdom, . . . he would be enabled to discharge the duties of his high position with success and honor. Under the influence of divine grace, every good quality would be gaining strength, while evil traits would as steadily lose their power.

This is the work which the Lord proposes to do for all who consecrate themselves to Him. . . . To all who will receive instruction He will impart grace and wisdom. . . . He will reveal to them their defects of character, and bestow upon all who seek His aid, strength to correct their errors. Whatever may be man's besetting sin, whatever bitter or baleful passions struggle for the mastery, he may conquer, if he will watch and war against them in the name and strength of Israel's Helper. The children of God should cultivate a keen sensitiveness to sin. . . . It is one of Satan's most successful devices, to lead men to the commission of little sins, to blind the mind to the danger of little indulgences, little digressions from the plainly stated requirements of God. Many who would shrink with horror from some great transgression, are led to look upon sin in little matters as of trifling consequence. But these little sins eat out the life of godliness in the soul. The feet which enter upon a path diverging from the right way are tending toward the broad road that ends in death.[62]

Whatever the position in which God has placed us, whatever our responsibilities or our dangers, we should remember that He has pledged Himself to impart needed grace to the earnest seeker. Those who feel insufficient for their position and yet accept it because God bids them, relying upon His power and wisdom, will go on from strength to strength.[63]

While Probation Lasts

He that is unjust, let him be unjust still: and he which is filthy, let him be filthy still: and he that is righteous, let him be righteous still: and he that is holy, let him be holy still. Rev. 22:11.

All the good that man enjoys comes because of the mercy of God. He is the great and bountiful Giver. His love is manifest to all in the abundant provision made for man. He has given us probationary time in which to form characters for the courts above.[64]

We believe without a doubt that Christ is soon coming. This is not a fable to us; it is a reality. . . . When He comes He is not to cleanse us of our sins, to remove from us the defects in our characters, or to cure us of the infirmities of our tempers and dispositions. If wrought for us at all, this work will all be accomplished before that time. When the Lord comes, those who are holy will be holy still. Those who have reserved their bodies and spirits in holiness, in sanctification and honor, will then receive the finishing touch of immortality. But those who are unjust, unsanctified, and filthy will remain so forever. No work will then be done for them to remove their defects and give them holy characters. The Refiner does not then sit to pursue His refining process and remove their sins and their corruption. This is all to be done in these hours of probation. It is now that this work is to be accomplished for us.[65]

During probationary time the grace of God is offered to every soul. But if men waste their opportunities in self-pleasing, they cut themselves off from everlasting life. No after-probation will be granted them. By their own choice they have fixed an impassable gulf between them and their God.[66]

Many are deceiving themselves by thinking that the character will be transformed at the coming of Christ, but there will be no conversion of heart at His appearing. Our defects of character must here be repented of, and through the grace of Christ we must overcome them while probation shall last. This is the place for fitting up for the family above.[67]

Probation is almost ended. . . . Get ready! get ready! Work while the day lasts, for the night cometh when no man can work.[68]

The Reward

Behold, I come quickly; and my reward is with me, to give every man according as his work shall be. Rev. 22:12.

In His divine arrangement, through His unmerited favor, the Lord has ordained that good works shall be rewarded. We are accepted through Christ's merit alone; and the acts of mercy, the deeds of charity, which we perform, are the fruits of faith; and they become a blessing to us; for men are to be rewarded according to their works. It is the fragrance of the merit of Christ that makes our good works acceptable to God, and it is grace that enables us to do the works for which He rewards us. Our works in and of themselves have no merit. . . . We deserve no thanks from God. We have only done what it was our duty to do, and our works could not have been performed in the strength of our own sinful natures.[69]

We need . . . to bring the light and grace of Christ into all our works. We need to take hold of Christ and to retain our hold of Him until we know that the power of His transforming grace is manifested in us. We must have faith in Christ if we would reflect the divine character. . . . Faith in the Word of God and in the power of Christ to transform the life will enable the believer to work His works.[70]

To His servants Christ commits "His goods"—something to be put to use for Him. He gives "to every man his work." . . . Not more surely is the place prepared for us in the heavenly mansions than is the special place designated on earth where we are to work for God. . . .

Christ has paid us our wages, even His own blood and suffering, to secure our willing service. He came to our world to give us an example of how we should work, and what spirit we should bring into our labor. He desires us to study how we can best advance His work and glorify His name in the world.[71]

The sanctification of the soul by the working of the Holy Spirit is the implanting of Christ's nature in humanity. Gospel religion is Christ in the life—a living, active principle. It is the grace of Christ revealed in character and wrought out in good works.[72]

For the Whole Man

The very God of peace sanctify you wholly; and I pray God your whole spirit and soul and body be preserved blameless unto the coming of our Lord Jesus Christ. 1 Thess. 5:23.

The sanctification set forth in the Scriptures embraces the entire being—spirit, soul, and body. . . . Christians are bidden to present their bodies, "a living sacrifice, holy, acceptable unto God" (Rom. 12:1). In order to do this, all their powers must be preserved in the best possible condition. Every practice that weakens physical or mental strength unfits man for the service of his Creator. . . . Said Christ: "Thou shalt love the Lord thy God with all thy heart" (Matt. 22:37). Those who do love God with all the heart will desire to give Him the best service of their life, and they will be constantly seeking to bring every power of their being into harmony with the laws that will promote their ability to do His will. They will not, by the indulgence of appetite or passion, enfeeble or defile the offering which they present to their heavenly Father.[73]

God would have us realize that He has a right to mind, soul, body, and spirit—to all that we possess. We are His by creation and by redemption. As our Creator, He claims our entire service. As our Redeemer, He has a claim of love as well as of right—of love without a parallel. . . . Our bodies, our souls, our lives, are His, not only because they are His free gift, but because He constantly supplies us with His benefits, and gives us strength to use our faculties. . . .

Shall we not, then, give to Christ that which He has died to redeem? If you will do this, He will quicken your conscience, renew your heart, sanctify your affections, purify your thoughts, and set all your powers at work for Him. Every motive, and every thought will be brought into captivity to Jesus Christ.

Those who are sons of God will represent Christ in character. Their works will be perfumed by the infinite tenderness, compassion, love, and purity of the Son of God. And the more completely mind and body are yielded to the Holy Spirit, the greater will be the fragrance of our offering to Him.[74]

In God's Image

And have put on the new man, which is renewed in knowledge after the image of him that created him. Col. 3:10.

When Adam came from the Creator's hand, he bore, in his physical, mental, and spiritual nature, a likeness to his Maker. . . .

Through sin the divine likeness was marred, and well-nigh obliterated. Man's physical powers were weakened, his mental capacity was lessened, his spiritual vision dimmed. He had become subject to death. Yet the race was not left without hope. By infinite love and mercy the plan of salvation had been devised, and a life of probation was granted. To restore in man the image of his Maker, to bring him back to the perfection in which he was created, to promote the development of body, mind, and soul, that the divine purpose in his creation might be realized—this was to be the great work of redemption.[75]

Though the moral image of God was almost obliterated by the sin of Adam, through the merits and power of Jesus it may be renewed. Man may stand with the moral image of God in his character; for Jesus will give it to him.[76]

It was a wonderful thing for God to create man, to make mind. The glory of God is to be revealed in the creation of man in God's image and in his redemption. One soul is of more value than a world. . . . The Lord Jesus Christ is the author of our being, and He is also the author of our redemption, and everyone who will enter the kingdom of God will develop a character that is the counterpart of the character of God.[77]

The Lord, by close and pointed truths for these last days, is cleaving out a people from the world and purifying them unto Himself. Pride and unhealthful fashions, the love of display, the love of approbation—all must be left with the world if we would be renewed in knowledge after the image of Him who created us.[78]

By the transforming agency of His grace, the image of God is reproduced in the disciple; he becomes a new creature.[79]

It is the Holy Spirit, the Comforter, which Jesus said He would send into the world, that changes our character into the image of Christ; and when this is accomplished, we reflect, as in a mirror, the glory of the Lord.[80]

Representatives of Christ

Ye are my witnesses, saith the Lord,
and my servant whom I have chosen. Isa. 43:10.

The life that Christ lived in this world, men and women can live through His power and under His instruction. In their conflict with Satan they may have all the help that He had. . . .

The lives of professing Christians who do not live the Christ life are a mockery to religion. Every one whose name is registered on the church roll is under obligation to represent Christ by revealing the inward adorning of a meek and quiet spirit. They are to be His witnesses, making known the advantages of walking and working as Christ has given them example. The truth for this time is to appear in its power in the lives of those who believe it, and is to be imparted to the world. Believers are to represent in their lives, its power to sanctify and ennoble. . . . They are to show forth the power of the grace that Christ died to give men. . . . They are to be men of faith, men of courage, whole-souled men, who, without questioning, trust in God and His promises. . . .

There must be no pretense in the lives of those who have so sacred and solemn a message as we have been called to bear. The world is watching Seventh-day Adventists because it knows something of their profession of faith and of their high standard, and when it sees those who do not live up to their profession, it points at them with scorn.

Those who love Jesus will bring all in their lives into harmony with His will. . . . Through the grace of God they are enabled to keep their purity of principle unsullied. Holy angels are close beside them, and Christ is revealed in their steadfast adherence to the truth. They are Christ's minutemen, bearing, as true witnesses, a decided testimony in favor of the truth. They show that there is a spiritual power that can enable men and women not to swerve an inch from truth and justice for all the gifts that men can bestow. Such ones, wherever they may be, will be honored of heaven because they have conformed their lives to the will of God, caring not what sacrifices they are called upon to make.[81]

Every Day, Everywhere

In all thy ways acknowledge him. Prov. 3:6.

Bible religion is not a garment which can be put on and taken off at pleasure. It is an all-pervading influence, which leads us to be patient, self-denying followers of Christ, doing as He did, walking as He walked. . . .

If no one ever came under your notice who needed your sympathy, your words of compassion and pity, then you would be guiltless before God for failing to exercise these precious gifts; but every follower of Christ will find opportunity to show Christian kindness and love; and in so doing he will prove that he is a possessor of the religion of Jesus Christ.

This religion teaches us to exercise patience and longsuffering when brought into places where we receive treatment that is harsh and unjust. . . . "Not rendering evil for evil, or railing for railing: but contrariwise blessing; knowing that ye are thereunto called, that we should inherit a blessing" (1 Peter 3:9). . . . When Christ was reviled, He reviled not again. . . . His religion brings with it a meek and quiet spirit. . . .

There is constant need of patience, gentleness, self-denial, and self-sacrifice in the exercise of Bible religion. But if the word of God is made an abiding principle in our lives, everything with which we have to do, each word, each trivial act, will reveal that we are subject to Jesus Christ. . . . If the word of God is received into the heart, it will empty the soul of self-sufficiency and self-dependence. Our lives will be a power for good, because the Holy Spirit will fill our minds with the things of God. . . .

Of ourselves, we can neither obtain nor practice the religion of Christ; for our hearts are deceitful above all things; but Jesus . . . has shown us how we may be cleansed from sin. "My grace is sufficient for thee" (2 Cor. 12:9), He says. . . . Looking unto Jesus, the author and the finisher of our faith, we shall catch the light of His countenance, reflect His image, and grow up unto the full stature of men and women in Christ Jesus. Our religion will be attractive, because it will possess the fragrance of the righteousness of Christ. We shall be happy; for our spiritual meat and drink will be to us righteousness and peace and joy.[82]

A Work of Reformation

Prepare ye the way of the Lord, make his paths straight. Every valley shall be filled, and every mountain and hill shall be brought low; and the crooked shall be made straight, and the rough ways shall be made smooth. Luke 3:4, 5.

The work of reformation here brought to view by John, the purging of heart and mind and soul, is one that is needed by many who today profess to have the faith of Christ. Wrong practices that have been indulged in need to be put away; the crooked paths need to be made straight, and the rough places smooth. The mountains and hills of self-esteem and pride need to be brought low. There is need of bringing forth "fruits meet for repentance" (Matt. 3:8). When this work is done in the experience of God's believing people, "all flesh shall see the salvation of God" (Luke 3:6). . . .

The fact that our names are on the church books will not secure for us an entrance into the kingdom of heaven. God asks, Have you used your opportunities for service and for the development of Christian character? Have you traded faithfully with your Lord's goods? Knowing the will of God concerning you, how have you obeyed that will? Have you sought to benefit and bless those who needed help and encouragement? . . .

There is no human being in the world but bears fruit of some kind, either good or evil; and Christ has made it possible for every soul to bear most precious fruit. Obedience to the requirements of God, submission to the will of Christ, will yield in the life the peaceable fruits of righteousness. The inhabitants of this world are dear to God's family. . . . He gave the richest gift that heaven could bestow, that men and women might return from their rebellion to His law, and accept into their hearts and lives the principles of heaven. If men would acknowledge the Gift, and accept His sacrifice, their transgressions would be pardoned, and the grace of God would be imparted to them to help them to yield in their lives the precious fruits of holiness.

"Every good tree bringeth forth good fruit." We have a representation to make to the world of pure principles, holy ambitions, noble aspirations, that will distinguish us from all other people, making us a separate nation, a peculiar people.[83]

Preparing for Heaven

Whosoever shall confess me before men, him shall the son of man also confess before the angels of God. Luke 12:8.

The thought that God can take a poor, sinful, sorrowful human being, and so transform him by grace that he may become an heir of God and joint heir with Jesus, is almost too great for our comprehension. . . . Christ takes upon Him the sins of the transgressor, and imputes to him His righteousness, and by His transforming grace makes him capable of associating with angels and communing with God.[84]

The refining influence of the grace of God changes the natural disposition of man. Heaven would not be desirable to the carnal-minded; their natural, unsanctified hearts would feel no attraction toward that pure and holy place, and if it were possible for them to enter, they would find there nothing congenial. The propensities that control the natural heart must be subdued by the grace of Christ before fallen man is fitted to enter heaven and enjoy the society of the pure, holy angels. When man dies to sin and is quickened to new life in Christ, divine love fills his heart; his understanding is sanctified; he drinks from an inexhaustible fountain of joy and knowledge, and the light of an eternal day shines upon his path, for with him continually is the Light of life.[85]

God desires that heaven's plan shall be carried out, and heaven's divine order and harmony prevail, in every family, in every church, in every institution. Did this love leaven society, we should see the outworking of noble principles in Christian refinement and courtesy, and in Christian charity toward the purchase of the blood of Christ. Spiritual transformation would be seen in all our families, in our institutions, in our churches. When this transformation takes place, these agencies will become instrumentalities by which God will impart heaven's light to the world and thus, through divine discipline and training, fit men and women for the society of heaven.

Jesus has gone to prepare mansions for those who are preparing themselves through His love and grace, for the abodes of bliss.[86]

Longing for Heaven and Home

My soul longeth, yea, even fainteth for the courts of the Lord: my heart and my flesh crieth out for the living God. Ps. 84:2.

Oh that the great interests of the world to come were appreciated! Why is it that men are so unconcerned about the salvation of the soul when it was purchased at such cost by the Son of God?

The heart of man may be the abode of the Holy Spirit. The peace of Christ that passeth understanding may rest in your soul, and the transforming power of His grace may work in your life, and fit you for the courts of glory. But if brain and nerve and muscle are all employed in the service of self, you are not making God and heaven the first consideration of your life. . . .

If the eye is single, if it is directed heavenward, the light of heaven will fill the soul, and earthly things will appear insignificant and uninviting. The purpose of the heart will be changed, and the admonition of Jesus will be heeded. . . . Your thoughts will be fixed upon the great rewards of eternity. All your plans will be made in reference to the future, immortal life. . . . Bible religion will be woven into your daily life.[87]

Some who profess to have true religion sadly neglect the guide-book given by God to point the way to heaven. They may read the Bible, but merely reading God's Word, as one would read words traced by a human pen, will give only a superficial knowledge. . . .

If we do not receive the religion of Christ by feeding upon the word of God, we shall not be entitled to an entrance into the city of God. Having lived on earthly food, having educated our tastes to love worldly things, we would not be fitted for the heavenly courts; we could not appreciate the pure, heavenly current that circulates in heaven. The voices of the angels and the music of their harps would not satisfy us. The science of heaven would be as an enigma to our minds. We need to hunger and thirst for the righteousness of Christ; we need to be molded and fashioned by the transforming influence of His grace, that we may be fitted for the society of heavenly angels.[88]

In order to be at home in heaven, we must have heaven enshrined in our hearts here.[89]

Seen and Heard

And we have seen and do testify that the Father sent the Son to be the Saviour of the world. 1 John 4:14.

As a witness for Christ, John entered into no controversy, no wearisome contention. He declared what he knew, what he had seen and heard. He had been intimately associated with Christ, had listened to His teachings, had witnessed His mighty miracles. Few could see the beauties of Christ's character as John saw them. For him the darkness had passed away; on him the true light was shining. His testimony in regard to the Saviour's life and death was clear and forcible. Out of the abundance of a heart overflowing with love for the Saviour he spoke; and no power could stay his words.[1]

He could testify: "That which was from the beginning, which we have heard, which we have seen with our eyes, which we have looked upon, and our hands have handled, of the Word of life; (for the Life was manifested, and we have seen it, and bear witness, and show unto you that eternal life, which was with the Father, and was manifested unto us;) that which we have seen and heard declare we unto you, that ye also may have fellowship with us: and truly our fellowship is with the Father, and with his Son Jesus Christ" (1 John 1:1-3).

So everyone may be able, through his own experience, to "set his seal to this, that God is true" (John 3:33, ARV). He can bear witness to that which he himself has seen and heard and felt of the power of Christ. He can testify: "I needed help, and I found it in Jesus. Every want was supplied, the hunger of my soul was satisfied; the Bible is to me the revelation of Christ. I believe in Jesus because He is to me a divine Saviour. I believe the Bible because I have found it to be the voice of God to my soul."[2]

How shall we know for ourselves God's goodness and His love? The psalmist tells us—not, hear and know, read and know, or believe and know; but—"*Taste* and see that the Lord is good" (Ps. 34:8). Instead of relying upon the word of another, taste for yourself. Experience is knowledge derived from experiment. Experimental religion is what is needed now. "Taste and see that the Lord is good."[3]

Power to Obey

For it is God which worketh in you both to will and to do of his good pleasure. Phil. 2:13.

The grace of God in Christ is the foundation of the Christian's hope, and that grace will be manifested in obedience.[4]

Christ is the sympathetic, compassionate Redeemer. In His sustaining power, men and women become strong to resist evil. As the convicted sinner looks at sin, it becomes to him exceeding sinful. . . . He sees that his faults must be overcome and that his appetites and passions must be subjected to God's will. . . . Having repented of his transgression of God's law, he strives earnestly to overcome sin. He seeks to reveal the power of Christ's grace, and he is brought into personal touch with the Saviour. Constantly he keeps Christ before him. Praying, believing, receiving the blessings he needs, he comes nearer and nearer to God's standard for him.

New virtues are revealed in his character as he denies self and lifts the cross, following where Christ leads the way. He loves the Lord Jesus with his whole heart, and Christ becomes his wisdom, his righteousness, his sanctification, and his redemption. . . .

The miracle-working power of Christ's grace is revealed in the creation in man of a new heart, a higher life, a holier enthusiasm. God says: "A new heart also will I give you" (Eze. 36:26). Is not this, the renewal of man, the greatest miracle that can be performed? What cannot the human agent do who by faith takes hold of the divine power?[5]

Human effort avails nothing without divine power; and without human endeavor, divine effort is with many of no avail. To make God's grace our own, we must act our part. His grace is given to work in us to will and to do, but never as a substitute for our effort. . . . Those who walk in the path of obedience will encounter many hindrances. Strong, subtle influences may bind them to the world; but the Lord is able to render futile every agency that works for the defeat of His chosen ones; in His strength they may overcome every temptation, conquer every difficulty.[6]

Resists Satan

There hath no temptation taken you but such as is common to man: but God is faithful, who will not suffer you to be tempted above that ye are able; but will with the temptation also make a way to escape, that ye may be able to bear it. 1 Cor. 10:13.

Will man take hold of divine power, and with determination and perseverance resist Satan, as Christ has given him example in His conflict with the foe in the wilderness of temptation? God cannot save man against his will from the power of Satan's artifices. Man must work with his human power, aided by the divine power of Christ, to resist and to conquer at any cost to himself. In short, man must overcome as Christ overcame. And then, through the victory that it is his privilege to gain by the all-powerful name of Jesus, he may become an heir of God and joint heir with Jesus Christ. This could not be the case if Christ alone did all the overcoming. Man must do his part; he must be victor on his own account, through the strength and grace that Christ gives him. Man must be a co-worker with Christ in the labor of overcoming.[7]

The victims of evil habit must be aroused to the necessity of making an effort for themselves. Others may put forth the most earnest endeavor to uplift them, the grace of God may be freely offered, Christ may entreat, His angels may minister; but all will be in vain unless they themselves are roused to fight the battle in their own behalf. . . .

Those who put their trust in Christ are not to be enslaved by any hereditary or cultivated habit or tendency. Instead of being held in bondage to the lower nature, they are to rule every appetite and passion. God has not left us to battle with evil in our own finite strength. Whatever may be our inherited or cultivated tendencies to wrong, we can overcome through the power that He is ready to impart.[8]

The strongest temptation cannot excuse sin. However great the pressure brought to bear upon the soul, transgression is our own act. It is not in the power of earth or hell to compel anyone to do evil. Satan attacks us at our weak points, but we need not be overcome. However severe or unexpected the assault, God has provided help for us, and in His strength we may conquer.[9]

Makes Us Overcomers

These things I have spoken unto you, that in me ye might have peace. In the world ye shall have tribulation: but be of good cheer; I have overcome the world. John 16:33.

Christ did not fail, neither was He discouraged, and His followers are to manifest a faith of the same enduring nature. They are to live as He lived, and work as He worked, because they depend on Him as the great Master Worker.

Courage, energy, and perseverance they must possess. Though apparent impossibilities obstruct their way, by His grace they are to go forward. Instead of deploring difficulties, they are called upon to surmount them. They are to despair of nothing, and to hope for everything. With the golden chain of His matchless love, Christ has bound them to the throne of God. It is His purpose that the highest influence in the universe, emanating from the Source of all power, shall be theirs. They are to have power to resist evil, power that neither earth, nor death, nor hell can master, power that will enable them to overcome as Christ overcame.[10]

Inspiration faithfully records the faults of good men, those who were distinguished by the favor of God; indeed, their faults are more fully presented than their virtues. . . .

Men whom God favored, and to whom He entrusted great responsibilities, were sometimes overcome by temptation and committed sin, even as we at the present day strive, waver, and frequently fall into error. Their lives, with all their faults and follies, are open before us, both for our encouragement and warning. If they had been represented as without fault, we, with our sinful nature, might despair at our own mistakes and failures. But seeing where others struggled through discouragements like our own, where they fell under temptation as we have done, and yet took heart again and conquered through the grace of God, we are encouraged in our striving after righteousness. As they, though sometimes beaten back, recovered their ground, and were blessed of God, so we too may be overcomers in the strength of Jesus.[11]

The life of Christ's disciples is to be like His, a series of uninterrupted victories, not seen to be such here, but recognized as such in the great hereafter.[12]

Self-Mastery

He that is slow to anger is better than the mighty; and he that ruleth his spirit than he that taketh a city. Prov. 16:32.

The highest evidence of nobility in a Christian is self-control. He who can stand unmoved amid a storm of abuse is one of God's heroes. To rule the spirit is to keep self under discipline; to resist evil; to regulate every word and deed by God's great standard of righteousness. He who has learned to rule his spirit will rise above the slights, the rebuffs, the annoyances, to which we are daily exposed, and these will cease to cast a gloom over his spirit.

It is God's purpose that the kingly power of sanctified reason, controlled by divine grace, shall bear sway in the lives of human beings. He who rules his spirit is in possession of this power.[13]

The body is a most important medium through which the mind and the soul are developed for the upbuilding of character. Hence it is that the adversary of souls directs his temptations to the enfeebling and degrading of the physical powers. . . . The body is to be brought into subjection to the higher powers of the being. The passions are to be controlled by the will, which is itself to be under the control of God. . . . Intellectual power, physical stamina, and the length of life depend upon immutable laws. Through obedience to these laws, man may stand conqueror of himself, conqueror of his own inclinations, conqueror of principalities and powers of "the rulers of the darkness of this world," and of "spiritual wickedness in high places" (Eph. 6:12). . . .

The spirit that possessed Daniel, the youth of today may have; they may draw from the same source of strength, possess the same power of self-control, and reveal the same grace in their lives, even under circumstances as unfavorable. Though surrounded by temptations to self-indulgence, especially in our large cities, where every form of sensual gratification is made easy and inviting, yet by divine grace their purpose to honor God may remain firm. Through strong resolution and vigilant watchfulness they may withstand every temptation that assails the soul.[14]

Angel Reinforcements

Behold, I give unto you power to tread on serpents and scorpions, and over all the power of the enemy. Luke 10:19.

Fallen man is Satan's lawful captive. The mission of Christ was to rescue him from the power of his great adversary. Man is naturally inclined to follow Satan's suggestions, and he cannot successfully resist so terrible a foe unless Christ, the mighty Conqueror, dwells in him, guiding his desires, and giving him strength. God alone can limit the power of Satan. . . . Satan knows better than God's people the power that they can have over him when their strength is in Christ. When they humbly entreat the mighty Conqueror for help, the weakest believer in the truth, relying firmly upon Christ, can successfully repulse Satan and all his host. . . .

Satan will call to his aid legions of his angels to oppose the advance of even one soul, and, if possible, wrest it from the hand of Christ. . . . But if the one in danger perseveres, and in his helplessness casts himself upon the merits of the blood of Christ, our Saviour listens to the earnest prayer of faith, and sends a reinforcement of those angels that excel in strength to deliver him. Satan cannot endure to have his powerful rival appealed to, for he fears and trembles before His strength and majesty. At the sound of fervent prayer, Satan's whole host trembles.[15]

Nothing but Christ's loving compassion, His divine grace, His almighty power, can enable us to baffle the relentless foe, and subdue the opposition of our own hearts. What is our strength? The joy of the Lord. Let the love of Christ fill our hearts, and then we shall be prepared to receive the power that He has for us. . . .

Beholding Christ for the purpose of becoming like Him, the seeker after truth sees the perfection of the principles of God's law, and he becomes dissatisfied with everything but perfection. . . . A battle must be fought with the attributes that Satan has been strengthening for his own use. . . . But he knows that with the Redeemer there is saving power that will gain for him the victory in the conflict. The Saviour will strengthen and help him as he comes pleading for grace and efficiency.[16]

For Disciplining the Mind

In thine hand is power and might; and in thine hand it is to make great, and to give strength unto all. 1 Chron. 29:12.

The mind is so constituted that it must be occupied with either good or evil. If it takes a low level, it is generally because it is left to deal with commonplace subjects. . . . Man has the power to regulate and control the workings of the mind, and give direction to the current of his thoughts. But this requires greater effort than we can make in our own strength. We must stay our minds on God, if we would have right thoughts, and proper subjects for meditation.

Few realize that it is a duty to exercise control over their thoughts and imaginations. It is difficult to keep the undisciplined mind fixed upon profitable subjects. But if the thoughts are not properly employed, religion cannot flourish in the soul. The mind must be preoccupied with sacred and eternal things, or it will cherish trifling and superficial thoughts. Both the intellectual and the moral powers must be disciplined, and they will strengthen and improve by exercise.

To understand this matter aright, we must remember that our hearts are naturally depraved, and we are unable, of ourselves, to pursue a right course. It is only by the grace of God, combined with the most earnest efforts on our part, that we can gain the victory. . . .

The intellect, as well as the heart, must be consecrated to the service of God. He has claims upon all there is of us. . . .

Pleasure-seeking, frivolity, and mental and moral dissipation, are flooding the world with their demoralizing influence. Every Christian should labor to press back the tide of evil, and save our youth from the influences that would sweep them down to ruin. May God help us to press our way against the current![17]

Without the power of God's grace and Spirit we cannot reach the high standard He has placed before us. There is a divine excellence of character to which we are to attain, and in striving to meet the standard of heaven, divine incentives will urge us on, the mind will become balanced, and the restlessness of the soul will be banished in repose in Christ.[18]

Our Strength and Security

Be strong in the Lord, and in the power of his might. Eph. 6:10.

Many are spiritually weak because they look at themselves instead of at Christ. . . . Christ is the great storehouse from which on every occasion we may draw strength and happiness. Why, then, do we withdraw our eyes from His sufficiency to look on and bemoan our weakness? Why do we forget that He is ready to help us in every time of need? We dishonor Him by talking of our inefficiency. Instead of looking at ourselves, let us constantly behold Jesus, daily becoming more and more like Him, more and more able to talk of Him, better prepared to avail ourselves of His kindness and helpfulness, and to receive the blessings offered us. As we thus live in communion with Him, we grow strong in His strength, a help and a blessing to those around us.

Christ has made every provision for us to be strong. He has given us His Holy Spirit, whose office is to bring to our remembrance all the promises that Christ has made, that we may have peace and a sweet sense of forgiveness. If we will but keep our eyes fixed on the Saviour, and trust in His power, we shall be filled with a sense of security; for the righteousness of Christ will become our righteousness. . . .

When temptations assail you, as they surely will, when care and perplexity surround you, when, distressed and discouraged, you are almost ready to yield to despair, look, O look, to where with the eye of faith you last saw the light; and the darkness that encompasseth you will be dispelled by the bright shining of His glory. When sin struggles for the mastery in your soul, and burdens the conscience, when unbelief clouds the mind, go to the Saviour. His grace is sufficient to subdue sin. He will pardon us, making us joyful in God.[19]

God wants our minds to expand. He desires to put His grace upon us. . . . We are to be one with Christ as He is one with the Father, and the Father will love us as He loves His Son. We may have the same help that Christ had, we may have strength for every emergency; for God will be our front guard and our rearward. He will shut us in on every side.[20]

All-Sufficient

Thou therefore, my son, be strong in the grace that is in Christ Jesus. 2 Tim. 2:1.

The lessons contained in the words of Paul to Timothy are of the greatest importance to us today. He charges him to "be strong"—in his own wisdom?—No, but "in the grace that is in Christ Jesus." He who would be a follower of Christ is not to rely upon his own capabilities, or to feel confident in himself. Neither is he to be dwarfed in his religious efforts, to shun responsibilities, and remain inefficient in the cause of God. . . . If the Christian feels his weakness, his inability, by putting his trust in God, he will find the grace of Christ sufficient for every emergency.

The soldier of Christ must meet many forms of temptation, and resist and overcome them. The fiercer the conflict, the greater the supply of grace to meet the need of the soul. . . . The true Christian will understand what it means to pass through severe conflicts and trying experiences; but he will steadily increase in the grace of Christ to meet successfully the enemy of his soul. . . . The darkness will press upon his soul at times; but the true light will shine, the bright beams of the Sun of righteousness will dispel the gloom; and . . . through the grace of Christ he will be enabled to be a faithful witness of the things which he has heard from the inspired messenger of God. . . . By thus communicating truth to others, the worker for Christ obtains a clearer view of the abundant provisions made for all, of the sufficiency of the grace of Christ for every time of conflict, sorrow, and trial. Through the mysterious plan of redemption, grace has been provided, so that the imperfect work of the human agent may be accepted in the name of Jesus our Advocate.

Man has little power, and can accomplish but a small work at his very best. . . . God is omnipotent, and at every point where we need divine help and seek for it in sincerity, it will be given. God has pledged His word that His grace will be sufficient for you in your greatest necessity, in your sorest distress. Christ will be to you a present help if you will appropriate His grace.[21]

For Today's Need

As thy days, so shall thy strength be. Deut. 33:25.

The promise is not that we will have strength today for a future emergency, that anticipated future trouble will be provided for beforehand, before it comes to us. We may, if we walk by faith, expect strength and provision for us as fast as our circumstances demand it. We live by faith, not by sight. The Lord's arrangement is for us to ask Him for the very things that we need. The grace of tomorrow will not be given today. Men's necessity is God's opportunity. . . . The grace of God is never given to be squandered, to be misapplied or perverted, or to be left to rust with disuse. . . .

While you are bearing daily responsibilities in the love and fear of God, as obedient children walking in all humility of mind, strength and wisdom from God will be given to meet every trying circumstance. . . .

We are to keep close to the Source of our strength day by day, and when the enemy comes in like a flood the Spirit of the Lord lifts up a standard for us against the enemy. The promise of God is sure, that strength shall be proportioned to our day. We may be confident for the future only in the strength that is given for the present necessities. . . . Do not borrow anxiety for the future. It is today that we are in need.[22]

Many are weighed down by the anticipation of future troubles. They are constantly seeking to bring tomorrow's burdens into today. Thus a large share of all their trials are imaginary. For these, Jesus has made no provision. He promises grace only for the day. He bids us not to burden ourselves with the cares and troubles of tomorrow. . . .

The Lord requires us to perform the duties of today and to endure its trials. We are today to watch that we offend not in word or deed. We must today praise and honor God. By the exercise of living faith today we are to conquer the enemy. We must today seek God and be determined that we will not rest satisfied without His presence. We should watch and work and pray as though this were the last day that would be granted us. How intensely earnest, then, would be our life. How closely would we follow Jesus in all our words and deeds.[23]

Gives Limitless Strength

God is my strength and power:
and he maketh my way perfect. 2 Sam. 22:33.

We have little idea of the strength that would be ours if we would connect with the Source of all strength. We fall into sin again and again, and think it must always be so. We cling to our infirmities as if they were something to be proud of. Christ tells us that we must set our face as a flint if we would overcome. He has borne our sins in His own body on the tree; and through the power He has given us, we may resist the world, the flesh, and the devil. Then let us not talk of our weakness and inefficiency, but of Christ and His strength. When we talk of Satan's strength, the enemy fastens his power more firmly upon us. When we talk of the power of the Mighty One, the enemy is driven back. As we draw near to God, He draws near to us.[24]

The Word of the eternal God is our guide. Through this Word we have been made wise unto salvation. This Word is ever to be in our hearts and on our lips. "It is written" is to be our anchor. Those who make God's Word their counselor realize the weakness of the human heart and the power of the grace of God to subdue every unsanctified, unholy impulse. Their hearts are ever prayerful, and they have the guardianship of holy angels. When the enemy comes in like a flood, the Spirit of God lifts up for them a standard against him. There is harmony in the heart; for the precious, powerful influences of truth bear sway.[25]

We must be better acquainted with our Bibles. We might close the door to many temptations, if we would commit to memory passages of Scripture. Let us hedge up the way to Satan's temptations with "It is written." We shall meet with conflicts to test our faith and courage, but they will make us strong if we conquer through the grace Jesus is willing to give. But we must believe; we must grasp the promises without a doubt.[26]

Bid the tempted one look not to circumstances, to the weakness of self, or to the power of temptation, but to the power of God's Word. All its strength is ours.[27]

Produces Loving, Lovable Christians

Grace be with all them that love our Lord Jesus Christ in sincerity.
Eph. 6:24.

Many take it for granted that they are Christians, simply because they subscribe to certain theological tenets. But they have not brought the truth into practical life. They have not believed and loved it, therefore they have not received the power and grace that come through sanctification of the truth. Men may profess faith in the truth; but if it does not make them sincere, kind, patient, forbearing, heavenly-minded, it is a curse to its possessors, and through their influence it is a curse to the world.[28]

The world needs evidences of sincere Christianity. Professed Christianity may be seen everywhere; but when the power of God's grace is seen in our churches, the members will work the works of Christ. Natural and hereditary traits of character will be transformed. The indwelling of His Spirit will enable them to reveal Christ's likeness, and in proportion to the purity of their piety will be the success of their work.[29]

Let us honor our profession of faith. Let us adorn our lives with beautiful traits of character. Harshness of speech and action is not of Christ, but of Satan. Shall we, by clinging to our imperfections and deformities, make Christ ashamed of us? His grace is promised to us. If we will receive it, it will beautify our lives. . . . Deformity will be exchanged for goodness, perfection. Our lives will be adorned with the graces that made Christ's life so beautiful. . . .

A true, lovable Christian is the most powerful argument that can be advanced in favor of Bible truth. Such a man is Christ's representative. His life is the most convincing evidence that can be borne to the power of divine grace.[30]

Every day of life is freighted with responsibilities which we must bear. Every day, our words and acts are making impressions upon those with whom we associate. . . . The true follower of Christ strengthens the good purposes of all with whom he comes in contact. Before an unbelieving, sin-loving world he reveals the power of God's grace and the perfection of His character.[31]

Points Out the Way

That the Lord thy God may shew us the way wherein we may walk, and the thing that we may do. Jer. 42:3.

To dwell upon the beauty, goodness, mercy, and love of Jesus is strengthening to the mental and moral powers, and while the mind is kept trained to do the works of Christ, to be obedient children, you will habitually inquire, Is this the way of the Lord? Will Jesus be pleased to have me do this? . . .

Many need to make a decided change in the tenor of their thoughts and actions, if they would please Jesus. We can seldom see our sins in the grievous light that God can. Many have habituated themselves to pursue a course of sin, and their hearts harden, under the influence of the power of Satan. . . .

But when in the strength and grace of God they place their minds against the temptations of Satan, their minds are made clear, their hearts and consciences by being influenced by the Spirit of God are made sensitive, and then sin appears as it is—exceedingly sinful.[32]

Every act of obedience to Christ, every act of self-denial for His sake, every trial well endured, every victory gained over temptation, is a step in the march to the glory of final victory. If we take Christ for our guide, He will lead us safely. The veriest sinner need not miss his way. Not one trembling seeker need fail of walking in pure and holy light. Though the path is so narrow, so holy that sin cannot be tolerated therein, yet access has been secured for all, and not one doubting, trembling soul need say, "God cares nought for me." . . .

And all the way up the steep road leading to eternal life are wellsprings of joy to refresh the weary. Those who walk in wisdom's ways are, even in tribulation, exceeding joyful; for He whom their soul loveth, walks, invisible, beside them. At each upward step they discern more distinctly the touch of His hand; at every step brighter gleamings of glory from the Unseen fall upon their path; and their songs of praise, reaching ever a higher note, ascend to join the songs of angels before the throne. "The path of the righteous is as the light of dawn, that shineth more and more unto the perfect day" (Prov. 4:18, RV, margin).[33]

For Him Who Believes

Therefore it is of faith, that it might be by grace. Rom. 4:16.

Without the grace of Christ, the sinner is in a hopeless condition; nothing can be done for him; but through divine grace, supernatural power is imparted. . . . It is through the impartation of the grace of Christ that sin is discerned in its hateful nature, and finally driven from the soul temple. It is through grace that we are brought into fellowship with Christ, to be associated with Him in the work of salvation. Faith is the condition upon which God has seen fit to promise pardon to sinners; not that there is any virtue in faith whereby salvation is merited, but because faith can lay hold of the merits of Christ, the remedy provided for sin. . . .

"Abraham believed God, and it was counted unto him for righteousness. Now to him that worketh is the reward not reckoned of grace, but of debt. But to him that worketh not, but believeth on him that justifieth the ungodly, his faith is counted for righteousness" (Rom. 4:3-5). Righteousness is obedience to the law. The law demands righteousness, and this the sinner owes to the law; but he is incapable of rendering it. The only way in which he can attain to righteousness is through faith. By faith he can bring to God the merits of Christ, and the Lord places the obedience of His Son to the sinner's account. Christ's righteousness is accepted in place of man's failure, and God receives, pardons, justifies, the repentant, believing soul, treats him as though he were righteous, and loves him as He loves His Son. This is how faith is accounted righteousness; and the pardoned soul goes on from grace to grace, from light to a greater light.[34]

The touch of faith opens to us the divine treasure house of power and wisdom; and thus, through instruments of clay, God accomplishes the wonders of His grace. This living faith is our great need today. We must know that Jesus is indeed ours; that His Spirit is purifying and refining our hearts. If the followers of Christ had genuine faith, with meekness and love, what a work they might accomplish! What fruit would be seen to the glory of God![35]

Power in the Promises

That ye be not slothful, but followers of them who through faith and patience inherit the promises. Heb. 6:12.

We must keep close to the Word of God. We need its warnings and encouragement, its threatenings and promises.[36]

The Scriptures are to be received as God's word to us, not written merely, but spoken. When the afflicted ones came to Christ, He beheld not only those who asked for help, but all who throughout the ages should come to Him in like need and with like faith. When He said to the paralytic, "Son, be of good cheer; thy sins be forgiven thee" (Matt. 9:2) . . . , He spoke to other afflicted, sin-burdened ones who should seek His help. So with all the promises of God's word. In them He is speaking to us individually, speaking as directly as if we could listen to His voice. It is in these promises that Christ communicates to us His grace and power. They are leaves from that tree which is "for the healing of the nations" (Rev. 22:2). Received, assimilated, they are to be the strength of the character, the inspiration and sustenance of the life. Nothing else can have such healing power.[37]

God loves His creatures with a love that is both tender and strong. He has established the laws of nature, but His laws are not arbitrary exactions. Every "thou shalt not," whether in physical or moral law, contains or implies a promise. If it is obeyed, blessings will attend our steps; if it is disobeyed, the result is danger and unhappiness. The laws of God are designed to bring His people closer to Himself. He will save them from the evil and lead them to the good if they will be led, but force them He never will.[38]

We are too faithless. Oh, how I wish that I could lead our people to have faith in God! They need not feel that in order to exercise faith they must be wrought up into a high state of excitement. All they have to do is to believe God's Word, just as they believe one another's word. He hath said it, and He will perform His Word. Calmly rely on His promise, because He means all that He says. Say, He has spoken to me in His Word, and He will fulfill every promise that He has made. Do not become restless. Be trustful. God's Word is true. Act as if your heavenly Father could be trusted.[39]

Not in Worldly Pomp

That your faith should not stand in the wisdom of men, but in the power of God. 1 Cor. 2:5.

Jesus was to do His work, . . . not with pomp and outward display, but through speaking to the hearts of men by a life of mercy and self-sacrifice. . . .

The followers of Christ are to be the light of the world; but God does not bid them make an effort to shine. He does not approve of any self-satisfied endeavor to display superior goodness. He desires that their souls shall be imbued with the principles of heaven; then, as they come in contact with the world, they will reveal the light that is in them. Their steadfast fidelity in every act of life will be a means of illumination. . . .

Worldly display, however imposing, is of no value in God's sight. Above the seen and temporal, He values the unseen and eternal. The former is of worth only as it expresses the latter. The choicest productions of art possess no beauty that can compare with the beauty of character which is the fruit of the Holy Spirit's working in the soul. . . .

Human effort will be efficient in the work of God just according to the consecrated devotion of the worker—by revealing the power of the grace of Christ to transform the life. We are to be distinguished from the world because God has placed His seal upon us, because He manifests in us His own character of love. Our Redeemer covers us with His righteousness.

In choosing men and women for His service, God does not ask whether they possess worldly wealth, learning, or eloquence. He asks, "Do they walk in such humility that I can teach them My way? Can I put My words into their lips? Will they represent Me?" God can use every person just in proportion as He can put His Spirit into the soul temple. The work that He will accept is the work that reflects His image. His followers are to bear, as their credentials to the world, the ineffaceable characteristics of His immortal principles.[40]

Jesus knew the worthlessness of earthly pomp, and He gave no attention to its display. In His dignity of soul, His elevation of character, His nobility of principle, He was far above the vain fashions of the world.[41]

Multiplied Blessings

Grace and peace be multiplied unto you through the knowledge of God, and of Jesus our Lord, according as his divine power hath given unto us all things that pertain unto life and godliness, through the knowledge of him that hath called us to glory and virtue. 2 Peter 1:2, 3.

In the first chapter of the second epistle of Peter you will find the promise that grace and peace will be multiplied unto you, if you will "add to your faith virtue; and to virtue knowledge; and to knowledge temperance; and to temperance patience; and to patience godliness; and to godliness brotherly kindness; and to brotherly kindness charity" (2 Peter 1:5-7). These virtues are wonderful treasures. . . .

Shall we not strive to use to the very best of our ability the little time that is left in this life, adding grace to grace, power to power, making it manifest that we have a source of power in the heavens above? Christ says: "All power is given unto me in heaven and in earth" (Matt. 28:18). What is this power given to Him for? For us. He desires us to realize that He has returned to heaven as our Elder Brother and that the measureless power given Him has been placed at our disposal. . . .

We are to represent Christ in all that we say and do. We are to live His life. The principles by which He was guided are to shape our course of action toward those with whom we are associated. When we are securely anchored in Christ, we have a power that no human being can take from us.[42]

The unstudied, unconscious influence of a holy life is the most convincing sermon that can be given in favor of Christianity. Argument, even when unanswerable, may provoke only opposition; but a godly example has a power that it is impossible wholly to resist.[43]

Through His Son, God has revealed the excellency to which man is capable of attaining. And before the world God is developing us as living witnesses of what man may become through the grace of Christ. . . .

What an honor He confers upon us, in urging us to be holy in our sphere, as the Father is holy in His sphere. And through His power we are able to do this; for He declares, "*All* power is given unto me in heaven and in earth" (Matt. 28:18). This unlimited power it is your privilege and mine to claim.[44]

The Youth Need It

Thou art my hope, O Lord God:
thou art my trust from my youth. Ps. 71:5.

There are among us many young men and women who are not ignorant of our faith, yet whose hearts have never been touched by the power of divine grace. How can we who claim to be the servants of God pass on day after day, week after week, indifferent to their condition? If they should die in their sins, unwarned, their blood would be required at the hands of the watchmen who failed to give them warning.

Why should not labor for the youth in our borders be regarded as missionary work of the highest kind? It requires the most delicate tact, the most watchful consideration, the most earnest prayer for heavenly wisdom. The youth are the objects of Satan's special attacks; but kindness, courtesy, and the sympathy which flows from a heart filled with love to Jesus, will gain their confidence, and save them from many a snare of the enemy.

The youth need more than a casual notice, more than an occasional word of encouragement. They need painstaking, prayerful, careful labor. . . . Often those whom we pass by with indifference, because we judge them from outward appearance, have in them the best material for workers, and will repay all the efforts bestowed on them.[45]

Seventh-day Adventist parents should more fully realize their responsibilities as character builders. God places before them the privilege of strengthening His cause through the consecration and labors of their children. He desires to see gathered out from the homes of our people a large company of youth who, because of the godly influences of their homes, have surrendered their hearts to Him, and go forth to give Him the highest service of their lives. Directed and trained by the godly instruction of the home, the influence of the morning and evening worship, the consistent example of parents who love and fear God, they have learned to submit to God as their Teacher, and are prepared to render Him acceptable service as loyal sons and daughters. Such youth are prepared to represent to the world the power and grace of Christ.[46]

For the Humble

Humble yourselves therefore under the mighty hand of God, that he may exalt you in due time. 1 Peter 5:6.

To be clothed with humility does not mean that we are to be dwarfs in intellect, deficient in aspiration, and cowardly in our lives, shunning burdens lest we fail to carry them successfully. Real humility fulfills God's purposes by depending upon His strength.

God works by whom He will. He sometimes selects the humblest instrument to do the greatest work, for His power is revealed through the weakness of men. We have our standard, and by it we pronounce one thing great and another small; but God does not estimate according to our rule. We are not to suppose that what is great to us must be great to God, or that what is small to us must be small to Him.[47]

All boasting of merit in ourselves is out of place. . . . The reward is not of works, lest any man should boast; but it is all of grace. . . .

There is no religion in the enthronement of self. He who makes self-glorification his aim will find himself destitute of that grace which alone can make him efficient in Christ's service. Whenever pride and self-complacency are indulged the work is marred. . . .

The Christian who is such in his private life, in the daily surrender of self, in sincerity of purpose and purity of thought, in meekness under provocation, in faith and piety, in fidelity in that which is least, the one who in the home life represents the character of Christ—such a one may in the sight of God be more precious than even the world-renowned missionary or martyr. . . .

Not in our learning, not in our position, not in our numbers or entrusted talents, not in the will of man, is to be found the secret of success. Feeling our inefficiency we are to contemplate Christ, and through Him who is the strength of all strength, the thought of all thought, the willing and obedient will gain victory after victory. . . . Blessed will be the recompense of grace to those who have wrought for God in the simplicity of faith and love.[48]

That We May Excel

The righteous is more excellent than his neighbour: but the way of the wicked seduceth them. Prov. 12:26.

The Lord expects His servants to excel others in life and character. He has placed every facility at the command of those who serve Him. The Christian is looked upon by the whole universe as one who strives for the mastery, running the race set before him, that he may obtain the prize, even an immortal crown; but if he who professes to follow Christ does not make it manifest that his motives are above those of the world in this great contest where there is everything to win and everything to lose, he will never be a victor. He is to make use of every entrusted power, that he may overcome the world, the flesh, and the devil through the power of the Holy Spirit, by grace abundantly provided. . . .

Those who would be victors should contemplate and count the cost of salvation. Strong human passions must be subdued; the independent will must be brought into captivity to Christ. The Christian is to realize that he is not his own. He will have temptations to resist, and battles to fight against his own inclinations; for the Lord will accept no half-way service. Hypocrisy is an abomination to Him. The follower of Christ must walk by faith, as seeing Him who is invisible. Christ will be his dearest treasure, his all and in all.

This experience is essential to those who profess the name of Christ, for its influence pervades the conduct, and sanctifies the influence of the Christian's life in its effect upon others. The business connections and intercourse of Christians with men of the world will be sanctified by the grace of Christ; and wherever they are, a moral atmosphere will be created, that will have power for good; for it will breathe the spirit of the Master.

He who has the mind of Christ knows that his only safe course is to keep close to Jesus, following the light of life. He will not accept work, or engage himself in business, that will hinder him from reaching the perfection of Christian character. . . . "No man that warreth entangleth himself with the affairs of this life; that he may please him who hath chosen him to be a soldier" (2 Tim. 2:4).[49]

Source of Right Influence

Then shall thy light break forth as the morning, and thine health shall spring forth speedily: and thy righteousness shall go before thee; the glory of the Lord shall be thy rereward. Isa. 58:8.

The Lord has a special work to do for us individually. As we see the wickedness of the world brought to light in the courts of justice and published in the daily papers, let us draw near to God, and by living faith lay hold of His promises, that the grace of Christ may be manifest in us. We may have an influence, a powerful influence, in the world. . . . We are to have an eye single to the glory of God. We are to work with all the intelligence that God has given us, placing ourselves in the channel of light, that the grace of God can come upon us to mold and fashion us to the divine similitude. Heaven is waiting to bestow its richest blessings upon those who will consecrate themselves to do the work of God in these last days of the world's history.[50]

There is nothing in us of ourselves by which we can influence others for good. If we realize our helplessness and our need of divine power, we shall not trust to ourselves. We know not what results a day, an hour, or a moment may determine, and never should we begin the day without committing our ways to our heavenly Father. His angels are appointed to watch over us, and if we put ourselves under their guardianship, then in every time of danger they will be at our right hand. When unconsciously we are in danger of exerting a wrong influence, the angels will be by our side, prompting us to a better course, choosing our words for us, and influencing our actions. Thus our influence may be a silent, unconscious, but mighty power in drawing others to Christ and the heavenly world.[51]

Personal influence is a power. It is to work with the influence of Christ, to lift where Christ lifts, to impart correct principles, and to stay the progress of the world's corruption. It is to diffuse that grace which Christ alone can impart. It is to uplift, to sweeten the lives and characters of others by the power of a pure example united with earnest faith and love.[52]

For the Race of Life

Let us lay aside every weight, and the sin which doth so easily beset us, and let us run with patience the race that is set before us, looking unto Jesus the author and finisher of our faith. Heb. 12:1, 2.

Envy, malice, evil thinking, evilspeaking, covetousness—these are weights that the Christian must lay aside if he would run successfully the race for immortality. Every habit or practice that leads into sin and brings dishonor upon Christ, must be put away, whatever the sacrifice. The blessing of heaven cannot attend any man in violating the eternal principles of right. . . .

The competitors in the ancient games, after they had submitted to self-denial and rigid discipline, were not even then sure of the victory. . . . However eagerly and earnestly the runners might strive, the prize could be awarded to but one. One hand only could grasp the coveted garland. Some might put forth the utmost effort to obtain the prize, but as they reached forth the hand to secure it, another, an instant before them, might grasp the coveted treasure.

Such is not the case in the Christian warfare. Not one who complies with the conditions will be disappointed at the end of the race. Not one who is earnest and persevering will fail of success. The race is not to the swift, nor the battle to the strong. The weakest saint, as well as the strongest, may wear the crown of immortal glory. All may win who, through the power of divine grace, bring their lives into conformity to the will of Christ. . . . Every act casts its weight into the scale that determines life's victory or defeat. And the reward given to those who win will be in proportion to the energy and earnestness with which they have striven. . . .

Paul knew that his warfare against evil would not end so long as life should last. Ever he realized the need of putting a strict guard upon himself, that earthly desires might not overcome spiritual zeal. With all his power he continued to strive against natural inclinations. Ever he kept before him the ideal to be attained, and this ideal he strove to reach by willing obedience to the law of God. His words, his practices, his passions—all were brought under the control of the Spirit of God.[53]

"Tell of His Power"

They shall speak of the glory of thy kingdom, and talk of thy power. Ps. 145:11.

If Christians would associate together, speaking to each other of the love of God, and of the precious truths of redemption, their own hearts would be refreshed, and they would refresh one another. We may be daily learning more of our heavenly Father, gaining a fresh experience of His grace; then we shall desire to speak of His love; and as we do this, our own hearts will be warmed and encouraged. If we thought and talked more of Jesus, and less of self, we should have far more of His presence.

If we would but think of God as often as we have evidence of His care for us, we should keep Him ever in our thoughts, and should delight to talk of Him and to praise Him. We talk of temporal things because we have an interest in them. We talk of our friends because we love them; our joys and our sorrows are bound up with them. Yet we have infinitely greater reason to love God than to love our earthly friends; it should be the most natural thing in the world to make Him first in all our thoughts, to talk of His goodness and tell of His power.[54]

Those who study the Word of God and day by day receive instruction from Christ bear the stamp of heaven's principles. A high, holy influence goes forth from them. A helpful atmosphere surrounds their souls. The pure, holy, elevated principles that they follow enable them to bear a living testimony to the power of divine grace.[55]

Christ wants His followers to be like Him, because He desires to be correctly represented in the family circle, in the church, and in the world. . . . We are to accept Christ as our efficiency, our strength, that we may reveal His character to the world. This is the work resting upon us as Christians. We are to witness to the power of heavenly grace. . . .

God wants His sons and daughters to reveal before the synagogue of Satan, before the heavenly universe, before the world, the power of His grace, that men and angels may know that Christ has not died in vain. Let us show the world that we have power from on high.[56]

Power to Shake the World

By the word of truth, by the power of God, by the armour of righteousness on the right hand and on the left. 2 Cor. 6:7.

The commission that Christ gave to the disciples, they fulfilled. As these messengers of the cross went forth to proclaim the gospel, there was such a revelation of the glory of God as had never before been witnessed by mortal man. By the cooperation of the divine Spirit, the apostles did a work that shook the world. To every nation was the gospel carried in a single generation.

Glorious were the results that attended the ministry of the chosen apostles of Christ. At the beginning of their ministry some of them were unlearned men, but their consecration to the cause of their Master was unreserved, and under His instruction they gained a preparation for the great work committed to them. Grace and truth reigned in their hearts, inspiring their motives and controlling their actions. Their lives were hid with Christ in God, and self was lost sight of, submerged in the depths of infinite love. . . . Jesus Christ, the wisdom and power of God, was the theme of every discourse. . . . As they proclaimed the completeness of Christ, the risen Saviour, their words moved hearts, and men and women were won to the gospel. Multitudes who had reviled the Saviour's name and despised His power, now confessed themselves disciples of the Crucified.

Not in their own power did the apostles accomplish their mission, but in the power of the living God. . . . The consciousness of the responsibility resting on them purified and enriched their experience; and the grace of heaven was revealed in the conquests they achieved for Christ. With the might of omnipotence God worked through them to make the gospel triumphant.[57]

As Christ sent forth His disciples, so today He sends forth the members of His church. The same power that the apostles had is for them. If they will make God their strength, He will work with them, and they shall not labor in vain. Let them realize that the work in which they are engaged is one upon which the Lord has placed His signet. . . . He bids us go forth to speak the words He gives us, feeling His holy touch upon our lips.[58]

The Christian's Badge

Now unto him that is able to do exceeding abundantly above all that we ask or think, according to the power that worketh in us. Eph. 3:20.

The Lord is waiting to manifest through His people His grace and power. But He requires that those who engage in His service shall keep their minds ever directed to Him. Every day they should have time for reading the Word of God and for prayer. . . .

Individually we are to walk and talk with God; then the sacred influence of the gospel of Christ in all its preciousness will appear in our lives.[59]

There is an eloquence far more powerful than the eloquence of words in the quiet, consistent life of a pure, true Christian. What a man is has more influence than what he says.

The officers who were sent to Jesus came back with the report that never man spoke as He spoke. But the reason for this was that never man lived as He lived. Had His life been other than it was, He could not have spoken as He did. His words bore with them a convincing power, because they came from a heart pure and holy, full of love and sympathy, benevolence and truth.

It is our own character and experience that determine our influence upon others. In order to convince others of the power of Christ's grace, we must know its power in our own hearts and lives. The gospel we present for the saving of souls must be the gospel by which our own souls are saved. Only through a living faith in Christ as a personal Saviour is it possible to make our influence felt in a skeptical world. If we would draw sinners out of the swift-running current, our own feet must be firmly set upon the Rock, Christ Jesus.

The badge of Christianity is not an outward sign, not the wearing of a cross or a crown, but it is that which reveals the union of man with God. By the power of His grace manifested in the transformation of character the world is to be convinced that God has sent His Son as its Redeemer. No other influence that can surround the human soul has such power as the influence of an unselfish life. The strongest argument in favor of the gospel is a loving and lovable Christian.[60]

Irresistible

Oh how great is thy goodness, which thou hast laid up for them that fear thee; which thou hast wrought for them that trust in thee before the sons of men! Ps. 31:19.

The Lord calls upon us for confession of His goodness. . . . Our confession of His faithfulness is Heaven's chosen agency for revealing Christ to the world. We are to acknowledge His grace as made known through the holy men of old; but that which will be most effectual is the testimony of our own experience. We are witnesses for God as we reveal in ourselves the working of a power that is divine. Every individual has a life distinct from all others, and an experience differing essentially from theirs. God desires that our praise shall ascend to Him, marked by our own individuality. These precious acknowledgments to the praise of the glory of His grace, when supported by a Christlike life, have an irresistible power that works for the salvation of souls.[61]

In order to confess Christ, we must have Him to confess. No one can truly confess Christ unless the mind and spirit of Christ are in him. . . . We must understand what it is to confess Christ and wherein we deny Him. . . . The fruits of the Spirit manifested in the life are a confession of Him. If we have forsaken all for Christ, our lives will be humble, our conversation heavenly, our conduct blameless. The powerful, purifying influence of truth in the soul, and the character of Christ exemplified in the life, are a confession of Him.[62]

Integrity, firmness, and perseverance are qualities that all should seek earnestly to cultivate; for they clothe the possessor with a power which is irresistible—a power which makes him strong to do good, strong to resist evil, strong to bear adversity. . . . Those who have placed themselves without reserve on the side of Christ will stand firmly by that which reason and conscience tell them is right.[63]

The life of the true believer reveals an indwelling Saviour. The follower of Jesus is Christlike in spirit and in temper. Like Christ, he is meek and humble. His faith works by love and purifies the soul. His whole life is a testimony to the power of the grace of Christ.[64]

Heirs of Immortality

Being justified by his grace, we should be made heirs according to the hope of eternal life. Titus 3:7.

Every earnest petition for grace and strength will be answered. . . . Ask God to do for you those things that you cannot do for yourselves. Tell Jesus everything. Lay open before Him the secrets of your heart; for His eye searches the inmost recesses of the soul, and He reads your thoughts as an open book. When you have asked for the things that are necessary for your soul's good, believe that you receive them and you shall have them. Accept His gifts with your whole heart; for Jesus has died that you might have the precious things of heaven as your own.[65]

The youth must not suppose that they can go on living careless and indulgent lives, seeking no preparation for the kingdom of God, and yet in time of trial be able to stand firm for the truth. They need to seek earnestly to bring into their lives the perfection that is seen in the life of the Saviour, so that when Christ shall come, they will be prepared to enter in through the gates into the city of God. God's abounding love and presence in the heart will give the power of self-control and will mold and fashion the mind and character. The grace of Christ in the life will direct the aims and purposes and capabilities into channels that will give moral and spiritual power—power which the youth will not have to leave in this world, but which they can carry with them into the future life and retain through the eternal ages.[66]

All heaven is interested in men and women whom God has valued so much as to give His beloved Son to die to redeem them. No other creature that God has made is capable of such improvement, such refinement, such nobility as man. Then when men become blunted by their own debasing passions, sunken in vice, what a specimen for God to look upon! Man cannot conceive what he may be and what he may become. Through the grace of Christ he is capable of constant mental progress. Let the light of truth shine into his mind and the love of God be shed abroad in his heart and he may, through the grace Christ has died to impart to him, be a man of power—a child of earth but an heir of immortality.[67]

Invincible

The blessing of the Lord, it maketh rich,
and he addeth no sorrow with it. Prov. 10:22.

When in his distress, Jacob laid hold of the Angel, and made supplication with tears, the heavenly Messenger, in order to try his faith, also reminded him of his sin, and endeavored to escape from him. But Jacob would not be turned away. He had learned that God is merciful, and he cast himself upon His mercy. He pointed back to his repentance for his sin, and pleaded for deliverance. As he reviewed his life, he was driven almost to despair; but he held fast the Angel, and with earnest, agonizing cries urged his petition until he prevailed.

Such will be the experience of God's people in their final struggle with the powers of evil. God will test their faith, their perseverance, their confidence in His power to deliver them. Satan will endeavor to terrify them with the thought that their cases are hopeless. . . . They will have a deep sense of their shortcomings, and as they review their lives, their hopes will sink. But remembering the greatness of God's mercy, and their own sincere repentance, they will plead His promises made through Christ to helpless, repenting sinners. Their faith will not fail because their prayers are not immediately answered. They will lay hold of the strength of God, as Jacob laid hold of the Angel, and the language of their souls will be, "I will not let thee go, except thou bless me" (Gen. 32:26). . . .

Jacob's history is an assurance that God will not cast off those who have been betrayed into sin, but who have returned unto Him with true repentance. It was by self-surrender and confiding faith that Jacob gained what he had failed to gain by conflict in his own strength. God thus taught His servant that divine power and grace alone could give him the blessing he craved. Thus it will be with those who live in the last days. As dangers surround them, and despair seizes upon the soul, they must depend solely upon the merits of the atonement. We can do nothing of ourselves. In all our helpless unworthiness we must trust in the merits of the crucified and risen Saviour. None will ever perish while they do this.[68]

"More Than Conquerors"

Who shall separate us from the love of Christ? shall tribulation, or distress, or persecution, or famine, or nakedness, or peril, or sword? . . . Nay, in all these things we are more than conquerors through him that loved us. Rom. 8:35-37.

God's servants receive no honor or recognition from the world. Stephen was stoned because he preached Christ and Him crucified. Paul was imprisoned, beaten, stoned, and finally put to death, because he was a faithful messenger of God to the Gentiles. The apostle John was banished to the Isle of Patmos, "for the word of God, and for the testimony of Jesus Christ" (Rev. 1:9). These examples of human steadfastness in the might of divine power are a witness to the world of the faithfulness of God's promises, of His abiding presence and sustaining grace.[69]

Jesus does not present to His followers the hope of attaining earthly glory and riches, of living a life free from trial. Instead He calls upon them to follow Him in the path of self-denial and reproach. He who came to redeem the world was opposed by the united forces of evil. . . .

In all ages Satan has persecuted the people of God. He has tortured them and put them to death, but in dying they became conquerors. They bore witness to the power of One mightier than Satan. Wicked men may torture and kill the body, but they cannot touch the life that is hid with Christ in God. They can incarcerate men and women in prison walls, but they cannot bind the spirit.

Through trial and persecution the glory—the character—of God is revealed in His chosen ones. The believers in Christ, hated and persecuted by the world, are educated and disciplined in the school of Christ. On earth they walk in narrow paths; they are purified in the furnace of affliction. They follow Christ through sore conflicts; they endure self-denial, and experience bitter disappointments; but thus they learn the guilt and woe of sin, and they look upon it with abhorrence. Being partakers of Christ's sufferings, they can look beyond the gloom to the glory, saying, "I reckon that the sufferings of this present time are not worthy to be compared with the glory which shall be revealed in us" (Rom. 8:18).[70]

"He Is Able"

I know whom I have believed, and am persuaded that he is able to keep that which I have committed unto him against that day. 2 Tim. 1:12.

The apostle [Paul] was looking into the great beyond, not with uncertainty or dread, but with joyous hope and longing expectation. As he stands at the place of martyrdom he sees not the sword of the executioner or the earth so soon to receive his blood; he looks up . . . to the throne of the Eternal.

This man of faith beholds the ladder of Jacob's vision, representing Christ, who has connected earth with heaven, and finite man with the infinite God. His faith is strengthened as he calls to mind how patriarchs and prophets have relied upon the One who is his support and consolation, and for whom he is giving his life. From these holy men who from century to century have borne testimony for their faith, he hears the assurance that God is true. His fellow apostles, who to preach the gospel of Christ, went forth to meet religious bigotry and heathen superstition, persecution, and contempt, who counted not their lives dear unto themselves that they might bear aloft the light of the cross amidst the dark mazes of infidelity—these he hears witnessing to Jesus as the Son of God, the Saviour of the world. From the rack, the stake, the dungeon, from dens and caves of the earth, there falls upon his ear the martyr's shout of triumph. He hears the witness of steadfast souls, who, though destitute, afflicted, tormented, yet bear fearless, solemn testimony for the faith, declaring, "I know whom I have believed." . . .

Ransomed by the sacrifice of Christ, washed from sin in His blood, and clothed in His righteousness, Paul has the witness in himself that his soul is precious in the sight of His Redeemer. His life is hid with Christ in God, and he is persuaded that He who has conquered death is able to keep that which is committed to His trust.[71]

I am so glad that we can come to God in faith and humility, and plead with Him until our souls are brought into such close relationship with Jesus that we can lay our burdens at His feet, saying, "I know whom I have believed, and am persuaded that he is able to keep that which I have committed unto him against that day."[72]

As Jesus Grew

And the child grew, and waxed strong in spirit, filled with wisdom: and the grace of God was upon him. Luke 2:40.

The Majesty of heaven, the King of glory, became a babe in Bethlehem, and for a time represented the helpless infant in its mother's care. In childhood He spoke and acted as a child, honoring His parents, and carrying out their wishes in helpful ways. But from the first dawning of intelligence He was constantly growing in grace and in a knowledge of truth.

Parents and teachers should aim so to cultivate the tendencies of the youth that at each stage of life they may represent the beauty appropriate to that period, unfolding naturally, as do the plants in the garden.[1]

As a child Jesus manifested a peculiar loveliness of disposition. His willing hands were ever ready to serve others. He manifested a patience that nothing could disturb, and a truthfulness that would never sacrifice integrity. In principle firm as a rock, His life revealed the grace of unselfish courtesy.

With deep earnestness the mother of Jesus watched the unfolding of His powers, and beheld the impress of perfection upon His character. With delight she sought to encourage that bright, receptive mind. Through the Holy Spirit she received wisdom to co-operate with the heavenly agencies in the development of this child, who could claim only God as His Father. . . . From her lips and from the scrolls of the prophets, He learned of heavenly things. The very words which He Himself had spoken to Moses for Israel He was now taught at His mother's knee. . . . And spread out before Him was the great library of God's created works. He who had made all things studied the lessons which His own hand had written in earth and sea and sky. . . . Heavenly beings were His attendants, and the culture of holy thoughts and communings was His. From the first dawning of intelligence He was constantly growing in spiritual grace and knowledge of truth.

Every child may gain knowledge as Jesus did. As we try to become acquainted with our heavenly Father through His Word, angels will draw near, our minds will be strengthened, our characters will be elevated and refined. We shall become more like our Saviour.[2]

The Divine Order of Growth

For the earth bringeth forth fruit of herself; first the blade, then the ear, after that the full corn in the ear. Mark 4:28.

He who gave this parable created the tiny seed, gave it its vital properties, and ordained the laws that govern its growth. And the truths which the parable teaches were made a living reality in His own life. In both His physical and His spiritual nature He followed the divine order of growth illustrated by the plant, as He wishes all youth to do. . . . In childhood He did the works of an obedient child. . . . But at each stage of His development He was perfect, with the simple, natural grace of a sinless life.[3]

The parable of the seed reveals that God is at work in nature. . . . There is life in the seed, there is power in the soil; but unless an infinite power is exercised day and night, the seed will yield no returns. . . . Every seed grows, every plant develops, by the power of God. . . .

The germination of the seed represents the beginning of spiritual life, and the development of the plant is a beautiful figure of Christian growth. As in nature, so in grace; there can be no life without growth. The plant must either grow or die. As its growth is silent and imperceptible, but continuous, so is the development of the Christian life. At every stage of development our life may be perfect; yet if God's purpose for us is fulfilled, there will be continual advancement. Sanctification is the work of a lifetime. As our opportunities multiply, our experience will enlarge, and our knowledge increase. We shall become strong to bear responsibility, and our maturity will be in proportion to our privileges.

The plant grows by receiving that which God has provided to sustain its life. It sends down its roots into the earth. It drinks in the sunshine, the dew, and the rain. It receives the life-giving properties from the air. So the Christian is to grow by cooperating with the divine agencies. . . . As the plant takes root in the soil, so we are to take deep root in Christ. As the plant receives the sunshine, the dew, and the rain, we are to open our hearts to the Holy Spirit. . . . By constantly relying upon Christ as our personal Saviour, we shall grow up into Him in all things who is our head.[4]

How to Grow

But grow in grace, and in the knowledge of our Lord and Saviour Jesus Christ. 2 Peter 3:18.

It is the privilege of the young, as they grow in Jesus, to grow in spiritual grace and knowledge. We may know more and more of Jesus through an interested searching of the Scriptures, and then following the ways of truth and righteousness therein revealed. Those who are ever growing in grace will be steadfast in the faith, and moving forward.

There should be an earnest desire in the heart of every youth who has purposed to be a disciple of Jesus Christ to reach the highest Christian standard, to be a worker with Christ. If he makes it his aim to be of that number who shall be presented faultless before the throne of God, he will be continually advancing. The only way to remain steadfast is to progress daily in divine life. Faith will increase if, when brought in contact with doubts and obstacles, it overcomes them. True sanctification is progressive. If you are growing in grace and the knowledge of Jesus Christ, you will improve every privilege and opportunity to gain more knowledge of the life and character of Christ.

Faith in Jesus will grow as you become better acquainted with your Redeemer by dwelling upon His spotless life and His infinite love. You cannot dishonor God more than to profess to be His disciple while you keep at a distance from Him, and are not fed and nourished by His Holy Spirit. When you are growing in grace, you will love to attend religious meetings, and you will gladly bear testimony of the love of Christ before the congregation. God, by His grace, can make the young man prudent, and He can give to the children knowledge and experience. They can grow in grace daily.[5]

As long as we continue to keep our eyes fixed upon the Author and Finisher of our faith, we shall be safe. But our affections must be placed upon things above, not on things of the earth. By faith we must rise higher and still higher in the attainment of the graces of Christ. By daily contemplating His matchless charms, we must grow more and more into His glorious image. While we thus live in communion with Heaven, Satan will lay his nets for us in vain.[6]

Conditions of Christian Growth

And this I pray, that your love may abound yet more and more in knowledge and in all judgment; . . . being filled with the fruits of righteousness, which are by Jesus Christ, unto the glory and praise of God. Phil. 1:9-11.

Where there is life, there will be growth and fruit-bearing; but unless we grow in grace, our spirituality will be dwarfed, sickly, fruitless. It is only by growing, by bearing fruit, that we can fulfill God's purpose for us. "Herein is my Father glorified," Christ said, "that ye bear much fruit" (John 15:8). In order to bear much fruit, we must make the most of our privileges. We must use every opportunity granted us for obtaining strength.

A pure, noble character, with all its grand possibilities, has been provided for every human being. But there are many who have not an earnest longing for such a character. They are not willing to part with the evil that they may have the good. . . . They neglect to grasp the blessings that would place them in harmony with God. . . . They cannot grow.

One of the divine plans for growth is impartation. The Christian is to gain strength by strengthening others. "He that watereth shall be watered also himself" (Prov. 11:25). This is not merely a promise; it is a divine law, a law by which God designs that the streams of benevolence, like the waters of the great deep, shall be kept in constant circulation, continually flowing back to their source. In the fulfilling of this law is the secret of spiritual growth. . . .

If we come to God in faith, He will receive us and give us strength to climb upward to perfection. If we watch every word and action, that we may do nothing to dishonor the One who has trusted us, if we improve every opportunity granted us, we shall grow into the full stature of men and women in Christ. . . .

Christians, is Christ revealed in us? Are we doing all in our power to gain a body that is not easily enfeebled, a mind that looks beyond self to the cause and effect of every movement, that can wrestle with hard problems and conquer them, a will that is firm to resist evil and defend the right? Are we crucifying self? Are we growing up into the full stature of men and women in Christ, preparing to endure hardness as good soldiers of the cross?[7]

A Mysterious Power

All that see them shall acknowledge them,
that they are the seed which the Lord hath blessed. Isa. 61:9.

In the plan of redemption there are mysteries that the human mind cannot fathom, many things that human wisdom cannot explain; but nature can teach us much concerning the mystery of godliness. Every shrub, every tree bearing fruit, all vegetation, has lessons for our study. In the growth of the seed are to be read the mysteries of the kingdom of God. To the heart softened by the grace of God, the sun, the moon, the stars, the trees, the flowers of the field, utter words of counsel. . . .

God's laws for nature are obeyed by nature. Cloud and storm, sunshine and shower, dew and rain, all are under the supervision of God and yield obedience to His command. In obedience to the law of God the spire of grain bursts through the earth, "first the blade, then the ear, after that the full corn in the ear" (Mark 4:28). The fruit is seen in the bud, and the Lord develops it in its proper season because it does not resist His working. . . .

Can it be that man, made in the image of God, endowed with reason and speech, shall alone be unappreciative of His gifts and disobedient to His laws? . . .

God desires us to learn from nature the lesson of obedience. . . . The book of nature and the written Word shed light upon each other. Both make us better acquainted with God by teaching us of His character and of the laws through which He works.[8]

Tell your children about the miracle-working power of God. As they study the great lesson book of nature, God will impress their minds. The farmer plows his land and sows his seed, but he cannot make the seed grow. He must depend on God to do that which no human power can do. The Lord puts His vital power into the seed, causing it to spring forth into life. Under His care the germ of life breaks through the hard crust encasing it, and springs up to bear fruit. . . . As the children are told of the work that God does for the seed, they learn the secret of growth in grace.[9]

From Childhood

Suffer the little children to come unto me, and forbid them not: for of such is the kingdom of God. Mark 10:14.

In the children who were brought in contact with Him, Jesus saw the men and women who should be heirs of His grace and subjects of His kingdom. . . . In His teaching He came down to their level. He, the Majesty of heaven, did not disdain to answer their questions and simplify His important lessons to meet their childish understanding. He planted in their minds the seeds of truth, which in after years would spring up, and bear fruit unto eternal life.

It is still true that children are the most susceptible to the teachings of the gospel; their hearts are open to divine influences, and strong to retain the lessons received. The little children may be Christians, having an experience in accordance with their years. They need to be educated in spiritual things, and parents should give them every advantage, that they may form characters after the similitude of the character of Christ. . . .

The Christian worker may be Christ's agent in drawing these children to the Saviour. By wisdom and tact he may bind them to his heart, . . . and through the grace of Christ may see them transformed in character, so that of them it may be said, "Of such is the kingdom of God."[10]

God wants every child of tender age to be His child, to be adopted into His family. Young though they may be, the youth may be members of the household of faith, and have a most precious experience. . . . They may have their hearts drawn out in confidence and love for Jesus, and live for the Saviour. Christ will make them little missionaries. The whole current of their thought may be changed, so that sin will not appear a thing to be enjoyed, but to be shunned and hated.[11]

The Saviour longs to save the young. He would rejoice to see them around His throne, clothed in the spotless robes of His righteousness. He is waiting to place upon their heads the crown of life, and to hear their happy voices join in ascribing honor and glory and majesty to God and the Lamb in the song of victory that will echo and re-echo through the courts of heaven.[12]

In the Home

Except the Lord build the house,
they labour in vain that build it. Ps. 127:1.

God designs that the families of earth shall be a symbol of the family in heaven. Christian homes, established and conducted in accordance with God's plan, are among His most effective agencies for the formation of Christian character and for the advancement of His work.[13]

The importance and the opportunities of the home life are illustrated in the life of Jesus. He who came from heaven to be our example and teacher spent thirty years as a member of the household at Nazareth.[14]

His mother was His first human teacher. From her lips, and from the scrolls of the prophets, He learned of heavenly things. He lived in a peasant's home, and faithfully and cheerfully He acted His part in bearing the household burdens. He had been the Commander of heaven, and angels had delighted to fulfill His word; now He was a willing servant, a loving, obedient son. . . .

Thus prepared, He went forth to His mission, in every moment of His contact with men exerting upon them an influence to bless, a power to transform, such as the world had never witnessed.[15]

Let your home be such that Christ can enter it as an abiding guest. Let it be such that people will take knowledge of you that you have been with Jesus, and have learned of Him. . . .

Angels of heaven often visit the home in which the will of God bears sway. Under the power of divine grace, such a home becomes a place of refreshing to worn, weary pilgrims. Self is kept from asserting itself. Right habits are formed. There is a careful recognition of the rights of others. The faith that works by love and purifies the soul stands at the helm, presiding over the entire household.[16]

The measure of your Christianity is gauged by the character of your home life. The grace of Christ enables its possessors to make the home a happy place, full of peace and rest.[17]

Let the light of heavenly grace irradiate your character, that there may be sunlight in the home.[18]

Daily Prayer Essential

If any man will come after me, let him deny himself, and take up his cross daily, and follow me. Luke 9:23.

If we would develop a character which God can accept, we must form correct habits in our religious life. Daily prayer is as essential to growth in grace, and even to spiritual life itself, as is temporal food to physical well-being. We should accustom ourselves to often lift the thoughts to God in prayer. If the mind wanders, we must bring it back; by persevering effort, habit will finally make it easy. We cannot for one moment separate ourselves from Christ with safety. We may have His presence to attend us at every step, but only by observing the conditions which He has Himself laid down.

Religion must be made the great business of life. Everything else should be held subordinate to this. All our powers of soul, body, and spirit, must be engaged in the Christian warfare. We must look to Christ for strength and grace, and we shall gain the victory as surely as Jesus died for us.[19]

At the beginning of the day, do not, dear youth, neglect to pray earnestly to Jesus that He will impart to you strength and grace to resist the temptations of the enemy in whatsoever form they may come; and if you pray earnestly, in faith and contrition of soul, the Lord will hear your prayer. But you must watch as well as pray. . . .

Children and youth may come to Jesus with their burdens and perplexities, and know that He will respect their appeals to Him, and give them the very things they need. Be earnest; be resolute. Present the promise of God, and then believe without a doubt. Do not wait to feel special emotions before you think the Lord answers. Do not mark out some particular way that the Lord must work for you before you believe you receive the things you ask of Him; but trust His word, and leave the whole matter in the hands of the Lord, with full faith that your prayer will be honored, and the answer will come at the very time and in the very way your heavenly Father sees is for your good; and then live out your prayers. Walk humbly and keep moving forward.[20]

Secret Prayer a Necessity

Seek the Lord and his strength, seek his face continually. 1 Chron. 16:11.

When Jesus was upon the earth, He taught His disciples how to pray. He directed them to present their daily needs before God, and to cast all their care upon Him. And the assurance He gave them that their petitions should be heard, is assurance also to us.[21]

Have a place for secret prayer. Jesus had select places for communion with God, and so should we. We need often to retire to some spot, however humble, where we can be alone with God. . . .

In the secret place of prayer, where no eye but God's can see, no ear but His can hear, we may pour out our most hidden desires and longings to the Father of infinite pity, and in the hush and silence of the soul that voice which never fails to answer the cry of human need will speak to our hearts. . . .

As we make Christ our daily companion we shall feel that the powers of an unseen world are all around us; and by looking unto Jesus we shall become assimilated to His image. By beholding we become changed. The character is softened, refined, and ennobled for the heavenly kingdom. The sure result of our intercourse and fellowship with our Lord will be to increase piety, purity, and fervor. There will be a growing intelligence in prayer. We are receiving a divine education, and this is illustrated in a life of diligence and zeal.

The soul that turns to God for its help, its support, its power, by daily, earnest prayer, will have noble aspirations, clear perceptions of truth and duty, lofty purposes of action, and a continual hungering and thirsting after righteousness. By maintaining a connection with God, we shall be enabled to diffuse to others, through our association with them, the light, the peace, the serenity, that rule in our hearts. The strength acquired in prayer to God, united with persevering effort in training the mind in thoughtfulness and care-taking, prepares one for daily duties and keeps the spirit in peace under all circumstances.[22]

Religion must begin with emptying and purifying the heart, and must be nurtured by daily prayer.[23]

A Continual Work

For this is the will of God, even your sanctification. 1 Thess. 4:3.

Sanctification is not the work of a moment, an hour, or a day. It is a continual growth in grace. We know not one day how strong will be our conflict the next. Satan lives, and is active, and every day we need to cry earnestly to God for help and strength to resist him. As long as Satan reigns we shall have self to subdue, besetments to overcome, and there is no stopping place, there is no point to which we can come and say we have fully attained. . . .

The Christian life is constantly an onward march. Jesus sits as a refiner and purifier of His people; and when His image is perfectly reflected in them, they are perfect and holy, and prepared for translation. A great work is required of the Christian. We are exhorted to cleanse ourselves from all filthiness of the flesh and spirit, perfecting holiness in the fear of God. Here we see where the great labor rests. There is a constant work for the Christian.[24]

None are living Christians unless they have a daily experience in the things of God and daily practice self-denial, cheerfully bearing the cross and following Christ. Every living Christian will advance daily in the divine life. As he advances toward perfection, he experiences a conversion to God every day; and this conversion is not completed until he attains to perfection of Christian character, a full preparation for the finishing touch of immortality. . . .

Religion is not merely an emotion, a feeling. It is a principle which is interwoven with all the daily duties and transactions of life. . . . It is continuance in well-doing that will form characters for heaven.[25]

We must live for Christ minute by minute, hour by hour, and day by day; then Christ will dwell in us, and when we meet together, His love will be in our hearts, welling up like a spring in the desert, refreshing all, and making those who are ready to perish, eager to drink of the waters of life.[26]

Through Simple, Trusting Faith

The grace of our Lord was exceeding abundant with faith and love which is in Christ Jesus. 1 Tim. 1:14.

It is your privilege ever to grow in grace, advancing in the knowledge and love of God, if you maintain the sweet communion with Christ it is your privilege to enjoy. In the simplicity of humble faith ask the Lord to open your understanding, that you may discern and appreciate the precious things of His Word. Thus you may grow in grace, grow in simple, trusting faith. . . .

Be sure that your spiritual life does not become poor, sickly, inefficient. There are many who have need of the words and example of a Christian. Weakness and indecision provoke the assaults of the enemy, and any one who fails to increase in spiritual growth, in a knowledge of truth and righteousness, will frequently be overcome by the enemy.[27]

Genuine faith always works by love. When you look to Calvary it is not to quiet your soul in the nonperformance of duty, not to compose yourself to sleep, but to create faith in Jesus, faith that will work, purifying the soul from the slime of selfishness. When we lay hold of Christ by faith, our work has just begun. Every man has corrupt and sinful habits that must be overcome by vigorous warfare. Every soul is required to fight the fight of faith. If one is a follower of Christ, he cannot be sharp in deal, he cannot be hardhearted, devoid of sympathy. . . . He cannot be overbearing, nor can he use harsh words, and censure and condemn.[28]

Let faith, like a palm tree, strike its penetrating roots beneath the things which do appear, and obtain spiritual refreshment from the living springs of God's grace and mercy. There is a well of water which springeth up into everlasting life. You must draw your life from this hidden spring. If you divest yourselves of selfishness, and strengthen your souls by constant communion with God, you may promote the happiness of all with whom you come in contact. You will notice the neglected, inform the ignorant, encourage the oppressed and desponding, and, as far as possible, relieve the suffering. And you will not only point the way to heaven, but will walk in that way yourselves.[29]

Abiding in Christ

I am the vine, ye are the branches: he that abideth in me, and I in him, the same bringeth forth much fruit: for without me ye can do nothing. John 15:5.

Many have an idea that they must do some part of the work alone. They have trusted in Christ for the forgiveness of sin, but now they seek by their own efforts to live aright. But every such effort must fail. Jesus says, "Without me ye can do nothing." Our growth in grace, our joy, our usefulness—all depend upon our union with Christ. It is by communion with Him, daily, hourly—by abiding in Him—that we grow in grace. He is not only the author, but the finisher of our faith. It is Christ first and last and always. He is to be with us, not only at the beginning and the end of our course, but at every step of the way. David says, "I have set the Lord always before me: because he is at my right hand, I shall not be moved" (Ps. 16:8).

Do you ask, "How am I to abide in Christ?"—In the same way as you received Him at first. "As ye have therefore received Christ Jesus the Lord, so walk ye in him" (Col. 2:6). . . . You gave yourself to God, to be His wholly, to serve and obey Him, and you took Christ as your Saviour. You could not yourself atone for your sins or change your heart, but having given yourself to God, you believed that He for Christ's sake did all this for you. By *faith* you became Christ's, and by faith you are to grow up in Him—by giving and taking. You are to *give* all—your heart, your will, your service—give yourself to Him to obey all His requirements; and you must *take* all—Christ, the fullness of all blessing, to abide in your heart, to be your strength, your righteousness, your everlasting helper—to give you power to obey. . . .

Your weakness is united to His strength, your ignorance to His wisdom, your frailty to His enduring might. So you are not to look to yourself, not to let the mind dwell upon self, but look to Christ. Let the mind dwell upon His love, upon the beauty, the perfection, of His character. Christ in His self-denial, Christ in His humiliation, Christ in His purity and holiness, Christ in His matchless love—this is the subject for the soul's contemplation. It is by loving Him, copying Him, depending wholly upon Him, that you are to be transformed into His likeness.[30]

Physically and Spiritually

Beloved, I wish above all things that thou mayest prosper and be in health, even as thy soul prospereth. 3 John 2.

God's purpose for His children is that they shall grow up to the full stature of men and women in Christ. In order to do this, they must use aright every power of mind, soul, and body. They cannot afford to waste any mental or physical strength.

The question of how to preserve the health is one of primary importance. When we study this question in the fear of God we shall learn that it is best, for both our physical and spiritual advancement, to observe simplicity in diet. Let us patiently study this question. . . .

Those who have received instruction regarding the evils of the use of flesh foods, tea and coffee, and rich and unhealthful food preparations, and who are determined to make a covenant with God by sacrifice, will not continue to indulge their appetite for food that they know to be unhealthful. God demands that the appetites be cleansed, and that self-denial be practiced in regard to those things which are not good. This is a work that will have to be done before His people can stand before Him a perfected people. . . .

God requires of His people continual advancement. We need to learn that indulged appetite is the greatest hindrance to mental improvement and soul sanctification. With all our profession of health reform, many of us eat improperly. Indulgence of appetite is the greatest cause of physical and mental debility, and lies largely at the foundation of feebleness and premature death. Let the individual who is seeking to possess purity of spirit bear in mind that in Christ there is power to control the appetite.[31]

The health of the body is to be regarded as essential for growth in grace and the acquirement of an even temper. . . . Erroneous eating and drinking result in erroneous thinking and acting. All are now being tested and proved. We have been baptized into Christ, and if we will act our part by separating from everything that would drag us down . . . there will be given us strength to grow up into Christ, who is our living head, and we shall see the salvation of God.[32]

Keeping the Heart

Keep thy heart with all diligence;
for out of it are the issues of life. Prov. 4:23.

Diligent heart-keeping is essential to a healthy growth in grace. The heart in its natural state is a habitation for unholy thoughts and sinful passions. When brought into subjection to Christ, it must be cleansed by the Spirit from all defilement. This cannot be done without the consent of the individual.

When the soul has been cleansed, it is the duty of the Christian to keep it undefiled. Many seem to think that the religion of Christ does not call for the abandonment of daily sins, the breaking loose from habits which have held the soul in bondage. They renounce some things condemned by the conscience, but they fail to represent Christ in the daily life. They do not bring Christlikeness into the home. They do not show a thoughtful care in their choice of words. Too often, fretful, impatient words are spoken, words which stir the worst passions of the human heart. Such ones need the abiding presence of Christ in the soul. Only in His strength can they keep guard over the words and actions. . . .

Many seem to begrudge moments spent in meditation, and the searching of the Scriptures, and prayer, as though the time thus occupied was lost. I wish you could all view these things in the light God would have you for you would then make the kingdom of heaven of the first importance. To keep your heart in heaven will give vigor to all your graces, and put life into all your duties. . . . As exercise increases the appetite, and gives strength and healthy vigor to the body, so will devotional exercises bring an increase of grace and spiritual vigor. . . .

Let the prayer go up to God, "Create in me a clean heart" (Ps. 51:10); for a pure, cleansed soul has Christ abiding therein, and out of the abundance of the heart are the issues of life. The human will is to be yielded to Christ. Instead of passing on, closing the heart in selfishness, there is need of opening the heart to the sweet influences of the Spirit of God. Practical religion breathes its fragrance everywhere. It is a savor of life unto life.[33]

First, an Empty Heart

Thou shalt love the Lord thy God with all thy heart, and with all thy soul, and with all thy mind, and with all thy strength: this is the first commandment. And the second is like, namely this, Thou shalt love thy neighbour as thyself. Mark 12:30, 31.

On these two commandments the whole interest and duty of moral beings hang. Those who do their duty to others as they would that others should do to them are brought into a position where God can reveal Himself to them. They will be approved of Him. They are made perfect in love, and their labors and prayers will not be in vain. They are continually receiving grace and truth from the Fountainhead, and as freely transmitting to others the divine light and salvation they receive. . . .

Selfishness is abomination in the sight of God and holy angels. Because of this sin many fail to attain the good which they are capable of enjoying. They look with selfish eyes on their own things, and do not love and seek the interest of others as they do their own. They reverse God's order. Instead of doing for others what they wish others to do for them, they do for themselves what they desire others to do for them, and do to others what they are most unwilling to have returned to them.[34]

How is it possible that we may grow in grace? It is possible to us only as we empty our hearts of self, and present them to Heaven, to be molded after the divine Pattern. We may have a connection with the living channel of light; we may be refreshed with the heavenly dew, and have the showers of Heaven descend upon us. As we appropriate the blessing of God, we shall be able to receive greater measures of His grace. As we learn to endure as seeing Him who is invisible, we shall become changed into the image of Christ. The grace of Christ will not make us proud, cause us to be lifted up in self, but we shall become meek and lowly in heart.[35]

Growth in grace will not lead you to be proud, self-confident, and boastful, but will make you more conscious of your own nothingness, of your entire dependence upon the Lord.[36]

Snares to Shun

For all that is in the world, the lust of the flesh, and the lust of the eyes, and the pride of life, is not of the Father, but is of the world. 1 John 2:16.

Pride and the love of the world are the snares which are so great a hindrance to spirituality and a growth in grace.

This world is not the Christian's heaven, but merely the workshop of God, where we are to be fitted up to unite with the sinless angels in a holy heaven. We should be constantly training the mind to noble, unselfish thoughts. This education is necessary to so bring into exercise the powers which God has given us that His name shall best be glorified upon the earth. We are accountable for all the noble qualities which God has given us, and to put these faculties to a use He never designed we should is showing base ingratitude to Him. The service of God demands all the powers of our being, and we fail of meeting the design of God unless we bring these powers to a high state of cultivation, and educate the mind to love to contemplate heavenly things, and strengthen and ennoble the energies of the soul by right actions, operating to the glory of God. . . .

Unless the mind is educated to dwell upon religious themes, it will be weak and feeble in this direction. But while dwelling upon worldly enterprises, it will be strong; for in this direction it has been cultivated, and has strengthened with exercise. The reason it is so difficult for men and women to live religious lives is because they do not exercise the mind unto godliness. It is trained to run in an opposite direction. Unless the mind is constantly exercised in obtaining spiritual knowledge and in seeking to understand the mystery of godliness, it is incapable of appreciating eternal things. . . . When the heart is divided, dwelling principally upon things of the world, and but little upon the things of God, there can be no special increase of spiritual strength.[37]

While worldlings are all earnestness and ambition to secure earthly treasure, God's people are not conformed to the world, but show by their earnest, watching, waiting position that they are transformed; that their home is not in this world, but that they are seeking a better country, even a heavenly.[38]

In Humility

Be clothed with humility: for God resisteth the proud, and giveth grace to the humble. 1 Peter 5:5.

The confiding love and unselfish devotion manifested in the life and character of John present lessons of untold value to the Christian church. John did not naturally possess the loveliness of character that his later experience revealed. By nature he had serious defects. He was not only proud, self-assertive, and ambitious for honor, but impetuous, and resentful under injury. . . . But beneath all this the divine Teacher discerned the ardent, sincere, loving heart. Jesus rebuked his self-seeking, disappointed his ambitions, tested his faith. But He revealed to him that for which his soul longed—the beauty of holiness, the transforming power of love.[39]

The lessons of Christ, setting forth meekness and humility and love as essential to growth in grace and a fitness for His work, were of the highest value to John. He treasured every lesson, and constantly sought to bring his life into harmony with the divine pattern. John had begun to discern the glory of Christ—not the worldly pomp and power for which he had been taught to hope, but "the glory as of the only begotten of the Father, full of grace and truth" (John 1:14). . . . John desired to become like Jesus, and under the transforming influence of the love of Christ he did become meek and lowly. Self was hid in Jesus.[40]

The Lord Jesus seeks the co-operation of those who will become unobstructed channels for the communication of His grace. The first thing to be learned . . . is the lesson of self-distrust; then they are prepared to have imparted to them the character of Christ. This is not to be gained through education in the most scientific schools. It is the fruit of wisdom that is obtained from the divine Teacher alone. . . .

Men of the highest education in the arts and sciences have learned precious lessons from Christians in humble life who were designated by the world as unlearned. But these obscure disciples had obtained an education in the highest of all schools. They had sat at the feet of Him who spoke as "never man spake" (John 7:46).[41]

In Kindness

Put on therefore, as the elect of God, holy and beloved, bowels of mercies, kindness, humbleness of mind, meekness, longsuffering. Col. 3:12.

Let the law of kindness be upon your lips and the oil of grace in your heart. This will produce wonderful results. You will be tender, sympathetic, courteous. You need all these graces. The Holy Spirit must be received and brought into your character; then it will be as holy fire, giving forth incense which will rise up to God, not from lips that condemn, but as a healer of the souls of men. Your countenance will express the image of the divine. . . . By beholding the character of Christ you will become changed into His likeness. The grace of Christ alone can change your heart and then you will reflect the image of the Lord Jesus. God calls upon us to be like Him—pure, holy, and undefiled. We are to bear the divine image. . . .

The Lord Jesus is our only helper. Through His grace we shall learn to cultivate love, to educate ourselves to speak kindly and tenderly. Through His grace our cold, harsh manners will be transformed. The law of kindness will be upon our lips, and those who are under the precious influences of the Holy Spirit, will not feel that it is an evidence of weakness to weep with those who weep, to rejoice with them that rejoice. We are to cultivate heavenly excellences of character. We are to learn what it means to have good-will toward all men, a sincere desire to be as sunshine and not as shadow in the lives of others.[42]

Seize every opportunity to contribute to the happiness of those around you, sharing with them your affection. Words of kindness, looks of sympathy, expressions of appreciation, would to many a struggling, lonely one be as a cup of cold water to a thirsty soul. . . .

Live in the sunshine of the Saviour's love. Then your influence will bless the world. Let the Spirit of Christ control you. Let the law of kindness be ever on your lips. Forbearance and unselfishness mark the words and actions of those who are born again, to live the new life in Christ.[43]

We Must Follow On

Then shall we know, if we follow on to know the Lord: his going forth is prepared as the morning. Hosea 6:3.

Christ came to teach the human family the way of salvation, and He made this way so plain that a little child can walk in it. He bids His disciples follow on to know the Lord; and as they daily follow His guidance, they learn that His going forth is prepared as the morning.

You have watched the rising sun, and the gradual break of day over earth and sky. Little by little the dawn increases, till the sun appears; then the light grows constantly stronger and clearer until the full glory of noontide is reached. This is a beautiful illustration of what God desires to do for His children in perfecting their Christian experience. As we walk day by day in the light He sends us, in willing obedience to all His requirements, our experience grows and broadens until we reach the full stature of men and women in Christ Jesus. . . .

Christ did not come to the earth as a king, to rule the nations. He came as a humble man, to be tempted, and to overcome temptation, to follow on, as we must, to know the Lord. In the study of His life we shall learn how much God through Him will do for His children. And we shall learn that, however great our trials may be, they cannot exceed what Christ endured that we might know the way, the truth, and the life. By a life of conformity to His example, we are to show our appreciation of His sacrifice in our behalf.[44]

As the flower turns to the sun, that the bright beams may aid in perfecting its beauty and symmetry, so should we turn to the Sun of Righteousness, that heaven's light may shine upon us, that our character may be developed into the likeness of Christ. . . .

You are just as dependent upon Christ, in order to live a holy life, as is the branch upon the parent stock for growth and fruitfulness. Apart from Him you have no life. You have no power to resist temptation or to grow in grace and holiness. Abiding in Him, you may flourish. Drawing your life from Him, you will not wither nor be fruitless. You will be like a tree planted by the rivers of water.[45]

Reflecting Jesus

Let no corrupt communication proceed out of your mouth,
but that which is good to the use of edifying,
that it may minister grace unto the hearers. Eph. 4:29.

I have a continual longing for Christ to be formed within, the hope of glory. I long to be beautified every day with the meekness and gentleness of Christ, growing in grace and in the knowledge of Jesus Christ up to the full stature of men and women in Christ Jesus. I must as an individual, through the grace given me of Jesus Christ, keep my own soul in health by keeping it as a divine channel through which His grace, His love, His patience, His meekness, shall flow to the world. This is my duty and no less the duty of every church member who claims to be a son or a daughter of God.

The Lord Jesus has made His church the depositary of sacred truth. He has left with her the work of carrying out His purposes and His plans to save the souls for whom He has manifested such interest, such unmeasured love. Like the sun in relation to our world, He rises amid the moral darkness—the Sun of Righteousness. He said of Himself, "I am the light of the world" (John 8:12). He said to His followers, "Ye are the light of the world" (Matt. 5:14). . . . By reflecting the image of Jesus Christ, by the beauty and holiness of their characters, by their continual self-denial and their separation from all idols, large or small, they reveal that they have learned in the school of Christ.[46]

The Scripture says of Christ that grace was poured into His lips that He might "know how to speak a word in season to him that is weary" (Ps. 45:2; Isa. 50:4). And the Lord bids us, "Let your speech be alway with grace" (Col. 4:6) "that it may minister grace unto the hearers" (Eph. 4:29).

In seeking to correct or reform others we should be careful of our words. They will be a savor of life unto life or of death unto death. . . . All who would advocate the principles of truth need to receive the heavenly oil of love. Under all circumstances reproof should be spoken in love. Then our words will reform but not exasperate. Christ by His Holy Spirit will supply the force and the power. This is His work.[47]

When We Fail

Rejoice not against me, O mine enemy: when I fall, I shall arise; when I sit in darkness, the Lord shall be a light unto me. Micah 7:8.

Nothing but divine power can regenerate the human heart and imbue souls with the love of Christ, which will ever manifest itself with love for those for whom He died. The fruit of the Spirit is love, joy, peace, long-suffering, goodness, faith, meekness, temperance. When a man is converted to God, a new moral taste is supplied, a new motive power is given, and he loves the things that God loves. . . . Love, joy, peace, and inexpressible gratitude will pervade the soul, and the language of him who is blessed will be, "Thy gentleness hath made me great" (Ps. 18:35).

But those who are waiting to behold a magical change in their characters without determined effort on their part to overcome sin, will be disappointed. We have no reason to fear while looking to Jesus, no reason to doubt but that He is able to save to the uttermost all that come unto Him; but we may constantly fear lest our old nature will again obtain the supremacy, that the enemy shall devise some snare whereby we shall again become his captives. We are to work out our own salvation with fear and trembling, for it is God that worketh in you to will and to do of His good pleasure. . . .

We are to grow daily in spiritual loveliness. We shall fail often in our efforts to copy the divine pattern. We shall often have to bow down to weep at the feet of Jesus, because of our shortcomings and mistakes; but we are not to be discouraged; we are to pray more fervently, believe more fully, and try again with more steadfastness to grow into the likeness of our Lord. As we distrust our own power, we shall trust the power of our Redeemer, and render praise to God, who is the health of our countenance, and our God. . . .

By beholding we are to become changed; and as we meditate upon the perfections of the divine Model, we shall desire to become wholly transformed, and renewed in the image of His purity. It is by faith in the Son of God that transformation takes place in the character, and the child of wrath becomes the child of God.[48]

Feasting on His Word

And now, brethren, I commend you to God, and to the word of his grace, which is able to build you up, and to give you an inheritance among all them which are sanctified. Acts 20:32.

The great and essential knowledge is the knowledge of God and His Word. . . . There should be a daily increasing of spiritual understanding; and the Christian will grow in grace, just in proportion as he depends upon and appreciates the teaching of the Word of God, and habituates himself to meditate upon divine things.[49]

In giving us the privilege of studying His Word, the Lord has set before us a rich banquet. Many are the benefits derived from feasting on His Word, which is represented by Him as His flesh and blood, His spirit and life. By partaking of this Word our spiritual strength is increased; we grow in grace and in the knowledge of the truth. Habits of self-control are formed and strengthened. The infirmities of childhood—fretfulness, willfulness, selfishness, hasty words, passionate acts—disappear, and in their place are developed the graces of Christian manhood and womanhood.[50]

The Lord, in His great mercy, has revealed to us in the Scriptures the rules of holy living. . . .

He has inspired holy men to record, for our benefit, instruction concerning the dangers that beset the path, and how to escape them. Those who obey His injunction to search the Scriptures will not be ignorant of these things. Amid the perils of the last days, every member of the church should understand the reasons of his hope and faith—reasons which are not difficult of comprehension. There is enough to occupy the mind, if we would grow in grace and in the knowledge of our Lord Jesus Christ.[51]

Whenever the people of God are growing in grace, they will be constantly obtaining a clearer understanding of His Word. They will discern new light and beauty in its sacred truths. This has been true in the history of the church in all ages, and thus it will continue to the end.[52]

From One Source Only

Grace and truth came by Jesus Christ. John 1:17.

Your strength and growth in grace come only from one source. If when you are tempted and tried you stand bravely for the right, victory is yours. You are one step nearer to perfection of Christian character. A holy light from heaven fills the chambers of your soul, and you are surrounded by a pure, fragrant atmosphere.[53]

It is our privilege to stand with the light of heaven upon us. It was thus that Enoch walked with God. It was no easier for Enoch to live a righteous life than it is for us at the present time. The world in his time was no more favorable to growth in grace and holiness than it is now.

It was by prayer and communion with God that Enoch was enabled to escape the corruption that is in the world through lust. We are living in the perils of the last days, and we must receive our strength from the same source. We must walk with God. A separation from the world is required of us, for we cannot remain free from its pollution unless we follow the example of the faithful Enoch. . . .

How many there are as weak as water who might have a never-failing source of strength. Heaven is ready to impart to us, that we may be mighty in God, and attain to the full stature of men and women in Christ Jesus. What increase of spiritual power have you gained during the last year? Who among us have gained one precious attainment after another, until envy, pride, malice, jealousy, and selfishness have been swept away, and only the graces of the Spirit remain—meekness, forbearance, gentleness, charity? God will help us if we take hold of the help He has provided.[54]

No other creature that God has made is capable of such improvement, such refinement, such nobility as man. . . . Man cannot conceive what he may be and what he may become. Through the grace of Christ he is capable of constant mental progress. Let the light of truth shine into his mind and the love of God be shed abroad in his heart and he may, through the grace Christ has died to impart to him, be a man of power—a child of earth but an heir of immortality.[55]

Helping Others

He that watereth shall be watered also himself. Prov. 11:25.

Christ presents to us who are athirst the water of life, that we may drink freely; when we do this we have Christ within us as a well of water springing up into everlasting life. Then our words are full of moisture. We are prepared to water others.[56]

No sooner does one come to Christ, than there is born in his heart a desire to make known to others what a precious friend he has found in Jesus; the saving and sanctifying truth cannot be shut up in his heart. If we are clothed with the righteousness of Christ, and are filled with the joy of His indwelling Spirit, we shall not be able to hold our peace. If we have tasted and seen that the Lord is good, we shall have something to tell. . . .

And the effort to bless others will react in blessings upon ourselves. This was the purpose of God in giving us a part to act in the plan of redemption. . . .

If you will go to work as Christ designs that His disciples shall, and win souls for Him, you will feel the need of a deeper experience and a greater knowledge in divine things, and will hunger and thirst after righteousness. You will plead with God, and your faith will be strengthened, and your soul will drink deeper drafts at the well of salvation. Encountering opposition and trials will drive you to the Bible and prayer. You will grow in grace and the knowledge of Christ, and will develop a rich experience.

The spirit of unselfish labor for others gives depth, stability, and Christlike loveliness to the character, and brings peace and happiness to its possessor. The aspirations are elevated. There is no room for sloth or selfishness. Those who thus exercise the Christian graces will grow, and will become strong to work for God. They will have clear spiritual perceptions, a steady, growing faith, and an increased power in prayer. The Spirit of God, moving upon their spirit, calls forth the sacred harmonies of the soul, in answer to the divine touch. Those who thus devote themselves to unselfish effort for the good of others, are most surely working out their own salvation. The only way to grow in grace is . . . to engage, to the extent of our ability, in helping and blessing those who need the help we can give them.[57]

Spiritual Exercise a Must

Watch ye, stand fast in the faith,
quit you like men, be strong. 1 Cor. 16:13.

An elevated standard is presented before the youth, and God is inviting them to come into real service for Him. True-hearted young men who delight to be learners in the school of Christ, can do a great work for the Master, if they will only give heed to the command of the Captain as it sounds down along the lines to our time, "Quit you like men, be strong."[58]

Strength comes by exercise. All who put to use the ability which God has given them will have increased ability to devote to His service. Those who do nothing in the cause of God will fail to grow in grace and in the knowledge of the truth. A man who would lie down and refuse to exercise his limbs would soon lose all power to use them. Thus the Christian who will not exercise his God-given powers not only fails to grow up into Christ, but he loses the strength which he already has; he becomes a spiritual paralytic. It is those who, with love for God and their fellow men, are striving to help others that become established, strengthened, settled, in the truth. The true Christian works for God, not from impulse, but from principle; not for a day or a month, but during the entire period of life.[59]

This world is not a parade ground, but a battlefield. All are called to endure hardness, as good soldiers. They are to be strong and quit themselves like men. . . . The true test of character is found in the willingness to bear burdens, to take the hard place, to do the work that needs to be done, though it bring no earthly recognition or reward.[60]

O that each one would place a proper estimate upon the capabilities that have been given him of God! Through Christ you may climb the ladder of progress, and bring every power under the control of Jesus. . . . In your own strength you can do nothing; but in the grace of Jesus Christ, you can employ your powers in such a way as to bring the greatest good to your own soul, and the greatest blessing to the souls of others. Lay hold of Jesus, and you will diligently work the works of Christ, and will finally receive the eternal reward.[61]

A Divine Prescription

That the name of our Lord Jesus Christ may be glorified in you, and ye in him, according to the grace of our God and the Lord Jesus Christ. 2 Thess. 1:12.

Many are longing to grow in grace; they pray over the matter, and are surprised that their prayers are not answered. The Master has given them a work to do whereby they shall grow. Of what value is it to pray when there is need of work? The question is, Are they seeking to save souls for whom Christ died? Spiritual growth depends upon giving to others the light that God has given to you. You are to put forth your best thoughts in active labor to do good, and only good, in your family, in your church, and in your neighborhood.

In place of growing anxious with the thought that you are not growing in grace, just do every duty that presents itself, carry the burden of souls on your heart, and by every conceivable means seek to save the lost. Be kind, be courteous, be pitiful; speak in humility of the blessed hope; talk of the love of Jesus; tell of His goodness, His mercy, and His righteousness; and cease to worry as to whether or not you are growing. Plants do not grow through any conscious effort. . . . The plant is not in continual worriment about its growth; it just grows under the supervision of God.[62]

If we will consecrate heart and mind to the service of God, doing the work He has for us to do and walking in the footsteps of Jesus, our hearts will become sacred harps, every chord of which will send forth praise and thanksgiving to the Lamb sent by God to take away the sins of the world. . . .

The Lord Jesus is our strength and happiness, the great storehouse from which, on every occasion, men may draw strength. As we study Him, talk of Him, become more and more able to behold Him—as we avail ourselves of His grace and receive the blessings He proffers us, we have something with which to help others. Filled with gratitude, we communicate to others the blessings that have been freely given us. Thus receiving and imparting, we grow in grace.[63]

No Place for Idleness

He that is not with me is against me: and he that gathereth not with me scattereth. Luke 11:23.

How is our light to shine forth to the world unless it be by our consistent Christian life? How is the world to know that we belong to Christ, if we do nothing for Him? . . . There is no neutral ground between those who work to the utmost of their ability for Christ and those who work for the adversary of souls. Everyone who stands as an idler in the vineyard of the Lord is not merely doing nothing himself, but he is a hindrance to those who are trying to work. Satan finds employment for all who are not earnestly striving to secure their own salvation and the salvation of others. . . . Whenever a Christian is off his guard, this powerful adversary makes a sudden and violent attack. Unless the members of the church are active and vigilant, they will be overcome by his devices.[64]

Many who should stand firm for righteousness and truth have manifested weakness and indecision that have encouraged the assaults of Satan. Those who fail to grow in grace, not seeking to reach the highest standard in divine attainments, will be overcome. . . .

In this season of conflict and trial we need all the support and consolation we can derive from righteous principles, from fixed religious convictions, from the abiding assurance of the love of Christ, and from a rich experience in divine things. We shall attain to the full stature of men and women in Christ Jesus only as the result of a steady growth in grace.[65]

It is the work that we do or do not do that tells with tremendous power upon our lives and destinies. God requires us to improve every opportunity for usefulness that is offered us. Neglect to do this is perilous to our spiritual growth. We have a great work to do. Let us not pass in idleness the precious hours that God has given us in which to perfect characters for heaven. We must not be inactive or slothful in this work, for we have not a moment to spend without a purpose or object. God will help us to overcome our wrongs if we will pray and believe on Him. We can be more than conquerors through Him who has loved us.[66]

In Life's Necessary Duties

Neither count I my life dear unto myself, so that I might finish my course with joy, and the ministry, which I have received of the Lord Jesus, to testify the gospel of the grace of God. Acts 20:24.

Your spiritual strength and growth in grace will be proportionate to the labor of love and good works which you do cheerfully for your Saviour, who has withheld nothing, not even His own life, that He might save you. . . .

Our good works alone will not save any of us, but we cannot be saved without good works. And after we have done all that we can do, in the name and strength of Jesus we are to say: "We are unprofitable servants" (Luke 17:10).[67]

If you have the riches of the grace of Christ in your heart, you will not keep them to yourselves while the salvation of souls depends upon a knowledge of the way of salvation that you can give. These may not come to you and tell you their heart longings, but many are hungry, unsatisfied, and Christ died that they might have the riches of His grace. What are you going to do that these souls may share the blessings that you enjoy? . . .

Growth in grace is shown in an increasing ability to work for God. He who learns in the school of Christ will know how to pray and how to speak for the Master. Realizing that he lacks wisdom and experience, he will place himself under the training of the Great Teacher, knowing that only thus he can obtain perfection in God's service. And daily he becomes better able to comprehend spiritual things. Every day of diligent labor finds him at its close better fitted to help others.[68]

The essential lesson of contented industry in the necessary duties of life is yet to be learned by many of Christ's followers. It requires more grace, more stern discipline of character, to work for God in the capacity of mechanic, merchant, lawyer, or farmer, carrying the precepts of Christianity into the ordinary business of life, than to labor as an acknowledged missionary in the open field. It requires a strong spiritual nerve to bring religion into the workshop and the business office, sanctifying the details of everyday life, and ordering every transaction according to the standard of God's Word. But this is what the Lord requires.[69]

Little Opportunities

Whatsoever thy hand findeth to do, do it with thy might. Eccl. 9:10.

Nothing will so arouse a self-sacrificing zeal and broaden and strengthen the character as to engage in work for others. . . . None need wait until called to some distant field before beginning to help others. Doors of service are open everywhere. All around us are those who need our help. The widow, the orphan, the sick and the dying, the heartsick, the discouraged, the ignorant, and the outcast are on every hand.

We should feel it our special duty to work for those living in our neighborhood. Study how you can best help those who take no interest in religious things. As you visit your friends and neighbors, show an interest in their spiritual as well as in their temporal welfare. Speak to them of Christ as a sin-pardoning Saviour. Invite your neighbors to your home, and read with them from the precious Bible and from books that explain its truths. Invite them to unite with you in song and prayer. In these little gatherings, Christ Himself will be present, as He has promised, and hearts will be touched by His grace. . . .

Many regret that they are living a narrow life. They themselves can make their life broad and influential if they will. Those who love Jesus with heart and mind and soul, and their neighbor as themselves, have a wide field in which to use their ability and influence. Let none pass by little opportunities, to look for larger work. You might do successfully the small work, but fail utterly in attempting the larger work, and fall into discouragement. It is by doing with your might what you find to do that you will develop aptitude for larger work. It is by slighting the daily opportunities, by neglecting the little things right at hand, that so many become fruitless and withered. . . .

In fields where the conditions are so objectionable and disheartening that many are unwilling to go to them, remarkable changes have been wrought by the efforts of self-sacrificing workers. Patiently and perseveringly they labored, not relying upon human power, but upon God, and His grace sustained them. The amount of good thus accomplished will never be known in this world, but blessed results will be seen in the great hereafter.[70]

Why Trials?

And he shall sit as a refiner and purifier of silver: and he shall purify the sons of Levi, and purge them as gold and silver, that they may offer unto the Lord an offering in righteousness. Mal. 3:3.

Here is the process, the refining, purifying process, to be carried on by the Lord of hosts. The work is most trying to the soul, but it is only through this process that the rubbish and defiling impurities can be removed. Our trials are all necessary to bring us close to our heavenly Father, in obedience to His will, that we may offer unto the Lord an offering in righteousness. God has given each of us capabilities, talents to improve. We need a new and living experience in the divine life, in order to do the will of God. No amount of past experience will suffice for the present, or will strengthen us to overcome the difficulties in our path. We must have new grace and fresh strength daily in order to be victorious. . . .

Abraham, Moses, Elijah, Daniel, and many others, were all sorely tried, but not in the same way. Everyone has his individual tests and trials in the drama of life, but the very same trial seldom comes twice. Each has his own experience, peculiar in its character and circumstances, to accomplish a certain work. God has a work, a purpose, in the life of each and all of us. Every act, however small, has its place. . . .

Would that all might feel that every step they take may have a lasting and controlling influence upon their own lives and the characters of others. Oh, how much need, then, of communion with God! What need of divine grace to direct every step, and show us how to perfect Christian characters!

Christians will have new scenes and new trials to pass through, where their past experience cannot be a sufficient guide. We need to learn of the divine Teacher as much now as at any period of our lives, and even more. And the more experience we gain, the nearer we draw toward the pure light of heaven, the more shall we discern in ourselves that needs reforming. . . . The path of the just is a progressive one, from strength to strength, from grace to grace, and from glory to glory. The divine illumination will increase more and more, corresponding with our onward movements, qualifying us to meet the responsibilities and emergencies before us.[71]

"Fulness of God"

And to know the love of Christ, which passeth knowledge, that ye might be filled with all the fulness of God. Eph. 3:19.

God calls upon those who know His will to be doers of His word. Weakness, halfheartedness, and indecision provoke the assaults of Satan; and those who permit these traits to grow will be borne helplessly down by the surging waves of temptation. . . .

Every means of grace should be diligently improved that the love of God may abound in the soul more and more, "that ye may approve things that are excellent; that ye may be sincere and without offense till the day of Christ; being filled with the fruits of righteousness" (Phil. 1:10, 11). Your Christian life must take on vigorous and stalwart forms. You can attain to the high standard set before you in the Scriptures, and you must if you would be children of God. You cannot stand still; you must either advance or retrograde. You must have spiritual knowledge, that you "may be able to comprehend with all saints what is the breadth, and length, and depth, and height; and to know the love of Christ," that you may "be filled with all the fulness of God." . . .

Will you have a stinted Christian growth, or will you make healthy progress in the divine life? Where there is spiritual health there is growth. The child of God grows up to the full stature of a man or woman in Christ. There is no limit to his improvement. . . .

We have great victories to gain, and a heaven to lose if we do not gain them. The carnal heart must be crucified; for its tendency is to moral corruption, and the end thereof is death. Nothing but the life-giving influences of the gospel can help the soul. Pray that the mighty energies of the Holy Spirit, with all their quickening, recuperative, and transforming power, may fall like an electric shock on the palsy-stricken soul, causing every nerve to thrill with new life, restoring the whole man from his dead, earthly, sensual state to spiritual soundness. You will thus become partakers of the divine nature, having escaped the corruption that is in the world through lust; and in your souls will be reflected the image of Him by whose stripes you are healed.[72]

Wages or Gift?

The wages of sin is death; but the gift of God is eternal life through Jesus Christ our Lord. Rom. 6:23.

Man was originally endowed with noble powers and a well-balanced mind. He was perfect in his being, and in harmony with God. His thoughts were pure, his aims holy. But through disobedience, his powers were perverted, and selfishness took the place of love. His nature became so weakened through transgression that it was impossible for him, in his own strength, to resist the power of evil. He was made captive by Satan, and would have remained so forever had not God specially interposed. It was the tempter's purpose to thwart the divine plan in man's creation, and fill the earth with woe and desolation.[1]

By nature we are alienated from God. The Holy Spirit describes our condition in such words as these: "Dead in trespasses and sins;" "the whole head is sick, and the whole heart faint;" "no soundness in it" (Eph. 2:1; Isa. 1:5, 6). We are held fast in the snare of Satan, "taken captive by him at his will" (2 Tim. 2:26). God desires to heal us, to set us free. But since this requires an entire transformation, a renewing of our whole nature, we must yield ourselves wholly to Him.

The warfare against self is the greatest battle that was ever fought. The yielding of self, surrendering all to the will of God, requires a struggle; but the soul must submit to God before it can be renewed in holiness. . . .

God does not force the will of His creatures. He cannot accept an homage that is not willingly and intelligently given. A mere forced submission would prevent all real development of mind or character; it would make man a mere automaton. Such is not the purpose of the Creator. He desires that man, the crowning work of His creative power, shall reach the highest possible development. He sets before us the height of blessing to which He desires to bring us through His grace. He invites us to give ourselves to Him, that He may work His will in us. It remains for us to choose whether we will be set free from the bondage of sin, to share the glorious liberty of the sons of God.[2]

Counting the Cost

But what things were gain to me, those I counted loss for Christ. Phil. 3:7.

Moses renounced a prospective kingdom, Paul the advantages of wealth and honor among his people, for a life of burden bearing in God's service. To many the life of these men appears one of renunciation and sacrifice. Was it really so? . . .

Moses was offered the palace of the Pharaohs and the monarch's throne; but the sinful pleasures that make men forget God were in those lordly courts, and he chose instead the "durable riches and righteousness" (Prov. 8:18). Instead of linking himself with the greatness of Egypt, he chose to bind up his life with God's purpose. Instead of giving laws to Egypt, he by divine direction enacted laws for the world. He became God's instrument in giving to men those principles that are the safeguard alike of the home and of society, that are the cornerstone of the prosperity of nations—principles recognized today by the world's greatest men as the foundation of all that is best in human governments.

The greatness of Egypt is in the dust. Its power and civilization have passed away. But the work of Moses can never perish. The great principles of righteousness which he lived to establish are eternal. . . .

With Christ in the wilderness wandering, with Christ on the mount of transfiguration, with Christ in the heavenly courts—his was a life on earth blessing and blessed, and in heaven honored.

Paul also in his manifold labors was upheld by the sustaining power of His presence. "I can do all things," he said, "through Christ which strengtheneth me" (Phil. 4:13). . . . Who can measure the results to the world of Paul's lifework? Of all those beneficent influences that alleviate suffering, that comfort sorrow, that restrain evil, that uplift life from the selfish and the sensual, and glorify it with the hope of immortality, how much is due to the labors of Paul and his fellow workers, as with the gospel of the Son of God they made their unnoticed journey from Asia to the shores of Europe?

What is it worth to any life to have been God's instrument in setting in motion such influences of blessing? What will it be worth in eternity to witness the results of such a lifework?[3]

Look and Live

As Moses lifted up the serpent in the wilderness, even so must the Son of man be lifted up: that whosoever believeth in him should not perish, but have eternal life. John 3:14, 15.

The lifting up of the brazen serpent [Num. 21:4-9] was to teach Israel an important lesson. They could not save themselves from the fatal effect of the poison in their wounds. God alone was able to heal them. Yet they were required to show their faith in the provision which He had made. They must look in order to live. It was their faith that was acceptable with God, and by looking upon the serpent their faith was shown. They knew that there was no virtue in the serpent itself, but it was a symbol of Christ; and the necessity of faith in His merits was thus presented to their minds. Heretofore many had brought their offerings to God, and had felt that in so doing they made ample atonement for their sins. They did not rely upon the Redeemer to come, of whom these offerings were only a type. The Lord would now teach them that their sacrifices, in themselves, had no more power or virtue than the serpent of brass, but were, like that, to lead their minds to Christ, the great sin offering. . . .

The Israelites saved their lives by looking upon the uplifted serpent. That look implied faith. They lived because they believed God's word, and trusted in the means provided for their recovery. So the sinner may look to Christ, and live. He receives pardon through faith in the atoning sacrifice. Unlike the inert and lifeless symbol, Christ has power and virtue in Himself to heal the repenting sinner.

While the sinner cannot save himself, he still has something to do to secure salvation. "Him that cometh to me," says Christ, "I will in no wise cast out" (John 6:37). But we must *come* to Him; and when we repent of our sins, we must believe that He accepts and pardons us. Faith is the gift of God, but the power to exercise it is ours. Faith is the hand by which the soul takes hold upon the divine offers of grace and mercy. . . .

Jesus has pledged His word; He will save all who come unto Him. Though millions who need it to be healed will reject His offered mercy, not one who trusts in His merits will be left to perish.[4]

When Satan Is Powerless

The Lord is nigh unto them that are of a broken heart; and saveth such as be of a contrite spirit. Ps. 34:18.

Satan knows that those who ask God for pardon and grace will obtain it; therefore he presents their sins before them to discourage them. Against those who are trying to obey God, he is constantly seeking occasion for complaint. Even their best and most acceptable service he seeks to make appear corrupt. By countless devices, the most subtle and the most cruel, he endeavors to secure their condemnation.

In his own strength, man cannot meet the charges of the enemy. In sin-stained garments, confessing his guilt, he stands before God. But Jesus, our Advocate, presents an effectual plea in behalf of all who by repentance and faith have committed the keeping of their souls to Him. He pleads their cause, and by the mighty arguments of Calvary, vanquishes their accuser. His perfect obedience to God's law has given Him all power in heaven and in earth, and He claims from His Father mercy and reconciliation for guilty man. To the accuser of His people He declares: "The Lord rebuke thee, O Satan. These are the purchase of My blood, brands plucked from the burning." And to those who rely on Him in faith, He gives the assurance, "Behold, I have caused thine iniquity to pass from thee, and I will clothe thee with change of raiment" (Zech. 3:4).

All who have put on the robe of Christ's righteousness will stand before Him as chosen and faithful and true. Satan has no power to pluck them out of the hand of the Saviour. Not one soul who in penitence and faith has claimed His protection will Christ permit to pass under the enemy's power. His word is pledged: "Let him take hold of my strength, that he may make peace with me; and he shall make peace with me" (Isa. 27:5). The promise given to Joshua is given to all: "If thou wilt keep my charge, . . . I will give thee places to walk among these that stand by" (Zech. 3:7). Angels of God will walk on either side of them, even in this world, and they will stand at last among the angels that surround the throne of God.[5]

For the Hungry and Thirsty

Blessed are they which do hunger and thirst after righteousness: for they shall be filled. Matt. 5:6.

Would that you could conceive of the rich supplies of grace and power awaiting your demand. Those who hunger and thirst for righteousness will be filled. We must exercise greater faith in calling upon God for all needed blessings.[6]

The strength acquired in prayer to God, united with individual effort in training the mind to thoughtfulness and care-taking, prepares the person for daily duties and keeps the spirit in peace under all circumstances, however trying. The temptations to which we are daily exposed make prayer a necessity. In order that we may be kept by the power of God through faith, the desires of the mind should be continually ascending in silent prayer for help, for light, for strength, for knowledge. But thought and prayer cannot take the place of earnest, faithful improvement of the time. Work and prayer are both required in perfecting Christian character.

We must live a twofold life—a life of thought and action, of silent prayer and earnest work. . . . God requires us to be living epistles, known and read of all men. The soul that turns to God for its strength, its support, its power, by daily, earnest prayer, will have noble aspirations, clear perceptions of truth and duty, lofty purposes of action, and a continual hungering and thirsting after righteousness.[7]

Let us realize the weakness of humanity, and see where man fails in his self-sufficiency. We shall then be filled with a desire to be just what God desires us to be—pure, noble, sanctified. We shall hunger and thirst after the righteousness of Christ. To be like God will be the one desire of the soul. This is the desire that filled Enoch's heart. And we read that he walked with God. He studied the character of God to a purpose. He did not mark out his own course, or set up his own will. . . . He strove to conform himself to the divine likeness.[8]

There is no excuse for defection or despondency, because all the promises of heavenly grace are for those who hunger and thirst after righteousness. The intensity of desire represented by hungering and thirsting is a pledge that the coveted supply will be given.[9]

With All Your Heart

And ye shall seek me, and find me,
when ye shall search for me with all your heart. Jer. 29:13.

Many are leaning upon a supposed hope without a true foundation. The fountain is not cleansed, therefore the streams proceeding from that fountain are not pure. Cleanse the fountain, and the streams will be pure. If the heart is right, your words, your dress, your acts, will all be right. True godliness is lacking. I would not dishonor my Master so much as to admit that a careless, trifling, prayerless person is a Christian. No; a Christian has victory over his besetments, over his passions. There is a remedy for the sin-sick soul. That remedy is in Jesus. Precious Saviour! His grace is sufficient for the weakest; and the strongest must also have His grace or perish.

I saw how this grace could be obtained. Go to your closet, and there alone plead with God: "Create in me a clean heart, O God; and renew a right spirit within me" (Ps. 51:10). Be in earnest, be sincere. Fervent prayer availeth much. Jacoblike, wrestle in prayer. Agonize. Jesus, in the garden, sweat great drops of blood; you must make an effort. Do not leave your closet until you feel strong in God; then watch, and just as long as you watch and pray you can keep these evil besetments under, and the grace of God can and will appear in you.

God forbid that I should cease to warn you. Young friends, seek the Lord with all your heart. Come with zeal, and when you sincerely feel that without the help of God you perish, when you pant after Him as the hart panteth after the water brooks, then will the Lord strengthen you speedily. Then will your peace pass all understanding. If you expect salvation, you must pray. . . . Beg of God to work in you a thorough reformation, that the fruits of His Spirit may dwell in you. . . . It is the privilege of every Christian to enjoy the deep movings of the Spirit of God. A sweet heavenly peace will pervade the mind, and you will love to meditate upon God and heaven. You will feast upon the glorious promises of His Word. But know first that you have begun the Christian course. Know that the first steps are taken in the road to everlasting life.[10]

"Not of Yourselves"

For by grace are ye saved through faith; and that not of yourselves: it is the gift of God. Eph. 2:8.

The apostle desired those to whom he was writing to remember that they must reveal in their lives the glorious change wrought in them by Christ's transforming grace. They were to be lights in the world, by their purified, sanctified characters exerting an influence counter to the influence of satanic agencies. They were ever to remember the words, "Not of yourselves." They could not change their own hearts. And when by their efforts souls were led from the ranks of Satan to take their stand for Christ, they were not to claim any credit for the transformation wrought.[11]

God calls upon all who will to come and drink of the waters of life freely. The power of God is the one element of efficiency in the grand work of obtaining the victory over the world, the flesh, and the devil. It is in accordance with the divine plan that we follow every ray of light given of God. Man can accomplish nothing without God, and God has arranged His plans so as to accomplish nothing in the restoration of the human race without the cooperation of the human with the divine. The part man is required to sustain is immeasurably small, yet in the plan of God it is just that part that is needed to make the work a success.[12]

The great change that is seen in the life of a sinner after conversion is not brought about by any human goodness. . . .

He who is rich in mercy has imparted His grace to us. Then let praise and thanksgiving ascend to Him, because He has become our Saviour. Let His love, filling our hearts and minds, flow forth from our lives in rich currents of grace. When we were dead in trespasses and sins, He quickened us into spiritual life. He brought grace and pardon, filling the soul with new life. Thus the sinner passes from death to life. He now takes up his new duties in Christ's service. His life becomes true and strong, filled with good works. "Because I live," Christ said, "ye shall live also." . . .

There will be no second probation. Now, while it is called today, if we will hear the voice of the Lord, and turn fully to Him, He will have mercy upon us, and abundantly pardon.[13]

Peace Restored

Grace be unto you, and peace, from God our Father and the Lord Jesus Christ. Col. 1:2.

Christ is "the Prince of Peace" (Isa. 9:6), and it is His mission to restore to earth and heaven the peace that sin has broken. "Being justified by faith, we have peace with God through our Lord Jesus Christ" (Rom. 5:1). Whoever consents to renounce sin and open his heart to the love of Christ, becomes a partaker of this heavenly peace.

There is no other ground of peace than this. The grace of Christ received into the heart, subdues enmity; it allays strife and fills the soul with love. He who is at peace with God and his fellow men cannot be made miserable. Envy will not be in his heart; evil surmisings will find no room there; hatred cannot exist. The heart that is in harmony with God is a partaker of the peace of heaven and will diffuse its blessed influence on all around. The spirit of peace will rest like dew upon hearts weary and troubled with worldly strife.

Christ's followers are sent to the world with the message of peace. Whoever, by the quiet, unconscious influence of a holy life, shall reveal the love of Christ; whoever, by word or deed, shall lead another to renounce sin and yield his heart to God, is a peacemaker. . . .

The spirit of peace is evidence of their connection with heaven. The sweet savor of Christ surrounds them. The fragrance of the life, the loveliness of the character, reveal to the world the fact that they are children of God. Men take knowledge of them that they have been with Jesus.[14]

The grace of Christ must be woven into every phase of the character. . . . Daily growth into the life of Christ creates in the soul a heaven of peace; in such a life there is continual fruit bearing. . . . In the lives of those who are ransomed by the blood of Christ, self-sacrifice will constantly appear. Goodness and righteousness will be seen. The quiet, inward experience will make the life full of godliness, faith, meekness, patience. This is to be our daily experience. We are to form characters free from sin—characters made righteous in and by the grace of Christ.[15]

Union With Christ

But put ye on the Lord Jesus Christ, and make not provision for the flesh, to fulfil the lusts thereof. Rom. 13:14.

To effect the salvation of men, God employs various agencies. He speaks to them by His word and by His ministers, and He sends by the Holy Spirit messages of warning, reproof, and instruction. These means are designed to enlighten the understanding of the people, to reveal to them their duty and their sins, and the blessings which they may receive; to awaken in them a sense of spiritual want, that they may go to Christ and find in Him the grace they need. . . .

Every individual, by his own act, either puts Christ from him by refusing to cherish His spirit and follow His example, or he enters into a personal union with Christ by self-renunciation, faith, and obedience. We must, each for himself, choose Christ, because He has first chosen us. This union with Christ is to be formed by those who are naturally at enmity with Him. It is a relation of utter dependence, to be entered into by a proud heart. This is close work, and many who profess to be followers of Christ know nothing of it. They nominally accept the Saviour, but not as the sole ruler of their hearts. . . .

To renounce their own will, perhaps their chosen objects of affection or pursuit, requires an effort, at which many hesitate and falter and turn back. Yet this battle must be fought by every heart that is truly converted. We must war against temptations without and within. We must gain the victory over self, crucify the affections and lusts; and then begins the union of the soul with Christ. . . . After this union is formed, it can be preserved only by continual, earnest, painstaking effort. Christ exercises His power to preserve and guard this sacred tie, and the dependent, helpless sinner must act his part with untiring energy, or Satan by his cruel, cunning power will separate him from Christ. . . .

Your birth, your reputation, your wealth, your talents, your virtues, your piety, your philanthropy, . . . will not form a bond of union between your soul and Christ. Your connection with the church . . . will be of no avail unless you believe in Christ. It is not enough to believe *about* Him. You must believe *in* Him. You must rely wholly upon His saving grace.[16]

What Is God's Glory?

For God, who commanded the light to shine out of darkness, hath shined in our hearts, to give the light of the knowledge of the glory of God in the face of Jesus Christ. 2 Cor. 4:6.

The glory of God is His character. While Moses was in the mount, earnestly interceding with God, he prayed, "I beseech thee, show me thy glory." In answer God declared, "I will make all my goodness pass before thee, and I will proclaim the name of the Lord before thee; and will be gracious to whom I will be gracious, and will show mercy on whom I will show mercy." The glory of God—His character—was then revealed: "The Lord passed by before him, and proclaimed, The Lord, The Lord God, merciful and gracious, longsuffering, and abundant in goodness and truth, keeping mercy for thousands, forgiving iniquity and transgression and sin, and that will by no means clear the guilty" (Ex. 33:18, 19; 34:6, 7).

This character was revealed in the life of Christ. That He might by His own example condemn sin in the flesh, He took upon Himself the likeness of sinful flesh. Constantly He beheld the character of God; constantly He revealed this character to the world.

Christ desires His followers to reveal in their lives this same character. In His intercessory prayer for His disciples He declared: "The glory [character] which thou gavest me I have given them; that they may be one, even as we are one; I in them, and thou in me, that they may be made perfect in one; and that the world may know that thou hast sent me, and hast loved them, as thou hast loved me" (John 17:22, 23).

Today it is still His purpose to sanctify and cleanse His church ". . . that he might present it to himself a glorious church, not having spot, or wrinkle, or any such thing . . ." (Eph. 5:26, 27). No greater gift than the character that He revealed, can Christ ask His Father to bestow upon those who believe on Him. What largeness there is in His request! What fullness of grace every follower of Christ has the privilege of receiving! . . . O that we might more fully appreciate the honor Christ confers upon us! By wearing His yoke and learning of Him, we become like Him in aspiration, in meekness and lowliness, in fragrance of character.[17]

Sanctified Perception

At that day shall a man look to his Maker, and his eyes shall have respect to the Holy One of Israel. Isa. 17:7.

The treasures of eternity have been committed to the keeping of Jesus Christ, to give to whomsoever He will; but how sad it is that so many quickly lose sight of the precious grace that is proffered unto them through faith in Him. He will impart the heavenly treasures to those who will believe in Him, look to Him, and abide in Him. . . . He calls upon His chosen, peculiar people who love and serve Him, to come unto Him and ask, and He will give them the bread of life, and endow them with the water of life, which shall be in them as a well of water springing up unto everlasting life.

Jesus brought to our world the accumulated treasures of God, and all who believe upon Him are adopted as His heirs. He declares that great shall be the reward of them who suffer for His name's sake.[18]

This world is but a little atom in the vast domain over which God presides, and yet this little fallen world is more precious in His sight than the ninety and nine which went not astray from the fold. If we will make Him our trust, He will not leave us to become the sport of Satan's temptations. God would have every soul for whom Christ has died become a part of the vine, connected with the parent stock, drawing nourishment from it. Our dependence on God is absolute, and should keep us very humble; and because of our dependence on Him, our knowledge of Him should be greatly increased. God would have us put away every species of selfishness, and come to Him, not as the owner of ourselves, but as the Lord's purchased possession.[19]

God will honor and uphold every truehearted, earnest soul who is seeking to walk before Him in the perfection of the grace of Christ. . . . Can we with keen, sanctified perception appreciate the strength of the promises of God, and appropriate them to our individual selves, not because we are worthy, but because Christ is worthy, not because we are righteous, but because by living faith we claim the righteousness of Christ in our behalf?[20]

The Sum and Substance

But the God of all grace, who hath called us unto his eternal glory by Christ Jesus, after that ye have suffered a while, make you perfect, stablish, strengthen, settle you. 1 Peter 5:10.

When the truth is received, it will work radical changes in life and character; for religion means the abiding of Christ in the heart, and where He is, the soul goes on in spiritual activity, ever growing in grace, ever going on to perfection. . . .

It is no real evidence that you are a Christian because your emotion is stirred, your spirit stirred by truth; the question is, Are you growing up into Christ, your living head? Is the grace of Christ manifested in your life? God gives His grace to men, that they may desire more of His grace. God's grace is ever working upon the human heart, and when it is received, the evidence of its reception will appear in the life and character of its recipient. . . . The grace of Christ in the heart will always promote spiritual life, and spiritual advancement will be made. . . . We do not see the plants grow in the field, and yet we are assured that they do grow, and may we not know of our own spiritual strength and growth? . . .

The sum and substance of the whole matter of Christian grace and experience is contained in believing on Christ, in knowing God and His Son whom He has sent. But here is where many fail, for they lack faith in God. Instead of desiring to be brought into fellowship with Christ in His self-denial and humiliation, they are ever seeking for the supremacy of self. . . .

O, if you loved Him as He has loved you, you would not shun an experience in the dark chapters of the suffering of the Son of God! . . . When we contemplate the humiliation of Christ, beholding His self-denial and self-sacrifice, we are filled with amazement at the manifestation of divine love for guilty man. When for Christ's sake we are called to pass through trials that are of a humiliating nature, if we have the mind of Christ, we shall suffer them with meekness, not resenting injury, or resisting evil. We shall manifest the spirit that dwelt in Christ. . . .

We are to bear Christ's yoke, to work as He worked for the salvation of the lost; and those who are partakers of His sufferings will also be partakers of His glory.[21]

Praise God!

I will mention the lovingkindnesses of the Lord, and the praises of the Lord, according to all that the Lord hath bestowed on us, and the great goodness toward the house of Israel. Isa. 63:7.

When a sense of the loving-kindness of God is constantly refreshing the soul, it will be revealed in the countenance by an expression of peace and joy. It will be manifest in the words and works. And the generous, holy Spirit of Christ, working upon the heart, will yield in the life a converting influence upon others. . . .

Have we not reason to talk of God's goodness and to tell of His power? When friends are kind to us we esteem it a privilege to thank them for their kindness. How much more should we count it a joy to return thanks to the Friend who has given us every good and perfect gift. Then let us, in every church, cultivate thanksgiving to God. Let us educate our lips to praise God in the family circle. . . . Let our gifts and offerings declare our gratitude for the favors we daily receive. In everything we should show forth the joy of the Lord. . . .

David declares, "I love the Lord, because he hath heard my voice and my supplications. Because he hath inclined his ear unto me, therefore will I call upon him as long as I live" (Ps. 116:1, 2). God's goodness in hearing and answering prayer places us under heavy obligation to express our thanksgiving for the favors bestowed upon us. We should praise God much more than we do. The blessings received in answer to prayer should be promptly acknowledged. . . .

We grieve the Spirit of Christ by our complaints and murmurings and repinings. We should not dishonor God by the mournful relation of trials that appear grievous. All trials that are received as educators will produce joy. The whole religious life will be uplifting, elevating, ennobling, fragrant with good words and works.[22]

Let the peace of God reign in your soul. Then you will have strength to bear all suffering, and you will rejoice that you have grace to endure. Praise the Lord; talk of His goodness; tell of His power. Sweeten the atmosphere that surrounds your soul. . . . Praise with heart and soul and voice, Him who is the health of your countenance, your Saviour, and your God.[23]

Nothing Withheld

For the Lord God is a sun and shield: the Lord will give grace and glory: no good thing will he withhold from them that walk uprightly. Ps. 84:11.

He that spared not his own Son, but delivered him up for us all, how shall he not with him also freely give us all things" (Rom. 8:32)? Let us appreciate the great sacrifice that God has made in our behalf. There will never be a time when we shall be more welcome to the gifts of His grace than now. Christ gave His life for men, that they might know how He loved them. He does not want any to perish, but longs to see all coming to repentance. All who will surrender the will to Him may have the life that measures with the life of God. . . . The sword of justice fell upon Him that they might go free. He died that they might live. . . .

We are to stand firmly for the principles of the Word of God, remembering that God is with us to give us strength to meet each new experience. Let us ever maintain the principles of righteousness in our lives, that in the name of the Lord we may go forward from strength to strength. . . . We are to cherish as very precious the work which the Lord has been carrying forward through His commandment-keeping people, and which, through the power of His grace, will grow stronger and more efficient as time advances. The enemy is seeking to becloud the discernment of God's people, and to weaken their efficiency; but if they will labor as the Spirit of God shall direct, He will open doors of opportunity before them for the work of building the old waste places. Their experience will be one of constant growth in assurance and power until the Lord shall descend from heaven with power and great glory to set His seal of final triumph on His faithful ones.

The Lord desires to see the work of the third angel's message carried forward with increasing efficiency. As He has worked in all ages to give courage and power to His people, so in this age He longs to carry to triumphant fulfillment His purposes for His church. He bids the saints advance unitedly, going from strength to greater strength, from faith to increased faith in the righteousness and truth of His cause.[24]

Thought Control?

Wherefore gird up the loins of your mind, be sober, and hope to the end for the grace that is to be brought unto you at the revelation of Jesus Christ. 1 Peter 1:13.

Few realize that it is a duty to exercise control over the thoughts and imaginations. It is difficult to keep the undisciplined mind fixed upon profitable subjects. But if the thoughts are not properly employed, religion cannot flourish in the soul. The mind must be pre-occupied with sacred and eternal things, or it will cherish trifling and superficial thoughts. Both the intellectual and the moral powers must be disciplined, and they will strengthen and improve by exercise.

In order to understand this matter aright, we must remember that our hearts are naturally depraved, and we are unable of ourselves to pursue a right course. It is only by the grace of God, combined with the most earnest effort on our part, that we can gain the victory.[25]

Every wrong tendency may be, through the grace of Christ, repressed, not in a languid, irresolute manner, but with firmness of purpose, with high resolves to make Christ the pattern. Let your love go out for those things that Jesus loved, and be withheld from those things that will give no strength to right impulses. With determined energy seek to learn, and to improve the character every day. You must have firmness of purpose to take yourself in hand and be what you know God would be pleased to have you.[26]

The intellect, as well as the heart, must be consecrated to the service of God. He has claims upon all there is of us. The follower of Christ should not indulge in any gratification, or engage in any enterprise, however innocent or laudable it may appear, which an enlightened conscience tells him would abate his ardor or lessen his spirituality. Every Christian should labor to press back the tide of evil, and save our youth from the influences that would sweep them down to ruin. May God help us to press our way against the current.[27]

In Debt

Forgive us our debts, as we forgive our debtors. Matt. 6:12.

A great blessing is here asked upon conditions. We ourselves state these conditions. We ask that the mercy of God toward us may be measured by the mercy which we extend to others. Christ declares that this is the rule by which the Lord will deal with us: "If ye forgive men their trespasses, your heavenly Father will also forgive you: but if ye forgive not men their trespasses, neither will your Father forgive your trespasses" (Matt. 6:14, 15). Wonderful terms! but how little are they understood or heeded. One of the most common sins, and one that is attended with most pernicious results, is the indulgence of an unforgiving spirit. How many will cherish animosity or revenge and then bow before God and ask to be forgiven as they forgive. Surely they can have no true sense of the import of this prayer or they would not dare take it upon their lips. We are dependent upon the pardoning mercy of God every day and every hour; how then can we cherish bitterness and malice toward our fellow sinners![28]

The fact that we are under so great obligation to Christ places us under the most sacred obligation to those whom He died to redeem. We are to manifest toward them the same sympathy, the same tender compassion and unselfish love, which Christ has manifested toward us.[29]

He who is unforgiving cuts off the very channel through which alone he can receive mercy from God. We should not think that unless those who have injured us confess the wrong we are justified in withholding from them our forgiveness. It is their part, no doubt, to humble their hearts by repentance and confession; but we are to have a spirit of compassion toward those who have trespassed against us, whether or not they confess their faults. However sorely they may have wounded us, we are not to cherish our grievances and sympathize with ourselves over our injuries; but as we hope to be pardoned for our offenses against God we are to pardon all who have done evil to us. . . .

As we come to God, this is the condition which meets us at the threshold, that, receiving mercy from Him, we yield ourselves to reveal His grace to others.[30]

In the School of Christ

I will instruct thee and teach thee in the way which thou shalt go: I will guide thee with mine eye. Ps. 32:8.

He who is seeking with diligence to acquire the wisdom of human schools should remember that another school also claims him as a student. Christ was the greatest teacher the world ever saw. He brought to man knowledge direct from heaven. . . .

In the school of Christ students are never graduated. Among the pupils are both old and young. Those who give heed to the instructions of the divine Teacher constantly advance in wisdom, refinement, and nobility of soul, and thus they are prepared to enter that higher school where advancement will continue throughout eternity.

Infinite Wisdom sets before us the great lessons of life—lessons of duty and happiness. These are often hard to learn, but without them we can make no real progress. . . . It is in this world, amid its trials and temptations, that we are to gain a fitness for the society of the pure and holy. Those who become so absorbed in less important studies that they cease to learn in the school of Christ are meeting with infinite loss. . . .

In the religion of Christ there is a regenerating influence that transforms the entire being, lifting man above every debasing, groveling vice, and raising the thoughts and desires toward God and heaven. . . . Every faculty, every attribute, with which the Creator has endowed the children of men is to be employed for His glory; and in this employment is found its purest, holiest, happiest exercise. While religious principle is held paramount, every advance step taken in the acquirement of knowledge or in the culture of the intellect is a step toward the assimilation of the human with the Divine, the finite with the Infinite. . . .

He who is following the divine guidance has found the only true source of saving grace and real happiness, and has gained the power of imparting happiness to all around him. . . . Love to God purifies and ennobles every taste and desire, intensifies every affection, and brightens every worthy pleasure. It enables men to appreciate and enjoy all that is true, and good, and beautiful.[31]

Examination Day

Examine me, O Lord, and prove me. Ps. 26:2.

The Lord in His providence brings men where He can test their moral powers and reveal their motives of action, that they may improve what is right in themselves and put away that which is wrong. God would have His servants become acquainted with the moral machinery of their own hearts. In order to bring this about, He often permits the fire of affliction to assail them that they may become purified. . . .

True grace is willing to be tried; if we are loath to be searched by the Lord, our condition is serious indeed. God is the refiner and purifier of souls; in the heat of the furnace the dross is separated forever from the true silver and gold of the Christian character. Jesus watches the test. He knows what is needed to purify the precious metal that it may reflect the radiance of His divine love.[32]

I entreat you to "examine yourselves, whether ye be in the faith; prove your own selves" (2 Cor. 13:5). To maintain the warmth and purity of Christian love requires a constant supply of the grace of Christ. . . .

In this season of conflict and trial we need all the support and consolation we can derive from righteous principles, from fixed religious convictions, from the abiding assurance of the love of Christ, and from a rich experience in divine things. We shall attain to the full stature of men and women in Christ Jesus only as the result of a steady growth in grace.[33]

Not in freedom from trial, but in the midst of it, is Christian character developed. Exposure to rebuffs and opposition leads the follower of Christ to greater watchfulness and more earnest prayer to the mighty Helper. Severe trial endured by the grace of God develops patience, vigilance, fortitude, and a deep and abiding trust in God. It is the triumph of the Christian faith that it enables its follower to suffer and be strong; to submit, and thus to conquer; to be killed all the day long, and yet to live; to bear the cross, and thus to win the crown of glory.[34]

What About Good Works?

We are his workmanship, created in Christ Jesus unto good works, which God hath before ordained that we should walk in them. Eph. 2:10.

Our acceptance with God is sure only through His beloved Son, and good works are but the result of the working of His sin-pardoning love. They are no credit to us, and we have nothing accorded to us for our good works by which we may claim a part in the salvation of our souls. Salvation is God's free gift to the believer, given to him for Christ's sake alone. The troubled soul may find peace through faith in Christ, and his peace will be in proportion to his faith and trust. He cannot present his good works as a plea for the salvation of his soul.

But are good works of no real value? Is the sinner who commits sin every day with impunity, regarded of God with the same favor as the one who through faith in Christ tries to work in his integrity? The Scripture answers, "We are His workmanship, created in Christ Jesus unto good works, which God hath before ordained that we should walk in them." In His divine arrangement, through His unmerited favor, the Lord has ordained that good works shall be rewarded. We are accepted through Christ's merit alone; and the acts of mercy, the deeds of charity, which we perform, are the fruits of faith; and they become a blessing to us; for men are to be rewarded according to their works. It is the fragrance of the merit of Christ that makes our good works acceptable to God, and it is grace that enables us to do the works for which He rewards us. Our works in and of themselves have no merit. When we have done all that it is possible for us to do, we are to count ourselves as unprofitable servants. We deserve no thanks from God. We have only done what it was our duty to do, and our works could not have been performed in the strength of our own sinful natures.

The Lord has bidden us to draw nigh to Him and He will draw nigh to us; and drawing nigh to Him, we receive the grace by which to do those works which will be rewarded at His hands.[35]

The labor of love springs from the work of faith. . . . While it is true that our busy activities will not in themselves ensure salvation, it is also true that faith which unites us to Christ will stir the soul to activity.[36]

Watch!

Watch and pray, lest ye enter into temptation. Mark 14:38.

Many today are asleep, as were the disciples. They are not watching and praying lest they enter into temptation.[37]

Let every soul be on the alert. The adversary is on your track. Be vigilant, watching diligently lest some carefully concealed and masterly snare shall take you unawares. Let the careless and indifferent beware lest the day of the Lord come upon them as a thief in the night. . . .

He who overcomes must watch; for, with worldly entanglements, error, and superstition, Satan strives to win Christ's followers from Him. It is not enough that we avoid glaring dangers and perilous, inconsistent moves. We are to keep close to the side of Christ, walking in the path of self-denial and sacrifice. We are in an enemy's country. He who was cast out of heaven has come down with great power. With every conceivable artifice and device he is seeking to take souls captive. Unless we are constantly on guard we shall fall an easy prey to his unnumbered deceptions.[38]

Warning, admonition, promise, all are for us, upon whom the ends of the world are come. "Therefore let us not sleep, as do others; but let us watch and be sober" (1 Thess. 5:6). . . . Watch against the stealthy approach of the enemy, watch against old habits and natural inclinations, lest they assert themselves; force them back, and watch. Watch the thoughts, watch the plans, lest they become self-centered. Watch over the souls whom Christ has purchased with His own blood. Watch for opportunities to do them good.[39]

If you draw close to Jesus and seek to adorn your profession by a well-ordered life and godly conversation, your feet will be kept from straying into forbidden paths. If you will only watch, continually watch unto prayer, if you will do everything as if you were in the immediate presence of God, you will be saved from yielding to temptation, and may hope to be kept pure, spotless, and undefiled till the last. If you hold the beginning of your confidence firm unto the end, your ways will be established in God; and what grace has begun, glory will crown in the kingdom of our God.[40]

Kept From Falling

Now unto him that is able to keep you from falling, and to present you before the presence of his glory with exceeding joy. Jude 24.

In these last days, when iniquity shall abound, and the love of many shall wax cold, God will have a people to glorify His name, and stand as reprovers of unrighteousness. They are to be a "peculiar people," who will be true to the law of God when the world shall seek to make void its precepts; and when the converting power of God works through His servants, the hosts of darkness will array themselves in bitter and determined opposition. . . . There will be a constant conflict from the time of our determination to serve the God of heaven, until we are delivered out of this present evil world. There is no release from this war. . . .

Our work is an aggressive one, and as faithful soldiers of Jesus, we must bear the blood-stained banner into the very strongholds of the enemy. . . . If we will consent to lay down our arms, to lower the blood-stained banner, to become the captives and servants of Satan, we may be released from the conflict and the suffering. But this peace will be gained only at the loss of Christ and heaven. We cannot accept peace on such conditions. Let it be war, war, to the end of earth's history, rather than peace through apostasy and sin.

The work of apostasy begins in some secret rebellion of the heart against the requirements of God's law. Unholy desires, unlawful ambitions, are cherished and indulged, and unbelief and darkness separate the soul from God. If we do not overcome these evils they will overcome us. . . .

The indulgence of spiritual pride, of unholy desires, of evil thoughts, of anything that separates us from an intimate and sacred association with Jesus, imperils our souls. . . . We must "fight the good fight of faith," if we would "lay hold on eternal life" (1 Tim. 6:12). We are "kept by the power of God through faith unto salvation" (1 Peter 1:5). If the thought of apostasy is grievous to you, . . . then "abhor that which is evil; cleave to that which is good" (Rom. 12:9); and believe in Him who is "able to keep you from falling, and to present you faultless before the presence of his glory with exceeding joy."[41]

Established

Now our Lord Jesus Christ himself, and God, even our Father, which hath loved us, and hath given us everlasting consolation and good hope through grace, comfort your hearts, and establish you in every good word and work. 2 Thess. 2:16, 17.

The Saviour made each work of healing an occasion for implanting divine principles in the mind and soul. This was the purpose of His work. He imparted earthly blessings, that He might incline the hearts of men to receive the gospel of His grace.[42]

For three years the disciples had before them the wonderful example of Jesus. Day by day they walked and talked with Him, hearing His words of cheer to the weary and heavy-laden, and seeing the manifestations of His power in behalf of the sick and afflicted. When the time came for Him to leave them, He gave them grace and power to carry forward His work in His name. They were to shed abroad the light of His gospel of love and healing. . . .

The work which the disciples did, we also are to do. Every Christian is to be a missionary. In sympathy and compassion we are to minister to those in need of help. . . . The Saviour identifies Himself with every child of humanity. . . . His followers are not to feel themselves detached from the perishing world around them. They are a part of the great web of humanity, and heaven looks upon them as brothers to sinners as well as to saints. . . . By all that has given us advantage over another—be it education and refinement, nobility of character, Christian training, religious experience—we are in debt to those less favored; and, so far as lies in our power, we are to minister unto them. . . .

He who becomes a child of God should henceforth look upon himself as a link in the chain let down to save the world, one with Christ in His plan of mercy, going forth with Him to seek and save the lost.[43]

The world needs a practical demonstration of what the grace of God can do in restoring to human beings their lost kingship, giving them mastery of themselves. There is nothing that the world needs so much as a knowledge of the gospel's saving power revealed in Christlike lives.[44]

Joy in Sharing

For what is our hope, or joy, or crown of rejoicing?
Are not even ye in the presence of our Lord Jesus Christ at his coming?
For ye are our glory and joy. 1 Thess. 2:19, 20.

God could have reached His object in saving sinners without our aid; but in order for us to develop a character like Christ's, we must share in His work. In order to enter into His joy—the joy of seeing souls redeemed by His sacrifice—we must participate in His labors for their redemption.[45]

Jesus saw in every soul one to whom must be given the call to His kingdom. He reached the hearts of the people by going among them as one who desired their good. He sought them in the public streets, in private houses, on the boats, in the synagogue, by the shores of the lake, and at the marriage feast. He met them at their daily vocations, and manifested an interest in their secular affairs. He carried His instruction into the household, bringing families in their own homes under the influence of His divine presence. His strong personal sympathy helped to win hearts. . . .

It was by personal contact and association that Jesus trained His disciples. Sometimes He taught them, sitting among them on the mountainside; sometimes beside the sea, or walking with them by the way, He revealed the mysteries of the kingdom of God. He did not sermonize as men do today. Wherever hearts were open to receive the divine message, He unfolded the truths of the way of salvation. He did not command His disciples to do this or that, but said, "Follow Me." On His journeys through the country and cities He took them with Him, that they might see how He taught the people. . . .

The example of Christ in linking Himself with the interests of humanity should be followed by all who preach His word, and by all who have received the gospel of His grace. . . . Not alone from the pulpit are the hearts of men touched by divine truth. There is another field of labor, humbler, it may be, but fully as promising. It is found in the home of the lowly, and in the mansion of the great; at the hospitable board, and in gatherings for innocent social enjoyment. . . . Wherever we go we are to carry Jesus with us, and to reveal to others the preciousness of our Saviour.[46]

To God Be the Glory

But we have this treasure in earthen vessels,
that the excellency of the power may be of God, and not of us.
2 Cor. 4:7.

All the good qualities that men possess are the gift of God; their good deeds are performed by the grace of God through Christ. Since they owe all to God, the glory of whatever they are or do belongs to Him alone; they are but instruments in His hands.

More than this—as all the lessons of Bible history—it is a perilous thing to praise or exalt men; for if one comes to lose sight of his entire dependence on God, and to trust to his own strength, he is sure to fall. Man is contending with foes who are stronger than he. . . . It is impossible for us in our own strength to maintain the conflict; and whatever diverts the mind from God, whatever leads to self-exaltation or to self-dependence, is surely preparing the way for our overthrow. The tenor of the Bible is to inculcate distrust of human power and to encourage trust in divine power.[47]

Our heavenly Father has not sent angels from heaven to preach salvation to men. He has opened to us the precious truths of His Word and implanted the truth in our hearts that we may give it to those who are in darkness. If we have indeed tasted of the precious gifts of God in His promises, we are to impart this knowledge to others. . . .

We are individually to work as though a great responsibility rested upon us. We are to manifest untiring energy and tact and zeal in this work and take the burden, feeling the peril in which our neighbors and friends are placed. We are to work as Christ worked. We are to present the truth as it is in Jesus, that the blood of souls shall not be upon our garments. At the same time we are to feel entire dependence and trust in God, for we know we cannot do anything without His grace and power to help. A Paul may plant, and an Apollos, water, but God alone can give the increase.[48]

Our duty, our safety, our happiness and usefulness, and our salvation call upon us each to use the greatest diligence to secure the grace of Christ.[49]

The Reaping

That in the ages to come he might shew the exceeding riches of his grace in his kindness toward us through Christ Jesus. Eph. 2:7.

No one can give place in his own heart and life for the stream of God's blessing to flow to others, without receiving in himself a rich reward. . . .

The grace of Christ in the soul is developing traits of character that are the opposite of selfishness—traits that will refine, ennoble, and enrich the life. Acts of kindness performed in secret will bind hearts together, and will draw them closer to the heart of Him from whom every generous impulse springs. The little attentions, the small acts of love and self-sacrifice, that flow out from the life as quietly as the fragrance from a flower—these constitute no small share of the blessings and happiness of life. And it will be found at last that the denial of self for the good and happiness of others, however humble and uncommended here, is recognized in heaven as a token of our union with Him, the King of glory, who was rich, yet for our sake became poor.

The deeds of kindness may have been done in secret, but the result upon the character of the doer cannot be hidden. If we work with whole-hearted interest as a follower of Christ, the heart will be in close sympathy with God, and the Spirit of God, moving upon our spirit, will call forth the sacred harmonies of the soul in answer to the divine touch.

He who gives increased talents to those who have made a wise improvement of the gifts entrusted to them is pleased to acknowledge the service of His believing people in the Beloved, through whose grace and strength they have wrought. Those who have sought for the development and perfection of Christian character by exercising their faculties in good works, will, in the world to come, reap that which they have sown. The work begun upon earth will reach its consummation in that higher and holier life to endure throughout eternity.[50]

He who is "rich unto all that call upon him," has said, "Give, and it shall be given unto you . . ." (Rom. 10:12; Luke 6:38). . . . Every sacrifice that is made in His ministry will be recompensed according to "the exceeding riches of his grace."[51]

The World Is Waiting

For all things are for your sakes, that the abundant grace might through the thanksgiving of many redound to the glory of God. 2 Cor. 4:15.

The church is God's appointed agency for the salvation of men. It was organized for service, and its mission is to carry the gospel to the world. From the beginning it has been God's plan that through His church shall be reflected to the world His fullness and His sufficiency. The members of the church, those whom He has called out of darkness into His marvelous light, are to show forth His glory. The church is the repository of the riches of the grace of Christ; and through the church will eventually be made manifest, even to "the principalities and powers in heavenly places" (Eph. 3:10), the final and full display of the love of God. . . .

The church is God's fortress, His city of refuge, which He holds in a revolted world. . . .

During ages of spiritual darkness the church of God has been as a city set on a hill. From age to age, through successive generations, the pure doctrines of heaven have been unfolding within its borders. Enfeebled and defective as it may appear, the church is the one object upon which God bestows in a special sense His supreme regard. It is the theater of His grace, in which He delights to reveal His power to transform hearts.[52]

As the rays of the sun penetrate to the remotest corners of the globe, so God designs that the light of the gospel shall extend to every soul upon the earth. . . . At this time, when the enemy is working as never before to engross the minds of men and women, we should be laboring with increasing activity. Diligently, disinterestedly, we are to proclaim the last message of mercy in the cities—in the highways and byways. All classes are to be reached. As we labor we shall meet with different nationalities. None are to be passed by unwarned. The Lord Jesus was the gift of God to the entire world—not to the higher classes alone, and not to one nationality, to the exclusion of others. His saving grace encircles the world. Whosoever will, may drink of the water of life. A world is waiting to hear the message of present truth.[53]

Christ Is Waiting

This gospel of the kingdom shall be preached in all the world for a witness unto all nations; and then shall the end come. Matt. 24:14.

The gospel of Christ is from beginning to end the gospel of saving grace. It is a distinctive and controlling idea. It will be a help to the needy, light for the eyes that are blind to the truth, and a guide to souls seeking for the true foundation. Full and everlasting salvation is within the reach of every soul. Christ is waiting and longing to speak pardon, and impart the freely offered grace. He is watching and waiting, saying as He said to the blind man at the gate of Jericho, "What wilt thou that I should do unto thee?" (Mark 10:51). I will take away thy sins; I will wash you in My blood.

In all the highways of life there are souls to be saved. The blind are groping in darkness. Give them the light, and God will bless you as His laborers.[54]

We need greater earnestness in the cause of Christ. The solemn message of truth should be given with an intensity that would impress unbelievers that God is working with our efforts, that the Most High is our living source of strength.[55]

It is the privilege of every Christian, not only to look for, but to hasten the coming of our Lord Jesus Christ. Were all who profess His name bearing fruit to His glory, how quickly the whole world would be sown with the seed of the gospel. Quickly the last harvest would be ripened, and Christ would come to gather the precious grain.[56]

The time has come when through God's messengers the scroll is being unrolled to the world. The truth contained in the first, second, and third angels' messages must go to every nation, kindred, tongue, and people; it must lighten the darkness of every continent, and extend to the islands of the sea. There must be no delay in this work.

Our watchword is to be, Onward, ever onward! Angels of heaven will go before us to prepare the way. Our burden for the regions beyond can never be laid down till the whole earth is lighted with the glory of the Lord.[57]

The Universe Is Waiting

Go out into the highways and hedges, and compel them to come in, that my house may be filled. Luke 14:23.

In this speck of a world the whole heavenly universe manifests the greatest interest, for Christ has paid an infinite price for the souls of its inhabitants.[58]

Everything in the universe calls upon those who know the truth to consecrate themselves unreservedly to the proclamation of the truth as it has been made known to them in the third angel's message. . . . The working of satanic agencies calls every Christian to stand in his lot.

The work given us is a great and important one, and in it are needed wise, unselfish men, men who understand what it means to give themselves to unselfish effort to save souls. But there is no need for the service of men who are lukewarm, for such men Christ cannot use. Men and women are needed whose hearts are touched with human suffering and whose lives give evidence that they are receiving and imparting light and life and grace.

The people of God are to come close to Christ in self-denial and sacrifice, their one aim being to give the message of mercy to all the world. Some will work in one way and some in another, as the Lord shall call and lead them. But they are all to strive together, seeking to make the work a perfect whole.[59]

The church will not retrograde while the members seek help from the throne of grace, that they may not fail to cooperate in the great work of saving the souls that are on the brink of ruin. . . .

The heavenly universe is waiting for consecrated channels, through which God can communicate with His people, and through them with the world. God will work through a consecrated, self-denying church, and He will reveal His Spirit in a visible and glorious manner, especially in this time, when Satan is working in a masterly manner to deceive the souls of both ministers and people. . . .

Will not the church awake to her responsibility? God is waiting to impart the Spirit of the greatest missionary the world has ever known to those who will work with self-denying, self-sacrificing consecration.[60]

Sons of God

Beloved, now are we the sons of God, and it doth not yet appear what we shall be: but we know that, when he shall appear, we shall be like him; for we shall see him as he is. 1 John 3:2.

Beloved, now are we the sons of God." Can any human dignity equal this? What higher position can we occupy than to be called the sons of the infinite God?[61]

What a stupendous thought, what unheard-of condescension, what amazing love, that finite men may be allied to the Omnipotent! "To them gave he power to become the sons of God, even to them that believe on his name" (John 1:12). "Beloved, now are we the sons of God." Can any worldly honor equal this?

Let us represent the Christian life as it really is; let us make the way cheerful, inviting, interesting. We can do this if we will. We may fill our own minds with vivid pictures of spiritual and eternal things, and in so doing help to make them a reality to other minds. Faith sees Jesus standing as our Mediator at the right hand of God. Faith beholds the mansions He has gone to prepare for those who love Him. Faith sees the robe and crown all prepared for the overcomer. Faith hears the songs of the redeemed, and brings eternal glories near. We must come close to Jesus in loving obedience, if we would see the King in His beauty.[62]

To have fellowship with the Father and His Son Jesus Christ is to be ennobled and elevated, and made a partaker of joys unspeakable and full of glory. Food, clothing, station, and wealth may have their value; but to have a connection with God and to be a partaker of His divine nature is of priceless value. Our lives should be hid with Christ in God; and although it "doth not yet appear what we shall be," "when Christ, who is our life, shall appear" (Col. 3:4), "we shall be like him; for we shall see him as he is." The princely dignity of the Christian character will shine forth as the sun, and the beams of light from the face of Christ will be reflected upon those who have purified themselves even as He is pure. The privilege of becoming sons of God is cheaply purchased, even at the sacrifice of everything we possess, be it life itself.[63]

In Sight of the Goal

I press toward the mark for the prize of the high calling of God in Christ Jesus. Phil. 3:14.

Know ye not that they which run in a race run all, but one receiveth the prize? So run, that ye may obtain. And every man that striveth for the mastery is temperate in all things. Now they do it to obtain a corruptible crown; but we an incorruptible. . . ." (1 Cor. 9:24-27). Those who engaged in running the race to obtain the laurel which was considered a special honor were temperate in all things, so that their muscles, their brains, and every part of them might be in the very best condition to run. . . . Only one received the prize. But in the heavenly race we can all run and all receive the prize. There is no uncertainty, no risk, in the matter. We must put on the heavenly graces, and, with the eye directed upward to the crown of immortality, keep the Pattern ever before us. . . . The humble, self-denying life of our divine Lord we are to keep constantly in view. And then as we seek to imitate Him, keeping our eye upon the mark of the prize, we can run this race with certainty.[64]

If heathen men, who were not controlled by enlightened conscience, who had not the fear of God before them, would submit to deprivation and the discipline of training, denying themselves of every weakening indulgence merely for a wreath of perishable substance and the applause of the multitude, how much more should they who are running the Christian race in the hope of immortality and the approval of High Heaven, be willing to deny themselves unhealthy stimulants and indulgences, which degrade the morals, enfeeble the intellect, and bring the higher powers into subjection to the animal appetites and passions. . . . With intense interest God and heavenly angels mark the self-denial, the self-sacrifice, and the agonizing efforts of those who engage to run the Christian race. . . .

To all those who fully comply with the conditions in God's word, and have a sense of their responsibility to preserve physical vigor and activity of body, that they may have well-balanced minds and healthy morals, the race is not uncertain. They all may gain the prize, and win and wear the crown of immortal glory that fadeth not away.[65]

God's Glory Seen in His Works

Holy, holy, holy, is the Lord of hosts:
the whole earth is full of his glory. Isa. 6:3.

As it came from the Creator's hand, not only the Garden of Eden but the whole earth was exceedingly beautiful. No taint of sin, or shadow of death, marred the fair creation. God's glory "covered the heavens, and the earth was full of his praise" (Hab. 3:3). "The morning stars sang together, and all the sons of God shouted for joy" (Job 38:7). Thus was the earth a fit emblem of Him who is "abundant in goodness and truth" (Ex. 34:6); a fit study for those who were made in His image. The Garden of Eden was a representation of what God desired the whole earth to become, and it was His purpose that, as the human family increased in numbers, they should establish other homes and schools like the one He had given. Thus in course of time the whole earth might be occupied with homes and schools where the words and the works of God should be studied, and where the students should thus be fitted more and more fully to reflect, throughout endless ages, the light of the knowledge of His glory.[1]

When Adam came from the Creator's hand, he bore, in his physical, mental, and spiritual nature, a likeness to his Maker. "God created man in his own image" (Gen. 1:27), and it was His purpose that the longer man lived the more fully he should reveal this image—the more fully reflect the glory of the Creator. All his faculties were capable of development; their capacity and vigor were continually to increase. Vast was the scope offered for their exercise, glorious the field opened to their research. The mysteries of the visible universe—the "wondrous works of him which is perfect in knowledge" (Job 37:16)—invited man's study. Face-to-face, heart-to-heart communion with his Maker was his high privilege. Had he remained loyal to God, all this would have been his forever. Throughout eternal ages he would have continued to gain new treasures of knowledge, to discover fresh springs of happiness, and to obtain clearer and yet clearer conceptions of the wisdom, the power, and the love of God. More and more fully would he have fulfilled the object of his creation, more and more fully have reflected the Creator's glory.[2]

Man Created for God's Glory

Whether therefore ye eat, or drink, or whatsoever ye do, do all to the glory of God. 1 Cor. 10:31.

God created man for His own glory, that after test and trial the human family might become one with the heavenly family. It was God's purpose to repopulate heaven with the human family, if they would show themselves obedient to His every word. Adam was to be tested, to see whether he would be obedient, as the loyal angels, or disobedient. If he stood the test, his instruction to his children would have been only of loyalty. His mind and thoughts would have been as the mind and thoughts of God. . . .

God made Adam after His own character, pure and upright. There were no corrupt principles in the first Adam, no corrupt propensities or tendencies to evil. Adam was as faultless as the angels before God's throne. These things are inexplainable, but many things which now we cannot understand will be made plain when we shall see as we are seen, and know as we are known.[3]

It is recorded of the holy men of old that God was not ashamed to be called their God [Heb. 11:16]. The reason assigned is that instead of coveting earthly possessions or seeking happiness in worldly plans or aspirations they placed their all upon the altar of God and made disposition of it to build up His kingdom. They lived only for God's glory and declared plainly that they were strangers and pilgrims on earth, seeking a better country, that is, an heavenly. Their conduct proclaimed their faith. God could entrust to them His truth and could leave the world to receive from them a knowledge of His will.

But how are the professed people of God today maintaining the honor of His name? How could the world infer that they are a peculiar people? What evidence do they give of citizenship in heaven? . . .

Puritan plainness and simplicity should mark the dwellings and apparel of all who believe the solemn truths for this time. . . . Our dress, our dwellings, our conversation, should testify of our consecration to God. What power would attend those who thus evinced that they had given up all for Christ.[4]

God's Glorious Plan

That as sin hath reigned unto death, even so might grace reign through righteousness unto eternal life by Jesus Christ our Lord. Rom. 5:21.

The plan by which alone man's salvation could be secured, involved all heaven in its infinite sacrifice. The angels could not rejoice as Christ opened before them the plan of redemption, for they saw that man's salvation must cost their loved Commander unutterable woe. In grief and wonder they listened to His words as He told them how He must descend from heaven's purity and peace, its joy and glory and immortal life, and come in contact with the degradation of earth, to endure its sorrow, shame, and death. He was to stand between the sinner and the penalty of sin; yet few would receive Him as the Son of God. He would leave His high position as the Majesty of heaven, appear upon earth and humble Himself as a man, and by His own experience become acquainted with the sorrows and temptations which man would have to endure. All this would be necessary in order that He might be able to succor them that should be tempted. When His mission as a teacher should be ended, He must be delivered into the hands of wicked men and be subjected to every insult and torture that Satan could inspire them to inflict. He must die the cruelest of deaths, lifted up between the heavens and the earth as a guilty sinner. He must pass long hours of agony so terrible that angels could not look upon it, but would veil their faces from the sight. He must endure anguish of soul, the hiding of His Father's face, while the guilt of transgression—the weight of the sins of the whole world—should be upon Him. . . .

He bade the angelic host to be in accord with the plan that His Father had accepted, and rejoice that, through His death, fallen man could be reconciled to God.

Then joy, inexpressible joy, filled heaven. The glory and blessedness of a world redeemed, outmeasured even the anguish and sacrifice of the Prince of life. Through the celestial courts echoed the first strains of that song which was to ring out above the hills of Bethlehem—"Glory to God in the highest, and on earth peace, good will toward men" (Luke 2:14).[5]

The Kingdom of Heaven in Miniature

Jesus taketh Peter, James, and John his brother, and bringeth them up into an high mountain apart, and was transfigured before them: and his face did shine as the sun, and his raiment was white as the light. Matt. 17:1, 2.

Evening is drawing on as Jesus calls to His side three of His disciples, Peter, James, and John, and leads them across the fields, and far up a rugged path, to a lonely mountainside. . . .

Stepping a little aside from them, the Man of Sorrows pours out His supplications with strong crying and tears. He prays for strength to endure the test in behalf of humanity. . . . And He pours out His heart longings for His disciples, that in the hour of the power of darkness their faith may not fail. . . .

Now the burden of His prayer is that they may be given a manifestation of the glory He had with the Father before the world was, that His kingdom may be revealed to human eyes, and that His disciples may be strengthened to behold it. He pleads that they may witness a manifestation of His divinity that will comfort them in the hour of His supreme agony with the knowledge that He is of a surety the Son of God and that His shameful death is a part of the plan of redemption.

His prayer is heard. While He is bowed in lowliness upon the stony ground, suddenly the heavens open, the golden gates of the city of God are thrown wide, and holy radiance descends upon the mount, enshrouding the Saviour's form. Divinity from within flashes through humanity, and meets the glory coming from above. Arising from His prostrate position, Christ stands in godlike majesty. The soul agony is gone. His countenance now shines "as the sun," and His garments are "white as the light."

The disciples, awaking, behold the flood of glory that illuminates the mount. In fear and amazement they gaze upon the radiant form of their Master. . . . Beside Him are two heavenly beings, in close converse with Him. They are Moses, who upon Sinai had talked with God; and Elijah, to whom the high privilege was given . . . never to come under the power of death. . . . Upon the mount the future kingdom of glory was represented in miniature—Christ the King, Moses a representative of the risen saints, and Elijah of the translated ones.[6]

Still Future

Thy kingdom come. Matt. 6:10.

The disciples of Christ were looking for the immediate coming of the kingdom of His glory, but in giving them this prayer Jesus taught that the kingdom was not then to be established. They were to pray for its coming as an event yet future. But this petition was also an assurance to them. While they were not to behold the coming of the kingdom in their day, the fact that Jesus made them pray for it is evidence that in God's own time it will surely come.

The kingdom of God's grace is now being established, as day by day hearts that have been full of sin and rebellion yield to the sovereignty of His love. But the full establishment of the kingdom of His glory will not take place until the second coming of Christ to this world.[7]

Not until the personal advent of Christ can His people receive the kingdom. The Saviour said: "When the Son of man shall come in his glory, and all the holy angels with him, then shall he sit upon the throne of his glory: and before him shall be gathered all nations. . . . Then shall the King say unto them on his right hand, Come, ye blessed of my Father, inherit the kingdom prepared for you from the foundation of the world" (Matt. 25:31-34). . . . When the Son of man comes, the dead are raised incorruptible and the living are changed. By this great change they are prepared to receive the kingdom. . . . Man in his present state is mortal, corruptible; but the kingdom of God will be incorruptible, enduring forever. Therefore man in his present state cannot enter the kingdom of God. But when Jesus comes, He confers immortality upon His people; and then He calls them to inherit the kingdom of which they have hitherto been only heirs.[8]

If "ye are Christ's," "all things are yours" (1 Cor. 3:23, 21). But you are as a child who is not yet placed in control of his inheritance. God does not entrust to you your precious possession, lest Satan by his wily arts should beguile you, as he did the first pair in Eden. Christ holds it for you, safe beyond the spoiler's reach.[9]

Why Not Now?

For they shall all know me, from the least of them unto the greatest of them, saith the Lord. Jer. 31:34.

Jesus said, "This gospel of the kingdom shall be preached in all the world for a witness unto all nations" (Matt. 24:14). His kingdom will not come until the good tidings of His grace have been carried to all the earth. Hence, as we give ourselves to God, and win other souls to Him, we hasten the coming of His kingdom. Only those who devote themselves to His service . . . pray in sincerity, "Thy kingdom come." . . .

The petition, "Thy will be done in earth, as it is in heaven," is a prayer that the reign of evil on this earth may be ended, that sin may be forever destroyed, and the kingdom of righteousness be established. Then in earth as in heaven will be fulfilled "all the good pleasure of his goodness" (2 Thess. 1:11).[10]

Christ will not be satisfied until the victory is complete, and "He shall see of the travail of his soul, and shall be satisfied" (Isa. 53:11). All the nations of the earth shall hear the gospel of His grace. Not all will receive His grace; but "a seed shall serve him; it shall be accounted to the Lord for a generation" (Ps. 22:30). "The kingdom and dominion, and the greatness of the kingdom under the whole heaven, shall be given to the people of the saints of the Most High," and the "earth shall be full of the knowledge of the Lord, as the waters cover the sea." "So shall they fear the name of the Lord from the west, and his glory from the rising of the sun" (Dan. 7:27; Isa. 11:9; 59:19).

"How beautiful upon the mountains are the feet of him that bringeth good tidings, that publisheth peace; that bringeth good tidings of good, that publisheth salvation; that saith unto Zion, Thy God reigneth! . . . Break forth into joy, sing together, ye waste places: . . . for the Lord hath comforted his people. . . . The Lord hath made bare his holy arm in the eyes of all the nations; and all the ends of the earth shall see the salvation of our God" (Isa. 52:7-10).[11]

Looking Into Eternity

Look up, and lift up your heads; for your redemption draweth nigh.
Luke 21:28.

If the church will put on the robe of Christ's righteousness, withdrawing from all allegiance with the world, there is before her the dawn of a bright and glorious day. God's promise to her will stand fast forever. . . . Truth, passing by those who despise and reject it, will triumph. Although at times apparently retarded, its progress has never been checked. . . . Endowed with divine energy, it will cut its way through the strongest barriers and triumph over every obstacle.

What sustained the Son of God during His life of toil and sacrifice? He saw the results of the travail of His soul and was satisfied. Looking into eternity, He beheld the happiness of those who through His humiliation had received pardon and everlasting life. His ear caught the shout of the redeemed. He heard the ransomed ones singing the song of Moses and the Lamb.

We may have a vision of the future, the blessedness of heaven. In the Bible are revealed visions of the future glory, scenes pictured by the hand of God, and these are dear to His church. By faith we may stand on the threshold of the eternal city, and hear the gracious welcome given to those who in this life cooperate with Christ, regarding it as an honor to suffer for His sake. As the words are spoken, "Come, ye blessed of my Father," they cast their crowns at the feet of the Redeemer, exclaiming, "Worthy is the Lamb that was slain to receive power, and riches, and wisdom, and strength, and honour, and glory, and blessing. . . . Honour, and glory, and power, be unto him that sitteth upon the throne, and unto the Lamb for ever and ever" (Matt. 25:34; Rev. 5:12, 13).

There the redeemed greet those who led them to the Saviour, and all unite in praising Him who died that human beings might have the life that measures with the life of God. The conflict is over. Tribulation and strife are at an end. Songs of victory fill all heaven as the ransomed ones take up the joyful strain, Worthy, worthy is the Lamb that was slain, and lives again, a triumphant conqueror.[12]

Who Are Eligible?

The wise shall inherit glory. Prov. 3:35.

God has elected a character in harmony with His law, and anyone who shall reach the standard of His requirement will have an entrance into the kingdom of glory. Christ Himself said, "He that believeth on the Son hath everlasting life: and he that believeth not on the Son shall not see life" (John 3:36). "Not every one that saith unto me, Lord, Lord, shall enter into the kingdom of heaven; but he that *doeth the will of my Father* which is in heaven" (Matt. 7:21). And in the Revelation He declares, "Blessed are they that do his commandments, that they may have right to the tree of life, and may enter in through the gates into the city" (Rev. 22:14). As regards man's final salvation, this is the only election brought to view in the Word of God.

Every soul is elected who will work out his own salvation with fear and trembling. He is elected who will put on the armor, and fight the good fight of faith. He is elected who will watch unto prayer, who will search the Scriptures, and flee from temptation. He is elected who will have faith continually, and who will be obedient to every word that proceedeth out of the mouth of God. The *provisions* of redemption are free to all; the *results* of redemption will be enjoyed by those who have complied with the conditions.[13]

Satan is ever at work endeavoring to pervert what God has spoken, to blind the mind and darken the understanding, and thus lead men into sin. This is why the Lord is so explicit, making His requirements so very plain that none need err. God is constantly seeking to draw men close under His protection, that Satan may not practice his cruel, deceptive power upon them. He has condescended to speak to them with His own voice, to write with His own hand the living oracles. And these blessed words, all instinct with life and luminous with truth, are committed to men as a perfect guide. . . .

Every chapter and every verse of the Bible is a communication from God to men. . . . If studied and obeyed, it would lead God's people, as the Israelites were led, by the pillar of cloud by day and the pillar of fire by night.[14]

Preparing to Live With Angels

I beseech you therefore, brethren, by the mercies of God, that ye present your bodies a living sacrifice, holy, acceptable unto God, which is your reasonable service. Rom. 12:1.

We have no doubt . . . that the doctrines we hold today are present truth, and that we are nearing the judgment. We are preparing to meet Him who, escorted by a retinue of holy angels, is to appear in the clouds of heaven to give the faithful and the just the finishing touch of immortality. . . .

We embrace the truth of God with our different faculties, and as we come under the influence of that truth, it will accomplish the work for us which is necessary to give us a moral fitness for the kingdom of glory and for the society of the heavenly angels. We are now in God's workshop. Many of us are rough stones from the quarry. But as we lay hold upon the truth of God, its influence affects us. It elevates us and removes from us every imperfection and sin, of whatever nature. Thus we are prepared to see the King in His beauty and finally to unite with the pure and heavenly angels in the kingdom of glory. It is here that this work is to be accomplished for us, here that our bodies and spirits are to be fitted for immortality.

We are in a world that is opposed to righteousness and purity of character, and to a growth in grace. Wherever we look we see corruption and defilement, deformity and sin. And what is the work that we are to undertake here just previous to receiving immortality? It is to preserve our bodies holy, our spirits pure, that we may stand forth unstained amid the corruptions teeming around us in these last days.[15]

The light shines clearly, and none need be ignorant, for the great God Himself is man's instructor. . . . He designs that the great subject of health reform shall be agitated and the public mind deeply stirred to investigate; for it is impossible for men and women, with all their sinful, health-destroying, brain-enervating habits, to discern sacred truth, through which they are to be sanctified, refined, elevated, and made fit for the society of heavenly angels in the kingdom of glory.[16]

Learn the Song of Triumph Now

I will sing unto the Lord, for he hath triumphed gloriously. Ex. 15:1.

This song and the great deliverance which it commemorates, made an impression never to be effaced from the memory of the Hebrew people. From age to age it was echoed by the prophets and singers of Israel, testifying that Jehovah is the strength and deliverance of those who trust in Him. That song does not belong to the Jewish people alone. It points forward to the destruction of all the foes of righteousness, and the final victory of the Israel of God. The prophet of Patmos beholds the white-robed multitude that "have gotten the victory," standing on the "sea of glass mingled with fire," having "the harps of God. And they sing the song of Moses the servant of God, and the song of the Lamb" (Rev. 15:2, 3).

"Not unto us, O Lord, not unto us, but unto thy name give glory, for thy mercy, and for thy truth's sake" (Ps. 115:1). Such was the spirit that pervaded Israel's song of deliverance, and it is the spirit that should dwell in the hearts of all who love and fear God. In freeing our souls from the bondage of sin, God has wrought for us a deliverance greater than that of the Hebrews at the Red Sea. . . . The daily blessings that we receive from the hand of God, and above all else the death of Jesus to bring happiness and heaven within our reach, should be a theme for constant gratitude. What compassion, what matchless love, has God shown to us, lost sinners, in connecting us with Himself, to be to Him a peculiar treasure! . . . We should praise God for the blessed hope held out before us in the great plan of redemption, we should praise Him for the heavenly inheritance and for His rich promises; praise Him that Jesus lives to intercede for us. . . .

All the inhabitants of heaven unite in praising God. Let us learn the song of the angels now, that we may sing it when we join their shining ranks. Let us say with the psalmist, "While I live, will I praise the Lord: I will sing praises unto my God while I have any being" (Ps. 146:2). "Let the people praise thee, O God; let all the people praise thee" (Ps. 67:5).[17]

While We Wait

Let your loins be girded about, and your lights burning; and ye yourselves like unto men that wait for their lord. Luke 12:35, 36.

Now is the time to prepare for the coming of our Lord. Readiness to meet Him cannot be attained in a moment's time. Preparatory to that solemn scene there must be vigilant waiting and watching, combined with earnest work. So God's children glorify Him. Amid the busy scenes of life their voices will be heard speaking words of encouragement, faith, and hope. All they have and are is consecrated to the Master's service. . . .

Christ tells us when the day of His kingdom shall be ushered in. He does not say that all the world will be converted, but that "this gospel of the kingdom shall be preached in all the world for a witness unto all nations; and then shall the end come" (Matt. 24:14). By giving the gospel to the world, it is in our power to hasten the coming of the day of God. Had the church of Christ done her appointed work as the Lord ordained, the whole world would before this have been warned, and the Lord Jesus would have come to the earth in power and great glory.

Living power must attend the message of Christ's second appearing. We must not rest until we see many souls converted to the blessed hope of the Lord's return. In the days of the apostles the message that they bore wrought a real work, turning souls from idols to serve the living God. The work to be done today is just as real, and the truth is just as much truth; only we are to give the message with as much more earnestness as the coming of the Lord is nearer. The message for this time is positive, simple, and of the deepest importance. We must act like men and women who believe it. Waiting, watching, working, praying, warning the world—this is our work.[18]

I have been deeply impressed by scenes that have recently passed before me in the night season. There seemed to be a great movement—a work of revival—going forward in many places. Our people were moving into line, responding to God's call. My brethren, the Lord is speaking to us. Shall we not heed His call? Shall we not trim our lamps, and act like men who look for their Lord to come?[19]

"Homeward Bound!"

Then shall the King say unto them on his right hand, Come, ye blessed of my Father, inherit the kingdom prepared for you from the foundation of the world. Matt. 25:34.

The coming of Christ is nearer than when we first believed. The great controversy is nearing its end. The judgments of God are in the land. They speak in solemn warning, saying: "Be ye also ready: for in such an hour as ye think not the Son of man cometh" (Matt. 24:44). . . .

We are living in the closing scenes of this earth's history. Prophecy is fast fulfilling. The hours of probation are fast passing. We have no time—not a moment—to lose. Let us not be found sleeping on guard. Let no one say in his heart or by his works: "My Lord delayeth his coming" (Matt. 24:48). Let the message of Christ's soon return sound forth in earnest words of warning. . . .

The Lord is soon to come, and we must be prepared to meet Him in peace. Let us be determined to do all in our power to impart light to those around us. We are not to be sad, but cheerful, and we are to keep the Lord Jesus ever before us. He is soon coming, and we must be ready and waiting for His appearing. Oh, how glorious it will be to see Him and be welcomed as His redeemed ones! Long have we waited, but our hope is not to grow dim. If we can but see the King in His beauty we shall be forever blessed. I feel as if I must cry aloud: "Homeward bound!" We are nearing the time when Christ will come in power and great glory to take His ransomed ones to their eternal home. . . .

Long have we waited for our Saviour's return. But nonetheless sure is the promise. Soon we shall be in our promised home. There Jesus will lead us beside the living stream flowing from the throne of God and will explain to us the dark providences through which on this earth He brought us in order to perfect our characters. There we shall behold with undimmed vision the beauties of Eden restored. Casting at the feet of the Redeemer the crowns that He has placed on our heads, and touching our golden harps, we shall fill all heaven with praise to Him that sitteth on the throne.[20]

What a Reward!

If any man's work abide . . . , he shall receive a reward. 1 Cor. 3:14.

Glorious will be the reward bestowed when the faithful workers gather about the throne of God and of the Lamb. When John in his mortal state beheld the glory of God, he fell as one dead; he was not able to endure the sight. But when the children of God shall have put on immortality, they will "see him as he is" (1 John 3:2). They will stand before the throne, accepted in the Beloved. All their sins have been blotted out, all their transgressions borne away. Now they can look upon the undimmed glory of the throne of God. They have been partakers with Christ in His sufferings, they have been workers together with Him in the plan of redemption, and they are partakers with Him in the joy of seeing souls saved in the kingdom of God, there to praise God through all eternity. . . .

In that day the redeemed will shine forth in the glory of the Father and the Son. The angels, touching their golden harps, will welcome the King and His trophies of victory. . . . A song of triumph will peal forth, filling all heaven. Christ has conquered. He enters the heavenly courts, accompanied by His redeemed ones, the witnesses that His mission of suffering and sacrifice has not been in vain. . . .

There are homes for the pilgrims of earth. There are robes for the righteous, with crowns of glory and palms of victory. All that has perplexed us in the providences of God will in the world to come be made plain. The things hard to be understood will then find explanation. The mysteries of grace will unfold before us. Where our finite minds discovered only confusion and broken promises, we shall see the most perfect and beautiful harmony. We shall know that infinite love ordered the experiences that seemed most trying. As we realize the tender care of Him who makes all things work together for our good, we shall rejoice with joy unspeakable and full of glory.[21]

I urge you to prepare for the coming of Christ in the clouds of heaven. . . . Prepare for the judgment, that when Christ shall come, to be admired in all them that believe, you may be among those who will meet Him in peace.[22]

Christ's Glorious Appearing

When the Son of man shall come in his glory, and all the holy angels with him, then shall he sit upon the throne of his glory. Matt. 25:31.

The voice of God is heard from heaven, declaring the day and hour of Jesus' coming, and delivering the everlasting covenant to His people. Like peals of loudest thunder His words roll through the earth. The Israel of God stand listening, with their eyes fixed upward. Their countenances are lighted up with His glory. . . .

Soon there appears in the east a small black cloud, about half the size of a man's hand. . . . The people of God know this to be the sign of the Son of man. In solemn silence they gaze upon it as it draws nearer the earth, becoming lighter and more glorious, until it is a great white cloud, its base a glory like consuming fire, and above it the rainbow of the covenant. Jesus rides forth as a mighty conqueror. . . . With anthems of celestial melody the holy angels, a vast, unnumbered throng, attend Him on His way. The firmament seems filled with radiant forms—"ten thousand times ten thousand, and thousands of thousands" (Rev. 5:11). No human pen can portray the scene; no mortal mind is adequate to conceive its splendor. . . .

The righteous cry with trembling: "Who shall be able to stand?" (Rev. 6:17). The angels' song is hushed, and there is a period of awful silence. Then the voice of Jesus is heard, saying: "My grace is sufficient for you" (2 Cor. 12:9). The faces of the righteous are lighted up, and joy fills every heart. And the angels strike a note higher and sing again. . . .

The King of kings descends upon the cloud, wrapped in flaming fire. The heavens are rolled together as a scroll, the earth trembles before Him, and every mountain and island is moved out of its place. . . . The wicked pray to be buried beneath the rocks of the mountains rather than meet the face of Him whom they have despised and rejected. . . . Those who would have destroyed Christ and His faithful people now witness the glory which rests upon them. In the midst of their terror they hear the voices of the saints in joyful strains exclaiming: "Lo, this is our God; we have waited for him, and he will save us" (Isa. 25:9).[23]

Victory Over Death

For the Lord himself shall descend from heaven with a shout, with the voice of the archangel, and with the trump of God: and the dead in Christ shall rise first: then we which are alive and remain shall be caught up together with them in the clouds, to meet the Lord in the air: and so shall we ever be with the Lord. 1 Thess. 4:16, 17.

The voice of the Son of God calls forth the sleeping saints. . . . From the prison house of death they come, clothed with immortal glory, crying: "O death, where is thy sting? O grave, where is thy victory?" (1 Cor. 15:55). . . .

The living righteous are changed "in a moment, in the twinkling of an eye." At the voice of God they were glorified; now they are made immortal and with the risen saints are caught up to meet their Lord in the air. . . .

Before entering the City of God, the Saviour bestows upon His followers the emblems of victory and invests them with the insignia of their royal state. . . . Upon the heads of the overcomers, Jesus with His own right hand places the crown of glory. For each there is a crown, bearing his own "new name," and the inscription, "Holiness to the Lord." In every hand are placed the victor's palm and the shining harp. Then, as the commanding angels strike the note, every hand sweeps the harp strings with skillful touch, awaking sweet music in rich, melodious strains. Rapture unutterable thrills every heart, and each voice is raised in grateful praise. . . .

Before the ransomed throng is the Holy City. Jesus opens wide the pearly gates, and the nations that have kept the truth enter in. . . . Then that voice, richer than any music that ever fell on mortal ear, is heard, saying: "Your conflict is ended." "Come, ye blessed of my Father, inherit the kingdom prepared for you from the foundation of the world" (Matt. 25:34).

Now is fulfilled the Saviour's prayer for His disciples, "I will that they also, whom thou hast given me, be with me where I am" (John 17:24). "Faultless before the presence of his glory with exceeding joy" (Jude 24), Christ presents to the Father the purchase of His blood. . . . Oh, the wonders of redeeming love! The rapture of that hour when the infinite Father, looking upon the ransomed, shall behold His image . . . ![24]

Joy Everlasting

The ransomed of the Lord shall return, and come to Zion with song and everlasting joy upon their heads: they shall obtain joy and gladness, and sorrow and sighing shall flee away. Isa. 35:10.

When Christ came to this earth the first time, He came in lowliness and obscurity, and His life here was one of suffering and poverty. . . . At His second coming all will be changed. Not as a prisoner surrounded by a rabble will men see Him, but as heaven's King. Christ will come in His own glory, in the glory of His Father, and in the glory of the holy angels. Ten thousand times ten thousand and thousands of thousands of angels, the beautiful, triumphant sons of God, possessing surpassing loveliness and glory, will escort Him on His way. In the place of a crown of thorns, He will wear a crown of glory—a crown within a crown. In the place of that old purple robe, He will be clothed in a garment of whitest white, "so as no fuller on earth can white" (Mark 9:3) it. And on His vesture and on His thigh a name will be written, "King of kings, and Lord of lords." . . .

To His faithful followers Christ has been a daily companion, a familiar friend. They have lived in close, constant communion with God. Upon them the glory of the Lord has risen. In them the light of the knowledge of the glory of God in the face of Jesus Christ has been reflected. Now they rejoice in the undimmed rays of the brightness and glory of the King in His majesty. They are prepared for the communion of heaven; for they have heaven in their hearts.

With uplifted heads, with the bright beams of the Sun of Righteousness shining upon them, with rejoicing that their redemption draweth nigh, they go forth to meet the Bridegroom. . . .

A little longer, and we shall see the King in His beauty. A little longer, and He will wipe all tears from our eyes. . . . Then by innumerable voices will be sung the song, "Behold, the tabernacle of God is with men, and he shall dwell with them, and they shall be his people, and God himself shall be with them, and be their God" (Rev. 21:3). . . .

"Wherefore, beloved, seeing that ye look for such things, be diligent that ye may be found of him in peace, without spot, and blameless" (2 Peter 3:14).[25]

Home At Last!

But as it is written, Eye hath not seen, nor ear heard, neither have entered into the heart of man, the things which God hath prepared for them that love him. 1 Cor. 2:9.

As your senses delight in the attractive loveliness of the earth, think of the world that is to come, that shall never know the blight of sin and death; where the face of nature will no more wear the shadow of the curse. Let your imagination picture the home of the saved, and remember that it will be more glorious than your brightest imagination can portray. In the varied gifts of God in nature we see but the faintest gleaming of His glory.[26]

And by and by the gates of heaven will be thrown open to admit God's children, and from the lips of the King of glory the benediction will fall on their ears like richest music—"Come, ye blessed of my Father, inherit the kingdom prepared for you from the foundation of the world" (Matt. 25:34). Then the redeemed will be welcomed to the home that Jesus is preparing for them.[27]

I saw Jesus lead the redeemed company to the gate of the city. He laid hold of the gate and swung it back on its glittering hinges, and bade the nations that had kept the truth enter in. Within the city there was everything to feast the eye. Rich glory they beheld everywhere. Then Jesus looked upon His redeemed saints; their countenances were radiant with glory; and as He fixed His loving eyes upon them, He said, with His rich, musical voice, "I behold the travail of My soul, and am satisfied. This rich glory is yours to enjoy eternally. Your sorrows are ended. There shall be no more death, neither sorrow nor crying, neither shall there be any more pain." . . .

Language is altogether too feeble to attempt a description of heaven. As the scene rises before me, I am lost in amazement. Carried away with the surpassing splendor and excellent glory, I lay down the pen, and exclaim, "Oh, what love! what wondrous love!" The most exalted language fails to describe the glory of heaven or the matchless depths of a Saviour's love.[28]

Eden Restored

To him that overcometh will I give to eat of the tree of life, which is in the midst of the paradise of God. Rev. 2:7.

The Garden of Eden remained upon the earth long after man had become an outcast from its pleasant paths. The fallen race were long permitted to gaze upon the home of innocence, their entrance barred only by the watching angels. At the cherubim-guarded gate of Paradise the divine glory was revealed. Hither came Adam and his sons to worship God. Here they renewed their vows of obedience to that law the transgression of which had banished them from Eden. When the tide of iniquity overspread the world, and the wickedness of men determined their destruction by a flood of waters, the hand that had planted Eden withdrew it from the earth. But in the final restitution, when there shall be "a new heaven and a new earth" (Rev. 21:1), it is to be restored more gloriously adorned than at the beginning.

Then they that have kept God's commandments shall breathe in immortal vigor beneath the tree of life; and through unending ages the inhabitants of sinless worlds shall behold, in that garden of delight, a sample of the perfect work of God's creation, untouched by the curse of sin—a sample of what the whole earth would have become, had man but fulfilled the Creator's glorious plan.[29]

Adam is reinstated in his first dominion. Transported with joy, he beholds the trees that were once his delight—the very trees whose fruit he himself had gathered in the days of his innocence and joy. He sees the vines that his own hands have trained, the very flowers that he once loved to care for. His mind grasps the reality of the scene; he comprehends that this is indeed Eden restored.[30]

Restored to the tree of life in the long-lost Eden, the redeemed will "grow up" to the full stature of the race in its primeval glory. The last lingering traces of the curse of sin will be removed, and Christ's faithful ones will appear in "the beauty of the Lord our God" (Ps. 90:17), in mind and soul and body reflecting the perfect image of their Lord. Oh, wonderful redemption! long talked of, long hoped for, contemplated with eager anticipation, but never fully understood.[31]

All Suffering Ended

And God shall wipe away all tears from their eyes; and there shall be no more death, neither sorrow, nor crying, neither shall there be any more pain: for the former things are passed away. Rev. 21:4.

Pain cannot exist in the atmosphere of heaven. In the home of the redeemed there will be no tears, no funeral trains, no badges of mourning. "The inhabitant shall not say, I am sick: the people that dwell therein shall be forgiven their iniquity" (Isa. 33:24). One rich tide of happiness will flow and deepen as eternity rolls on.[32]

The time has come to which holy men have looked with longing since the flaming sword barred the first pair from Eden, the time for the "redemption of the purchased possession" (Eph. 1:14). The earth originally given to man as his kingdom, betrayed by him into the hands of Satan, and so long held by the mighty foe, has been brought back by the great plan of redemption. All that was lost by sin has been restored. . . . God's original purpose in the creation of the earth is fulfilled as it is made the eternal abode of the redeemed. . . .

There, "the wilderness and the solitary place shall be glad for them; and the desert shall rejoice, and blossom as the rose" (Isa. 35:1). "Instead of the thorn shall come up the fir tree, and instead of the brier shall come up the myrtle tree" (Isa. 55:13). "The wolf also shall dwell with the lamb, and the leopard shall lie down with the kid; . . . and a little child shall lead them" (Isa. 11:6). "They shall not hurt nor destroy in all my holy mountain" (verse 9), saith the Lord.[33]

One reminder alone remains: our Redeemer will ever bear the marks of His crucifixion. Upon His wounded head, upon His side, His hands and feet, are the only traces of the cruel work that sin has wrought. . . .

The great controversy is ended. Sin and sinners are no more. The entire universe is clean. One pulse of harmony and gladness beats through the vast creation. From Him who created all, flow life and light and gladness, throughout the realms of illimitable space. From the minutest atom to the greatest world, all things, animate and inanimate, in their unshadowed beauty and perfect joy, declare that God is love.[34]

Eden Life Renewed

They shall build houses, and inhabit them; and they shall plant vineyards, and eat the fruit of them. They shall not build, and another inhabit; they shall not plant, and another eat: for as the days of a tree are the days of my people, and mine elect shall long enjoy the work of their hands. Isa. 65:21, 22.

There will be employment in heaven. The redeemed state is not one of idle repose.[35]

In the earth made new, the redeemed will engage in the occupations and pleasures that brought happiness to Adam and Eve in the beginning. The Eden life will be lived, the life in garden and field. . . .

There every power will be developed, every capability increased. The grandest enterprises will be carried forward, the loftiest aspirations will be reached, the highest ambitions realized. And still there will appear new heights to surmount, new wonders to admire, new truths to comprehend, fresh objects of study to call forth the powers of body and mind and soul.[36]

"His servants shall serve him" (Rev. 22:3). The life on earth is the beginning of the life in heaven; education on earth is an initiation into the principles of heaven; the lifework here is a training for the lifework there. What we now are, in character and holy service, is the sure foreshadowing of what we shall be.

"The Son of man came not to be ministered unto, but to minister" (Matt. 20:28). Christ's work below is His work above, and our reward for working with Him in this world will be the greater power and wider privilege of working with Him in the world to come. "Ye are my witnesses, saith the Lord, that I am God" (Isa. 43:12). This also we shall be in eternity. . . .

In our life here, earthly, sin-restricted though it is, the greatest joy and the highest education are in service. And in the future state, untrammeled by the limitations of sinful humanity, it is in service that our greatest joy and our highest education will be found—witnessing, and ever as we witness learning anew "the riches of the glory of this mystery;" "which is Christ in you, the hope of glory" (Col. 1:27).[37]

Everlasting Happiness

Thou wilt shew me the path of life: in thy presence is fulness of joy; at thy right hand there are pleasures for evermore. Ps.16:11.

During His ministry Jesus lived to a great degree an outdoor life. . . . Much of His teaching was given in the open air.[38]

In the Bible the inheritance of the saved is called "a country" (Heb. 11:16). There the heavenly Shepherd leads His flock to fountains of living waters. The tree of life yields its fruit every month, and the leaves of the tree are for the service of the nations. There are ever-flowing streams, clear as crystal, and beside them waving trees cast their shadows upon the paths prepared for the ransomed of the Lord. There the wide-spreading plains swell into hills of beauty, and the mountains of God rear their lofty summits. On those peaceful plains, beside those living streams, God's people, so long pilgrims and wanderers, shall find a home.[39]

The Bible presents to our view the unsearchable riches and immortal treasures of heaven. Man's strongest impulse urges him to seek his own happiness, and the Bible recognizes this desire and shows us that all heaven will unite with man in his efforts to gain true happiness. It reveals the condition upon which the peace of Christ is given to men. It describes a home of everlasting happiness and sunshine, where no tears nor want shall ever be known.[40]

Let all that is beautiful in our earthly home remind us of the crystal river and green fields, the waving trees and living fountains, the shining city and the white-robed singers, of our heavenly home—that world of beauty which no artist can picture, no mortal tongue describe. . . .

To dwell forever in this home of the blest, to bear in soul, body, and spirit, not the dark traces of sin and the curse, but the perfect likeness of our Creator, and through ceaseless ages to advance in wisdom, in knowledge, and in holiness, ever exploring new fields of thought, ever finding new wonders and new glories, ever increasing in capacity to know and to enjoy and to love, and knowing that there is still beyond us joy and love and wisdom infinite—such is the object to which the Christian's hope is pointing.[41]

With My Guardian Angel

Take heed that ye despise not one of these little ones; for I say unto you, That in heaven their angels do always behold the face of my Father which is in heaven. Matt. 18:10.

Not until the providences of God are seen in the light of eternity shall we understand what we owe to the care and interposition of His angels. Celestial beings have taken an active part in the affairs of men. They have appeared in garments that shone as the lightning; they have come as men, in the garb of wayfarers. They have accepted the hospitalities of human homes; they have acted as guides to benighted travelers. . . .

Though the rulers of this world know it not, yet often in their councils angels have been spokesmen. Human eyes have looked upon them. Human ears have listened to their appeals. In the council-hall and the court of justice, heavenly messengers have pleaded the cause of the persecuted and oppressed. They have defeated purposes and arrested evils that would have brought wrong and suffering to God's children. To the students in the heavenly school, all this will be unfolded.

Every redeemed one will understand the ministry of angels in his own life. The angel who was his guardian from his earliest moment; the angel who watched his steps, and covered his head in the day of peril; the angel who was with him in the valley of the shadow of death, who marked his resting-place, who was the first to greet him in the resurrection morning—what will it be to hold converse with him, and to learn the history of divine interposition in the individual life, of heavenly cooperation in every work for humanity![42]

With the Word of God in his hands, every human being . . . may have such companionship as he shall choose. . . . He may dwell in this world in the atmosphere of heaven, . . . drawing nearer and nearer the threshold of the eternal world, until the portals shall open, and he shall enter there. He will find himself no stranger. The voices that will greet him are the voices of the holy ones, who, unseen, were on earth his companions—voices that here he learned to distinguish and to love. He who through the Word of God has lived in fellowship with heaven, will find himself at home in heaven's companionship.[43]

Heaven's School

And all thy children shall be taught of the Lord;
and great shall be the peace of thy children. Isa. 54:13.

Heaven is a school; its field of study, the universe; its teacher, the Infinite One. A branch of this school was established in Eden; and the plan of redemption accomplished, education will again be taken up in the Eden school. . . .

Between the school established in Eden at the beginning and the school of the hereafter there lies the whole compass of this world's history—the history of human transgression and suffering, of divine sacrifice, and of victory over death and sin. Not all the conditions of the first school of Eden will be found in the school of the future life. No tree of knowledge of good and evil will afford opportunity for temptation. No tempter is there, no possibility of wrong. Every character has withstood the testing of evil, and none are longer susceptible to its power. . . .

There, when the veil that darkens our vision shall be removed, and our eyes shall behold that world of beauty of which we now catch glimpses through the microscope; when we look on the glories of the heavens, now scanned afar through the telescope; when, the blight of sin removed, the whole earth shall appear in "the beauty of the Lord our God" (Ps. 90:17), what a field will be open to our study! There the student of science may read the records of creation and discern no reminders of the law of evil. He may listen to the music of nature's voices, and detect no note of wailing or undertone of sorrow. In all created things he may trace one handwriting—in the vast universe behold "God's name writ large," and not in earth or sea or sky one sign of ill remaining.[44]

Those who have made the most of their privileges to reach the highest attainments here, will take these valuable acquisitions with them into the future life. They have sought and obtained that which is imperishable. The capability to appreciate the glories that "eye hath not seen, nor ear heard," will be proportionate to the attainments reached in the cultivation of the faculties in this life.[45]

Christ Our Teacher Still

My people shall know my name: . . . they shall know in that day that I am he that doth speak: behold, it is I. Isa. 52:6.

Restored to His presence, man will again, as at the beginning, be taught of God.[46]

We have not the slightest idea of what will then be opened before us. With Christ we shall walk beside the living waters. He will unfold to us the beauty and glory of nature. He will reveal what He is to us, and what we are to Him. Truth we cannot know now, because of finite limitations, we shall know hereafter.[47]

In the world to come Christ will lead the redeemed beside the river of life and will teach them wonderful lessons of truth. . . . They will see that a master hand holds the world in position. They will behold the skill displayed by the great Artist in coloring the flowers of the field, and will learn of the purposes of the merciful Father, who dispenses every ray of light, and with the holy angels the redeemed will acknowledge in songs of grateful praise God's supreme love to an unthankful world.[48]

There will be open to the student, history of infinite scope and of wealth inexpressible. . . . The history of the inception of sin; of fatal falsehood in its crooked working; of truth that, swerving not from its own straight lines, has met and conquered error—all will be made manifest. The veil that interposes between the visible and the invisible world will be drawn aside, and wonderful things will be revealed. . . .

With unutterable delight we shall enter into the joy and the wisdom of unfallen beings. We shall share the treasures gained through ages upon ages spent in contemplation of God's handiwork. And the years of eternity, as they roll, will continue to bring more glorious revelations. "Exceeding abundantly above all that we ask or think" (Eph. 3:20), will be, forever and forever, the impartation of the gifts of God.[49]

Every right principle, every truth learned in an earthly school, will advance us just that much in the heavenly school.[50]

We must get an education here that will enable us to live with God through the eternal ages. The education we begin here will be perfected in heaven. We will only just enter a higher grade.[51]

Our Curriculum

For our knowledge is imperfect . . . ; but when the perfect comes, the imperfect will pass away. 1 Cor. 13:9, 10, RSV.

By faith we should look to the hereafter and grasp the pledge of God of a growth of intellect, the human faculties uniting with the divine, and every power of the soul being brought into direct contact with the Source of light. We may rejoice that all that has perplexed us in the providences of God will then be made plain; things hard to be understood will find an explanation.[52]

There all who have wrought with unselfish spirit will behold the fruit of their labors. The outworking of every right principle and noble deed will be seen. Something of this we see here. But how little of the result of the world's noblest work is in this life manifest to the doer! How many toil unselfishly and unweariedly for those who pass beyond their reach and knowledge! Parents and teachers lie down in their last sleep, their lifework seeming to have been wrought in vain; they know not that their faithfulness has unsealed springs of blessing that can never cease to flow; only by faith they see the children they have trained become a benediction and an inspiration to their fellow men, and the influence repeat itself a thousandfold. Many a worker sends out into the world messages of strength and hope and courage, words that carry blessings to hearts in every land; but of the results he, toiling in loneliness and obscurity, knows little. So gifts are bestowed, burdens are borne, labor is done. Men sow the seed from which, above their graves, others reap blessed harvests. They plant trees, that others may eat the fruit. They are content here to know that they have set in motion agencies for good. In the hereafter the action and reaction of all these will be seen.

Of every gift that God has bestowed, leading men to unselfish effort, a record is kept in heaven. To trace this in its wide-spreading lines, to look upon those who by our efforts have been uplifted and ennobled, to behold in their history the outworking of true principles—this will be one of the studies and rewards of the heavenly school.[53]

Exploring the Universe

Now we see through a glass, darkly; but then face to face: now I know in part; but then shall I know even as also I am known. 1 Cor. 13:12.

Now we see through a glass, darkly." We behold the image of God reflected, as in a mirror, in the works of nature and in His dealings with men; but then we shall see Him face to face, without a dimming veil between. . . .

The loves and sympathies which God Himself has planted in the soul shall there find truest and sweetest exercise. The pure communion with holy beings, the harmonious social life with the blessed angels and with the faithful ones of all ages who have washed their robes and made them white in the blood of the Lamb, the sacred ties that bind together "the whole family in heaven and earth"—these help to constitute the happiness of the redeemed.

There, immortal minds will contemplate with never-failing delight the wonders of creative power, the mysteries of redeeming love. There will be no cruel, deceiving foe to tempt to forgetfulness of God. . . .

All the treasures of the universe will be open to the study of God's redeemed. Unfettered by mortality, they wing their tireless flight to worlds afar—worlds that thrilled with sorrow at the spectacle of human woe and rang with songs of gladness at the tidings of a ransomed soul. . . . With undimmed vision they gaze upon the glory of creation—suns and stars and systems, all in their appointed order circling the throne of Deity. Upon all things, from the least to the greatest, the Creator's name is written, and in all are the riches of His power displayed.

And the years of eternity, as they roll, will bring richer and still more glorious revelations of God and of Christ. As knowledge is progressive, so will love, reverence, and happiness increase. The more men learn of God, the greater will be their admiration of His character. As Jesus opens before them the riches of redemption and the amazing achievements in the great controversy with Satan, the hearts of the ransomed thrill with more fervent devotion, and with more rapturous joy they sweep the harps of gold; and ten thousand times ten thousand and thousands of thousands of voices unite to swell the mighty chorus of praise.[54]

Rejoice With Jerusalem

And I John saw the holy city, new Jerusalem, coming down from God out of heaven, prepared as a bride adorned for her husband. Rev. 21:2.

There is the New Jerusalem, the metropolis of the glorified new earth, "a crown of glory in the hand of the Lord, and a royal diadem in the hand of thy God." "Her light was like unto a stone most precious, even like a jasper stone, clear as crystal." "The nations of them which are saved shall walk in the light of it: and the kings of the earth do bring their glory and honour into it." Saith the Lord: "I will rejoice in Jerusalem, and joy in my people." "The tabernacle of God is with men, and he will dwell with them, and they shall be his people, and God himself shall be with them, and be their God" (Isa. 62:3; Rev. 21:11, 24; Isa. 65:19; Rev. 21:3).

In the City of God "there shall be no night." None will need or desire repose. There will be no weariness in doing the will of God and offering praise to His name. We shall ever feel the freshness of the morning and shall ever be far from its close. "And they need no candle, neither light of the sun; for the Lord God giveth them light" (Rev. 22:5). The light of the sun will be superseded by a radiance which is not painfully dazzling, yet which immeasurably surpasses the brightness of our noontide. The glory of God and the Lamb floods the Holy City with unfading light. The redeemed walk in the sunless glory of perpetual day.[55]

In the visions of the prophet, those who have triumphed over sin and the grave are now seen happy in the presence of their Maker, talking freely with Him as man talked with God in the beginning. "Be ye glad," the Lord bids them, "and rejoice forever in that which I create: for, behold, I create Jerusalem a rejoicing, and her people a joy. And I will rejoice in Jerusalem, and joy in my people: and the voice of weeping shall be no more heard in her, nor the voice of crying" (Isa. 65:18, 19). . . .

As the prophet beholds the redeemed dwelling in the City of God, free from sin and from all marks of the curse, in rapture he exclaims, "Rejoice ye with Jerusalem, and be glad with her, all ye that love her: rejoice for joy with her" (Isa. 66:10).[56]

Eternal Security

*And the Lord shall be king over all the earth:
in that day shall there be one Lord, and his name one. Zech. 14:9.*

The great plan of redemption results in fully bringing back the world into God's favor. All that was lost by sin is restored. Not only man but the earth is redeemed, to be the eternal abode of the obedient. For six thousand years, Satan has struggled to maintain possession of the earth. Now God's original purpose in its creation is accomplished. "The saints of the most High shall take the kingdom, and possess the kingdom for ever, even for ever and ever" (Dan. 7:18).

"From the rising of the sun unto the going down of the same the Lord's name is to be praised" (Ps. 113:3). . . . "All his commandments are sure. They stand fast for ever and ever" (Ps. 111:7, 8). The sacred statutes which Satan has hated and sought to destroy, will be honored throughout a sinless universe.[57]

Through Christ's redeeming work the government of God stands justified. The Omnipotent One is made known as the God of love. Satan's charges are refuted, and his character unveiled. Rebellion can never again arise. Sin can never again enter the universe. Through eternal ages all are secure from apostasy. By love's self-sacrifice, the inhabitants of earth and heaven are bound to their Creator in bonds of indissoluble union.

The work of redemption will be complete. In the place where sin abounded, God's grace much more abounds. The earth itself, the very field that Satan claims as his, is to be not only ransomed but exalted. Our little world, under the curse of sin the one dark blot in His glorious creation, will be honored above all other worlds in the universe of God. Here, where the Son of God tabernacled in humanity; where the King of glory lived and suffered and died—here, when He shall make all things new, the tabernacle of God shall be with men, "and he will dwell with them, and they shall be his people, and God himself shall be with them, and be their God" (Rev. 21:3). And through endless ages as the redeemed walk in the light of the Lord, they will praise Him for His unspeakable gift—Immanuel, "God with us."[58]

Full Compensation

Cast not away therefore your confidence, which hath great recompence of reward. For ye have need of patience, that, after ye have done the will of God, ye might receive the promise. For yet a little while, and he that shall come will come, and will not tarry. Heb. 10:35-37.

The long-suffering of God is wonderful. Long does justice wait while mercy pleads with the sinner. But "righteousness and judgment are the establishment of his throne" (Ps. 97:2, margin). . . . The world has become bold in transgression of God's law. Because of His long forbearance, men have trampled upon His authority. . . . But there is a line beyond which they cannot pass. The time is near when they will have reached the prescribed limit. Even now they have almost exceeded the bounds of the long-suffering of God, the limits of His grace, the limits of His mercy. The Lord will interpose to vindicate His own honor, to deliver His people, and to repress the swellings of unrighteousness. . . .

In this time of prevailing iniquity we may know that the last great crisis is at hand. When the defiance of God's law is almost universal, when His people are oppressed and afflicted by their fellow men, the Lord will interpose. . . .

"There shall be a time of trouble, such as never was since there was a nation even to that same time; and at that time thy people shall be delivered, every one that shall be found written in the book" (Dan. 12:1). From garrets, from hovels, from dungeons, from scaffolds, from mountains and deserts, from the caves of the earth and the caverns of the sea, Christ will gather His children to Himself. . . . By human tribunals the children of God have been adjudged the vilest criminals. But the day is near when "God is judge himself" (Ps. 50:6). Then the decisions of earth shall be reversed. "The rebuke of his people shall he take away" (Isa. 25:8). White robes will be given to every one of them. . . .

Whatever crosses they have been called to bear, whatever losses they have sustained, whatever persecution they have suffered, even to the loss of their temporal life, the children of God are amply recompensed. "They shall see his face; and his name shall be in their foreheads" (Rev. 22:4).[59]

Look Up!

Comfort ye, comfort ye my people, saith your God. Speak ye comfortably to Jerusalem, and cry unto her, that her warfare is accomplished, that her iniquity is pardoned. Isa. 40:1, 2.

In the darkest days of her long conflict with evil, the church of God has been given revelations of the eternal purpose of Jehovah. His people have been permitted to look beyond the trials of the present to the triumphs of the future, when, the warfare having been accomplished, the redeemed will enter into possession of the promised land. These visions of future glory, scenes pictured by the hand of God, should be dear to His church today, when the controversy of the ages is rapidly closing and the promised blessings are soon to be realized in all their fullness.[60]

To us who are standing on the very verge of their fulfillment, of what deep moment, what living interest, are these delineations of the things to come—events for which, since our first parents turned their steps from Eden, God's children have watched and waited, longed and prayed!

Fellow pilgrim, we are still amid the shadows and turmoil of earthly activities; but soon our Saviour is to appear to bring deliverance and rest. Let us by faith behold the blessed hereafter as pictured by the hand of God. He who died for the sins of the world is opening wide the gates of Paradise to all who believe on Him. Soon the battle will have been fought, the victory won. Soon we shall see Him in whom our hopes of eternal life are centered. And in His presence the trials and sufferings of this life will seem as nothingness. The former things "shall not be remembered, nor come into mind." "Cast not away therefore your confidence, which hath great recompense of reward. For ye have need of patience, that, after ye have done the will of God, ye might receive the promise. For yet a little while, and he that shall come will come, and will not tarry." "Israel shall be saved . . . with an everlasting salvation: ye shall not be ashamed nor confounded world without end."

Look up, look up, and let your faith continually increase. Let this faith guide you along the narrow path that leads through the gates of the city into the great beyond, the wide, unbounded future of glory that is for the redeemed.[61]

God's Justice Vindicated

As I live, says the Lord, to me every knee shall bow and every tongue acknowledge God. Rom. 14:11, NEB.

For what was the great controversy permitted to continue throughout the ages? Why was it that Satan's existence was not cut short at the outset of his rebellion? It was that the universe might be convinced of God's justice in His dealing with evil; that sin might receive eternal condemnation. In the plan of redemption there are heights and depths that eternity itself can never exhaust, marvels into which the angels desire to look. The redeemed only, of all created beings, have in their own experience known the actual conflict with sin; they have wrought with Christ, and, as even the angels could not do, have entered into the fellowship of His sufferings; will they have no testimony as to the science of redemption—nothing that will be of worth to unfallen beings? . . .

"In his temple doth everyone speak of his glory" (Ps. 29:9), and the song which the ransomed ones will sing . . . will declare the glory of God: "Great and marvelous are thy works, O Lord God, the Almighty; righteous and true are thy ways, thou King of the ages. Who shall not fear, O Lord, and glorify thy name? for thou only art holy" (Rev. 15:3, 4, RV).[62]

As if entranced, the wicked have looked upon the coronation of the Son of God. They see in His hands the tables of the divine law, the statutes which they have despised and transgressed. . . . Every question of truth and error in the longstanding controversy has now been made plain. The results of rebellion, the fruits of setting aside the divine statutes, have been laid open to the view of all created intelligences. The working out of Satan's rule in contrast with the government of God has been presented to the whole universe. Satan's own works have condemned him. God's wisdom, His justice, and His goodness stand fully vindicated. It is seen that all His dealings in the great controversy have been conducted with respect to the eternal good of His people and the good of all the worlds that He has created. . . . With all the facts of the great controversy in view, the whole universe, both loyal and rebellious, with one accord declare: "Just and true are thy ways, thou King of saints" (Rev. 15:3).[63]

Key to Abbreviations

AA—*Acts of the Apostles, The*
AH—*Adventist Home, The*
1BC—Ellen G. White Comments in *SDA Bible Commentary, The,* vol. 1 (2BC, etc., for vols. 2-7)
CG—*Child Guidance*
CH—*Counsels on Health*
COL—*Christ's Object Lessons*
CS—*Counsels on Stewardship*
CT—*Counsels to Parents, Teachers, and Students*
CW—*Counsels to Writers and Editors*
DA—*Desire of Ages, The*
Ed—*Education*
Ev—*Evangelism*
EW—*Early Writings*
FE—*Fundamentals of Christian Education*
FL—*Faith I Live By, The*
GC—*Great Controversy, The*
GW—*Gospel Workers*
HC—*Our High Calling*
HP—*In Heavenly Places*
KH—*That I May Know Him*
MB—*Thoughts From the Mount of Blessing*
MH—*Ministry of Healing, The*
ML—*My Life Today*
MM—*Medical Ministry, The*
MS—Ellen G. White Manuscript
MYP—*Messages to Young People*
PK—*Prophets and Kings*
PP—*Patriarchs and Prophets*
RH—*Review and Herald*
SC—*Steps to Christ*
SD—*Sons and Daughters of God*
1SG—*Spiritual Gifts*, vol. 1 (2SG, etc., for vols. 2-4)
SL—*Sanctified Life, The*
SP—*Spirit of Prophecy, The*, vol. 3
SR—*Story of Redemption, The*
ST—*Signs of the Times*
Sufferings—*Sufferings of Christ, The*
1T—*Testimonies for the Church*, vol. 1 (2T, etc., for vols. 2-9)
Te—*Temperance*
TM—*Testimonies to Ministers and Gospel Workers*
YI—*Youth's Instructor*

Source References

JANUARY

1. MB 6-9
2. RH Sept. 15, 1896
3. *Ibid.*
4. DA 32-38
5. *Ibid.*, 232-234
6. *Ibid.*, 509, 510
7. RH Aug. 18, 1896
8. 4BC 1171
9. PP 68
10. 1SM 237-241
11. DA 509
12. *Ibid.*, 506
13. MH 36, 37
14. COL 77-79
15. *Ibid.*, 96-102
16. GC 345-348
17. *Ibid.*, 467-469
18. MB 98, 99
19. AA 467
20. DA 176
21. *Ibid.*, 168-175
22. GC 347, 348
23. DA 22
24. 1BC 1084
25. *Ibid.*, 1085
26. COL 307-311
27. KH 302
28. 5T 220, 221
29. Ed 249
30. COL 252-254
31. AA 20
32. MB 42
33. AA 109-111
34. GW 27
35. *Ibid.*, 26, 27
36. RH Aug. 18, 1896
37. GW 13-15
38. AA 371
39. 9T 116
40. 5T 394, 395
41. HP 179
42. 5T 707-710
43. 8T 162
44. 6BC 1119
45. 2T 453
46. SL 11
47. PK 587
48. 9T 182, 183
49. MH 142, 143
50. GC 47
51. DA 302, 305
52. *Ibid.*, 312
53. 7T 237
54. 1T 407
55. 3SG 145, 146
56. CT 182, 183
57. COL 60
58. 2T 265, 266
59. HC 113
60. AA 502
61. 5BC 1129
62. FE 100
63. RH Feb. 28, 1888
64. SD 242
65. *Ibid.*, 160
66. 3T 472
67. 6T 140
68. 8T 55, 56
69. 6BC 1119
70. TM 296
71. 4T 25-28
72. GW 274
73. 7T 108
74. 6T 140
75. 4T 348, 349
76. EW 46

FEBRUARY

1. 1BC 1082
2. Ed 20
3. PP 48-50
4. Ed 26, 27
5. PP 67

6. DA 129-131
7. PP 63, 64
8. ML 323
9. PP 366, 367
10. HC 358
11. 2SM 312
12. SL 39, 40
13. DA 19-23
14. *Ibid.*, 377-379
15. *Ibid.*, 569-572
16. 3SP 15
17. GC 17-21
18. *Ibid.*, 28
19. 6BC 1053
20. 3SP 254, 255
21. *Ibid.*, 262, 263
22. Ed 173-178
23. 9T 92-94
24. 5T 208-210
25. RH Mar. 26, 1895
26. SD 11
27. *Ibid.*, 12
28. PP 64
29. COL 314
30. 6BC 1114
31. 6T 268
32. 3BC 1147, 1148
33. DA 638-641
34. 5T 623, 624
35. SD 225
36. *Ibid.*, 229
37. PP 140, 141
38. *Ibid.*, 133, 134.
39. *Ibid.*, 447
40. FE 481
41. TM 130, 131
42. MYP 329
43. RH Mar. 9, 1897
44. GW 288
45. 9T 234, 235
46. AA 68, 69
47. RH Mar. 26, 1895
48. CT 454
49. TM 121, 122
50. CS 116
51. 5T 731-737
52. 6T 448
53. COL 124, 125
54. 5BC 1100
55. CT 278, 279
56. COL 349, 350
57. *Ibid.*, 348
58. RH Aug. 24, 1897
59. *Ibid.*
60. *Ibid.*, July 4, 1907
61. *Ibid.*

MARCH

1. GC 347
2. 6T 363, 364
3. GC 415, 416
4. *Ibid.*, 489, 490
5. DA 493
6. 6BC 1071, 1072
7. TM 157
8. EW 54, 55
9. *Ibid.*, 252
10. 7BC 948
11. GW 21
12. MB 104
13. PP 522
14. 1SM 155, 156
15. 5T 197
16. DA 762
17. 1SM 349
18. 6T 364-367
19. 6T 365-368
20. 5T 318, 319
21. DA 480, 483
22. 5T 173, 174
23. *Ibid.*, 337
24. *Ibid.*, 345-347
25. RH Feb. 28, 1888
26. DA 24-26
27. 2SM 318
28. 1SM 239, 240
29. 2BC 1014
30. DA 680
31. 5T 573, 574
32. *Ibid.*, 578, 579
33. SC 52-55
34. RH Feb. 28, 1888
35. DA 113
36. SL 89-91
37. 5T 221
38. COL 174
39. 8T 178, 179
40. 4T 616
41. 6BC 1059
42. 5T 648, 649
43. 2SG 257
44. 2BC 1034, 1035
45. *Ibid.*, 1035
46. PK 156, 157
47. 3T 115
48. 4T 143
49. 9T 287
50. 3T 67
51. 5T 215
52. PK 545
53. MB 30
54. 2SM 315
55. RH Nov. 30, 1905
56. PP 252
57. GW 176, 178
58. 1T 410
59. PK 48, 49
60. Ed 243
61. MB 106, 107
62. 6T 418, 419
63. 6BC 1118
64. *Ibid.*, 1088
65. CS 27, 28
66. 6BC 1098
67. 5T 553
68. SD 98
69. AH 127, 128
70. CH 591-593
71. GC 651, 652

APRIL

1. MYP 137
2. SD 139
3. 1SM 323, 324
4. 4BC 1164, 1165
5. 4T 552, 553
6. MB 135
7. DA 336
8. MH 179
9. CT 257, 258
10. MB 48, 49
11. 4T 312
12. SD 365
13. 1SM 309
14. CT 249
15. MH 114, 115
16. PK 233
17. DA 148, 149
18. MH 428
19. 1SM 384, 385
20. DA 340
21. SD 122
22. PK 68, 69
23. DA 409
24. *Ibid.*, 294
25. *Ibid.*, 649
26. AA 476-478
27. MYP 73, 74
28. GC 506
29. 2T 409
30. MH 25
31. *Ibid.*, 249, 250
32. 2SM 231, 232
33. 7BC 907
34. AA 164
35. TM 488, 489
36. 5T 278
37. MM 264
38. MYP 147, 148
39. MM 144
40. CG 165, 166
41. MYP 99
42. DA 312
43. GW 366
44. 6T 413
45. AA 57
46. 4T 560, 561

47. 7T 297, 298
48. 1T 309, 310
49. SD 19
50. MB 117
51. MH 248, 249
52. *Ibid.*, 356
53. RH Dec. 10, 1908
54. MH 199
55. SC 100
56. 7T 297
57. SD 191
58. AA 55, 56
59. DA 568
60. CT 491
61. DA 187
62. *Ibid.*, 195
63. 5BC 1134
64. AA 51
65. SC 18
66. 6BC 1117
67. MYP 108
68. 3T 376
69. CG 423, 424
70. 6T 96
71. AA 523, 524
72. MB 13
73. HP 273
74. SD 268
75. HC 64
76. PP 667
77. AA 595-599
78. Ev 596
79. RH Aug. 22, 1899
80. DA 152, 153
81. GC 459
82. 8T 46, 47
83. SD 192
84. MH 148-151
85. AA 13
86. Ev 355
87. MB 127, 128
88. 1SM 89, 90
89. MH 168, 169
90. 7T 170
91. AA 600
92. 7T 148, 149

MAY

1. ST Apr. 25, 1892
2. *Ibid.*, Aug. 24, 1891
3. 7BC 934
4. PP 338
5. *Ibid.*, 373
6. PK 186, 187
7. PP 370
8. 1BC 1104
9. 1SM 220
10. *Ibid.*, 230
11. MB 48, 49
12. 1SM 90
13. 3SG 65
14. *Ibid.*, 73, 74
15. PP 107
16. 1BC 1092
17. PP 370, 371
18. 1BC 1092
19. 4T 524
20. PK 178
21. 1BC 1105
22. SC 62
23. COL 391
24. MB 76
25. PP 371
26. *Ibid.*, 303
27. *Ibid.*, 371, 372
28. PK 294
29. PP 372
30. 7BC 931
31. PP 372
32. SC 59-64
33. MS 28, 1905
34. 1SM 340
35. *Ibid.*, 350-353
36. DA 347
37. MH 62
38. PP 373
39. FE 403
40. 1SM 211, 212
41. COL 305
42. SD 215
43. 1BC 1103
44. 6BC 1114
45. 4BC 1167
46. SD 137
47. 6BC 1075
48. FL 89
49. 6BC 1072
50. 4T 294, 295
51. 6BC 1073
52. DA 677, 678
53. COL 384, 385
54. 5BC 1097
55. SD 42
56. COL 331
57. TM 378
58. MH 503
59. CH 41
60. *Ibid.*, 586-588
61. DA 826
62. 9T 17
63. COL 315
64. TM 419, 420
65. MS 67, 1907
66. *Ibid.*
67. PK 707, 708
68. CS 74, 75
69. *Ibid.*, 19
70. Ev 273-276
71. DA 165
72. *Ibid.*, 790
73. 1SM 341
74. 7BC 933
75. AA 552, 553
76. 2T 591
77. 6BC 1077, 1078
78. 7BC 932, 933
79. *Ibid.*, 932
80. TM 130
81. 6T 349, 350
82. 9T 18
83. 8T 23
84. 7T 30, 31
85. PK 631, 632
86. 7BC 932
87. CT 248, 249
88. 8T 38, 39
89. 3SG 74, 75
90. 1BC 1091

JUNE

1. 2T 200, 201
2. 1SM 321
3. 4T 563
4. RH Oct. 22, 1895
5. *Ibid.*, Oct. 29, 1895
6. 5BC 1129
7. DA 92
8. *Ibid.*, 111
9. *Ibid.*, 565
10. Sufferings, 10-12
11. 7BC 927
12. 1SM 253
13. 5T 421, 422
14. 3T 378-380
15. *Ibid.*, 378
16. 2T 508, 509
17. 5BC 1103
18. *Ibid.*
19. 2T 203-207
20. *Ibid.*, 207-211
21. *Ibid.*, 213-215
22. 4T 458
23. 1SM 322
24. 6T 479
25. COL 326
26. TM 423
27. 4T 261
28. MH 396, 397
29. 2T 289
30. 6BC 1118
31. HP 43
32. COL 156
33. *Ibid.*, 196, 197
34. 2T 634, 635
35. KH 134
36. COL 49
37. SD 11

38. 1SM 134
39. 5T 614
40. 1SM 363, 364
41. 4T 119
42. 8T 287, 288
43. 5T 730
44. RH Mar. 15, 1887
45. HP 50
46. COL 245, 246
47. *Ibid.*, 115-117
48. *Ibid.*, 145
49. 5T 167
50. 1SM 394
51. HP 34
52. *Ibid.*, 50
53. 1SM 398
54. 1T 167
55. 1SM 331-335
56. 4BC 1183
57. MB 8, 9
58. 6T 308, 309
59. EW 73
60. SC 45
61. 5T 199, 200
62. 1SM 403-405
63. GC 652
64. COL 419
65. 5T 730
66. AA 567
67. SC 12-15
68. 5BC 1108
69. Ed 263, 264
70. DA 356
71. Ed 270
72. *Ibid.*, 264
73. *Ibid.*, 271

JULY

1. CH 222
2. GC v
3. AA 53, 54
4. DA 668, 669
5. RH June 10, 1902
6. DA 669, 670
7. AA 30
8. *Ibid.*, 35-37
9. *Ibid.*, 38, 39
10. 6BC 1055
11. DA 671
12. COL 354
13. GW 285-287
14. Ev 615
15. AA 51
16. KH 171
17. RH Nov. 30, 1897
18. MYP 17
19. *Ibid.*, 55, 56
20. Ed 104-106
21. GC vi, vii
22. 2SM 39
23. PK 376, 377
24. DA 671
25. SC 109
26. CT 360, 361
27. SC 91
28. GC 343
29. 2SM 406, 407
30. 5T 87
31. *Ibid.*, 427
32. 7BC 907
33. SD 295
34. DA 527
35. 5T 120
36. GW 174
37. 5T 69, 70
38. 6T 167
39. 8T 301
40. SD 294
41. TM 223
42. 8T 40
43. AA 49-53
44. 1SM 190-192
45. SD 107
46. GW 127
47. HP 283
48. SD 98
49. EW 72
50. MB 132
51. HP 336
52. CT 22, 23
53. 8T 14
54. MH 159, 160
55. 6T 415
56. ML 318
57. CT 237, 238
58. 8T 241-243
59. *Ibid.*, 242, 243
60. 5T 239
61. *Ibid.*, 47, 48
62. *Ibid.*, 537
63. 6BC 1090
64. 9T 187, 188
65. GW 284-287
66. MB 20, 21
67. HP 307
68. DA 370
69. COL 406-414
70. TM 104
71. DA 322-324
72. *Ibid.*, 324
73. SC 118, 119
74. GW 261
75. CH 561
76. 6BC 1118
77. AA 530-532
78. HP 80
79. MB 19
80. 7T 213
81. AA 48, 49
82. 8T 20-22
83. 5T 157, 158
84. 7T 32
85. AA 50
86. GW 288, 289
87. AA 54, 55
88. 7BC 983
89. Ev 700
90. AA 55
91. TM 508

AUGUST

1. DA 407
2. 7T 229
3. *Ibid.*
4. TM 18, 19
5. 6T 457
6. Ed 79, 80
7. HC 336
8. RH July 7, 1904
9. 2T 478, 479
10. CG 164
11. *Ibid.*, 165
12. *Ibid.*, 165, 166
13. MB 143
14. ML 97
15. COL 332
16. 2BC 1003
17. ML 221
18. KH 42
19. 4T 348, 349
20. RH Dec. 20, 1881
21. HC 243
22. SD 123
23. ML 252
24. SC 87, 88
25. 2SM 125
26. TM 389
27. 6T 11-13
28. KH 45
29. SC 65
30. RH Apr. 22, 1909
31. KH 130
32. DA 664
33. KH 331
34. COL 339-341
35. 4T 294, 295
36. RH Nov. 17, 1885
37. 4T 626
38. AA 532
39. *Ibid.*, 558, 559
40. 5T 603-606
41. *Ibid.*, 612, 613
42. KH 200
43. RH Apr. 24, 1900
44. 7T 9, 10
45. KH 156
46. *Ibid.*, 173

47. AA 550, 551
48. 1SM 86
49. SC 68
50. COL 298
51. 6T 43, 44
52. 9T 40
53. AA 564
54. HC 29
55. SC 98, 99
56. MH 471
57. SD 117
58. *Ibid.*, 349
59. FE 303
60. HC 68
61. 4T 444-446
62. 2BC 1016, 1017
63. *Ibid.*, 1017
64. 6T 385
65. 2T 355
66. COL 260
67. AH 319
68. 2T 401
69. HC 122
70. 9T 279
71. COL 326-331
72. *Ibid.*, 384
73. GC 473, 474
74. 7BC 909
75. Ed 15, 16
76. 6BC 1078
77. *Ibid.*, 1105
78. 3T 52
79. DA 391
80. 6BC 1097
81. 9T 22-24
82. RH May 4, 1897
83. *Ibid.*, Apr. 22, 1909
84. YI Jan. 19, 1893
85. AA 273
86. 8T 140
87. RH Jan. 24, 1888
88. *Ibid.*, May 4, 1897
89. 4T 442

SEPTEMBER

1. AA 555
2. 8T 321
3. 5T 221
4. GC 256
5. 9T 151, 152
6. PK 487
7. 4T 32, 33
8. MH 174-176
9. PP 421
10. DA 679, 680
11. PP 238
12. 6T 307
13. MYP 134
14. PK 488-490
15. 1T 341-346
16. RH Mar. 31, 1904
17. *Ibid.*, Jan. 4, 1881
18. KH 85
19. RH Oct. 1, 1908
20. 1SM 416
21. RH June 16, 1896
22. HC 125
23. 5T 200
24. MYP 105
25. 6T 160, 161
26. FL 8
27. MH 181
28. DA 309, 310
29. TM 416
30. RH Jan. 14, 1904
31. PK 348
32. 3BC 1150
33. MB 140, 141
34. 1SM 366, 367
35. ML 13
36. 5T 198
37. MH 122
38. 5T 445
39. 1SM 83, 84
40. MH 36, 37
41. 1SM 259, 260
42. 9T 186, 187
43. AA 511
44. HC 108
45. GW 207, 208
46. CT 131
47. COL 363, 364
48. *Ibid.*, 401-404
49. RH June 16, 1896
50. MYP 26
51. COL 341, 342
52. PK 232
53. AA 312-315
54. SC 101, 102
55. HP 311
56. *Ibid.*, 321
57. AA 593-595
58. *Ibid.*, 599, 600
59. 6T 253
60. MH 469, 470
61. DA 347
62. 1T 303, 304
63. CT 226
64. 7T 67
65. ML 16
66. YI Nov. 12, 1907
67. HP 195
68. PP 201-203
69. GW 18
70. AA 576, 577
71. *Ibid.*, 511-513
72. MM 203

OCTOBER

1. Ed 107
2. DA 68-70
3. COL 82, 83
4. *Ibid.*, 63, 67
5. MYP 121, 122
6. *Ibid.*, 104
7. ST June 12, 1901
8. 8T 326-328
9. CT 124, 125
10. DA 512-517
11. CT 169
12. *Ibid.*, 48
13. 6T 430
14. MH 349
15. 8T 222, 223
16. FL 254
17. ML 102
18. *Ibid.*
19. MYP 114, 115
20. *Ibid.*, 122, 123
21. SC 93
22. MB 84, 85
23. 4T 535
24. 1T 340
25. 2T 505-507
26. 5T 609
27. HC 279
28. 6BC 1111
29. 4T 567
30. SC 69-71
31. 9T 153-156
32. *Ibid.*, 160
33. 3BC 1157
34. 2T 550, 551
35. 7BC 947
36. ML 104
37. 2T 187-189
38. *Ibid.*, 194
39. AA 539
40. *Ibid.*, 544
41. DA 249-251
42. 3BC 1164
43. 7T 50
44. MYP 15, 16
45. SC 68, 69
46. HC 247
47. COL 336, 337
48. 1SM 336-338
49. RH Apr. 17, 1888
50. CT 207
51. MYP 282
52. GW 297
53. HP 231
54. RH Jan. 9, 1900
55. HP 195
56. 6T 51
57. SC 78-80
58. MYP 24

59. 5T 393
60. Ed 295
61. SD 118
62. ML 103
63. *Ibid.*, 171
64. 5T 393, 394
65. *Ibid.*, 104, 105
66. 3T 540
67. 4T 228
68. HP 320
69. CT 279
70. MH 151-154
71. RH June 22, 1886
72. 5T 263-267

NOVEMBER

1. SC 17
2. *Ibid.*, 43, 44
3. Ed 68-70
4. PP 430-432
5. PK 586, 587
6. 5T 17
7. 4T 459, 460
8. 1BC 1087
9. 7T 213
10. 1T 158, 159
11. RH May 10, 1906
12. MS 113, 1898
13. RH May 10, 1906
14. MB 27, 28
15. CH 633, 634
16. 5T 46-49
17. ST Sept. 3, 1902
18. 1SM 138
19. TM 324, 325
20. 1SM 108
21. RH May 24, 1892
22. *Ibid.*, May 7, 1908
23. ML 174
24. RH Jan. 11, 1912
25. CT 544
26. KH 135
27. CT 544
28. 5T 170
29. *Ibid.*
30. MB 113-115
31. CT 50-53
32. 4T 85, 86
33. 5T 103-105
34. AA 467, 468
35. 5BC 1122
36. 6BC 1111
37. 8T 100
38. *Ibid.*, 99, 100
39. 6T 410
40. 5T 148
41. RH May 8, 1888
42. MH 20
43. *Ibid.*, 104, 105
44. *Ibid.*, 132, 133
45. DA 142
46. *Ibid.*, 151, 152
47. PP 717
48. HP 331
49. *Ibid.*, 184
50. MB 81-83
51. DA 249
52. AA 9-12
53. HP 340
54. Ev 552, 553
55. *Ibid.*, 697
56. 8T 22
57. GW 470
58. COL 176
59. 9T 25, 26
60. 1SM 117
61. 4T 365
62. Te 212, 213
63. 4T 357
64. 2T 357, 358
65. 4T 34, 35

DECEMBER

1. Ed 22
2. *Ibid.*, 15, 16
3. 1BC 1082, 1083
4. 5T 188, 189
5. PP 64, 65
6. DA 419-422
7. MB 107, 108
8. GC 322, 323
9. MB 110, 111
10. *Ibid.*, 108-110
11. DA 827, 828
12. AA 601, 602
13. PP 207, 208
14. *Ibid.*, 503, 504
15. 2T 355, 356
16. 3T 162
17. PP 289, 290
18. RH Nov. 13, 1913
19. TM 515
20. 8T 252-254
21. 9T 285, 286
22. *Ibid.*, 285
23. GC 640-644
24. *Ibid.*, 644-646
25. RH Nov. 13, 1913
26. SC 86, 87
27. *Ibid.*, 125, 126
28. EW 288, 289
29. PP 62
30. GC 648
31. *Ibid.*, 645
32. 9T 286
33. GC 674-676
34. *Ibid.*, 674-678
35. 3BC 1164
36. PK 730, 731
37. Ed 307-309
38. MH 52
39. GC 675
40. ML 160
41. CT 55
42. Ed 304, 305
43. *Ibid.*, 127
44. *Ibid.*, 301-303
45. FE 49
46. Ed 302
47. CT 162
48. ML 361
49. Ed 304, 307
50. CT 208, 209
51. ML 361
52. 5T 706
53. Ed 305, 306
54. CC 676-678
55. *Ibid.*, 676
56. PK 729
57. PP 342
58. DA 26
59. COL 177-180
60. PK 722
61. *Ibid.*, 731, 732
62. Ed 308, 309
63. GC 668-671

Scripture Index

MARK

LUKE

JOHN

ACTS

ROMANS

1 CORINTHIANS

2 CORINTHIANS

GALATIANS

EPHESIANS